A CRISIS IN CONFEDERATE COMMAND

A CRISIS IN CONFEDERATE COMMAND

EDMUND KIRBY SMITH,

RICHARD TAYLOR,

AND THE ARMY OF THE

TRANS-MISSISSIPPI

Jeffery S. Prushankin

LOUISIANA STATE UNIVERSITY PRESS
BATON ROUGE

Designer: *Amanda McDonald Scallan*
Typeface: *Whitman*
Typesetter *G&S Typesetters, Inc.*

ISBN 0-8071-3088-5

And you ought to take very great care when you are about to praise or blame any man, that you speak correctly.

—PLATO, THE *MINOS*

CONTENTS

Illustrations follow page 90

MAPS

ACKNOWLEDGMENTS

Conscientious study will not perhaps make
them great, but it will make them respectable.
—RICHARD TAYLOR

Soon after beginning my investigation into Smith and Taylor, I found myself alone one day in the back of a dark and dusty used-book store somewhere in the depths of Los Angeles. Having had no luck at all finding what I wanted, I turned to wind my way back through the stacks, looked down, and there at my feet was a tattered copy of *Strategy and Tactics* magazine with a cover story on the Red River campaign. How it got there I do not know, because I had told no one at the store what I was looking for, and I doubt that anyone even knew I was back there. A coincidence? Or perhaps the ghost of some long-forgotten Confederate soldier had laid the magazine at my feet and then vanished in a wisp of gray, having shaped the destiny of this poor mortal from the Great Beyond. I found out later that J. E. Sligh, a soldier from the Twenty-eighth Louisiana Infantry, moved to Los Angeles after the war, and he had much to say on the Smith–Taylor relationship in an article written for *Confederate Veteran* in 1923. So I suppose the first person I should thank for his help on this manuscript is Sligh, or perhaps the Gray Ghost of Dutton's Books.

I also wish to thank four historians who provided advice, counsel, and support far beyond the call of academic duty. Anne J. Bailey and Daniel E. Sutherland, two of the brightest stars in the Civil War field, each provided extraordinary guidance during and after my doctoral studies at the University of Arkansas. I am fortunate to have worked with these people and consider them my friends, despite Bailey's fondness for the Dallas Cowboys and Sutherland's attachment to the Detroit Red Wings. Joseph Speakman, professor of history at Montgomery County Community College, was the first to see the potential in my work on Smith and Taylor and urged me to take the topic as far as I could. He encouraged me to go to graduate school and later helped me land my first job in academia, teaching Civil War history at Montgomery County Community College. Lawrence S. Little, my thesis director at Villanova, took on Smith and Taylor when many others dismissed my subject as too politically incorrect. I am sure the sight of an African American professor hashing out Confederate history with a white grad student turned many heads out on the Philadelphia Main Line.

In addition, I want to thank historians Arthur W. Bergeron Jr., Gary D. Joiner, Terry L. Beckenbaugh, Steve Bounds, Scott Dearman, and Dana M. Mangham. All are experts on one facet or another of the Trans-Mississippi and have given of their time, energy, and knowledge toward this project.

And now that this book is finished, I appreciate the opportunity to express my heartfelt gratitude to the following historians, buffs, archivists, and librarians for their assistance and encouragement during my work on the various phases of the project. Some of these people made tremendous contributions, while others helped in some small but significant way. Thanks to: T. Michael Parrish, Edwin C. Bearss, Donald S. Frazier, Richard Lowe, John R. House III, Henry O. Robertson, Glynn Maxwell, Eliot West, Albert J. Dorley, Wayne Huss, Kevin Brock, Beth Juhl, Sherrie S. Pugh, Sylvia Frank Rodrigue, the late Jerry Russell, Don Montgomery, Larry Beane, Noel Estes, Barron T. Smith.

Further, I wish to acknowledge the contributions made by the fellows and faculty at the 2002 West Point Summer Seminar on military history, particularly Carol Reardon's "Civil Warriors." I also want to thank the folks who staff the manuscript repositories listed in the bibliography, the overwhelming majority of whom graciously took the time to help in my research. And thank you to MaryKatherine Callaway, Rand Dotson, Lee Sioles, Mary Yates, Cynthia Williams, and all those at LSU Press who facilitated the production of this book.

Finally, I wish to thank my friends and family for putting up with Smith and Taylor and me for all these years. Journalist Bill German and computer tech David Stahl helped me cope with nearly every imaginable nonhistorian problem. My son Keith (a.k.a. Jake), my daughter Bishon, my mother, and my mother-in-law all exhibited a tremendous degree of understanding and support during this project, and I appreciate every bit of it. My wife, Janet, has read every word I have ever written on Smith and Taylor at least a dozen times. Her aid and comfort were of paramount importance to this book and to my sanity, or what is left of it. I hope she caught all my mistakes.

I dedicate this book to the memory of two World War II veterans: my father,

James Franklin Prushankin, USAAF, and my father-in-law, Howard Vernon Hart, USMC—two guys who loved history, politics, baseball, and their country. One was a Democrat, the other a Republican, one rooted for the Phillies, the other for the Red Sox, but somehow they worked things out. I wish they were still around to read the story of Smith and Taylor.

INTRODUCTION

You will hear rumor and reports of every description . . . but do not
believe the truth of what you hear. I care not for the censure of those
who allege that I have exhibited a want of capacity.

—EDMUND KIRBY SMITH

Men without knowledge have at all times usurped the right to
criticise campaigns and commanders . . . knowing that the
greatest is he who commits the fewest blunders.

—RICHARD TAYLOR

A recent work by Civil War historian Joseph T. Glatthaar, *Partners in Command*,
examines the professional relationships between several of the war's most famous
military leaders: Robert E. Lee and Stonewall Jackson, William Tecumseh Sherman
and Ulysses S. Grant, and other well-known figures whose reliance upon one another proved crucial to the successes and failures of their governments. Notably
absent from Glatthaar's fine work is the most notorious of all military relationships
chiseled from the hardships of the Civil War: Confederate generals Richard Taylor
and Edmund Kirby Smith.[1]

This is not an indictment of Glatthaar's book but rather an observation on the
historiography of the war. The Trans-Mississippi theater, in which Taylor served
under Smith's command, has long suffered from scholarly neglect. Many historians have considered the Trans-Mississippi a backwater, while Civil War buffs
have often dismissed the battles west of the river as insignificant. The classic work
on leadership in the Confederate military, *Lee's Lieutenant's*, by Douglas Southall
Freeman, and its counterpart for the Federal army, *Lincoln Finds a General*, by Kenneth P. Williams, both discount the importance of the Trans-Mississippi. Both
works are products of and contributors to the notion that significant events in the
war occurred only in the eastern or western theaters. Even more recent standards,
such as Richard M. McMurry's *Two Great Rebel Armies* and James M. McPherson's
Battle Cry of Freedom, fail to explore the strategic concerns of the Trans-Mississippi
in the context of the larger war.[2]

The focus on the eastern and western theaters is understandable. The momentous events at Antietam, Gettysburg, Vicksburg, and Atlanta were among the many such that occurred east of the Mississippi. Events in the Trans-Mississippi seem, by comparison, peripheral. Further, more soldiers served east of the river, leaving a greater paper trail for historians to follow. Moreover, throughout the victorious postbellum North, many veterans of these battles sanctified the Union's struggles as an example of might making right. Given the strategic aims and their tactical execution by Federal armies in the Trans-Mississippi, warfare west of the river did not always meet the nineteenth-century northern standard of political correctness.

Southerners, meanwhile, embraced the concept of the Lost Cause and deified Lee and his Army of Northern Virginia, often at the expense of other commands and generals. Richard Taylor's Army of Western Louisiana, while every bit as ferocious a fighting force as their Virginia brethren, failed to engender much respect outside of the Red River Valley. Nevertheless, Tom Green's Texas cavalry performed feats rivaling those of Jeb Stuart's horsemen on the Peninsula, while John G. Walker's Greyhounds covered ground that would have exhausted Stonewall Jackson's foot cavalry in the Shenandoah, and Alfred Mouton's Louisiana brigade, like Lewis Armistead's Virginians at Gettysburg, made a heroic charge into the guns of a foe entrenched on high ground. The glory of battle aside, Louisiana historian Terry L. Jones reminds us that in the Trans-Mississippi, "the heart-break of the dead's loved ones was just as tearful in a piney-hill cabin as it was in a pillared Virginia mansion."[3]

Increasingly, though, an appreciation for the Trans-Mississippi has emerged in works presenting a broad view of the war. Many historians now argue that events in the Trans-Mississippi had considerable impact on the southern war effort. Archer Jones points out, in *Civil War Command and Strategy*, that Jefferson Davis entrusted autonomous management of the Trans-Mississippi to the "competent direction" of Smith. In fact, turning over complete control of every aspect of a department to one individual was something the president did with no other general officer, including Lee. Moreover, in his landmark work *The Confederate Nation*, Emory Thomas describes Smith as the embodiment of the Confederate government to southerners west of the Mississippi. In *The Confederate War*, Gary Gallagher emphasizes the impact that Taylor's battlefield victories had on the home front and argues that the Louisianan's success in April 1864 served to boost morale from Shreveport to Richmond during the waning months of the struggle.[4]

The importance of the Trans-Mississippi as a vital theater of military operations has surfaced as a fertile frontier for research. Several historians have made important new contributions to Civil War literature exploring the experiences of soldiers who served west of the river. M. Jane Johansson's examination of the Twenty-eighth Texas Infantry and Stanley McGowen's treatment of the First Texas Cavalry are both fine examples of fresh scholarship at the regimental level. Richard Lowe's exposé on Walker's Greyhounds paints a vivid portrait of Trans-Mississippi infantry at the division level, while Anne Bailey's *Between the Enemy and Texas* provides a stirring ride with Confederate cavalry at the brigade level. Jeff Kinard's depiction of the French general Camille Polignac contributes a unique view on warfare west of the Mississippi, as does Arthur W. Bergeron's *Reminiscences of Major Silas T. Grisamore*, a skillfully edited collection of articles first published in a small-town Louisiana newspaper immediately following the war.[5]

As the number of authors and historians examining the Trans-Mississippi continues to grow, several works have emerged as standards in the field. *Kirby Smith's Confederacy*, by Robert L. Kerby, and John D. Winters's *The Civil War in Louisiana* are classic studies that address a wide range of Trans-Mississippi subjects, including the Smith–Taylor axis. However, these historians examine Smith and Taylor primarily in terms of specific events and do not investigate how their acrimonious relationship affected the Confederate war effort.[6]

Ludwell Johnson's *Red River Campaign* provides a well-defined context in which to explore the relationship between Smith and Taylor. Although Johnson does not probe the genesis of the feud, he describes the working relationship between the quarrelsome generals. Johnson asserts that the "estrangement between Smith and Taylor was unfortunate from every point of view, the more so because both men were fundamentally sincere and upright individuals." Nevertheless, Johnson concludes that while Taylor was guilty of insubordination, he had ample justification for criticizing Smith's strategy. Another monograph on the campaign, *War along the Bayous*, written by William R. Brooksher, condemns Smith's strategy as "incomprehensible" and denounces Taylor's views as "grandiose." On the issue of blame, however, Brooksher holds Smith accountable for the "deteriorating relationship between the senior Confederate commanders" in the Trans-Mississippi. In *One Damn Blunder from Beginning to End*, historian Gary D. Joiner argues that while Smith's decisions "left Taylor with inadequate resources" to defend his district, Taylor's attitude degenerated to the point that he "could not stand the sight of the commanding general." Joiner maintains that this animosity filtered down to the ranks, where Taylor's partisans nearly came to blows with Smith's supporters.[7]

Biographers of each general have also explored the Smith–Taylor relationship as it pertained to their respective subjects. T. Michael Parrish's *Richard Taylor: Soldier Prince of Dixie* and Joseph H. Parks's *General Edmund Kirby Smith C.S.A.* provide great insight into the flaws and quirks of the generals. Parrish contends that the only blemish on Taylor's wartime record was his "strident personal reaction to General Edmund Kirby Smith's foolish ambition." Parks, on the other hand, characterizes Smith's policy as strategically sound and maintains that "resentment and bitterness" toward Smith nearly destroyed Taylor's "many soldierly qualities."[8]

Missing from this collection is an all-encompassing approach to the relationship between Smith and Taylor. How did their dependence upon and animosity toward one another shape events during the war and interpretations afterward? *A Crisis in Confederate Command* suggests that while their conflicting styles of leadership saved the Trans-Mississippi from an external threat, their equally conflicting personalities damaged the department from within.

Arthur W. Hyatt, a Trans-Mississippi Confederate, recorded his impressions of Smith and Taylor in his diary. "Smith is a most gifted gentleman," Hyatt asserted, "with a mind sufficiently large to cover the states of Louisiana, Arkansas, and Texas, at the same time that it is occupied with picnics, blackberry and crawfish parties, and his young wife. Most men could only attend to one of these at a time, and do them justice." Taylor, on the other hand, was a "very quiet, unassuming little fellow, except on a retreat," when he became uncharacteristically noisy. "On these occasions he has been known to curse and sware at mules and wagons, but this is overlooked as it is known it was only done for effect." Smith's policy in Louisiana was to trade territory for time. The territory, however, was Taylor's. Incessant retreat gave him ample opportunity to curse mules, wagons, and soldiers, including his commanding officer.[9]

The seeds of acrimony between Smith and Taylor were sown not in the Red River Valley but in Richmond, Virginia, where the generals received irreconcilable orders from the War Department that undermined their working relationship and made a dispute almost inevitable. Jefferson Davis's rigid command structure not only inhibited cooperation between the Trans-Mississippi and departments east of the river but also aggravated differences between Smith and Taylor. States' rights and state politics too played a role. Smith felt obligated to politicians from Arkansas and Missouri who had helped to secure his appointment, while Taylor's devotion to his native Louisiana impaired his ability to accept his commander's methods.

At the center of the feud lay John G. Walker's Texas division. Throughout 1863 each general insisted that Walker's presence was essential for his own operations and accused the other of misusing the infantry. In 1864 Smith and Taylor found themselves caught between a two-pronged Federal advance from Little Rock and New Orleans, and Walker's division once again found itself caught between Smith and Taylor.

During the Red River campaign, Smith and Taylor clashed over strategy. A disciple of Joseph E. Johnston, Smith ordered a Fabian retreat on both fronts and planned to use interior lines to concentrate against whichever arm of the Federal pincer presented the most immediate danger. To Taylor's chagrin, this policy meant the continued surrender of his territory without a fight. A veteran of Stonewall Jackson's Valley campaign, Taylor valued the offensive and hoped to seize the initiative. Taylor's pedigree as an aristocrat and his background as a politician prevented him from following a course of action that he considered foolhardy. Smith's experience in the prewar army and his West Point training prevented him from indulging the views of an arrogant amateur soldier. The dynamics of the internal conflict between the generals, and the external pressures exerted upon them by a massive army of conquest, provide the archetypal underpinnings of their story.

Taylor disobeyed Smith's orders and attacked the enemy in northwestern Louisiana, forcing the Federals there to abandon the campaign. Rather than continue concentration in Louisiana, however, Smith withdrew two-thirds of Taylor's infantry, including Walker, to pursue the subsequent Federal retreat across Arkansas. As a result, both enemy columns escaped, and Taylor, embittered by the outcome of the campaign, launched a vindictive war of words with Smith. Taylor continued his tirade even after Smith relieved him from command, through the end of the war and beyond.

Yet despite their differences, Smith and Taylor prevented the Federals from achieving several objectives. First, the Confederates ended the Federal military and political presence in western Louisiana. Accordingly, the state would not have a reconstructed Unionist government in place at the time of Abraham Lincoln's reelection bid. Second, the Federals were unable to meet New England's enormous demand for baled cotton, a key political motivation for the Red River campaign. Third, Smith and Taylor prevented the Federals from establishing a military presence in Texas, one that would have severely hampered the flow of supplies, both medical and military, from Mexico. Despite the extreme handicap under which they conducted operations in the Trans-Mississippi, Smith and Taylor worked together to achieve one of the Confederacy's greatest military accomplishments of the war. Unfortunately, they tarnished their own reputations in the process.

A CRISIS IN CONFEDERATE COMMAND

1

Prologue

THE GENTLEMAN AND THE OFFICER

By dawn, the Louisiana summer rain had slackened enough to let the small boat continue on its way through the mist that shrouded Bayou Courtableau. Four black oarsmen labored to navigate the tangle of cypress trees and Spanish moss that bowed across the sluggish branch of the Atchafalaya. Another black man sat silently alongside his white master, a rather frail looking Confederate officer. The two men waited anxiously until their boat finally docked at the village of Washington. From there, after a brief visit with family, they made their way six miles south to Opelousas, the Confederate state capital, where, on August 20, 1862, thirty-six-year-old Richard Taylor assumed command of the Confederate District of West Louisiana. Promoted one month earlier to the rank of major general, Taylor returned from Virginia to his home state as the youngest non–West Point graduate to achieve such high rank in the Confederate army.[1]

In the decades before the Civil War, the only son of Zachary Taylor eschewed army life, choosing a Yale education over West Point. Although he gained a reputation as a somewhat lackadaisical student, Taylor cultivated a strong interest in military history. Following graduation in 1845, Taylor gained brief military experience during a stint as an aide to his father during the Mexican War. Illness cut short this training and forced his return to the United States, where he soon began pursuit of the more genteel lifestyle of a cavalier southern aristocrat. In 1850 Taylor acquired a large sugar plantation in St. Charles Parish along the banks of the Mississippi River near New Orleans, where he became ensconced in the opulent world of gambling and horse racing.[2]

Although Taylor considered himself ill suited for a career in politics, he won election to the Louisiana state senate in 1855. In 1860 he served as a delegate to the Democratic national convention at Charleston and, nine months later, as a delegate to Louisiana's secession convention. On January 26, 1861, just one day short of his thirty-fifth birthday, Taylor sided reluctantly with the majority to vote Louisiana out of the Union.[3]

Afterward the convention selected Taylor to oversee Louisiana's Committee on Military and Naval Affairs. His belief that war was inevitable led to repeated clashes with Governor Thomas O. Moore over Louisiana's desultory preparations. Taylor left the convention disillusioned and "determined to accept such responsibility only as came . . . unsought." Such responsibility came in May in the form of a personal appeal from Louisianan Braxton Bragg, a brigadier in the Provisional Army of the Confederacy. Taylor accepted a civilian position on Bragg's staff to assist in organizing Confederate military units at Pensacola, Florida.[4]

Early in July, Taylor received word of his selection as colonel of the Ninth Louisiana Infantry. His election by the regiment was less an acknowledgment of his military acumen and more an affirmation of Taylor's unique relationship with President Jefferson Davis. While a young lieutenant in the United States Army, Davis had married one of Taylor's sisters. Although his wife died after just a few months of marriage, Davis had remained close to the Taylor family. The men of the Ninth Louisiana were cognizant of the relationship between politics and the military, and many crowed that with Taylor in command, they would see action in Virginia rather than remain idle in Louisiana. The speculation proved correct, and the regiment left for Richmond in mid-July. To their dismay, the troops arrived too late for the battle at Manassas and for the next several months found themselves mired behind the lines in Virginia.[5]

Disease was among the worst hardships the soldiers endured during the early months of the war. In late September, Taylor himself became a casualty, stricken with an attack of rheumatoid arthritis. He suffered symptoms that ranged from severe migraine headaches and fever to partial paralysis. The condition forced him to leave the regiment for several weeks, but by late October he had rejoined his men at Centerville, Virginia.[6]

During his absence the regiment became part of the Louisiana brigade, and the War Department promoted Taylor to brigadier general. While his own men were not troubled by Taylor's political connections, the promotion angered many enlistees and officers in the brigade's other regiments. Charges of nepotism swirled through the camp, and the accusations stung Taylor's pride. He petitioned Davis to rescind the promotion, but the president refused. As the firestorm subsided, Taylor took the opportunity to prove himself beyond reproach in the eyes of his men. He soon developed a reputation as a strict disciplinarian with a razor-quick temper and a propensity for profanity and punishment.[7]

Chronic health problems often kept Taylor either incapacitated or in a foul mood during the long months of training and drill. "Taylor well was charming company," acknowledged Major David French Boyd. But when Taylor fell ill, Boyd noticed, soldiers scrambled to avoid him. An enlisted man noted that failure to follow the general's instructions "caused much swearing," while another Louisianan professed that Taylor was "proud as Lucifer." Taylor's displays of wrath did not stop with enlisted men or junior officers. Division commander Richard S. Ewell reprimanded him for upbraiding his courier, and some weeks later Thomas J. "Stonewall" Jackson reacted with "reproachful surprise" to Taylor's liberal use of profanity. "I am afraid you are a wicked fellow," the pious Jackson told Taylor after hearing the brigadier swear at his troops.[8]

Despite their objections to Taylor's temperament, Ewell and Jackson found him an extraordinary soldier, eager to learn the art of war. Ewell spent many hours with Taylor immersed in discussions on military history and Napoleonic maxims. In a letter to his brother Ewell praised "Taylor's genius and military ability." Taylor recalled appreciatively, "Our talks were of more value to me than to him."[9]

As a result of these meetings, Taylor developed two fundamental principles that underlay the strategies and tactics he developed throughout the war. The first "was to examine at every halt the adjacent roads and paths, their direction and condition; distances of nearest towns and cross-roads; the country, its capacity to furnish supplies, as well as the general topography." The second was to draw a map that reflected the features and characteristics of each position and thereupon devise two battle plans, the first to attack the position and the second to defend it. The exercise allowed Taylor to correct potential blunders without sacrificing his men. "I . . . can safely affirm," Taylor wrote after the war, "that such slight success as I had in command was due to these customs."[10]

As for Jackson, although the generals eventually forged a strong working relationship, Taylor initially served under him with some trepidation. Jackson's reputation had suffered since Manassas, and both Ewell and Taylor balked when they received orders to join him for a spring campaign in the Shenandoah Valley. Ewell and Taylor conspired to either seek a transfer for the division or secure the appointment of a new commanding general in the Valley. Ewell sent Taylor to Richmond to broach the subject with Davis. Confident that his influence with the president would remedy the situation, Taylor announced, "We won't be under this damn old crazy fool long." Evidently Taylor's standing with Davis was not as great as either he or many of his contemporaries thought. Within days of Taylor's return, the War Department notified Ewell that his orders stood, and Jackson was to remain in command.[11]

Once Taylor finally met Jackson, his reservations about the general vanished.

During the Valley campaign Jackson often rode with Taylor at the head of the column, and in the evenings he frequently made his way to the Louisianan's campfire for a discussion of the day's events. Speed and efficiency during the march were among their topics of conversation, and the emergence of Jackson's "foot-cavalry" during the campaign enabled Confederate forces to neutralize the overall numerical superiority of the Federals in the theater by swift concentration at the point of attack. Taylor's appreciation of the rapid march as a means to strike and pursue a divided foe would serve him well in later campaigns.[12]

Jackson also affirmed Taylor's conviction that an understanding of topography was a crucial element of success. Jackson relied heavily on his cartographer to tutor him on the lay of the land. This helped to minimize the unnecessary movement of men and enabled the general to react quickly to developments as they unfolded. Taylor learned that Jackson's stealth produced the key elements of deception and surprise. Several times during the campaign the enemy had no idea where Jackson was or what he was going to do next. This helped to paralyze Federal commanders and prevented them from a timely concentration of their forces. Subsequently, Jackson was able to choose the time and place for battle. Despite their numerical advantage, the Federals in the Valley played a reactive role rather than a proactive one. "The value of the initiative in war cannot be overstated," Taylor stressed in his memoirs. It was a lesson that he would carry with him throughout his military career.[13]

On the battlefields of the Shenandoah, Taylor's brigade performed exceedingly well and played a conspicuous role in sweeping the Federals from Front Royal and Winchester. At Port Republic, Taylor personally led an assault that marked the turning point of the battle and secured success in the campaign for Jackson's Confederates. His leadership qualities earned him high praise from Jackson and Ewell. Jackson's report on Port Republic cited "the gallant and successful charge of General Taylor on the Federal left and rear," and Ewell acknowledged that "the honor of deciding two battles" in the campaign belonged to Taylor. Indeed, Taylor had made crucial contributions and in doing so erased any question of his personal mettle on the battlefield.[14]

With the Valley campaign closed, Jackson recommended Taylor for promotion to major general. "The success with which he has managed his Brigade in camp, on the march, and when engaged with the enemy," Jackson advised the Confederate high command, "makes it my duty as well as my pleasure to recommend him for promotion." One month later, Taylor became the second youngest major general in the Confederacy. The promotion ended accusations that he had attained his rank through preferential treatment.[15]

Despite this good fortune, Taylor's health suffered, and at the close of the campaign he traveled to Richmond for medical attention. Upon his return he found his brigade on the move as a part of Robert E. Lee's army operating on the Peninsula. On June 25 an attack of rheumatoid arthritis again felled Taylor, this time forcing him to relinquish field command. As he drifted in and out of consciousness during the next twenty-four hours, he became unable to move his arms and legs or to understand messages sent to him from the front. Two days later he struggled onto his horse, and with one leg hanging limp "like a rope from his saddle" he rode to join his command at the battle of Gaines' Mill. Although he was physically unable to lead the men into combat, his presence behind the lines for the duration of the Seven Days battles provided some solace to the Louisiana troops.[16]

At the end of the campaign Taylor suffered another debilitating relapse. Paralyzed from the waist down, he returned to Richmond for therapy. On July 24, after nearly a month of convalescence, he met with the president to discuss his future and how best to serve the Confederacy. Coincidentally, Governor Thomas O. Moore had recently petitioned Davis to send a general officer to Louisiana to coordinate the state's men and resources. Davis realized that an officer of Taylor's stature—a war hero, the son of an American president, and a Louisianan to boot—was precisely what Moore needed to organize conscripts, control partisans, and calm the fears of an anxious citizenry. Taylor agreed that an assignment to command in Louisiana would benefit both him and the Confederacy. "No appointment could have been more satisfactory to me or to my people," Moore affirmed gratefully. On behalf of the state's citizens, the governor assured Davis that "[Taylor] shall have everything Louisiana has to give."[17]

Two weeks later Taylor left Virginia for Louisiana, where, he later wrote, "beyond the father of waters, two years of hard work and much fighting awaited." En route he stopped in Chattanooga, Tennessee, to confer with Braxton Bragg. Recently promoted to full general, Bragg outlined a strategy to secure middle Tennessee and perhaps Kentucky. Taylor thought the plan "excellent, giving promise of large results if vigorously executed." Its successful prosecution, however, would depend heavily on the cooperation of the commander of the Department of East Tennessee, Edmund Kirby Smith.[18]

In the summer of 1862, thirty-eight-year-old Edmund Kirby Smith was a rising gray star in the Confederacy. His promotion to major general and subsequent assignment to lead the Department of East Tennessee seemed logical steps in his expeditious ascent up the ladder of Confederate command. Despite the missteps that had marked his early career, Smith appeared poised to fulfill the expectations of those around him who believed that he would someday become a great military leader.[19]

Such expectations stretched back to Smith's boyhood in St. Augustine, Florida. His family ancestry was steeped in American history, with the maternal Kirby bloodlines flowing back to the American Revolution and the Smith lineage running through the War of 1812. The youngest son of the Kirby-Smith children, Edmund was born on May 16, 1824, and, following in the footsteps of his brother Ephraim, he entered West Point at age sixteen.[20]

Smith maintained a respectable class rank during his first two years at the academy, but during his third year his parents separated, and the young cadet found himself caught between sniping factions of the Kirby and Smith families. The troubled domestic situation affected him. His grades began to suffer, demerits began to accumulate, and his class rank plummeted from twelfth to twenty-sixth. Smith continued to struggle for the next two years but managed to graduate, ranked twenty-fifth out of forty-one cadets in the class of 1845.[21]

In September 1845, twenty-one-year-old lieutenant Smith joined the infantry at Corpus Christi, Texas. During the adjustment to army life, he endeavored to modify his behavior from that of a brooding youth to that of an honorable soldier. The following spring Mexican forces clashed with United States troops at Palo Alto, and in the ensuing battle of Resaca de la Palma, Smith reportedly fought "with great gallantry." Afterward, however, General Zachary Taylor refused to pursue the enemy and did not cross into Mexico for nine days. The decision angered Smith. He believed that Taylor had violated a tactical principle held by many young West Pointers that the offensive was of greater strategic value than the defensive. To press the advantage of victory on the battlefield with an aggressive pursuit of the vanquished foe exemplified the offensive principle.[22]

In September 1846 Taylor again violated military theory and divided his force for a two-pronged assault on Monterrey. The plan succeeded, but Smith's regiment suffered heavy casualties, especially among the officer corps. "Our officers died like heroes," Smith wrote, but of the strategy he complained, "A great mistake was made somewhere." Afterward the level of support for Taylor in Washington began to wither. In March 1847 Winfield Scott took four thousand veterans from Taylor, including Smith's unit, and began a campaign that would culminate in the capture of Mexico City.[23]

On April 18, less than thirty miles from Mexico City, Smith led a charge against the Mexican position at El Telegrafo during the battle of Cerro Gordo. After the battle a citation filed by the regiment's colonel omitted reference to Smith's heroics. At first Smith was despondent, but his gloom turned quickly to anger, and he filed an exasperated protest with Scott. Although Smith suspected the oversight to be intentional, his colonel changed the report to reflect the young lieutenant's bravery. The revised summary included a section dedicated to Smith's acts of valor and characterized him as "an officer of much merit and promise." Smith was somewhat mollified, and five months later, at war's end, he received a promotion to first lieutenant.[24]

Smith's Mexican War experience influenced his thinking on warfare. Scott and Taylor relied on the strategic turning movement and the tactics of a frontal assault. Although effective, these maneuvers presented great risk and were often costly. The price of victory was over seventeen hundred American battlefield deaths, among them Smith's brother Ephraim, who fell at Molino del Rey. After the war Smith reflected, "The greatness of victory is measured, not by the immensity of loss on either side, but by the accomplishment of the result with the smallest possible loss." Indeed, during the Civil War, Smith invariably challenged the wisdom of the tactical offensive and chose repeatedly to proceed with caution, stressing the strength of the defensive.[25]

Similarly, at several engagements Scott and Taylor exhibited a tendency to divide their armies rather than to bring a concentration of force to bear against the enemy. To Smith, this seemed incongruous with West Point teachings. During the Civil War he increasingly sought concentration before offering battle. While this was consistent with Napoleonic theory, other West Pointers, such as Stonewall Jackson, refined the theory to fit the changing nature of warfare. In addition, Smith's reluctance to assume the tactical offensive did not reflect Napoleonic theory. His propensity to favor the defensive often led to sluggish or ill-timed concentration that made his strategy ineffective.[26]

The concept of glory was also important to Smith. Throughout the campaigning he demonstrated great courage and leadership under fire, yet he was hungry for recognition and complained bitterly when overlooked for a citation. His perception that the slight was intentional indicates that Smith felt underappreciated, if not persecuted, by his superiors. In fact, his desire for accolades became a motivating factor throughout his career, and his quest for glory increased greatly during the Civil War.[27]

The issue of pursuit played a crucial role in Smith's Mexican War education. He criticized Taylor's decision not to pursue the enemy after the victory at Resaca de la Palma and lauded Scott's drive from Vera Cruz through the gates of Mexico

City. By the time of the Civil War, however, Smith had adapted his views on pursuit to satisfy his own vision of warfare and to satiate a thirst for glory. During the Civil War he refused to permit a subordinate to pursue a shattered Union army. Instead, Smith detached troops and led the pursuit of another enemy column over one hundred miles away. Ironically, the subordinate was Zachary Taylor's son.[28]

In the months following the Mexican War, Smith became active in a soldiers' lobby that represented the interests of war orphans and widows. The cause touched Smith personally, as his brother Ephraim had left behind a wife and three children. Smith's military career soon carried him to a variety of posts, including a three-year stint at West Point as professor of mathematics and assignment to the elite Second Cavalry.[29]

In 1859 Smith took command of Camp Colorado, a seventy-four-man garrison northwest of San Antonio, Texas. During that time, tempers east of the Mississippi flared over the issues of slavery and secession. Smith rejected the doctrine of states' rights and acknowledged the evils of slavery, but he feared that Abraham Lincoln's election would drive many southern states from the Union. To avoid confronting his divided loyalties, Smith contemplated resigning his commission and remaining in Texas to become a cattle rancher. "God grant that we may weather the storm without dismantling the ship," he wrote his family just prior to the 1860 election. Lincoln's victory decided the issue, and on Christmas Eve, Smith confided to his mother, "Right or wrong I go with the land of my birth."[30]

Despite Florida's secession, in January 1861, Smith was wary of the viability of a southern nation and decided to remain at his post to await further developments. While he pondered his fate, Texas passed its own ordinance of secession, and on February 22 several hundred Texans encircled the fort and demanded Smith's surrender. Although he expressed a degree of sympathy with the Texans, Smith bristled at the thought of surrender and warned that he would not submit to a mob of rebels. Only after David E. Twiggs, United States commander of the Department of Texas, acquiesced to the surrender terms of the state legislature did Smith agree to relinquish the fort, and on February 26 he ordered the Stars and Stripes lowered. For his heroism he received a promotion to major. Smith briefly considered remaining in the army, reasoning that rapid advancement in rank would surely follow. Nevertheless, he resigned his commission on March 1 and offered his services to the Southern Confederacy.[31]

From the new nation's capital in Montgomery, Alabama, the Confederate high command determined that Smith's talents made him best suited to coordinate the vital defenses around New Orleans. Instead of reporting directly to Louisiana, however, Smith went to Florida to visit his mother. When he failed to turn up, state officials grew nervous and the War Department became impatient. "Your presence is wanted here, come at once," Adjutant General Samuel Cooper commanded in a wire to St. Augustine. Smith indicated that he could fulfill certain duties such as making staff appointments before going to Louisiana. The War Department was not pleased and revoked the assignment, ordering him back to Texas. Before Smith left, however, Virginia seceded from the Union, and the War Department issued new instructions: he was to help organize recruits in Lynchburg. Smith's first task in Confederate service was far less glamorous than the duty to which he aspired.[32]

Upon his arrival in Virginia, Smith expressed skepticism about enlistees, supplies, and officers. He described the recruits as "uncouth and intractable" and characterized the selection of Robert E. Lee to lead the Virginians as "unfortunate." Lee had more faith in Smith and placed him in command of the operation. The Confederates were not disappointed, and Smith's administrative skill helped to assemble an army from scratch. Still, Smith did not share in the martial enthusiasm that swept through the encampment. He accused others of bungling their assignments and claimed that a regiment of regulars was worth more than the entire Confederacy.[33]

In late May, Smith received an appointment as chief of staff to General Joseph E. Johnston. "The first military man of the day," he boasted of Johnston. Indeed, Johnston's reputation followed him from West Point through the Mexican War and now to his assignment at Harpers Ferry. The strategic importance of Harpers Ferry made Smith's responsibilities vitally important. His hopes of coordinating a proper military force there were dashed, however, when he arrived to find conditions as chaotic as those in Lynchburg.[34]

While stationed at Harpers Ferry, Smith forged a close relationship with Johnston. He did double duty as Johnston's adjutant and used the opportunity to learn from the general's experience. The men shared similar views, and Smith took Johnston's pronouncements to heart. In a letter to Richmond written May 26, Johnston labeled Harpers Ferry untenable, complained that the army was improperly supplied, and insisted that the lack of discipline among the troops would "render it difficult to use them in the field." Within days Smith wrote a series of letters home that expressed the identical sentiments. Smith also noted that given the caliber of soldier under arms to the Confederacy, a defensive policy with reliance upon interior lines was the only way for the South to win the war. This manner of thinking not only mirrored Johnston's approach but became an influential precept that guided Smith's Confederate career.[35]

In June, Johnston's green Army of the Shenandoah moved to Winchester, and on the seventeenth Davis promoted eleven colonels, including Smith, to the rank of brigadier. One month later the army began to travel by rail forty miles southeast to Manassas Junction, where a Confederate force of twenty-two thousand under P. G. T. Beauregard prepared to meet a Federal army of thirty-three thousand. Johnston directed Smith to remain in the Shenandoah and coordinate the movement. Once the task was complete, he was to bring up the rear with his own brigade. The operation took three days, and Smith chafed at the protracted pace. Yet at 3:00 A.M. on July 21 his own brigade was still unprepared to board the train for Manassas. This placed Smith in a quandary. If he stayed with his men he would miss the battle, but his responsibilities dictated that he remain until the last elements of the army had departed. The temptation to take part in the war's first battle proved too great to resist. Smith left his men behind, boarded a train to the front, and assumed command of Colonel Arnold Elzey's brigade.[36]

The train arrived at Manassas shortly after midday on July 21, and Smith received instructions to halt the brigade in the rear. He challenged the orders and demanded to speak directly with Johnston. Moments later the generals met, and Smith lobbied fervently for a chance to join the fighting. Johnston acquiesced and told him to take up a position on the left flank. Smith hesitated and requested that Johnston lead the brigade to the front. "I cannot direct you," replied the commander. "[Use] the fire as your guide." Smith continued to pressure his commander to accompany him until Johnston relented and led the troops forward.[37]

When the men reached the Confederate left, Johnston instructed Smith to extend the flank and turn the Union right. A Confederate soldier reported that "cheer after cheer now rent the air" as Smith rode along the lines and moved the brigade into position. Before the deployment was complete, however, Smith's men became entangled with John B. Kershaw's brigade. As the two bickered over placement of the troops, a ball pierced Smith below the right collarbone, traveled through his body, and exited from his left breast. "The reins [fell] from his grasp, he reeled in the saddle, threw out his arms and fell to the ground," recalled one of the soldiers. Feeling a warm stream of water from his pierced canteen trickle slowly down his torso, Smith believed he was wounded mortally. He lost consciousness and was carried from the field.[38]

Although the incident seemed serious, Smith soon recovered. Meanwhile, the media portrayed him as a hero, even though his participation had been limited to, in his own words, "moving on the double quick so as to bring my command on the flank of the enemy's victorious column." Southern newspapers trumpeted his actions: "The tide of battle was turned . . . by the arrival of Gen. Kirby Smith," and "Kirby Smith had . . . driven the wedge that was to split the Yankee army to pieces." Smith believed his press clippings and noted privately that his mere arrival at the front had caused the Federal "panic and flight." Publicly, however, he was more modest, claiming that God, rather than Kirby Smith, had "spread a panic . . . and turned [the enemy] in dismay & ultra confusion at the very moment of their victory."[39]

The Confederate high command was less laudatory than the press. In fact, Rebel brass implied that Smith had performed a greater service by suffering a battle wound than by any action he had taken. Johnston noted specifically that Smith had declined to lead the troops onto the field, and Davis asserted that Smith had disobeyed orders. Regardless of his role, Smith emerged as one of the Confederacy's first war heroes. For the remainder of his career he embraced this status and sought to erase any stains of controversy.[40]

Although Smith received a promotion for his service at Manassas, Davis seemed unsure of what to do with him. During the winter months of 1861–1862 Smith commanded a division in northern Virginia that included Richard Taylor's brigade. "For soldierly appearance," he noted, "they excelled anything I have seen." However, he disapproved of the rowdy behavior that plagued the army, from "the highest in command to the lowest in rank." In December two of Taylor's soldiers received the death penalty for storming a guardhouse to free several intoxicated compatriots. Both Smith and Taylor reviled drunkenness among the soldiers, and despite their personal revulsion at overseeing the executions, they carried out the orders of the court martial with the Louisiana brigade drawn up as observers.[41]

After Smith's brief stint as a division commander in northern Virginia, the War Department sent him to command the Department of East Tennessee. Davis believed that the leadership provided by Smith, an acknowledged war hero, would help to stabilize and pacify the restless population of a region opposed to Tennessee's secession. Upon his arrival in Knoxville, Smith found the department "a disorganized mob without head or discipline." He described the state of the civilian population as one of "open rebellion" against Confederate authority. Smith sent Davis a blistering assessment of the situation and accused the president of deceiving him about the assignment. "All accounts given me were far short of the truth," he snarled, and he complained to his wife, "I am overwhelmed with cares and troubles."[42]

For the next several months Smith juggled his interior lines to protect a two-hundred-mile stretch between the Cumberland Gap to the north and Chattanooga to the south. By late spring, however, Federal pressure from Don Carlos Buell, to the southwest, forced Smith to abandon the gap in favor of Chattanooga. Smith had only eight thousand men and requested reinforcements at once. In response, Davis turned to Braxton Bragg in Tupelo, Mississippi. Grudgingly, Bragg agreed to send Smith a division. "I have hoped you would be able to cope with [the enemy's] force," he scolded Smith.[43]

At this point Smith began discussions with Bragg about a campaign to secure middle Tennessee. He urged Bragg to shift his base to Chattanooga and emphasized that without such cooperation the Federals would soon overrun the state. Although Smith's evaluation was correct, his pleas for aid from Bragg were duplicitous. His real goal was Kentucky. With Bragg holding the Federals at bay in front of Chattanooga, the road would lie open for Smith to march all the way to the Ohio River. Smith failed to mention this stratagem to Bragg or to Davis. In late July, Bragg notified Richmond of plans to take his thirty-thousand-man army to Chattanooga and join Smith. Smith was elated by the news and alerted a subordinate to this "most favorable opportunity" to push into Kentucky.[44]

Of concern to Bragg was the command structure and its effect on the working relationship between the generals. He confessed as much to Smith and emphasized, "My only desire is to know the precise limits of my responsibilities, not to interfere in the least with your operations and command." Smith dismissed Bragg's angst and offered to "cheerfully place my command under you subject to your orders." Despite the offer, Bragg remained uneasy about the arrangement and asked Richmond to place Smith's department under his jurisdiction. This would have made Smith subordinate to Bragg's orders and reduced the potential confusion or misunderstanding between them. The War Department refused, and Davis scolded Bragg, urging him to cooperate fully with Smith, whom he called "one of our ablest and purest officers." This flaw in the command structure turned Bragg into an intruder in Smith's department and forced him to render advice rather than issue orders.[45]

In July the generals devised a strategy that called for Smith to retake the Cumberland Gap and then unite with Bragg for a drive into middle Tennessee. Less than two weeks after their agreement, Smith notified Bragg of a change in plans. He would leave a division to check the enemy at Cumberland Gap and push the rest of his command into Kentucky. Bragg would have to handle Chattanooga on his own. The abrupt, unilateral change in strategy angered Bragg, yet without unity of command, he was unable to stop Smith. Instead, he could only urge caution. Still, Smith counseled Bragg to expect nothing short of the "most brilliant results." Smith's ego allowed for nothing less. In letters to his wife Smith likened himself to the Spanish conquistador Cortés and to the Carthaginian general Hannibal. He considered his plan to invade Kentucky "a stroke of inspiration and genius."[46]

In mid-August, with an army of nearly ten thousand, Smith moved into the Blue Grass state, and by September 3 he held Lexington and Frankfort. Smith characterized the operation as one of liberation, not conquest, and confided to his wife, "[Kentuckians] have flocked to me and with tears in their eyes have thanked God for their deliverance." In a letter to Davis he indicated that Bragg had sanctioned the movement and pledged that the generals would act "in concert" throughout the campaign. In fact, Smith had seized command initiative, and all thoughts of turning over control to Bragg had vanished.[47]

Once Smith reached Lexington, he began a markedly conservative approach to the campaign. At least one member of his staff, William R. Boggs, expressed shock at Smith's decision not to push on toward the Ohio. Boggs believed that another staff member, Dr. Sol Smith, had counseled the general to exercise caution. Although not related to Smith, the surgeon was a trusted family friend. Smith took the doctor's advice to heart and for the next three weeks remained in Lexington. His army of liberation became one of occupation, spread across the Kentucky countryside in search of recruits and supplies. Amid persistent rumors of Federal forces converging on Lexington, Smith's grand vision turned rapidly to thoughts of retreat. "Unless . . . you can either speedily move your column in this direction or make with me a combined attack at Louisville," he warned Bragg, "I shall be compelled to fall back upon you for support."[48]

Bragg, meanwhile, had not remained idle in Chattanooga. When Smith's change in plans forced him to rethink his part in the campaign, Bragg elected to move into Kentucky and hoped to join Smith at Louisville. Unable to issue orders, Bragg suggested concentration at Bardstown, southeast of the city. Smith protested, arguing that the disposition of his troops made concentration below Louisville impractical and that he would do so only under orders.[49]

On October 1 Bragg arrived in Lexington to discuss the situation with Smith. By then Bragg had had enough, and he assumed operational control of all forces in the theater. Intelligence indicated that a Federal attack would come at Frankfort, and Bragg ordered Smith to concentrate his army there while Leonidas Polk led the remaining troops north from Bardstown. Bragg did not yet realize that Buell's movement toward Frankfort was a feint and that the main Federal force was advancing on Bardstown itself.[50]

Even as the enemy closed in, Smith continued to balk at Bragg's orders and attempted to reassert his autonomy. He sent erroneous reports of a large Federal force massing on his front and persuaded Bragg to shift two divisions from Polk to bolster his line. Meanwhile, on October 7 Buell's main force collided with Polk's rear strung out at Perryville, nearly forty miles south of Smith's position. The following day Bragg ordered Polk to attack, not realizing that he faced nearly sixty thousand Federals. The battle at Perryville raged inconclusively until nightfall when Bragg withdrew north to Harrodsburg, where he expected to find Smith.[51]

Smith was not there. Instead, his army still held its position below Frankfort. The previous afternoon, while Bragg fought at Perryville, Smith realized that Buell's strategy had fooled him, and he put his army in motion, clashing with the enemy rear guard near Lawrenceburg. The fight did little more than drive the Federals in the direction in which they were already moving. Afterward Smith rode to Harrodsburg to confer with Bragg. Upon his arrival he learned of the misfortune at Perryville.[52]

Smith implored Bragg not to abandon the campaign, but the general responded that he would not "risk the destruction of his army" and ordered an immediate withdrawal back to Tennessee. "For the first time in the history of the Confederacy," protested Smith, "an army of veterans retreated before an inferior force." During the arduous retreat Smith complained that Bragg had intentionally assigned him a treacherous route as punishment for the failure in Kentucky.[53]

Upon his return to Tennessee, Smith became despondent and considered resigning from the army to become a minister. He changed his mind, however, with word of a promotion to lieutenant general and a request to come to Richmond for an audience with the president. Smith arrived in the capital in November and, using the interview as an opportunity to denounce Bragg, placed blame for the failure of the campaign squarely on the stooped shoulders of the Louisiana general.[54]

Certainly Bragg was not without fault, but Smith was also culpable for compromising the strategic and tactical integrity of the campaign on several fronts. In August he deceived Bragg about his true intentions and unilaterally initiated a change of plans after the campaign had already gotten under way. He repeatedly refused concentration and filed misleading reports concerning Federal troop movements. The erroneous information prompted Bragg to move away from the real threat at Perryville. Smith's aspirations to live up to the expectations of others, and to his press clippings from Manassas, were critical factors in his abdication of responsibility for the unsuccessful campaign. His reluctance to push the initiative and to risk his discreetly honed reputation led directly to Confederate failure on the battlefield at Perryville and to Bragg's downfall in Kentucky.

Despite Smith's assurances to Davis of continued cooperation, the president took the dispute with Bragg to heart. In early January 1863 the War Department transferred Smith to command of the Southwestern Army, operating in Texas and Louisiana. While Smith began preparations for his new assignment, Davis and Robert E. Lee discussed reassigning him to command the Department of North Carolina and Southern Virginia. Smith balked at this assignment primarily out of deference to his friend Gustavus W. Smith, the officer he was to replace. Davis sustained the original orders. Nevertheless, Smith was unhappy with his assignment to the Trans-Mississippi, a theater far removed from his exploits in Kentucky and Virginia. "You might as well bury me," he moaned to the president.[55]

In late January, Smith gathered his family, servants, and staff for the journey across the Mississippi. However grim his prospects appeared to be, Lee's earlier pronouncement that Smith was "one of our best officers" must have carried weight with Davis, for when Smith and his entourage reached Montgomery, there was a telegram from Richmond waiting. The War Department had amended Smith's orders and in doing so made his assignment even more burdensome: "The command of Lieut. Gen. E. Kirby Smith is extended so as to embrace the Trans-Mississippi Department." It did not take Smith long to appreciate what he was up against, and he complained to Joseph E. Johnston, "I have a herculanian task before me . . . no army—no means . . . no system, no order, all to be done from the beginning."[56]

2

To Baffle the Enemy in His Designs

While Edmund Kirby Smith was busy fighting Federals in Kentucky, Richard Taylor assumed command in Louisiana. Of Taylor's homecoming Governor Thomas O. Moore announced, "Nothing can exceed the gratification, both personal and official, which is occasioned here by the arrival of Gen. Taylor." Yet the situation was unstable at best, and Taylor faced a plethora of problems, most of which stemmed from the fall of New Orleans in April. "I found almost a total want of everything necessary for troops in the field," Taylor noted, and he complained that the district "had no soldiers, no arms or munitions, and no money." The extensive system of navigable rivers and bayous left Louisiana's interior vulnerable to invasion, and Taylor was agonizingly aware of the Federal forces that prowled the Lafourche region. The danger of an enemy incursion into the district's heartland was something that Taylor would have to contend with for the remainder of his tenure. Moreover, Confederate authority throughout the state had effectively ceased. Taylor's job was to reestablish that authority.[1]

Taylor was to serve under General Theophilus H. Holmes, the commander of the Trans-Mississippi Department, headquartered in Little Rock, Arkansas. Holmes was a partially deaf fifty-seven-year-old Mexican War veteran. Though he had once been described as a "brave [and] true . . . patriot and gentleman," some men under his command now considered him "weak, vacillating, and totally devoid of [the] energy" necessary to handle the complicated demands of a department as extensive as the Trans-Mississippi. Upon his arrival Taylor notified Holmes of the district's needs but did not receive an immediate reply. When a response finally came, Holmes indicated that his primary concern was Arkansas, and he offered little advice for Taylor and no assistance for Louisiana. Taylor realized that the burden of command had fallen on him alone.[2]

Taylor's official assignment was twofold. First, he was to marshal fresh troops, by means of either conscription or enlistment, and select those most suited to fill out the Louisiana regiments in Virginia. The remainder of the recruits, along with state militia and scattered partisan troops, was to be reorganized and deployed throughout the district as Taylor saw fit. The second task was to prevent the Federals from using the rivers and bayous as a means to establish a position in the Louisiana interior. By disrupting Federal navigation and harassing enemy troop movements, the Confederate command hoped that Taylor could "confine the enemy within the narrowest limits and recover . . . any and all positions . . . which had fallen into his hands."[3]

Although his written orders did not specify which Federal positions warranted consideration for recapture, a meeting with President Davis and Secretary of War George Wythe Randolph, held just before Taylor's departure for Louisiana, left no doubt that New Orleans was the top priority. Randolph recognized the importance of the Trans-Mississippi to the war effort and insisted that the recapture of New Orleans was essential to assure a steady flow of supplies to the east. In addition, Moore had characterized the Federal garrison in New Orleans as little more than "an ordinary city mob" and implied that there was a strong possibility for military success. Ideally, Taylor would fuel the passions of southern nationalism among the citizens, who would then rise up to help the army drive the enemy from the city. Given the depleted resources of Taylor's district, the paucity of troops at his command, and the number of Federals in and around New Orleans, the plan to recapture the city was highly speculative. Still, despite these obstacles, circumstances along the Mississippi River dictated that Davis take action. Accordingly, he assigned the task to Taylor.[4]

Immediately upon his arrival in Louisiana, Taylor began to prepare for the campaign. The Randolph-Davis plan for New Orleans granted him virtual autonomy within his district and sweeping authority in districts outside of his direct control. But although the plan authorized him to detach units from surrounding states, Davis and Randolph chose to keep the New Orleans mission secret from other Confederate government and military officials. The covert nature of the operation undermined Taylor's ability to mobilize his resources and put him at odds with several of his counterparts, most notably Daniel Ruggles, the officer whose command encompassed eastern Louisiana.[5]

Nevertheless, Taylor prepared to take the offensive. He established his new headquarters in Alexandria, located on the Red River sixty miles north of Opelousas and sixty-five river miles from the confluence of the Red and Mississippi. From Alexandria, Taylor maintained that the "geographical center of the State and of steam navigation" provided him a better command axis. It was an excellent choice. Forty-five miles east of Alexandria, on the northern banks of the Red, Taylor had access to the Ouachita River and, twenty miles further, on the south bank, to the Bayou Atchafalaya. Below Alexandria the Bayou Teche flowed south through Opelousas, Vermilionville, and on to Brashear City at the southern tip of

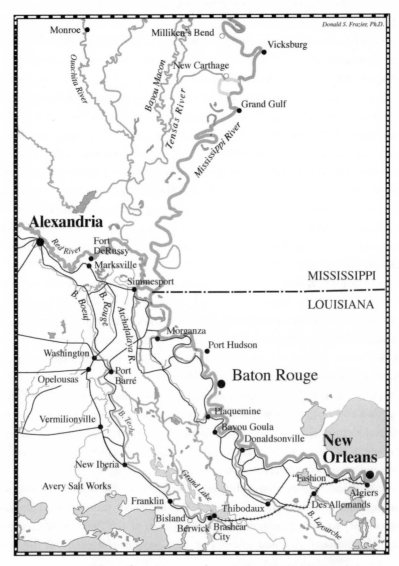

Theater of operations, southeastern Louisiana, 1862

Grand Lake. From Brashear City a railroad line ran sixty-five miles east, through the Lafourche region, and directly into New Orleans. Accordingly, Alexandria not only provided for the defense of western Louisiana and the important waterways but also afforded access to the Lafourche region, a prime staging area for the planned attack on New Orleans.[6]

In early September, Taylor pushed into the Lafourche region and attacked the Federal garrison at Bayou Des Allemands, halfway between Brashear City and New Orleans. The operation was significant in that the engagement marked the first Confederate victory in Louisiana since the fall of New Orleans, and it netted Taylor a cache of much needed munitions and supplies. The action also provided an important boost to the sagging morale of the state's civilians and soldiers while serving as a reminder to the Federals that Rebel forces in Louisiana still posed a threat. Despite the initial success, Federal reinforcements soon drove the Confederates from the area. This reversal prompted Taylor to criticize Colonel Edward Waller, the field commander of the operation. He accused Waller of failing to follow specific orders for the defense of his position. The vigilance necessary to win the war could "only be secured by discipline," Taylor admonished him. "Nothing compensates for absence of discipline." This incident marked the first time Taylor as a district commander leveled criticism at a subordinate for failure to perform up to expectations.[7]

Despite Waller's inability to hold the position, Taylor was pleased with the sortie. His satisfaction proved short-lived, however, when he learned that Federal raiding parties had vandalized his plantation home in St. Charles Parish. Taylor was livid and threatened to execute prisoners of war in reprisal. Federal commander Benjamin Butler acknowledged Taylor's grievance but urged him to rescind the death threats. Correctly perceiving that Taylor had personalized the war, Butler reminded him that the destruction of property, though regrettable, was an inevitable consequence of war. Taylor regained his composure and his perspective, and no prisoners were executed. Across the lines, however, Butler vowed to drive the Rebels from western Louisiana.[8]

By October 1862 Taylor was operating his district as an independent command, without direction from Holmes in Little Rock. Taking advantage of the wide latitude granted him by the department commander, he had combined a successful overhaul of district administration with a fervent invocation of Louisiana nationalism to swell his ranks to nearly six thousand effectives. Most significantly, Taylor worked to establish foundries at Alexandria, Franklin, Monroe, and New

Iberia. These installations not only repaired and reissued hundreds of previously unusable arms but also manufactured quantities of munitions sufficient to send a surplus across the Mississippi to Vicksburg and Charleston, thus relieving Richmond of the responsibility to fill Taylor's requisitions for arms.[9]

Not all the news was encouraging for Richmond or for Taylor. By mid-October, Confederate failures at Corinth and in Kentucky had damaged hopes for the rescue of New Orleans. These defeats elevated the defense of Vicksburg and Port Hudson to the highest priority for the War Department, relegating New Orleans to secondary strategic status. Davis confided to Moore that Louisiana's only hope lay in Taylor's ability to "baffle the enemy in his designs on the Mississippi Valley." Yet Davis did not abandon the plans for New Orleans completely. Nor did he notify Taylor of any change in policy toward the mission to take the city. Accordingly, Taylor refused to surrender New Orleans as his ultimate objective. He recognized, however, that for the moment the only actions he could undertake were of a defensive nature.[10]

On October 1, 1862, Brigadier General Alfred Mouton received an assignment to Taylor's command. Mouton, the thirty-three-year-old son of Louisiana's former governor, and a West Pointer, shared a common background with his new commanding officer. As members of the state's elite, each had political influence and maintained a sense of responsibility not only to the Confederacy but also to Louisiana. Taylor instructed Mouton to establish headquarters at Thibodaux, a central point in the Lafourche region near Boutte Station. Mouton deployed his skeleton regiments, which consisted of twenty-five hundred troops, along a sixty-mile stretch of the Bayou Lafourche that extended south from Donaldsonville to Des Allemands. He ordered Mouton to gather intelligence on the enemy's movements and to guard against further Federal encroachment.[11]

Taking advantage of Mouton's presence, Taylor traveled to Vicksburg to discuss the situation along the Mississippi with John C. Pemberton, department commander in Mississippi. During the meeting Taylor proposed to threaten New Orleans in order to deter the enemy from increasing pressure on Vicksburg. Pemberton gave tacit approval to the plan, and Taylor, believing that his counterpart would support the operation with reinforcements, returned to Louisiana with renewed hope.[12]

While Taylor was still in Vicksburg, though, the Federals drove Confederate forces from Donaldsonville and conducted a sweeping descent along both sides of the Lafourche. After two days of fighting, Mouton withdrew from Thibodaux and escaped through Brashear City, west across Berwick Bay, to the safety of the Bayou Teche. In his official report Mouton noted emphatically, "The presence of General Taylor is indispensably necessary here." When Taylor returned to find the country west of New Orleans under Federal control, he was quick to blame Mouton for the loss and condemned him for failing to concentrate against divided elements of the Federal column. Upon closer analysis of the tactical situation, however, and in light of Mouton's orders to picket such a large region with such a small force, Taylor soon softened his criticism.[13]

Taylor contacted Pemberton at once to apprise him of developments in Louisiana. Federal occupation of the Lafourche compromised not only the tenuous security of Taylor's district but also the supply routes from western Louisiana to the Mississippi. Yet Pemberton was indifferent. "I cannot send a regiment unless of vital importance," he replied to Taylor's request for help. With no recourse, Taylor turned his attention to the defense of his district and ordered immediate construction of water batteries along the Red River, the Ouachita, the Atchafalaya, and the Bayou Teche. With few men and fewer guns to protect these installations, he again requested aid from Vicksburg, and Pemberton again refused. "I regard the defense of this valley of much greater importance than that of West Louisiana," he scolded Taylor. Taylor was less stung by Pemberton's rebuff than he was disgusted with President Davis for placing a man with an "incapacity . . . for independent command" in such a strategically crucial position. Unlike his anger with subordinates Mouton and Waller, however, Taylor saved this vitriolic assessment of a senior officer for his postwar memoirs.[14]

By the end of 1862 a steady increase in the number of Federal forays probing the Louisiana interior forced Taylor to marshal all of his resources to protect the Teche region. For Taylor, the new year brought with it a new Union general and an old battlefield foe. Massachusetts politician-turned-general Nathaniel P. Banks arrived in New Orleans with orders to move against points along the Mississippi held by Taylor's Confederates. Less than one year earlier, Banks had faced Taylor during Jackson's Valley campaign. Then, the luckless New Englander had suffered the humiliating capture of his trains and his stores, earning him the title "Commissary to the Confederacy." Now, in Louisiana, Banks's mission was to open the Mississippi to Federal navigation. His secondary objective was to clear the Confederates from the Red River Valley. With the Louisiana heartland thus secured, he was to turn his attention to a third task, the occupation of Texas.[15]

Although Taylor believed Banks to be an officer prone to "ignorance and arrogance," he did not underestimate his enemy. He recognized that unless the Federals launched a direct assault on the fortifications at Port Hudson, a bloody prospect upon which few politicians would dare risk their reputation, they would first have to gain control of the Teche region. In anticipation of Banks's movements up the Teche, Taylor strengthened Confederate positions on the roads along its banks. He selected the high ground above the bayou west of Brashear City for construction of an earthworks called Fort Bisland. Bisland would serve as the center of military operations, and Confederate numbers soon rose by thirteen hundred when Louisianan Henry Hopkins Sibley's brigade of Texas cavalry joined Taylor's command. The brigade was originally ordered from Texas to Vicksburg, but Pemberton had refused assistance from Sibley. To Taylor, though, Sibley's ill-equipped and undisciplined troops made up for their deficiencies with their bravery and zeal. During this time Taylor also received word that the War Department had decided to make a change in leadership west of the river. Richmond reduced Holmes's command to the District of Arkansas and ordered Edmund Kirby Smith to take charge of the Trans-Mississippi Department. "Smith, from his training and services," Taylor reasoned, "seemed an excellent selection."[16]

President Davis and his new secretary of war, James A. Seddon, also considered Smith an outstanding choice for command in the Trans-Mississippi. Their primary concerns were to protect the Mississippi River and defend the lower Mississippi Valley. Although there was no mention of the plan to recapture New Orleans, Smith's instructions indicated that Louisiana had become a strategic priority. Smith acknowledged that his most important task would be to aid Taylor in the defense of the lower Mississippi. He concurred with Seddon that the area encompassed by Taylor's command was "among the most defensible in the world, and that comparatively few . . . men could repel a host of invaders." While Davis reportedly held Smith "in the highest esteem," the new Trans-Mississippi commander accepted his assignment reluctantly and out of a sense of duty. "I feel my responsibilities are great and that my troubles will soon commence," he confessed to his wife, and he indicated to at least one staff member that he fully expected to shoulder the blame "for the inroads which the enemy may make." By March 7 Smith had crossed the Mississippi at Port Hudson and, on a boat provided by Taylor, traveled up the Red River to his new headquarters in Alexandria, Louisiana.[17]

Although Davis and Seddon directed him to concentrate on securing the lower Mississippi, Smith remained in Louisiana just long enough to coordinate his staff and meet with Taylor. During the interview Smith echoed Davis's concern for

Vicksburg and insisted that "something should be done on our side of the river." Taylor indicated that the dearth of troops in Louisiana hampered all operations. Smith acknowledged the problem and stated that he had "positive instructions" from the president to send John G. Walker's Texas infantry division from Arkansas to Louisiana. With that the meeting adjourned, and Smith promptly turned his attention to Arkansas. Ten days after crossing into Louisiana he arrived in Little Rock for a series of meetings with authorities in Arkansas. This action mystified even his own chief of staff, William R. Boggs. En route to Little Rock, Smith confided to Boggs that "Davis was very much annoyed with the manner in which . . . Holmes had been conducting the department," and that Holmes "had centered his thoughts and ideas on Arkansas alone . . . leaving the rest of the department to take care of itself." Yet Smith remained in Arkansas for three weeks and, despite orders to the contrary, strengthened the northern portions of his department at the expense of the lower Mississippi.[18]

Boggs later maintained that Smith had "fallen under the same influences" in Arkansas as had Holmes. His suspicions were at least partially accurate. Smith's assignment to the Trans-Mississippi came largely in response to pressure from the Arkansas congressional delegation. A highly placed member of the War Department, Robert Garlick Hill Kean, recorded that the Arkansas politicians "insist[ed] on a change in commanders" for their state. He stressed that these congressmen displayed serious "indications of dissatisfaction with the Government and complain[ed] of neglect in the Trans-Mississippi." Josiah Gorgas, the Confederacy's chief of ordnance, thought that Arkansas suffered from a "lamentable record of bad management and of failures," and that Smith's appointment could only help. Seddon's evaluation mirrored these assessments. In a letter to Smith he noted that "disorder, confusion, and demoralization" were prevalent throughout Arkansas and that conditions justified "serious anxiety and apprehensions." The targets of the dissatisfaction among Arkansans were Holmes and his subordinate Thomas C. Hindman, whose policies had left the state destitute of supplies and bereft of morale. The clamor in Arkansas newspapers and among the state's politicians for a capable general with a good record and reputation, rather than a military derelict like Holmes, prompted Davis to select Smith. Consequently, Smith felt beholden to the Arkansas contingent of Congress that had lobbied successfully for his appointment as commander of the Trans-Mississippi.[19]

Seddon understood that the uproar in Arkansas would not subside with the mere appointment of Smith. The change in leadership required action by the new commander. On March 18 he advised Smith, "A pressing necessity requires your personal presence and influence." The secretary proceeded to paint a picture of lawlessness, disease, and gloom among soldiers and civilians alike. He urged Smith to go to Arkansas and to use his "ability and influence to restore order and confidence" among the people. Seddon did not, however, forget the crisis in Louisiana. He prefaced the directive by emphasizing "the primary importance of maintaining . . . command of the Lower Mississippi" and instructing Smith to "plan and direct operations" in Louisiana before leaving for Arkansas. But Smith had already decided to leave Louisiana for Arkansas and arrived in Little Rock on the day Seddon composed his letter. As a result, Smith's absence left Taylor free to plan and direct operations in the lower Mississippi while the department commander turned his attention to the politics and policies in Arkansas.[20]

The pressure for Smith to take action in the northern sector of his department did not stop at the Arkansas border. On April 1 General Sterling Price, the former Missouri governor who had been serving under Pemberton, arrived in Little Rock. Missouri's Confederate governor, Thomas C. Reynolds, had pressured Richmond for Price's return to the Trans-Mississippi more for his popularity than for his military expertise. Although Smith managed to effect Price's reassignment, he failed to secure the transfer of his command, thus depriving the Trans-Mississippi of badly needed troops.[21]

Smith gave Price command of an Arkansas division. In turn, Price and Reynolds beseeched Smith to invade Missouri as a means of relieving pressure on Vicksburg. Smith's name was "a household word" in Missouri, Reynolds told the commanding general, and failure to liberate the state would lead its loyal Confederates to believe that Richmond did not care. Smith understood the strategic importance of the state and agreed to lead an expedition into Missouri. He refused to launch the campaign, though, until he had enough troops to hold the state. By the close of the meetings, Price, Reynolds, and even Holmes had made such an impression on Smith that he decided to keep Walker's division in Arkansas rather than send it to Taylor in Louisiana.[22]

As a result, Smith opened his tenure as commander of the Trans-Mississippi by making the identical mistake his predecessor had made. By concentrating on Arkansas, he left Taylor to fend for himself in Louisiana. This perpetuated the pattern of de facto autonomy that Taylor had enjoyed since his arrival in the Trans-Mississippi. For Smith, Taylor's district was simply one piece in a larger puzzle. By going to Arkansas just days after his arrival in the department, he flagrantly disobeyed orders from Davis and Seddon. His failure to follow explicit instructions regarding protection of the lower Mississippi placed the security of Taylor's entire district in jeopardy. Moreover, Smith's neglect of Louisiana undermined the command structure in the Trans-Mississippi and reinforced Taylor's notion of self-sufficiency.[23]

By April 1863 Taylor had received little guidance from department head-quarters and was still operating, in effect, an independent command in western Louisiana. On April 9 Colonel Henry Gray reported from Fort Bisland that large numbers of Federals, protected by gunboats, had begun crossing Berwick Bay from Brashear City. That evening Taylor rode to Bisland to inspect the fortifica-tions and analyze the situation at Gray's front. The next morning he found three divisions of enemy troops preparing to move up the Bayou Teche toward the Confederate position.[24]

Taylor believed that he could hold Bisland with four thousand troops against a frontal assault even by sixteen thousand Federals. Yet he realized that the fort was vulnerable to an amphibious flanking movement by way of Grand Lake, four miles to his rear. Taylor suspected just such a maneuver by the Federals, and at noon on April 12, blue troop movements confirmed his suspicions. As the Federals advanced slowly toward the front at Bisland, Taylor received reports of a Union gunboat and several transports in Grand Lake. In response, he divided the small gray force and deployed Mouton and Sibley, each with fifteen hundred men, along the east and west banks of the Teche, respectively. Taylor sent the remainder of the troops to Hutchins' Point on Grand Lake to monitor the Federals.[25]

Taylor's anticipation of the Federal strategy proved correct. Yet as the afternoon sun fell below the tangle of swamp ash and cypress trees, a frontal attack against Bisland failed to materialize. Banks seemed content to engage in an artillery duel while awaiting the advance of fellow New Englander Cuvier Grover southward from Grand Lake. That night Taylor hatched a plan to take the offensive. He be-lieved that Banks would continue waiting for Grover. Accordingly, Taylor ordered Sibley to launch a predawn assault on the Union left. By seizing the offensive in what was clearly a defensive situation, Taylor chose to wrest the initiative from Banks. In striking the Federals to his front, Taylor hoped to "drive the enemy back, throw him into confusion," and force Grover to withdraw from Grand Lake in or-der to reinforce Banks. Attacking the southern arm of the pincer would effectively break the northern arm of the movement. Likewise, once the Federals broke off the threat from the north, the danger from the south would be neutralized.[26]

This was a strategy that Taylor employed at various times against Banks during ensuing Federal operations across Louisiana. In the Teche campaign of 1863 and the Red River campaign of 1864, the Federals sent large but separate columns to oper-

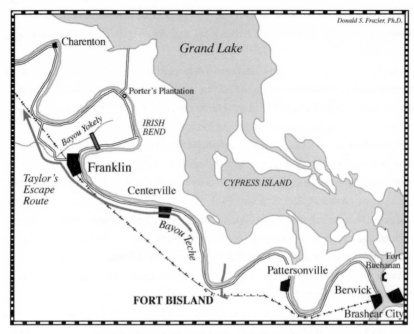

Teche campaign, Fort Bisland and Irish Bend, 1863

ate against Taylor's modest forces. This compelled Taylor to gamble on his army's ability to launch a swift and convincing tactical strike and thus require the enemy to alter its own strategy. Perhaps less out of design than necessity, Taylor consistently sought to take the initiative against a larger force, deliver a stunning blow to the enemy, and disrupt Federal operations. Although the strategy was sound, the officers upon whom Taylor relied, both superior and subordinate, proved to be a variable that he could not control. Such was the case at Bisland.

In the predawn hours of April 13 Taylor rode north to Grand Lake to assess the situation personally while leaving command at Bisland to Sibley. Although Sibley had established a reputation in the Seminole and Mexican wars as a hard fighter, he had also earned notoriety as a hard drinker and more recently as a malcontent. On the morning of April 13 Sibley failed to initiate the attack as ordered. This forced the Confederates at Bisland to weather another daylong firestorm of shot and shell. As Taylor had predicted, Banks continued the artillery barrage rather than launch an infantry assault without Grover's force in position. Sibley's failure to force Banks's hand further compromised the vulnerable position at Bisland. Nevertheless, Sibley's unwillingness to advance could not have come as a complete surprise to Taylor. During a council of war held on the night of April 12, Sibley had argued that Bisland was the wrong place to make a stand. Now, with Taylor out of the way at Grand Lake, Sibley resolved that an attack against the Federal left was impracticable and refused to execute Taylor's orders.[27]

Taylor was furious when he returned to Bisland that evening. Although he discovered no evidence to indicate that drunkenness had played a part in the insubordination, he angrily condemned Sibley's failure to carry out instructions. "The supineness of that officer," he seethed in his report to Smith, "and his positive declaration of the impracticability of carrying the plan into execution . . . frustrated the scheme." The strategy to take the offensive against Banks, Taylor concluded, "would have accomplished the most favorable results if actively attempted." Taylor's bitterness towards Sibley intensified when, at 9:00 P.M. he learned that Grover had finally landed at Grand Lake. The Federals marched to a position near the town of Franklin on the Teche's Irish Bend. With fourteen thousand enemy troops to his front and four thousand poised to spring a trap to his rear, Taylor had no choice but to abandon Bisland.[28]

Fortunately, Grover had made a tactical mistake. Confederate skirmishers between Hutchins' Point and Franklin put up such stiff resistance that he decided to delay his move on the town until morning. By halting his troops short of Franklin, Grover failed to cut off the lone road and bridge by which Taylor's entire force could escape. Seizing the opportunity, Taylor again took the initiative, this time to cover the withdrawal from Bisland. At dawn on April 14, with fewer than twelve hundred men, he led an attack on Grover's unsuspecting force and drove the enemy far enough for the rest of the Confederates to slip through Franklin. Before Grover could regroup, the Confederate gunboat *Diana* steamed into position along Taylor's right and swept the field with deadly fire. Upon Mouton's arrival at 8:00 A.M, Taylor turned operations over to his brigadier and rode to Franklin to direct the retreating columns to New Iberia twenty-five miles to the northwest. "The salvation of our retiring army was entirely owing to the bold and determined attack of our troops under the immediate command of Major-General Taylor," reported Mouton. Taylor left Mouton with instructions to contain Grover until the remainder of the troops from Bisland, including Sibley, had passed safely through Franklin.[29]

Thus far Taylor's revised plan had worked to near perfection. He had stolen a march on Banks, held Grover in check, and extricated his forces from the jaws of a lethal trap. As Mouton continued to fight the delaying action against Grover, Sibley's division hurried through Franklin. Yet Sibley's mind was apparently elsewhere. He was still smarting from Taylor's reprimand and angered by the subsequent appointment of Mouton, a subordinate officer, to command the operation. Earlier in the day Sibley had complained of feeling ill and evidently did not understand the tactical situation. At Franklin he did not realize that Mouton was still across the Bayou Yokely, holding off the Federal counterattack. Sibley issued orders for his rear guard, under Texan Thomas Green, to fire the bridge across the bayou. This cut off Mouton's only escape route. Mouton, recognizing what had happened, ordered a headlong retreat through the flames. "I succeeded in eluding pursuit and extricated the troops from a very perilous attitude," Mouton reported candidly, "and saw every man file over a burning bridge in the rear of the village, myself and staff crossing when it was almost entirely consumed." Taylor took the news far less amicably. He not only relieved Sibley of command but also filed charges against him and ordered a court martial.[30]

Having just returned to Alexandria from Arkansas, Smith did not learn of the battle at Bisland until the day after Taylor's narrow escape. In the mistaken belief that the Federals had launched a pincer movement toward Alexandria, with Banks coming up the Teche and John A. McClernand descending from the northeast, Smith called immediately for troops to support Taylor. He ordered Holmes to send Walker's infantry from Arkansas to Monroe in northern Louisiana and directed General John Bankhead Magruder, in command of the District of Texas, New Mexico, and Arizona, to move his disposable force toward Opelousas, between Alexandria and the enemy. By the time three regiments of Texas cavalry under Colonel James P. Major reached the Red River, Banks had already driven Taylor past Opelousas, thus forcing the horsemen to ride to Alexandria. For the time being, the pressing situation in Louisiana took precedence over Smith's desire to make Arkansas and Missouri the primary theater of operations.[31]

As the Federal invasion force continued to cut its way deeper into central Louisiana, both Smith and Taylor realized that the situation was indeed grave. Taylor, his men starving and exhausted, sent Mouton and Green, Sibley's replacement, west to forage along the Sabine River. He held the remainder of the troops in Alexandria. Concern over an invasion of Texas prompted Smith to order Brigadier General William Scurry, stationed in Houston, to concentrate his forces at Niblett's Bluff, on the Sabine. With Port Hudson partially relieved by Banks's movement up the Teche, Smith asked Pemberton for reinforcements from Vicksburg to assist Taylor. Pemberton refused and suggested that Smith begin operations toward

Baton Rouge in order to relieve Vicksburg. Only then would Pemberton "endeavor to co-operate" from east of the Mississippi.[32]

Smith had neither the personnel nor the time to devote to a movement on Baton Rouge. Both he and Pemberton labored under the constraints of a Confederate command system that inhibited cooperation and fostered uncoordinated actions between departments. Pemberton struggled with increasing threats against Vicksburg, yet despite instructions from Richmond to hold the city at all costs, he was unable to enlist cooperation from west of the river. Similarly, Smith's undermanned department was effectively cut off from any cis-Mississippi aid. Circumstances forced him to rely on poorly trained and ill-equipped troops from Texas, many of whom resisted leaving their state and openly defied Confederate authority. Unable to reach across the river for aid, both Smith and Pemberton sought to concentrate their forces, shorten their lines, and, if necessary, risk a siege rather than a pitched battle against a numerically superior Union host.[33]

On April 24, as Banks closed in, Smith issued orders to abandon Alexandria and reestablish headquarters at Shreveport. Several weeks earlier, during their first meeting, Taylor had suggested just such a move. He explained to Smith at that time that Shreveport, the geographical center of the Trans-Mississippi, would be the most appropriate site for department headquarters. Further, the city's strategic location on the Red River and its proximity to Arkansas and Texas had helped make it the hub of munitions manufacturing and ordnance supply for the department. Despite the logic of Taylor's argument, Smith apparently took the advice of his surgeon and close friend Dr. Sol Smith and elected to remain in Alexandria, the doctor's home town. Reluctant to change his headquarters, the commanding general described Shreveport to his wife as "a miserable place with a miserable population." Nevertheless, Banks's advance had forced the evacuation of Alexandria, and Smith had to acknowledge the strategic advantage inherent in his new location. The geography made it easier for Confederate troops from across the department to concentrate at Shreveport. This made the use of interior lines more practicable for both the defense of the capital and an attack on the Federal advance.[34]

At the same time, Smith did not want to relinquish Fort DeRussy, a battery on the Red River just below Alexandria. He suspected, however, that DeRussy's defenses could not withstand a large-scale assault, and he gave Taylor discretionary orders to remove the guns and withdraw the garrison. Taylor agreed with Smith's assessment and deemed DeRussy "untenable." The garrison dismantled the fortifications and began their evacuation, thus removing the last military obstacle from the Federal path into Alexandria.[35]

Before leaving Alexandria, Smith filed his official report concerning Taylor's retreat along the Teche. He praised Taylor's "skill and ability" in extricating his army from "irretrievable destruction" and noted that Taylor's performance under such difficult circumstances stamped him "as a leader of no ordinary merit." Smith blamed Taylor's inability to prevent the Federal incursion on the Confederate departmental system and Pemberton's refusal to furnish troops for operations in Western Louisiana. "General Taylor has done everything that was possible with the resources at his command," he stressed to Richmond. He then delivered an insightful assessment of the situation: "Could General Taylor have drawn upon Port Hudson for re-enforcements, or had troops in East and West Louisiana been under one control, the force at Port Hudson might have been marched across to the Atchafalaya and rapidly transported to the scene of the action in time to have defeated General Banks." Given the tentative manner in which Banks carried out the campaign, and Taylor's propensity to take the offensive, Smith's contention had merit. Smith's inability to remedy the overwhelming numerical discrepancy that confronted Taylor forced the Confederates to retreat deep into the interior. The remnants of Taylor's command left Alexandria just days ahead of the advancing Union column and prepared to march fifty miles north to Natchitoches. "We are now in a regular race from the enemy," wrote one of his officers. "I shall remember this retreat as long as I live."[36]

Smith and his staff traveled to Shreveport on board one of many steamers loaded with supplies and refugees. Among the passengers were Taylor's wife and four young children. During the trip all of Taylor's children were stricken with scarlet fever. His five-year-old son Zack died before the boat reached Shreveport, and three-year-old Richard Jr. died just days later. The tragedy stunned Taylor, but he recalled that duties in the field left little time "for the indulgence of private grief." Smith compassionately "attended to [Mrs. Taylor's] requests in regard to her little boys' graves." After the funerals Taylor had only an hour to spend with his daughters, both of whom had recovered from the illness, and with his grieving wife. He lamented that his wife was "left alone with the dead and dying, deprived of the consolation of [his] presence." She never fully recovered from the loss of her sons.[37]

By May 8 the Federals controlled the central Red River Valley. Alexandria and Opelousas, both Confederate strongholds, fell under the sway of Banks's occupation. "How galling to our feelings," fumed one Louisianan, "that we are compelled thus to retreat before an enemy who destroys everything as he advances." Upon his arrival in Alexandria, Banks ordered the arrest of former governor Alexandre Mouton on the grounds that a man of his influence "should at least be quiet[ed]." Afterward Banks announced to the citizens, "As if you heard God himself speak it: I will lay waste to your country, [and] destroy your crops, stock, and agricultural implements." The general was true to his word and ordered cotton, livestock, and other spoils of war sent downriver to Brashear City and New Orleans while his soldiers ransacked and plundered the town. Many slaves sought refuge behind Union lines, although some suffered violent physical abuse at the hands of the northerners. Although Banks instructed his men to cease their wanton destruction of civilian property and issued orders to ration supplies of surplus food to local residents, the decree had little effect. The sacking of central Louisiana continued and spread like a blue plague across the Red River Valley.[38]

Smith feared that the Federal rampage would continue along the Red River and into Shreveport. If Banks captured the city, he could take advantage of Shreveport's central location and send his armies north into Arkansas and west into Texas. Smith accordingly urged Holmes "to make arrangements for the protection of property and dispositions for the defense" of Arkansas and instructed Scurry and Magruder to organize the citizenry of eastern Texas into "minute companies" in preparation for an invasion. Taylor did not share Smith's fear of a Federal crusade through the heart of the Trans-Mississippi. He surmised that from Alexandria, Banks would turn his attention to the east and begin to invest Port Hudson. On May 14, less than one week after he arrived in Alexandria, Banks withdrew from central Louisiana and marched back down the Red River to prepare for the reduction of Port Hudson.[39]

On May 20 Taylor and his army left Natchitoches to reoccupy Alexandria. By June the Confederates had refurbished fortifications at DeRussy and Bisland, and Taylor again controlled the Teche. With the addition of Walker's four-thousand-man division to his command, Taylor believed he could secure Berwick Bay and seize control of the Lafourche region. The successful execution of such a bold strategy would cut Banks's communication with New Orleans and threaten Union control of the city. Taylor held that the citizens of New Orleans remained "bitterly hostile to Federal rule, and [that] the appearance of a Confederate force . . . would raise such a storm as to bring General Banks from Port Hudson." He presumed that the Confederate garrison at Port Hudson would then unite with Joseph E. Johnston in Mississippi to strike Ulysses S. Grant outside of Vicksburg.

This strategy certainly fit Taylor's directive from Richmond to recapture "any and all positions in the State of Louisiana which by the fortunes of war had fallen into [enemy] hands." Further, the plan strengthened the de facto position as an independent commander that Taylor had enjoyed before the Federal invasion of the Teche region.[40]

Smith, however, operated under a different set of orders. As a result, his interpretation of events in Louisiana and his criteria for an effective military operation in the district ran contrary to Taylor's expectations. To Smith, instructions from the War Department to "aid in the defense of the Lower Mississippi" rendered Taylor's plan to recapture New Orleans immaterial. In his estimation, Confederate control of the city would afford only a "minor advantage" toward what emerged as Smith's preeminent goal: to aid Pemberton at Vicksburg.[41]

Moreover, despite the earlier glowing report of Taylor's actions during the recent campaign, Smith held him responsible for the surrender of territory. In a letter to Taylor dated May 20 he blamed his subordinate for the losses at Bisland and Alexandria. Smith also insinuated that Taylor's aspiration to take New Orleans was founded in the failure of the Teche campaign. "I know your desire is naturally great to recover what you have lost in Lower Louisiana, and to push on toward New Orleans," he chided, and he cautioned, "The stake contended for near Vicksburg is the Valley of the Mississippi and the Trans-Mississippi Department; the defeat of General Grant is the *terminus ad quem* of all operations in the west this summer." Smith's failure to grasp the nature of Taylor's plan created a division between them regarding prosecution of the war in Louisiana. His unfounded criticism of Taylor's performance during the Teche campaign fostered tension between the two. The accusation that Taylor's interest in New Orleans was personal rather than professional began to erode the tenuous working relationship between the generals.[42]

3

The Golden Opportunity Has Passed

Once the Federals broke off the invasion of central Louisiana and turned toward Port Hudson, the pressure on Smith to aid his compatriots across the Mississippi began to intensify. John C. Pemberton in particular lobbied vigorously, arguing that an attack on Federal supply lines west of the river would ease the mounting threat to Vicksburg. Smith agreed and ordered Taylor to strike the Federals in northeastern Louisiana along the west bank of the Mississippi between New Carthage and Milliken's Bend. In Taylor's opinion, the "peculiar position of Vicksburg" combined with the presence of Union gunboats made the plan unfeasible. Upon learning of Taylor's challenge, Smith defended the decision to his lieutenant. "Confederate authorities in the east were urgent for some effort on our part in behalf of Vicksburg," he explained. "Public opinion would condemn us if we did not try to do something." Taylor disagreed and insisted that the solution was to withdraw Pemberton's garrison, not support it. Arguments against the operation failed to convince Smith. "Remonstrances," Taylor recalled, "were of no avail."[1]

In late May, John G. Walker's division and James C. Tappan's Arkansas brigade marched south to join Taylor in Monroe. By June 2, only Walker's Texans had arrived. Nevertheless, Taylor began preparations for the operation and assembled a strike force of forty-five hundred at Delhi, west of the Tensas River and thirty miles from the Mississippi. The movements stirred Smith to comment that Taylor's progress exceeded his "most sanguine expectations." Unfortunately, the intelligence reports on which Smith pinned his hopes were several weeks out of date. Unbeknownst to Smith or Taylor, Grant was no longer using Milliken's Bend as a primary staging area for resupply. The Federals had relocated their base of operation several miles away on the Yazoo River, where, Taylor later recalled, "transports were beyond the reach of annoyance from the west bank of the Mississippi."[2]

Another intelligence communiqué reported that Federal outposts along the Mississippi were "guarded by convalescents and some negro troops." The report led Smith to underestimate the resolve of the Union defenders. He counseled Taylor not to expect strong opposition and directed him to move against the position at once. Taylor consequently ordered the operation to commence before Tappan's men arrived and shifted his base across the Tensas to Richmond, just a dozen miles from the Mississippi.[3]

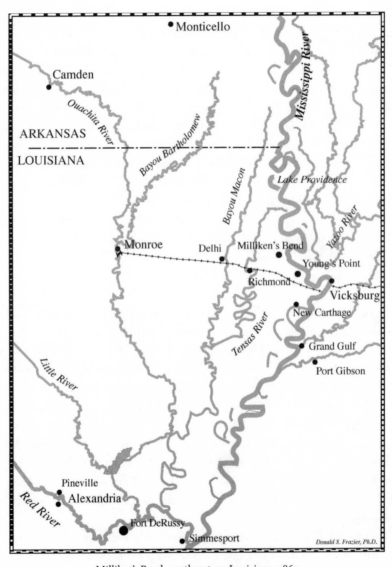

Milliken's Bend, northeastern Louisiana, 1863

Taylor determined that the Federal position stretched north along the Mississippi for over thirty-five miles from Young's Point to Lake Providence, with Milliken's Bend at the strategic center. Rather than assault the center with his entire force, he divided Walker's infantry and planned to strike simultaneously at three points. Taylor made his dispositions accordingly: Henry E. McCulloch's brigade was to advance directly against Milliken's Bend while James M. Hawes moved his command south to attack Young's Point. Horace Randal would remain in reserve within supporting distance of the other two. Taylor also directed Frank A. Bartlett to lead a regiment of Texas cavalry and a battalion of Louisiana partisan rangers against the garrison at Lake Providence. Anticipating little resistance from the enemy, Taylor delegated field command of the operation to Walker and remained behind at Richmond.[4]

As the Confederate infantry began to move into position, Isaac Harrison's cavalry screen clashed with a Federal probe three miles east of Richmond. While the skirmish protected the disposition of Confederate troop movements, it also alerted the Federals to an imminent attack. The element of surprise was lost and the operation compromised, yet Taylor did not alter his plans. As a result, Walker and his men went into battle overconfident and unprepared for what lay ahead.[5]

At about 4:00 A.M. on June 7, 1863, the first of Taylor's columns stormed the Federal position at Milliken's Bend. McCulloch's Texans drove the Federals to an area between two levees where, in bloody hand-to-hand combat, the defenders slowly broke. The advance continued beyond the second levee until, at 7:00 A.M., Union gunboats churned into action and sprayed the attackers with grape and canister. Walker and Randal rushed to the front only to find McCulloch in full retreat. "After making a personal reconnaissance," reported Walker, "I determined not to order another assault." McCulloch's men limped back to Richmond with nearly two hundred casualties.[6]

Hawes was to strike Young's Point at the same time McCulloch launched his assault on Milliken's Bend. However, Hawes became lost in the thickets and briars of the outlying area and, arriving at Young's Point around 11:00 A.M., found himself under attack by Union gunboats. Exhausted from their twenty-mile march, which had taken sixteen hours, Hawes's men stood under a broiling sun in the face of superior enemy firepower. Despite peremptory orders to attack Young's Point, Hawes withdrew without a fight. The brigade lost more men to heatstroke than McCulloch lost in combat. Similarly, the strike at Lake Providence did not materialize until June 9 and resulted in little more than a firefight. "As foreseen," Taylor sniped, "our movement resulted, and could result, in nothing."[7]

The failures along the Mississippi reflected badly on both Smith and Taylor—on the former as a strategist and on the latter as a tactician. Contributing to these failures was the overall lack of agreement regarding their primary responsibilities within the Trans-Mississippi. By insisting that Taylor retain Walker's division in an effort to relieve Vicksburg, Smith was responding to direct pressure not only from Pemberton but also from his friend and former commanding officer Joseph E. Johnston. Johnston's jurisdiction included Vicksburg, and he was actively soliciting troops for relief of the beleaguered city. Smith, after receiving the Trans-Mississippi assignment, had confided to Confederate senator Louis T. Wigfall that he would treat suggestions from Johnston as if they were orders. This sentiment encouraged Johnston to view Smith's department as an ancillary district to his own command, in effect relegating the Trans-Mississippi to the status of providing supply and support for other theaters. Only days before the repulse at Milliken's Bend, Smith complained to Johnston of his situation in the Trans-Mississippi and expressed a longing for the "halcyon days" of service in Virginia: "I would willingly be back under your command at any personal sacrifice." Further complicating his position in Louisiana, Smith still wanted a free hand in Arkansas and Missouri. He believed he had an obligation to politicians from both states who had helped secure his appointment as Trans-Mississippi commander.[8]

By keeping Walker in northern Louisiana and ordering Taylor to strike the Federals west of Vicksburg, Smith chose a politically expedient path. In deference to his allies in the Confederate military and the government hierarchy, he ignored the New Orleans option presented by Taylor. To approve Taylor's strategy for a campaign in the Lafourche would have prevented Walker from joining Smith in the event of an opportunity to strike into Arkansas and Missouri. At the same time, to endorse Taylor's plan would have put Smith at odds with Pemberton and Johnston, thus risking criticism and censure from the southern citizenry as well as from President Davis if Vicksburg fell before the recovery of New Orleans. Smith's experience with Bragg in Kentucky had taught him the meaning of such criticism, so he concerned himself more with what was politically advantageous than with what was militarily viable. Smith had "given much of his mind to the recovery of his lost empire," Taylor brooded years later. "The substance of Louisiana and Texas was staked against the shadow of Missouri and northern Arkansas."[9]

Taylor, with his plantation sacked, two children dead, and much of his state ravaged by the enemy, had likewise suffered a "lost empire." He believed that from a strategic standpoint the Lafourche, not northeastern Louisiana, was the legitimate theater of operations. Yet Smith's May 20 letter had dismissed the New Orleans campaign as merely an attempt on Taylor's part to recover something of what he had lost. The letter and the disagreement over how best to utilize Walker's division had marked the beginning of a sharp deterioration in the working rapport between Smith and Taylor. The defeat at Milliken's Bend and the failures at Young's Point and Lake Providence only served to increase the dissension between them.[10]

Despite his duty to execute Smith's orders regardless of any personal disagreement, Taylor lacked enthusiasm for a fight at Milliken's Bend. He went into the operation convinced of its futility, and his tactical approach reflected that perspective. Taylor underestimated enemy resources and accepted at face value Smith's pronouncement that black Federal recruits would not put up a fight against Confederate regulars. As a result, Taylor's battle plan squandered his advantage of superior numbers. By dividing his force to strike multiple objectives, Taylor sought to use the same blueprint that he had employed at Bisland and Irish Bend. But this was not the Teche, and Taylor did not devise a battle plan to exploit Confederate strengths in northeastern Louisiana.[11]

Taylor made several fundamental mistakes. During the Teche campaign he had raced back and forth between Grand Lake and Fort Bisland to direct operations. At the battle of Irish Bend he had personally led the army from Franklin to New Iberia. At Milliken's Bend, however, he relied on others to reconnoiter the ground and to direct the army's line of march. Poor reconnaissance of bridges, roads, and terrain prevented Randal from reinforcing McCulloch in a timely manner and doomed Hawes's brigade before it had even moved into position. Moreover, the miscalculation of Federal troop strength, particularly gunboats at Milliken's Bend, contributed significantly to the Confederate defeat. Taylor was familiar with the tactical use of gunboats and had used the *Diana* to support his infantry during the Teche campaign. Yet he failed to take into account the Federal use of gunboats as a response to his own troop movements. Taylor addressed these problems in his report but criticized Walker's men for their "dread of gunboats," adding that their lack of mobility had led to the "meager results of the expedition." He did not shoulder any responsibility for neglecting to reconnoiter the area or failing to ascertain enemy troop strength before ordering the assault.[12]

Moreover, as he had done at Bisland, Taylor delegated operational control to a subordinate, despite assurances to Smith that he had "used every personal exertion in order to insure success." He confessed to Smith that the failure at Milliken's Bend "satisfies me that it is necessary that I should rely upon myself not only to devise the plans, but also to execute them, in order to insure their being carried out vigorously." Taylor condemned McCulloch for his "injudicious handling of troops" and denounced Hawes's failure to follow orders. He also delivered a stinging indictment of Walker's performance as division commander. "Nothing was wanted but vigorous action in the execution of the plans," he complained, adding that Walker had previously expressed an "ardent desire to undertake this . . . expedition" and yet did not personally direct any of the attacks. Walker took offense at Taylor's report and construed it as personal criticism of his leadership skills. Taylor soon clarified his comments and claimed that nothing in the account "was intended to reflect, directly or indirectly, on General Walker," whom he then characterized as "a meritorious officer."[13]

Nevertheless, this marked the fourth time in as many engagements that Taylor's subordinates had suffered the sting of blame for the failure of his battle plan: Waller at Des Allemands, Mouton in the Lafourche, Sibley at Bisland, and now Walker at Milliken's Bend. Both Mouton and Walker saw fit to accept the apology implicit in Taylor's subsequent remarks, and in the coming months they would emerge as staunch allies in his struggle against the Federals and against Smith.[14]

The burgeoning dispute between Smith and Taylor assumed two additional characteristics following the Milliken's Bend fiasco. First, rumors emanated from Alexandria that Smith was preparing to relieve Taylor and assume field command of the army in Louisiana. From department headquarters, Smith denied the allegations and claimed that they were deliberate misrepresentations of his relations with Taylor. Smith complained to Taylor's adjutant, Eustace Surget, that someone at district headquarters had spread the rumors in order to slander him. He insisted that Surget act at once to "counteract any misstatement in circulation." Astonishingly, Smith then effectively confirmed the rumors he had just denied by telling Surget that should it become "necessary to send an officer senior to [Taylor]" to lead the troops in the field, he would go himself. Apparently the leak had originated at Smith's own headquarters. By first denying the rumors and then creating a subjective loophole by means of which he could relieve Taylor, Smith contributed to the confusion and helped foster distrust between the generals.[15]

The second problem concerned the disposition of captured black Federal troops. When Smith learned that a number of these soldiers had been taken prisoner, he incredulously asked Taylor for immediate confirmation: "I hope this may not be so, and you and your subordinates . . . may have recognized the propriety of giving no quarter to armed negroes and their officers." Smith recognized the serious problem that the capture of runaway-slaves-turned-soldiers presented to the Confederacy. If black Federals received equal treatment as prisoners of war, the Confederate military would be repudiating the racial hierarchy of southern society. Yet should the Confederates execute black prisoners of war, they would be in violation of military guidelines that required humane treatment of all soldiers taken prisoner. Smith assumed that Taylor would have a similar understanding of this "delicate and important question" and would have instructed his officers to show no quarter to black troops. But this was not the case.[16]

For Taylor, Smith's instructions came too late. He acknowledged the "unfortunate" capture of the black troops and "respectfully ask[ed] instructions as to the disposition of these prisoners." Smith was uncertain about Confederate policy toward escaped slaves in military service of the enemy and turned for guidance to General Order 111, issued in December 1862. The order directed the following: "That all negro slaves captured in arms be at once delivered over to the executive authorities of the respective States to which they belong to be dealt with according to the laws of said States." Yet the order did not address the issue of quarter in combat conditions. Smith determined that until Richmond clarified the order, Trans-Mississippi troops were to show no quarter to black soldiers under arms in Federal regiments.[17]

Smith's policy included an unintended loophole. In accordance with General Order 111, Smith instructed officers to turn over all black Federal prisoners to state authorities. The directive created a paradox. Smith admonished his subordinates not to take black soldiers prisoner but also provided instructions for handling black prisoners of war. He had given commanders in the field too much latitude, which could well lead to a breakdown in discipline. Without discipline, the officers risked losing control over their men. In effect, Smith's policy was no policy at all. Two months after Smith's appeal, the War Department issued an official reply: a policy of no quarter exceeded the guidelines established in General Order 111, and Smith was to consider black Federal soldiers "deluded victims [to be] treated with mercy and returned to their owners." In his reply Secretary of War James Seddon nevertheless conceded that white officers leading black troops were subject to execution at the discretion of the commanding officer.[18]

The problem also reached across the lines and into Grant's camp near Vicksburg. One week after Milliken's Bend, a Confederate deserter informed the Federals that Taylor had ordered the execution of black prisoners and their white officers. Despite this melodramatic testimony, Grant remained unconvinced of the veracity of the charges and of Taylor's role in the alleged incident. He dispatched two officers with a letter to Taylor that summarized the accusations and demanded an explanation. The correspondence reminded Taylor that all men serving in the Union army were entitled to equal protection regardless of race and threatened like retaliation against captured Confederates if the allegations proved true.[19]

Taylor reacted immediately and denied the accusations, characterizing such acts as "disgraceful . . . to humanity and to the reputation of soldiers." He promised Grant that he would investigate the charges thoroughly and mete out severe punishments should he uncover evidence of any executions. "My orders at all times," he assured Grant, "have been to treat all prisoners with every consideration." Taylor also explained that Confederate policy required the military to turn over all black prisoners of war "to civil authorities, to be dealt with according to the laws of the State wherein they were captured." The response was acceptable to Grant, and both he and Taylor returned their focus to the campaigns for Vicksburg, Port Hudson, and New Orleans.[20]

Upon his return to Alexandria on June 10, Taylor turned his attention to the Teche. Several days earlier Smith had received a request from Johnston for additional help to aid Port Hudson. Following the failure of his own plan to assist Vicksburg by striking Milliken's Bend, Smith could not object to reviving Taylor's plan to relieve Port Hudson by threatening New Orleans. He authorized Taylor to return to the Lafourche and pursue the same strategy he had vetoed weeks earlier. Although Smith expressed his confidence in the mission to Taylor, he confessed to Johnston that he had "little hopes of [Taylor's] affording any assistance to the garrison at Port Hudson," or for the relief of Vicksburg.[21]

While Mouton and Green reestablished control in the Teche region, Taylor directed Walker to march his division south from their position opposite Vicksburg toward Alexandria. He had advised Smith of his intention to do so in a report written just after Milliken's Bend. Almost immediately, though, Taylor reversed himself. He determined that he had sufficient troop strength in southeastern Louisiana without Walker and instructed the division to remain in place. On June 11 Taylor notified Smith that he had decided to hold Walker's division "in its present position until the enemy's movements and the condition of affairs around Vicksburg are more fully developed." Taylor had thus established two precedents for actions he would subsequently undertake. First, Taylor had implied that he, not Smith, would determine the strategic situation and the disposition of troops in the District of Western Louisiana. Second, he had claimed operational control over Walker's division. Smith did not explicitly agree to either of these points, but he also failed to dispute them, and Taylor took this to imply consent. Each of these elements became increasingly important to Taylor's development of strategy in Louisiana, and each helped to heighten the tension between the generals.[22]

To provide a better understanding of conditions east of the river, Smith urged Taylor to communicate directly with Johnston in Mississippi. Taylor sent a member of his staff, C. L. Elgee, to meet with Johnston and ascertain how they might best cooperate. Johnston had no specific advice for Taylor except to suggest that he continue attempts to relieve Vicksburg and Port Hudson. In a followup letter to Smith, however, Johnston charged that Trans-Mississippi troops had "done nothing" to alleviate pressure on Confederate positions across the Mississippi. He implored Smith to take personal control of operations and to do whatever he deemed best to "accomplish the immense result of saving Vicksburg." Given the limited resources of the Trans-Mississippi Department, Smith could not have been optimistic upon reading Johnston's decree: "Our only hope of saving Vicksburg . . . depends on the operations of your troops."[23]

The situation left Smith in a quandary. Earlier he had pledged to treat Johnston's suggestions as if they were orders. Yet his strategy for Milliken's Bend had failed, and the only operation currently under way was Taylor's. For Taylor to succeed required concentration in south central Louisiana. This troop movement would forestall Smith's desired campaign through Arkansas and Missouri. Moreover, Johnston wanted Smith to take field command. Should Smith move to supersede Taylor, he would further alienate his temperamental subordinate. However, should Taylor lead the operations, and should they succeed, Smith would not receive his share of the accolades. While Taylor began operations in the Lafourche, Smith traveled to Monroe to hear Walker's suggestions for the relief of Vicksburg. The Federals had just moved a large force into Richmond and compelled the Confederates to abandon positions east of the Tensas. Walker characterized the situation opposite Vicksburg as "utterly impracticable."[24]

From the Teche region Taylor targeted Brashear City, a town that served as the terminus of the New Orleans and Opelousas Railroad. Because of its location near Grand Lake and the confluence of the Bayou Teche and Atchafalaya River, Brashear City was vital for control of the lower Teche and Lafourche regions. Again Taylor arranged to divide his force. He ordered Mouton and Green to march on Fort Buchanan, the Federal installation north of Brashear City on Berwick Bay.

To coincide with this line of attack, Taylor proposed a turning movement with James P. Major's cavalry brigade. The Texans were to ride southeast along the Lafourche to Thibodaux where the railroad crossed the bayou. From there Major would cut the lines of communication in the Federal rear that led from Brashear City to New Orleans. Once all of his forces were in position, Taylor planned to spring a trap similar to the one Banks and Grover had designed for him at Bisland ten weeks earlier. Unlike his Federal counterparts, Taylor had just over three thousand men for this daring and complex plan. If successful, the operation would open the Lafourche for a move on New Orleans.[25]

Taylor instructed Major to be in position and ready for the attack on June 23. The mission was a dangerous one. Major was to ride through nearly one hundred miles of enemy-occupied territory without giving away the nature of the operation or exposing the disposition of Taylor's infantry. He was a practiced veteran, however, a West Pointer with service in the elite United States Second Cavalry, and the experience paid off handsomely. Taylor rode with Major east across the Atchafalaya and down the Bayou Fordoche to a point so close to Port Hudson that "the noise of the battle . . . could be heard" by the troopers. From there the general turned southwest to join Mouton and Green while Major made for the Lafourche. The cavalry skirmished its way past Federal outposts at Plaquemine and Bayou Goula and then stole down the Mississippi below Baton Rouge. Just above the confluence of the Mississippi and the Lafourche, Major learned of a strong Federal garrison occupying nearby Donaldsonville. Rather than engage the enemy and jeopardize the security of the operation, he guided his column around the outpost and advanced swiftly to Thibodaux, a distance of twenty-five miles. Major had his troops in position on June 22, the same day that Taylor joined Mouton and Green at Bisland.[26]

Taylor sought to exploit the terrain around Brashear City and the element of surprise so as to catch the Federals off guard. He divided his forces once more and sent most of Green's men to Berwick, a small hamlet directly across from Brashear City on the western banks of Berwick Bay. Mouton's command then took a position just north on Gibbons Point, across from Fort Buchanan. The balance of the forces prepared for an amphibious assault on the enemy rear. That night the detachment assembled a small flotilla to carry the strike force east across Berwick Bay into the swamps behind Brashear City. Three hundred volunteers, led by Major Sherod Hunter of the Second Arizona Cavalry, crossed at Berwick Bay in fifty-three assorted "boats, skiffs, flats, [and] even sugar-coolers" to land on the eastern shore just before dawn. Dubbed the "the mosquito fleet" by Taylor's marines, this array of vessels was, in the words of Confederate Joseph A. Breaux, "a promiscuous collection for such an enterprise." Taylor hoped that Green's movements at Berwick would draw the Federals' attention and allow Hunter to close from the rear. With Major in place to cut off their escape, the Federals would have no choice but surrender.[27]

At daybreak, Green's artillery opened from the west. With the sound of the guns, Hunter sprang into action and, striking from the east, took the enemy by surprise. Although greatly outnumbered, Hunter's graybacks routed the Federals in Brashear City and forced the surrender of the garrison at Fort Buchanan "after a short and desultory fight." Meanwhile, a train carrying four hundred Federals narrowly escaped capture at Brashear City, only to find Major's cavalry several miles outside of town blocking the tracks. The Federals surrendered quietly and quickly. In all, Taylor's trap bagged seventeen hundred men and cleared the immediate area of Federal troops. One of the northern prisoners described the Rebels as "the most ragged, dirty-looking set of rascals" he had ever seen.[28]

Taylor arranged to have the wealth of supplies and military wares sent north to Natchitoches and west to Niblett's Bluff. He recalled, "For the first time since I reached western Louisiana I had supplies," and he informed Smith, "The quantity of quartermaster's and commissary ordnance stores captured at this place exceeds belief." Smith offered cordial congratulations for the "brilliant successes at Berwick Bay." As he had been in Virginia's Shenandoah Valley a year earlier, "Banks was once more Commissary for the Confederacy." These supplies would be of immense importance to Smith and Taylor the following spring in the Red River campaign.[29]

Following previous operations that had met with failure, Taylor had been quick to blame his subordinates for the defeat. After the success at Brasher City, he praised his lieutenants generously. Taylor lauded "the zeal, energy, and ardor manifested by . . . Mouton" and emphasized that Green's conduct "fully justified the high expectations." He was particularly delighted with the bold performance that took Major and his six hundred Texas horsemen on a perilous ride around the Federal flank. Citing Major's "energy, industry, and capacity [for command]," Taylor recommended him for promotion to brigadier.[30]

Building on his success at Brashear City, Taylor divided the army once more and pushed the two wings deeper into the Lafourche. Mouton was to advance east along the rail line to Thibodaux. His orders were to establish a base there and throw pickets forward to Bayou Des Allemands, just twenty-five miles from New Orleans. To protect Mouton's rear, Taylor sent Green and Major northeast to reduce the enemy outpost at Donaldsonville. Taylor hoped to increase the pressure on the Federal occupation force in New Orleans by capturing strategic locations and continuing to concentrate his troops in the Lafourche. The strategy, he believed, would force Banks to divest from Port Hudson in order to meet the threat.[31]

Taylor planned to execute the same strategy to relieve Port Hudson that he had outlined for Smith before the operation at Milliken's Bend. Now that the campaign in the Lafourche had commenced, he acknowledged the need to bolster Confederate troop strength, and on June 27 he ordered Walker's division to Berwick Bay. The decision to summon Walker was reasonable. Smith had not initiated any further attempt to aid Vicksburg, and Walker's men were reportedly suffering from "the unhealthiness" of their position. Better to put the division to use, thought Taylor, than to let them waste away in northeastern Louisiana. In a letter advising Smith of the decision, Taylor cited these reasons and explained that "a change of the disposition of troops [was] necessary." He announced, "I have ordered Major-General Walker's division to proceed immediately to Berwick Bay; thence I shall send it into the Lafourche country." Taylor believed that if Vicksburg could hold on, the Lafourche campaign would relieve Port Hudson and change the outlook of the war along the Mississippi.[32]

Smith countermanded the orders and held Walker in place. He admonished Taylor, "I shall order Walker's division to you whenever operations about Vicksburg permit." Smith based the decision on an urgent plea from Johnston received the day before stating that the Trans-Mississippi held the key to the salvation of Vicksburg. In his desperation, Johnston even went so far as to suggest that Smith send troops, perhaps Walker's, to reinforce Pemberton in Vicksburg. When Smith broached the subject with Walker, the latter bristled. "As far as I am concerned," he scoffed, ". . . unless the enemy are blind and stupid, . . . no part of my command would escape capture or destruction if such an attempt should be made."[33]

In fact, there were not operations of any military significance in northeastern Louisiana. Since Milliken's Bend, Walker's "Greyhounds," so named for their pace during numerous marches, had remained mired along the Mississippi bottoms between Monroe and the river. During that time Smith failed to devise any sort of cohesive plan to relieve Vicksburg. Instead, he used Walker, along with a portion of William H. Parsons's Texas cavalry and Tappan's infantry, to raid plantations that had fallen under Federal control. The limited operations, which consisted of burning crops and capturing runaway slaves, squandered one of the Trans-Mississippi's largest fighting units on marginally important targets and weak, undermanned Federal garrisons. Walker lost more men battling disease than fighting Federals, and by July he could count only two-thirds of his division fit for duty. Walker held Smith responsible for the sorry condition of his men. "These actions [opposite Vicksburg]," he complained, "leading to no result if they had succeeded, wasted the Confederate strength and dispirited the troops." Walker had emerged a non-combatant in Smith and Taylor's battle over the deployment of his division.[34]

To date, Taylor had enjoyed greater success with the enemy than with his commanding officer. In rapid succession, Mouton swept the Federals from Thibodaux and stormed through the Lafourche to take Raceland, Des Allemands, and Boutte Station, on the outskirts of New Orleans. Taylor reported that the city was "greatly excited" at the renewed show of Confederate force. His spies in New Orleans relayed intelligence that by establishing "important relations" within the city, he could "justify a coup" and spark an uprising by the citizenry. As Green moved on Donaldsonville, Taylor's strategy appeared poised to bring about results in the Lafourche that would reverberate across the Mississippi.[35]

The Federal installation at Donaldsonville presented a formidable obstacle for Green. Fort Butler had an impressive parapet surrounded by a deep moat and enjoyed the protection of gunboats on the Mississippi and Bayou Lafourche. In an attempt to minimize these strengths, Green started his assault at 2 : 00 A.M. on June 28. The stubborn Federal garrison of two hundred held off the Confederates until dawn, when gunboats forced Green to break off the attack. Some Confederates complained that they were ill equipped to take the position. Officers issued orders to charge the works but, according to one private, did not provide "scaling ladders nor any other preparation." Many of the men refused to advance under fire, and most of those who did attempt to scale the parapet were killed or captured. Green blamed faulty reconnaissance for the repulse and reported that "the fort was much stronger than it was represented to be, or than we expected to find it."[36]

Notwithstanding Green's tactical defeat, the Confederates took up positions along the Mississippi near Donaldsonville. From behind their earthworks the Texans poured "continuous fire on the enemy's gunboats and transports." Green reported, "This interruption of the navigation of the river caused great uneasiness on the part of the enemy." Taylor's strategy disrupted Federal shipping on the Mississippi for the next several weeks.[37]

Although Smith had no faith in Taylor's strategy, it had become a cause for consternation at Banks's headquarters. "Taylor's plans were well laid, and had been brilliantly executed," admitted Banks's adjutant. "In no other way, with the force at his disposal, could he have performed a greater service for his cause." Indeed, the pressure on New Orleans had thrown Banks into a quandary. As Banks pondered his next move, he complained, "If I detach from my command in the field a sufficient force to defend [New Orleans] . . . my assistance to General Grant is unimportant, and I leave an equal or larger number of the enemy to re-enforce Johnston. If I defend New Orleans and its adjacent territory, the enemy will go against Grant. If I go with a force sufficient to aid him, my rear will be seriously threatened." Putting Banks in this predicament was exactly what Taylor had planned. Even without Walker, operations in the Lafourche had stirred such panic within the Federal army that the Union command began to discuss abandoning the siege of Port Hudson. From New Orleans, General William Emory advised Banks to "choose between Port Hudson and New Orleans," for he could not hope to hold both.[38]

Having seized control of the territory between Banks and New Orleans, Taylor notified Smith on July 4, "If any opportunity, however slight, offers, I will throw myself into New Orleans." He then added a sarcastic jab: "I trust the lieutenant general commanding will not feel disappointed at these results. At all events, I have used every exertion to relieve Port Hudson, and shall continue to the last." Eight days later, amid unconfirmed rumors of Confederate capitulation at Vicksburg, Smith relented and sent Walker south to Alexandria. In a letter announcing the move, Smith praised Taylor for recent victories in the Lafourche: "I take pleasure in expressing my satisfaction at your operations. The results are beyond my expectation. Should the siege of Port Hudson be raised, your campaign will be crowned with entire success." Smith then warned Taylor that despite his triumph in the Lafourche, the probable loss of Vicksburg, and the possible loss of Port Hudson, would render Confederate reoccupation of New Orleans temporary at best. In anticipation of these setbacks, and a subsequent renewal of the Federal offensive along the Teche, Smith suggested that Taylor change his base of operations to better "defend the upper valley of the Red River."[39]

By the time Smith's letter reached Taylor, the Trans-Mississippi Department had received confirmation of the surrender at Vicksburg and the fall of Port Hudson. Increased Federal pressure along the Lafourche began immediately. On July 13 Major and Green confronted two enemy divisions at Kock's plantation just below Donaldsonville. Although the Confederates defeated a force three times their size, it was clear that the enemy would soon bring superior numbers to bear throughout the region. The day after the battle Taylor acknowledged that the fall of Vicksburg and Port Hudson made his position in the Lafourche "extremely hazardous" and that he could no longer justify the campaign strategically or militarily. To continue the campaign was futile, and he arranged a hasty withdrawal to the Teche. Taylor expressed bitterness about having missed an opportunity to relieve Port Hudson via New Orleans, and he placed the blame squarely on Smith. "The plan I had arranged for an attack," he reported, "fell through as soon as I was advised that J. G. Walker's division would not join me." In his memoirs Taylor charged that Smith had wasted Walker on "absurd movements" in northeastern Louisiana and cited "the unwise movement toward Vicksburg" as having "retarded operations at Berwicks and on the river." Walker concurred: "The golden opportunity had been allowed to pass."[40]

Unlike his response to Taylor's plan in Louisiana, Smith had approved operations against Helena, Arkansas, as a means of diverting enemy forces from Vicksburg. That suggestion originated with Seddon in late May and made its way to Smith through Johnston. Smith asserted that he had no knowledge of the situation at Helena and therefore left Theophilus Holmes to formulate and execute the battle plan. Although the seventy-five hundred Missourians and Arkansans under Sterling Price and John S. Marmaduke outnumbered the enemy nearly two to one, Holmes botched the July 4 attack by issuing contradictory instructions that led to a series of uncoordinated assaults against fortified positions. After several hours of fighting, Holmes retired with heavy losses. The breakdown at Helena served to increase criticism of Smith. The decision to appoint Holmes to lead the attack, particularly in view of his own refusal to take the field, undermined Smith's credibility in the department. "He could have hardly done anything more unwise," noted Thomas L. Snead, one of Price's staff officers.[41]

On the eve of Vicksburg's demise, Taylor sent Smith a copy of two letters from Johnston that accused Trans-Mississippi commanders of failing to provide support. "I feel pained at the contents," Taylor protested. Smith too was stung by his friend's accusations. "The extract from General Johnston's letter, quoted by you, was unjust both in fact and implication," he complained. Unlike Taylor, Smith took Johnston's criticism personally: "Had I not known the nobleness and generosity of his disposition, I should have credited him with the wrong motives." In an attempt at solidarity with Taylor, Smith portrayed the Trans-Mississippi Department as the aggrieved party: "I shall communicate the facts to the War

Department . . . in the event of any attempt being made to throw the blame on the troops in this command." He cited the weakness of Confederate positions west of the river and "corrected the exaggerated estimation" of troop strength in the department.[42]

The basic elements of Smith's rebuttal were valid. Still, his reluctance to support Taylor's strategy of concentration in the Lafourche had prevented the Confederates from undertaking the only campaign that had any real potential for success. Had Smith allowed Walker to join Taylor in mid-May, immediately following Banks's removal from Alexandria, the Confederates would have had the troop strength to draw a Federal response from Port Hudson. Similarly, had Smith timed the operations in Louisiana to coincide with a strike against the Federal fortifications in Helena, he could have drawn troops away from both Vicksburg and Port Hudson. Instead, he chose to demonstrate against Federal supply depots at Milliken's Bend, an operation that, even if successful, would have siphoned very few Federals away from Vicksburg. Moreover, after this operation failed, Smith refused to release Walker to Taylor and, by holding the division in northeastern Louisiana, undercut Confederate gains in the Lafourche. Certainly Tappan and Parsons could have provided Smith with enough manpower to raid Federal plantations along the Tensas. His reluctance to lead his troops against either Helena or Milliken's Bend, despite Johnston's earlier suggestion that he take the field personally, suggests that Smith did not truly expect success in either operation. His willingness to allow Holmes complete control in Arkansas while limiting Taylor's movements in Louisiana indicates that the commanding general neither understood nor appreciated the capabilities of his subordinates and their men. In fact, Smith may have feared a success by Taylor. The expectations held by Johnston, Pemberton, and others east of the river may have been excessive, but in mid-1863 Smith failed to provide the type of leadership in the Trans-Mississippi that the situation required.

4

The Devil's Own Time

After the fall of Vicksburg, Smith and Taylor faced more pressing matters than accusations and criticism from Confederates across the Mississippi. Federal control of the great river severed the Trans-Mississippi Department from the rest of the nation. Smith announced that, subsequent to the loss of communication with Richmond, "all officers and agents connected with the army . . . would receive their instructions from the department commander." He assumed "extraordinary powers" over his isolated command and vowed to temper his actions with "caution and forbearance." Jefferson Davis did not seem worried by Smith's self-proclaimed expansion of powers. "My confidence in the discretion and ability of General Smith," the president affirmed, "assures me that I shall have no difficulty in sustaining any assumption of authority which may be necessary."[1]

Smith was not in a desirable position. "Affairs and difficulties over here are on a larger scale," wrote a staff officer, and Smith had his hands "full of political as well as military matters." The task before Smith was in fact much more than the military defeat of the Union army. It entailed the resuscitation of a populace suffocated by the spreading malignancy of war and an economy cut off from the rest of the country. One Texan's lament on the eve of the fall of Vicksburg exemplified the misfortune of many Trans-Mississippians: "Money once would buy goods but now goods buyes money." Smith organized efficient departmental agencies to integrate areas such as cotton procurement and sales with the acquisition of munitions and machinery. "He soon brought his department to the highest standard of efficiency," declared one Trans-Mississippi Confederate. The timely consolidation of interrelated areas of the Trans-Mississippi bureaucracy would be the single most important factor in keeping Confederate hope alive west of the Mississippi River.[2]

In addition, Smith worked to strengthen the power of the Confederate government throughout the Trans-Mississippi. He expanded the postal service, extended the Treasury Department, and opened diplomatic channels with the

French in Mexico. On this last point, Smith acknowledged that matters of foreign policy were beyond his jurisdiction, but he justified his actions by insisting that circumstances compelled him to take on "great responsibilities, and to exercise powers with which I am not legally vested."[3]

Smith's enhanced authority alarmed many Trans-Mississippi politicians. Secretary of War James Seddon suggested that he sit down with state officials to discuss their concerns formally. On August 15 Smith met with Trans-Mississippi governors at Marshall, Texas, and reassured them of two things. First, he would continue to support their authority, and second, he would not abandon any state to the Federals. At the close of the proceedings the governors issued a proclamation declaring their confidence in and support of Smith's administration.[4]

Problems in the army also increased after the fall of Vicksburg and Port Hudson. Jayhawking and desertion became so rampant in Louisiana that Smith ordered Taylor to take action. Taylor sent a cavalry force on a sweep of the northern parishes to arrest deserters and break up "bands of jayhawkers infesting that section of the country." The raids enjoyed only moderate success, and the forewarning of harsh punishment seemed an empty threat. Alfred Mouton, the Creole general, "feared to shoot a conscript," one Louisianan revealed, "lest it should make him unpopular in his State, and affect his chances for the Gunernational [sic] chair." The lack of manpower grew so critical that Smith offered a general pardon and amnesty to all absent officers and soldiers who returned to duty by the end of September.[5]

The troop shortage also compelled Smith to look to Trans-Mississippi slave owners for help. He hoped that an appeal to their patriotism would persuade the planter class to volunteer their chattel for service in the growing military-industrial complex. Smith advised his lieutenants that "the temper of the people is now favorable for such a step" and directed them to submit estimates of the number of slaves required to fill their district needs. While the "temper of the people" might have supported such a step, the temper of Arkansas senator R. W. Johnson did not. Johnson, who had lobbied for Smith's appointment to command, lodged a formal protest at Trans-Mississippi headquarters. Regardless of the department's pressing needs, Smith owed Johnson a political debt, and the senator had come to collect. While he was willing to cross the lines of social propriety, Smith was not able to cross the line drawn by one of the politicians to whom he owed his appointment. He promised to amend the program to suit Johnson's wishes.[6]

Two weeks after the request for slaves, Smith took the idea a dramatic step further. Just prior to the general amnesty deadline, he considered "calling out a military force from among the slave population" to restore the Trans-Mississippi's dwindling numbers. He selected chief quartermaster Major J. F. Minter to prepare for the recruitment of three thousand slaves and to enlist white officers to train and lead them. Although Smith was well aware of the explosive potential of arming slaves, the military needs of the Trans-Mississippi outweighed the political and social ramifications of such a bold move. Moreover, Smith recognized that if the Confederacy did not marshal slaves for military service, the Federals would turn southern plantations into recruiting stations. In fact, they already had. "Every sound black male left for the enemy becomes a soldier, whom we have afterward to fight," he explained. His plan did not develop beyond the exploratory stage, and Smith reflected that preliminary preparation for the recruitment of slaves was "as near a military organization" as he "dare[d] venture upon."[7]

Although Louisiana remained relatively quiet during the late summer, the situation in Arkansas worsened considerably. Following the defeat at Helena, Smith advised Theophilus Holmes to expect no further threats from the Federals in his district. Nevertheless, Holmes was emotionally shaken and physically ill after the battle, and his ability to provide even a semblance of capable leadership deteriorated rapidly. As a result, Sterling Price assumed temporary district command. Price assessed the situation and warned of an impending Federal advance on Little Rock. With just eight thousand troops dispersed across Arkansas, he appealed to Smith for reinforcements. Smith concluded that Price had "overestimated" the threat. Federal movements in Arkansas, he told Taylor, were a reconnaissance force, not a general advance. As a precaution, Smith sent Price a small brigade from Texas and ordered Tappan back to Arkansas.[8]

Smith's forecast for Arkansas proved incorrect and his response to Price inadequate. The fall of Vicksburg had enabled the Federals to transfer additional troops to Helena for operations against Little Rock. Smith failed to anticipate or prepare for this contingency. In mid-August, Union general Frederick Steele advanced nearly twelve thousand men toward the state capital. Price complained that he possessed neither the strength nor the fortifications to hold the city, and on September 10 he withdrew to Arkadelphia. Afterward Smith characterized the retreat as "unfortunate" but forecast that the enemy would advance no further. A Confederate officer recalled that Price's decision to abandon Little Rock without a fight "produced feelings of profound discouragement in the public mind." By autumn the Confederates controlled only the southwest corner of the state, and Governor

Harris Flanagin expressed alarm that Smith would forsake Arkansas completely in favor of a position on the Red River in northwest Louisiana or northeast Texas.[9]

In response to the worsening situation, Smith turned to Texas for help. He ordered district commander John B. Magruder to concentrate his forces near the Red River and prepare to lead them into Arkansas. This action, combined with the presence of five thousand Texas troops already in Louisiana, infuriated Magruder, who responded angrily to Smith's directive: "The question now presents itself, and cannot be avoided, as to the relative importance of . . . Texas." Magruder warned Smith that the Federals were about to "attempt to get possession of the Sabine River from its mouth." Four days later, on September 8, six thousand Federals on board transports protected by gunboats tried just that. A small southern garrison repulsed the clumsy invasion attempt and inflicted heavy casualties on the stunned Federal force. The action at Sabine Pass left Magruder in a panic. In anticipation of another attack, he halted the troops en route to Arkansas and ordered them to Beaumont and Orange in hopes of preventing the Federals from ascending the Sabine.[10]

Magruder persuaded Smith that the bid at Sabine Pass was the precursor to a full-scale invasion of Texas, with the occupation of Houston as the prize. Smith called for Taylor to concentrate his forces at once along Niblett's Bluff, just a few miles west of Lake Charles on the Louisiana side of the Sabine. He feared that Taylor's command, made up primarily of Texans, might desert if not "engaged in active operations against the enemy [threat]" to their home state. Taylor argued that the Union foray into the Sabine Pass was nothing more than a diversion. On September 17 Smith instructed Taylor and Magruder to hold their positions until the enemy's intentions became clear. To each, he stressed cooperation between the districts.[11]

Fallout from Smith's response to events in Arkansas and Texas rippled across Louisiana. Governor Moore feared that Smith's troop deployments betrayed "an intention to give up the state without a determined effort." He was also concerned that Smith would send Walker back to Arkansas. Smith defended his actions in a brusque letter to Moore declaring that he had no plans to abandon Louisiana and insisting, "There has been no order issued from department headquarters for the removal of any portion of Walker's division from General Taylor's command." Contrary to his recent instructions at Milliken's Bend and his subsequent unwillingness to send Walker to the Lafourche, Smith acknowledged that he considered the division a part of Taylor's command and therefore subject to Taylor's orders.[12]

Despite his attempt to calm the governor, Smith in fact aggravated the situation. In his letter he blamed Louisiana for the recent losses in Arkansas and scolded Moore for questioning troop movements within the department. Smith charged that had it not been for the earlier transfer of Walker's division, the Confederates would probably "be in possession of the Arkansas Valley, instead of being forced back to the line of the Washita." As for Moore's fears of an invasion, Smith indicated that the responsibility for the defense of Louisiana belonged to Taylor. If Moore thought Taylor's force inadequate, Smith suggested that the governor issue a call "to bring out every able-bodied man in the State for the defense of his fireside."[13]

In Shreveport, Smith conferred with Holmes, who was preparing to resume command in his district. They determined that conditions in Arkansas required Smith's personal attention, and on September 26 he left for Arkadelphia. On the eve of his departure Smith notified Taylor that "should the enemy advance from Little Rock, Arkansas is decidedly the place for concentration." Despite his assurances to Moore that he would not abandon Louisiana, Smith prepared to do exactly that if an opportunity arose.[14]

Just one week after Smith pledged that he would not take Walker from Taylor's command, he ordered the division to join James P. Major's cavalry on a march north from Alexandria to Natchitoches. The orders were a response to fresh intelligence from Price forecasting a Federal advance from Little Rock. Smith established a supply depot at Minden, in northern Louisiana, and began to assemble forces for a campaign into Arkansas. Although reports from Taylor of a Federal buildup around Berwick Bay soon persuaded Smith to suspend Walker's movement, the commanding general had made his intentions clear: Arkansas was the place for concentration. Smith's duplicity regarding Walker had two adverse effects: it weakened his credibility with Moore and undermined Taylor's ability to defend Louisiana. Despite the volatile situation that continued to unfold across western Louisiana, Smith sought to tilt the playing field toward Arkansas, where the stakes could carry him to glory.[15]

Smith arrived in Arkadelphia at the end of September and was shocked to find Holmes's army in an appallingly jaded condition. Under the circumstances there could be no concentration in Arkansas until the troops received sustenance and reinforcements. He directed Holmes to establish a base at Camden, on the Ouachita River southwest of Arkadelphia. From there the army could readily secure the necessary aid from Shreveport. In addition to protecting Camden, the position would allow the Arkansans to reinforce Shreveport if the enemy ascended the Red River. Likewise, Smith indicated to Holmes that he would instruct Taylor to gather his forces in the Red River Valley and prepare to move through Shreveport to support Arkansas if the Federals marched south from Little Rock. The plan to operate along interior lines put the Trans-Mississippi capital directly at the center of Smith's strategy.[16]

Concentration at Shreveport provided Smith with two alternatives. First, it gave him the flexibility to consolidate the department's resources against a Federal column advancing from either Arkansas or Louisiana. This allowed him to maximize the impact of his smaller force against a larger army. Second, concentration at Shreveport gave Smith the opportunity to take command of Confederate forces in the field. "I have made my arrangements for taking command in person," he announced to Holmes and Taylor, "[as soon as] the enemy's plans are developed." Smith then returned to Shreveport to monitor Federal activity along both fronts.[17]

According to Smith, Taylor understood and approved of these plans. Taylor had no intention, however, of waiting for orders to abandon Louisiana. He directed Walker to march from Alexandria toward Opelousas and instructed Mouton to proceed toward the south central portion of the state and probe the Federal perimeter. Accompanied by Tom Green's cavalry, the Confederates moved cautiously into the Teche region from Opelousas and across the Atchafalaya to Morganza. Several miles outside the town Taylor's forces overwhelmed a Federal division along Bayou Fordoche and took nearly five hundred prisoners. From these men Taylor ascertained that Federal strategy did indeed call for an invasion of Texas. "There is no doubt that the enemy is advancing in very large force," he warned. "Whether it is his intention to march to the Red River Valley before going to Texas has not yet been developed." Smith assured Taylor that the Federals would not move along the Red River because seasonal rains would make "the difficulties of campaigning in the upper country . . . almost insurmountable." The Federals were not so sure.[18]

Major General William B. Franklin led the Federal forces along the Teche. Franklin was a Pennsylvania West Pointer who had borne much of the blame for the Union defeat at Fredericksburg and hoped to restore his tarnished reputation by campaigning with Banks in the Louisiana bayous. Banks was unsure which route the army should take into Texas, the northern route through Shreveport or the southern route through Niblett's Bluff. He directed Franklin to push the army cautiously up the Bayou Teche toward Opelousas while he remained in New Orleans to monitor the situation. Banks's previous experiences with Taylor gave him reason to employ discretion. "While rapidity is desirable," Banks cautioned, "the movement should be secure." In early October, Franklin inched his way along the Teche through New Iberia and Vermilionville. Outnumbered five to one, Taylor's six-thousand-man army began another retreat.[19]

On October 8, as Franklin's columns continued their deliberate ascent, Taylor received valuable intelligence from a network of civilian operatives that included a local judge and a Catholic priest. Father Gilbert Raymond not only provided the Confederates with information regarding enemy troop strength and disposition but also brought to light the Federal operational strategy. He reported that the enemy "would advance cautiously, driving you before him, until he could force an engagement, or in default of that, by pushing you, . . . demoralize your army so that he would have nothing to apprehend from your army in his march to Texas." Taylor apprised Smith of the news and suggested that Federal movements pointed to Niblett's Bluff as the immediate objective.[20]

Upon receipt of the letter, Smith instructed Taylor to prepare his forces at once to aid Magruder in defense of Texas. He indicated that operations might require the Confederates to abandon Louisiana altogether. "This you will unhesitatingly do," Smith commanded. In a letter to Magruder, written on the same day, Smith was far less decisive. A Federal movement on Niblett's Bluff was still uncertain, and the Teche remained a viable option. While Magruder could expect Taylor to hang on the enemy's flanks and harass the advance, Smith did not affirm that Taylor's command would cross the Sabine. This news did not sit well with Magruder, particularly since most of Taylor's men were Texans. Yet Smith characterized troop deployment as a district matter and shifted the burden of support for Texas onto Taylor. Smith also emphasized that it was "utterly impossible" to send any help from Arkansas. If Texas needed assistance, it must come from Louisiana.[21]

Taylor did not move toward the Sabine. Instead, he continued to give ground ahead of Franklin while the cavalry gathered intelligence. William G. Vincent's Second Louisiana Cavalry rode to harass the enemy rear while Green's horsemen slashed at Franklin's flanks, skirmished with the vanguard, attacked pickets, plagued foraging parties, and devoured stragglers by the score. Although these strikes did not stop the enemy, they did unnerve many northern soldiers. The operations also served to embolden the Confederates.[22]

At daybreak on October 15 Green offered battle to Federal advance units at Buzzard's Prairie, ten miles north of Vermilionville. The challenge took Franklin by surprise and forced him to deploy two corps before the stubborn Rebels finally dispersed. Buzzard's Prairie achieved little for Taylor beyond verifying reports concerning the enemy position and strength. For the Texans in Louisiana, the campaigning helped bring into focus the magnitude of the threat to their home state. "I tremble for the consequences," wrote Captain Elijah Petty to his wife. "I will do my best to send them to hell as they come."[23]

Taylor reported that Franklin continued his march "with the greatest caution," confining his cavalry's movements to within five hundred yards of infantry support. As the head of the Federal column drove the Confederates out of Opelousas, Vincent's cavalry thundered into the Union rear, which still languished near Vermilionville. The raid netted several prisoners from Franklin's signal corps, including one of the officers. Vincent raced north to Taylor's headquarters at Washington to deliver his bounty. "The lieutenant had on him a signal book," Taylor reported to Smith, "with copies of many important dispatches between Franklin . . . and Banks." Taylor spent the night analyzing the information and concluded, "All thought of the enemy moving to Texas may now be dismissed, unless after first marching up the valley of Red River to Shreveport." He relayed the intelligence to Smith and stressed that Franklin intended to advance his force northwest through Alexandria and along the Red River into Texas. He also apprised an anxious Governor Moore, "If the Yanks still mean Texas they will have the devil's own time getting there."[24]

Smith disputed the reliability of the captured intelligence. On October 28 he replied that the Red River remained, at best, a "probable" invasion route, and that the enemy had "not sufficiently developed their plans to decide certainly upon [a] true line of operations." His orders to Taylor remained unchanged. "You must restrain your own impulses as well as the desires of your men," he insisted, and he instructed Taylor to enlist a policy of delay and harassment.[25]

Taylor was to fall back toward Alexandria, the gateway to the Red River Valley. If the Federal columns turned west toward the Sabine, Taylor would be in position to operate against the flanks. Only if the Federals marched along the Red past Alexandria would Smith permit Taylor to confront the advance. "Should [the enemy] push up the Red River Valley, I shall concentrate everything to meet him," Smith pledged. But evidently "everything" did not include troops from Magruder, whom Smith portrayed as unwilling to leave their district, or

Holmes's five thousand men, whom Smith planned to bring no further than Minden. From Minden, he reasoned, Holmes was "still within supporting distance" of the garrison at Camden. Although there was no immediate threat of a Federal offensive in Arkansas, Smith still could not bring himself to commit fully to a defense of Louisiana.[26]

Despite his avowed determination to wait until the intentions of the enemy became clear, Smith pushed toward concentration in Shreveport. He interpreted events in such a way that they supported his strategy. On October 8 he notified Holmes of plans for Taylor to evacuate the Teche region and take a position above Alexandria. "Taylor will draw in and concentrate his command in the Red River Valley," he explained, "and when the enemy advances, a concentration will be made." This plan would surrender, unnecessarily, all of lower Louisiana and much of central Louisiana to the Federals. In addition, a withdrawal to northwestern Louisiana would open a clear path across southern Louisiana to Niblett's Bluff, the Sabine, and Texas. Smith's desire to make Arkansas the theater of operations colored his assessment of the situation in Louisiana and jeopardized the security of Texas.[27]

To Taylor, Smith painted a jumbled picture. On the same day that Smith notified Holmes of his intent to concentrate near Shreveport, he had dismissed the notion of a Federal advance along the Red River. Yet he issued instructions for Taylor to collect his forces in the Red River Valley "with as little delay as possible" and ordered him to "be prepared to march when called upon." On October 20, in the face of solid intelligence that the Federals were marching toward Alexandria, Smith determined that an advance along the Red River was not yet a certainty. He told Taylor that should the Federals move on Texas by way of Niblett's Bluff, the Confederates must seize the opportunity to fortify positions in the Red River Valley. Given the commanding general's correspondence with Magruder and Holmes, the suggestion was at best foolish and at worst mendacious.[28]

Taylor faced the continued erosion of his territory and a prolonged retreat before a plodding enemy. Anxieties over surrendering territory haunted many of Mouton's Louisianans. "The men are very much dissatisfied, and disertions are numerous," wrote Lieutenant Arthur W. Hyatt, whose Louisiana troops feared they were about to be withdrawn to Texas. Nevertheless, Taylor continued to fall back. Should he resist the dilatory advance of the Federals, he would be doing so without orders from Smith and without hope of reinforcements. Should he continue his retreat, he risked the loss not only of his state but of his army. In late

October, Taylor decided to contest the Federal invasion. Smith's most recent directive had told him to strike "only with strong hopes of success," and Taylor was aware that the region between Washington and Alexandria offered poor defensive terrain. Accordingly, he took the measure of his enemy and decided that the benefits outweighed the risks. He summoned Walker's infantry and Major's cavalry to the front and planned to take the offensive.[29]

Near Moundville, three miles above Washington, Taylor prepared an elaborate ambush. He deployed Confederate forces along the edge of an abandoned sugar plantation astride the main road to Alexandria. The men used a series of drainage ditches as trenches and stationed sharpshooters in sugarhouses, in slave cabins, and in the woods. Here they waited for the enemy. "Every minute seemed like an hour to us," wrote one of Walker's Texans, but the advance never came. On October 24, Union skirmishers approached Taylor's lines only to fall back after a brief firefight. Confident in the strength of his position, Taylor waited, hoping that the Federals would return in force. A Texan recalled, "Taylor was determined to give battle if the enemy advanced." The Confederates held their lines for nearly twenty-four hours until Taylor ordered the troops back to camp. Most did not know it at the time, but the Federal advance had turned into a retreat.[30]

Uncertainty and anxiety had plagued Franklin throughout the campaign. Requests for instructions from Banks had gone unanswered, and his army began to suffer from the unexpectedly stiff resistance. Unbeknownst to Franklin, Banks intended to land an expeditionary force at Brownsville, Texas. That crusade would amount to little more than a symbolic planting of the Union flag on Texas soil, and Banks would soon return to New Orleans. However, Banks's lack of a strategic vision had left Franklin to his own devices in the heart of Taylor's territory. Citing the lack of forage and poor road conditions, Franklin declined to continue the campaign. Following the skirmish at Moundville, he turned his army toward New Iberia and began a deliberate retreat down the Teche.[31]

Taylor was not content to let Franklin slip away unpunished. The Yankees had pillaged their way across the Teche for the second time in less than a year. The thinly strung blue column stretched for several miles between Washington and Opelousas, and Taylor ordered Green and Walker to strike. On November 3 the Confederates waylaid a Union division eight miles below Opelousas on Bayou Bourbeau, just above the Buzzard's Prairie battlefield. In a vicious scrap, the Confederates exacted a measure of revenge and inflicted a casualty rate of 44 percent on their foe. Despite warnings from Smith not to risk an engagement without "strong hopes of success," Taylor had seized the initiative that Franklin surrendered at Moundville. In a letter home one Confederate officer described the spirit of his men after the battle at Bayou Bourbeau: "All that we lacked of a battle was the advance of the enemy which he prudently failed to do thereby spoiling a great battle in the Trans Miss Dept—much anticipated fun on our part and escaping a good sound thrashing upon his part." For the remainder of the campaign Franklin declined to fight anything more than rear-guard actions, and by November 17 his army was safely ensconced in New Iberia.[32]

Franklin's inglorious retreat ended the campaigning in Louisiana for 1863. Smith publicly praised Taylor's successful efforts to contest the invasion. In his report to Richmond he described Taylor as "cautious, yet bold; always prepared for and anticipating the enemy; concentrating skillfully upon his main force, holding it in check, and crippling its movements; promptly striking his detached columns, routing and destroying them." Smith went on to declare, "The enemy have been completely foiled in the objectives of their campaign, and have fallen back for a new plan and a new line of operations." The glowing report did not give any hint of the disagreements between Smith and Taylor over the disposition of troops or the development of strategy in the district.[33]

Privately, tensions between the generals grew worse. The catalyst was a scathing editorial published in an Alexandria newspaper that accused Smith of planning to abandon Louisiana. The article concluded with a call for his immediate resignation. Smith held Taylor responsible for the editorial and initiated a confrontation. "I should not notice this attack, but that it comes from a paper printed at your headquarters," he snapped. He accused Taylor of complicity in stirring up trouble within the district and in turning the citizens of Louisiana against him: "I know not why it is that the people of this section for whom I have exerted myself most, and for the defense of whose country I have made [the] most sacrifices, are the only people in the whole department who misappreciate my motives and falsify my acts." This episode marked the second time since June that Smith had blamed Taylor for his own bad publicity. Taylor was in fact not directly responsible for the allegations. Indeed, the editorial echoed many of Governor Moore's previous accusations. Nevertheless, Taylor responded with a letter to the paper in defense of his commanding officer. Although Smith insisted that he would not let the incident influence his feelings or affect what he called the "cordial relations existing between us," he withdrew Green's cavalry from Taylor and sent the division to Texas.[34]

Green's was not the only division that Smith sought to take from Taylor. On December 12 he traveled to Camden for a conference with Holmes to devise a plan to recapture Little Rock. To bolster Holmes's army, Smith arranged to transfer Mouton's division to Arkansas. Much to his dismay, Smith soon discovered that the Federal army in Little Rock was stronger and larger than Holmes had intimated. Reluctantly, he abandoned plans for Little Rock and instructed all district commanders to expect no further campaigning until spring. He directed Taylor to retain Mouton for resupply operations in Louisiana.[35]

The stratagem with Mouton's division came three weeks after Smith had assured Taylor that the season for campaigning was over and he would not transfer any more units. On November 18 Taylor had offered to lead troops to Arkansas, but Smith rejected the suggestion. "As regards the removal of your force from your district, I do not think yet that it would be safe or advisable," Smith concluded on November 23. If the enemy were to advance during the winter, he speculated, the Red River Valley would be the theater. Likewise, Smith nixed Taylor's proposal to move back toward the Lafourche and probe Federal positions. Franklin remained a potent threat, and Smith therefore insisted that Taylor stay in central Louisiana to guard against an advance on Alexandria. Still, Arkansas weighed heavily on Smith's mind. "Great as is my anxiety and desire to drive the Federals from Little Rock and occupy the Arkansas Valley, the season has now too far advanced to avail myself of re-enforcements from your army," he informed Taylor. Whether it was because he needed Taylor to hold the line in the Red River Valley or because he wanted to lead the campaign in Arkansas personally, Smith schemed to deceive Taylor as to his true intentions. If not for Holmes's misrepresentation of Federal troop strength in Little Rock, Smith would have taken Mouton and inaugurated a winter campaign in Arkansas.[36]

By the close of 1863 Smith had weakened Taylor's army by shuffling troops across district lines. His confusion regarding Federal movements along Bayou Teche and the Red River kept him from grasping the strategic importance of Louisiana. Having tied his personal aspirations to a successful resolution of the situation in Arkansas, Smith undervalued the impact that Taylor's army had on Federal strategy in Louisiana. Smith's myopic approach to departmental command during his first year in the Trans-Mississippi severely hindered operations to recover New Orleans, to aid Vicksburg and Port Hudson, and to thwart enemy advances up Bayou Teche.

To many soldiers, civilians, and politicians across the department it appeared that Smith lacked a grand strategy for the Trans-Mississippi. Captain William A. Freret, a member of Smith's staff since the Kentucky campaign, complained that politicians swarmed constantly around headquarters, making demands and offering advice to the general. Freret noted that the bureaucrats were "not as true to [Smith] as those he had with him before—they hold him responsible if he should make a mistake, and herald their own part in the affairs if successful."[37]

To Smith's lieutenants, successes in their individual districts were paramount, and emergencies warranted concentration to repel the enemy at once. From their point of view, Smith's constant redeployment of troops seemed impulsive and his orders to fall back ill conceived. But despite his weak response to Federal gains in Arkansas and Louisiana, and his complete lack of response to the threat in Texas, Smith did have a strategic vision: to concentrate Trans-Mississippi forces and resources around Shreveport. From there he could operate along interior lines to confront the enemy anywhere in the department. Smith explained his strategy to Taylor: "Our policy is clearly not to engage the enemy without some chance of success, but to draw him back from his base, weakening his column, and enabling us to strike a decisive blow."[38]

From a military perspective, this strategy would offset the discrepancy in numbers between the armies and give Smith an opportunity to destroy isolated elements of the enemy force in detail. But the strategy would also require the surrender of territory, and with the Trans-Mississippi cut off from Richmond, Smith was more than just the commanding general; he was the political representative of the Confederate government. The dual role forced Smith to balance his duties as a military man with those of a statesman. "The President impresses it upon me, the representative and the leading men of the States urge it upon me, that the States must be defended," he confessed to Taylor. The politicians were convinced that once a state had fallen to the Federals it would be "irretrievably lost to the Confederacy." Thus, Smith's strategy developed along mutually exclusive lines. To achieve his military goal of concentration, he must surrender territory. To achieve his political goal of territorial control, he must disperse his forces.[39]

Smith's military training and experience suggested that he follow a Fabian strategy. His newfound responsibilities as chief executive officer of the Trans-Mississippi demanded otherwise. Immediately following the fall of Vicksburg, Richmond made sure Smith understood that his obligations extended beyond the battlefield. "The great duty of defending the Trans-Mississippi States and of holding them firm to the Confederacy must now devolve mainly upon you," wrote Seddon on August 3. Perhaps the Confederate government should have sent a nonmilitary official to administer the department and let Smith concentrate on his military duties. Reflecting on the constraints that Confederate politics had put upon his strategy, Smith complained openly to Taylor: "But for these considerations I would long since have followed the military principle of abandoning a part to save the whole, and, concentrating in advance, been ready to strike decisively and boldly when the campaign would have been materially influenced." Although Smith was cut off physically from Richmond, the politics of command governed his attempt to consolidate power and maintain control in the Trans-Mississippi.[40]

As a result, Smith's strategy lacked coherence. His policy vacillated between concentration and confrontation. To each of his three district commanders he presented a different picture of circumstances in the department. The commanders, Taylor in particular, as well as Trans-Mississippi politicians, did not want to surrender their territory to hoards of marauding Yankees. The politicians demanded protection, Holmes and Magruder demanded support, and Taylor sought to exert his independence. In each case Smith attempted to explain away his predicament when he should have simply stated his policy in a firm, decisive manner to all involved. By vacillating, Smith relinquished psychological command and material control to his lieutenants and to the politicians. In an attempt to pacify each, he alienated all.

In Taylor, Smith was complaining to the wrong man. More so than either of his district counterparts, Taylor was committed to and capable of directing a fierce defense of his territory. Unlike Magruder, a Virginian, or Holmes, a North Carolinian, Taylor was defending his home state. The Louisianan did not intend to surrender his district willingly so that Smith could lead the combined forces of the Trans-Mississippi elsewhere. Instead, he would join with Louisiana politicians and officers to fight both the Federals and Smith.

Although Smith acknowledged that Taylor was the strongest of his district commanders, the sheer intensity of his subordinate may have played a role in Smith's desire to pursue operations elsewhere. His pride stung by public ridicule as well as professional criticism, Smith was well aware that in an Arkansas theater of operations, he would no longer be laboring under the shadow of a popular and successful native son. Having come to regard Taylor as a rival, he belittled the value of his subordinate's intelligence reports and ignored his recommendations.

Smith's failure to support Taylor's strategy in 1863 would lead to more serious problems for the Confederates in 1864. It would also lead to more serious problems between the generals.

Neither Smith nor Taylor was happy about the situation in the Trans-Mississippi. Exasperated by his commanding officer's insincerity and constant complaining, and by his reluctance to allow a defense of Louisiana, Taylor wrote that he was "fatigued and jaded beyond belief." Smith, in turn, was frustrated by his inability to make Arkansas the primary theater of operations as well as by the political pressures of command and the military weakness of his department. Freret acknowledged that troubles in the Trans-Mississippi had taken their toll on the general and that he seemed "somewhat more quiet and older." Smith confided to his wife, "Everything has gone wrong—I am miserable, discontented, unhappy."[41]

5

A Battle for Louisiana

As early as January 1864, Richard Taylor's intelligence sources in New Orleans reported that the Federals planned to launch a spring campaign along the Red River, with the capture of Shreveport as the objective. By the end of February, Confederate spies had confirmed that enemy troop movements were about to commence. The Union ground force, led by Nathaniel P. Banks, included over twenty thousand soldiers from the Department of the Gulf and ten thousand on loan from William T. Sherman's rugged Army of the Tennessee. Admiral David Dixon Porter's fleet of warships, the largest yet assembled in North America, was to accompany the army in its advance along the Red River. Together the joint operations would move as one arm of a massive pincer movement aimed at the Trans-Mississippi capital. A force of twelve thousand under General Frederick Steele, a veteran professional soldier, was to strike south from Arkansas and join Banks at Shreveport to close the pincer. Taylor assured Edmund Kirby Smith that the information could "be relied upon with as much confidence as if the plans had been laid here instead of New Orleans."[1]

Across Louisiana, citizens, soldiers, and politicians were all well aware of the peril. Previous campaigns through the Teche region had revealed just how vulnerable the Louisiana interior was to invasion. On January 25, newly elected Confederate governor Henry Watkins Allen assumed office and took immediate action to help defend the state. Elected with the overwhelming support of the army, Allen enjoyed a mandate as a hawkish governor. As his first official act he offered to transfer control of munitions in the state arsenals to Taylor. In addition, Allen called for the creation of a mounted state guard and proposed to expand the militia to include "every able bodied white male in the State, between the ages of fifteen and fifty-five." Taylor welcomed the support, but his district needed much more than militia and small arms to defend western Louisiana. Taylor needed Confederate troops.[2]

During the early months of 1864 there were barely seven thousand Confederate regulars still stationed in the District of Western Louisiana. Taylor requested additional troops to meet the invasion, but only a handful of Louisiana independent companies had arrived by March 1, Banks's projected launch date for the campaign. In anticipation of the enemy movements, Taylor stretched his threadbare forces between Simmesport, on the Atchafalaya just west of the confluence of the Red and the Mississippi, and Alexandria, nearly forty-five miles above on the Red. He hoped that reinforcements would arrive before the Federals could move into the Louisiana heartland.[3]

Despite his intention to make Arkansas the theater of operations, Smith realized that a greater threat loomed in Louisiana. In January he notified Jefferson Davis, "The only true line of operation by which the enemy can penetrate the department is the valley of the Red River." Such a movement did not necessarily preclude a campaign in Arkansas. An advance along the Red would allow Smith to hold a central position at Shreveport. From there he could still lead the army into Arkansas if an opportunity arose. Accordingly, during the winter months Smith drained troops from Taylor's command to refurbish fortifications along the Red River and staff the growing bureaucracy at Shreveport.[4]

As the cornerstone of his defense, Smith directed Taylor to restore Fort De-Russy, situated on the Red just below Alexandria. During the Teche campaign the previous spring the Federals had driven Taylor's men from DeRussy and taken temporary possession of the works. Despite later attempts to rebuild the fort, DeRussy remained little more than a river battery. Any hope of halting the blue advance with the guns of DeRussy was unrealistic, according to Taylor, and he considered its loss inevitable. He advised Smith that the garrison could "make a formidable defense against gun-boats" but maintained that the fort was vulnerable by land and could not withstand a sustained assault. Smith weighed Taylor's objections but overruled him and insisted on strengthening the works. Recalling this incident after the war, Taylor remarked cynically, "We shall see what became of DeRussy."[5]

In addition to demanding a comprehensive strategy for the defense of Louisiana, the impending Federal threat reignited tensions between Smith and Taylor. While Smith developed plans for a defensive strategy with Shreveport as the hub, Taylor mapped out plans to intercept the Federals before they entered the Red River Valley. He maintained that an attack in the Federal rear, at Plaquemine, southwest of Baton Rouge, would stall the enemy advance long enough for the river to fall. A low water level would prevent Union gunboats from ascending the Red and stop the invasion before it could start. Although the rapid buildup of enemy forces around Simmesport soon nullified Taylor's hopes, Smith's conservative approach worried him. A strictly defensive posture ran counter to the strategy that had underpinned Taylor's earlier successes against Banks in Virginia in 1862 and in Louisiana in 1863. To grant Banks the initiative seemed little more than surrender.[6]

Meanwhile, Taylor began to complain that rheumatoid arthritis was sapping his strength, and he asked Smith for time off to regain his stamina. Smith refused to grant a furlough, suspecting that his lieutenant suffered from personal problems and professional concerns unrelated to his health. He even coaxed Taylor, "Let me know what the matter really is." Smith's concern was genuine. Since the death of Taylor's sons in 1863, Smith had felt a paternalistic attachment to the Louisianan's wife and daughters. Further, he realized that Taylor was the most reliable district commander in the department. Their differences notwithstanding, Smith needed Taylor's experience and leadership to defend the Red River Valley.[7]

Smith remained hopeful that the fortifications at DeRussy would prevent the Federal advance. Reluctantly, Taylor directed a detail of soldiers and slaves to strengthen the works. In early March he instructed John G. Walker to deploy his division of thirty-eight hundred Texans in a defensive alignment designed to protect DeRussy from an overland assault. Walker also assigned several companies to garrison DeRussy itself. On March 12, before work was complete, lead elements of the Federal advance pushed through Simmesport. The following day Union infantry overran a Rebel outpost dubbed Fort Humbug, on Yellow Bayou north of Simmesport. "[DeRussy] must fall as soon almost as invested by the force marching against it," Walker informed Taylor. "It will be unsafe to linger here." Taylor obeyed Smith's orders and insisted that Walker hold his position to buy time for DeRussy. To support Walker, he ordered down Henry Gray's Louisianans and a brigade of Texas infantry under Camille J. Polignac, a highly regarded French officer. Taylor issued specific instructions to Walker for the tactical defense of the fort. Despite his objections to refurbishing DeRussy, he understood the strategic importance of the place. Taylor implored Walker to be aggressive and "take more than ordinary hazards in fighting." [8]

Walker warned that eighteen thousand Federals were closing on his position. While Taylor had been expecting such news, the number seemed high, and he disputed the estimate. He believed that, given the time constraints and the number of reported Federal transports, the enemy could not have moved more than six thousand troops into the theater that quickly. Accordingly, he directed Walker to take the offensive and strike the head of the Federal column. Taylor hoped that with "close, sharp, and quick fighting" the Texans could "break up this expedition." Above all, he encouraged Walker to risk engaging the enemy where there was "any reasonable chance of success." Taylor's assessment of the situation proved incorrect. The overwhelming numbers that Walker faced, combined with the naval firepower protecting the Federal advance, precluded any chance of success, reasonable or otherwise.[9]

By March 14 the Federal fleet had drawn to within range of DeRussy. After intermittent shelling from gunships, two Federal infantry brigades brushed aside Confederate pickets and struck DeRussy from the rear. "It seemed so hopeless for us to hold the fort," wrote one of the defenders, "[that] the officers were in favor of surrendering." After several headlong attacks, the Federals stormed the works and smothered the southern garrison. There were some who "screamed in demonic tones" at their captors, but otherwise the Confederates capitulated quietly. Walker, outnumbered and outgunned, had assessed the situation and chosen to abandon the field. The Federals promptly resumed their advance along the Red River and on March 15 occupied Alexandria.[10]

The loss of DeRussy created dissension within the ranks of Taylor's officers. Captain Edmund T. King, a member of the DeRussy garrison, insisted that "Taylor expected us to hold the enemy in check" and that the men "felt safe until we found [Walker] had retreated and left us at the mercy of the whole Federal Army." Polignac also blamed Walker for failing to support the garrison and accused him of disobeying Taylor's orders. He claimed that had Walker established a position consistent with Taylor's instructions, "the enemy could not have attacked the Fort, as by such an attack his flank and rear would have been exposed." In fact, Walker had expected a junction with Polignac and Gray for a movement to raise the siege at DeRussy. Both brigades, however, failed to arrive in time to support the Texans, and Walker had little choice but to withdraw. He defended the decision and asserted that covering DeRussy would have meant disaster for his command. Walker argued that it would have required at least ten thousand men to mount a successful defense of the ground surrounding the fort. He went even further in his official report and blamed Smith for the "wretched judgment displayed in the selection of the position." Taylor concurred with the criticism. "Thus much," he noted sardonically, "for our Red River Gibraltar."[11]

Immediately following the fall of DeRussy, Taylor ordered his forces to march to one of several previously selected forage depots. The selection of these sites had been yet another source of disagreement between Smith and Taylor. Taylor reported that he had established a series of supply depots in the summer of 1863, after the fall of Vicksburg, as insurance against a Federal incursion into the Red River Valley. In a letter to Davis, Smith contradicted Taylor's claim and asserted that he himself had established the network of supply depots in the autumn of 1863 in anticipation of a Federal invasion along the Red River. Given Taylor's intimate knowledge of the Louisiana interior, and the fact that many in his command were from the northwestern parishes, Smith's claim seems suspect. However, William R. Boggs, Smith's chief of staff, claimed that Smith had set up the depots as a part of a road-refurbishing plan in late 1863 and early 1864. That disagreement aside, Taylor directed his soldiers to the plantation of Carroll Jones, an affluent free black man. Here, in the piney woods thirty miles northwest of occupied Alexandria, the Confederates rested and recuperated while awaiting reinforcements. During this time Taylor designated Gray's and Polignac's brigades as a new division under the command of Alfred Mouton. Including Walker's division, the entire force consisted of just sixty-five hundred troops.[12]

While at Jones's plantation, Taylor sent William Vincent's Second Louisiana Cavalry toward the river to scout enemy movements from Alexandria. On the cold, rainy night of March 21 a Federal division, acting on information obtained from Union sympathizers in the area, surrounded Vincent's secluded campsite on Henderson's Hill. A southern courier on his way from Vincent to Taylor mistook the enemy for Confederate reinforcements and gave the countersign to Union pickets. Federal brigadier James A. Mower moved quickly to take advantage of the error. Mower approached the courier personally and purportedly "passed himself off as General Taylor seeking the camp of the Second Louisiana." The courier obliged and led the Federals directly into the Confederate camp. Mower's troops caught Vincent by surprise and captured over two hundred cavalrymen and their horses. "Reb prisoners pronounce it a mean Yankee trick not at all military," cackled one Union officer. The bespectacled Vincent, whom Taylor later criticized for a lack of discipline, "escaped in his slippers" and hid in a henhouse to avoid capture.[13]

Despite the blinding loss at Henderson's Hill, Taylor's official report did not hold Vincent directly responsible. In a subsequent report, however, he described Vincent as "one of a class of officers that have done more harm to the service than many good soldiers can repair. Never coming exactly in reach of a court-martial," he charged, "Colonel Vincent has never done any duty satisfactorily." On the eve of the fiasco at Henderson's Hill, Taylor had implored Vincent to maintain a vigilant watch for "some unusual occurrence." The lack of cavalry early in the campaign had forced Taylor to "overlook many of [Vincent's] failures" and to rely on him for hazardous reconnaissance work. Ultimately, Taylor considered the loss Smith's fault. Despite continued requests for additional cavalry, Smith did not issue orders for Thomas Green's return to Louisiana until March 5, nearly two months after he had received confirmation of the Federal invasion along the Red River.[14]

The ruin of the Second Louisiana Cavalry left Taylor with "little or no means of obtaining information" on Federal movements around Alexandria. This forced the Confederates to abandon Jones's plantation and retreat further upriver. Along their line of march the sight and smell of burning cotton fields, destroyed by Louisiana farmers ahead of the Federal invasion, darkened the mood of the gray-clad soldiers. The order to destroy civilian cotton had come from Smith in mid-February. Having failed to secure an agreement with the Federals to trade cotton for supplies, Smith ordered the burning to keep the commodity from falling into enemy hands. Although Taylor had initially protested the order, he later came to agree with the decision. "[Despite the] tendency of the destruction of [civilians' property] to alienate their affections from the Government," he admitted to Smith, "it is now my deliberate judgment that every ounce of cotton ought to be destroyed before an advance of the enemy." The road along the Red River was "a solid flame," recalled one of Taylor's men. The sight of ashes fluttering through the air reminded one officer of a "snow scene in a cold climate," while a Texan lamented, "The clouds seem to be lowering over the Trans Miss Dept Louisiana."[15]

While his army trudged north to a forage depot outside Natchitoches, Taylor hurried directly to the little river town. There he welcomed the first elements of Green's cavalry from Texas. The band of six hundred ragged horsemen, one-third of whom were unarmed, straggled into town on March 30. Taylor had been reminding Smith since February 21, "I can do nothing until I have more cavalry at my disposition." Once the enemy began their advance, he begged Smith to send him every available soldier in Texas and offered to serve under Texas district commander John B. Magruder if that would facilitate defense of the department. Without reinforcements and outnumbered nearly five to one, Taylor stressed, he stood little chance of stopping the Federals in Louisiana.[16]

Despite intelligence at the outset of the campaign confirming the Federal advance along the Red River, Smith had remained indecisive. One week after receiving Taylor's request for reinforcements, he ordered a brigade of cavalry down from Arkansas. Five days later, he rescinded the order. On March 18 Smith again ordered Arkansas troopers to Louisiana, only to reverse himself once more just hours later. He finally directed four brigades of infantry in Arkansas to join Taylor. The delays and false starts enraged Taylor. As the ill-equipped and over-due Texans finally began to arrive, his temper flared. On March 29 he vented his frustration to Smith: "Two weeks have elapsed since the fall of Alexandria, and I have cherished the hope from day to day that assistance would reach me before I was forced to give up the producing country." Twenty-four hours later he made a second, more restrained complaint: "I most respectfully call attention to the fact that sixteen days after the fall of DeRussy and the opening of the campaign by the enemy only 250 re-enforcements have reached me." On the same day that the jaded Texans rode into Natchitoches, the Federal advance carried the enemy to within twelve miles of the town. That afternoon Taylor left Natchitoches and resumed his retreat.[17]

The developing crisis in Louisiana was not Smith's only departmental con-cern. The conspicuous decline of Theophilus Holmes demanded his attention in Arkansas. On January 21 Smith petitioned Davis to replace the aging general with an officer "who would excite the enthusiasm and win the confidence of the troops and people." When Holmes learned of the appeal for his dismissal, he accused Smith of subverting Confederate authority in the district and angrily tendered his resignation.[18]

Smith's initial reaction was to lash back and demand that Richmond hold Holmes accountable for making slanderous accusations. Six days later Smith tried to soothe the general's wounded pride with a patronizing letter insisting that, with the exception of the request for a change in command, he had always "spoken [of Holmes] in the highest terms." Smith then assumed the role of the injured party and claimed that Holmes's embarrassing behavior following the defeat at Helena had created the need for a change. The allegation was to some extent true, as the perception of Holmes as unfit for command had begun to spread throughout the department. "Nobody cares any thing for him & nobody has any respect for him," jeered one Texan, adding, "I don't want to see nor hear of him any more."[19]

The groundswell against Holmes did not stop with the military. For nearly a year many of the same politicians from Arkansas and Missouri who had lob-bied for Smith's appointment to command had been pressing hard for Holmes's removal. During his trip to Camden the previous December, Smith had realized that the appalling conditions in Holmes's district made a campaign through Arkansas utterly impracticable. The only way to take the offensive was to increase Confederate authority in the district. A new commander would be both a military and a political expediency. While Smith's handling of the incident may have been arrogant, he had sufficient grounds to ask for a change and made the correct decision in seeking to install fresh leadership for Arkansas.[20]

Although Smith did not necessarily respect Sterling Price's skills as a general officer, he tapped the former Missouri governor to replace Holmes. Smith knew

Theater of operations, Red River and Arkansas campaigns, 1864

that he could count on Price to support him in an expedition through Arkansas and Missouri, even though that campaign would have to wait. By the time Price took command on March 16, the Red River campaign was already under way, and the Federals again forced Smith to turn his attention away from Missouri and toward the preservation of his department.[21]

In late March reports poured into Smith's headquarters confirming that the Federals had launched the northern arm of the Red River campaign. As Banks continued his relentless advance on Shreveport from the south, Frederick Steele marched eight thousand troops southwest from Little Rock toward Arkadelphia, where he planned to unite with John M. Thayer's four-thousand-man Army of the Frontier and move against the Trans-Mississippi capital. At his headquarters, Smith pondered his next move. Price seized the opportunity to renew pressure on Smith to take the offensive in Arkansas. Despite his keen desire to make Arkansas the theater of operations, Smith dismissed the call as premature. Instead, he directed Price to convert all "inefficient and ill-mounted cavalry" to infantry and advised him to "introduce order and discipline" among the remaining troopers. Smith appreciated the urgent need for a well-disciplined cavalry in Arkansas to provide reliable reconnaissance of enemy movements. He instructed Price to "retard the enemy's advance . . . [and] fall back towards re-enforcements" in Shreveport, but not to "risk a general action" unless he held the advantage.[22]

Rather than support Price against Steele, Smith ordered the infantry in Arkansas to march to Louisiana. He anticipated that Banks's advance from Alexandria would develop more rapidly than Steele's movement from Little Rock. On March 20 Smith apprised Price of his intention to "bring matters to an issue" in Louisiana and then "transfer a sufficient force to . . . regain the Arkansas Valley." Ten days later Steele's bluecoats swept through Arkadelphia, and the projected Federal line of march toward Washington convinced Smith of the need to modify his plans. Rather than commit to a strike against Banks, he decided to concentrate against whichever column posed the greater danger. Once Price's infantry reached Shreveport, Smith could use them to operate along interior lines in Arkansas or Louisiana, depending upon where the Federal threat developed first. Although this policy remained the foundation of his strategy throughout the campaign, Smith sought to adapt the plan to allow for concentration in Arkansas rather than Louisiana. The line of Steele's advance from Arkadelphia to Washington, and the relative isolation of the column, left the Federal flanks and rear susceptible to attack. Smith recognized Steele's vulnerability and quickly revived his plans to lead a drive into Arkansas. He notified Price on March 31 that the Confederates would concentrate against whichever column offered "the best prospect of success." On the same day, he advised Taylor that Steele was moving along a line "most favorable to our operations."[23]

Smith ordered Taylor to fall back toward Shreveport and trade territory for time. He explained his reasoning in a letter dated March 31: "Our role must be a defensive policy where the enemy is largely our superior, and where our columns come within a practicable distance of each other, concentrating rapidly upon and crushing one or the other of the enemy's column." Although Smith admitted that the situation in Louisiana appeared "extremely favorable" for concentration, he neglected to tell Taylor that four thousand troops from Arkansas were en route to Shreveport. As Taylor continued to retreat, the lack of substantial reinforcements raised his suspicion that Smith was withholding troops in favor of a move against Steele in Arkansas.[24]

Earlier in the campaign Smith had advised Taylor, "The only field for great results in this department is the District of Arkansas." At that time Taylor had assured Smith that should Steele's advance prove a greater threat, he would relinquish command of Louisiana troops for service in Arkansas. The offer, however, was contingent upon the prompt arrival of Green's division from Texas. Although Smith was not to blame for Green's tardiness, he had dallied in ordering the Texans to Louisiana, and Taylor held the commanding general personally responsible for the lack of cavalry. Green's delay, in conjunction with his own orders to retreat and Smith's intent to concentrate against Steele, seemed to Taylor a surrender of Louisiana. He voiced his bitter disappointment to Smith: "Had I conceived for an instant that such astonishing delay would ensue before re-enforcements reached me, I would have fought a battle even against heavy odds." Although such a battle would have violated Smith's instructions to avoid a general engagement, Taylor pressed the issue. "It would have been better to lose the State after a defeat than surrender it without a fight," he fumed. "Expecting every hour to receive promised re-enforcements, I did not feel justified in hazarding a general engagement with my little army. I shall never cease to regret my error."[25]

Southern soldiers and civilians in the district shared Taylor's view. "We have already run away & given up nearly all and quite the best part of Louisiana," Captain Elijah P. Petty wrote to his wife. The citizens of Louisiana had lost faith in the army's ability to protect them. A corporal in Walker's division, Joseph P. Blessington, recalled that the "inhabitants, all along the route of our retreat, were hurriedly quitting their homes, and flying before the approach of the invader." As the Confederate rear guard passed through Natchitoches, Private Frank L. Richardson noted that those civilians who remained behind "ran out to meet us with food in the streets, but . . . the enemy did not give us time to eat." [26]

Prior to the Federal occupation of Natchitoches, Taylor had boasted to Smith, "I shall assume the offensive as soon as Green joins me." However, with Green's main body long overdue and the Federals advancing steadily, Taylor had no choice but to follow orders and fall back. Sullenly, he marched his gray army away from the enemy, away from the river, and toward another forage depot at Pleasant Hill, just forty miles southwest of Shreveport. The Confederates traveled along a narrow stagecoach road that wound through a deep pine forest, described by one as a "howling wilderness" with "no good resting place for man or beast." [27]

Intelligence reports indicated that Green could not possibly push the remainder of his two thousand troopers to Pleasant Hill in less than a week. That information came as no surprise to Taylor, although a letter from his brother-in-law Duncan Kenner, a Confederate congressman in Shreveport, delivered a shock. On March 26 Kenner informed Taylor that four thousand reinforcements from Arkansas had been in Shreveport for nearly a week and that Smith had not yet decided whether to send them to Taylor or return them to Price. With the Federals in Louisiana just eighty miles from Shreveport, Taylor had assumed that Smith's strategy of rapid concentration would assure him command of the reinforcements. Two days after the arrival of Kenner's letter, Taylor demanded an explanation from headquarters.[28]

Smith took umbrage at Taylor's challenge and responded the next day by listing several reasons for withholding the reinforcements. Their ammunition was in "bad order," he explained, and the troops would thus remain at Shreveport until resupplied. Once outfitted properly, he planned to reorganize the brigades into two divisions, with Kentucky-born Thomas Churchill leading the Arkansans and Missourian Mosby M. Parsons in command of troops from his home state. More important, however, Smith disclosed that Steele was advancing on Washington and that, "should he move rapidly, so as to come within reach, it may be best to fight him first." The dispatch incensed Taylor. Steele was nearly twice as far from Shreveport as Banks and had far fewer men to threaten the capital. Taylor fired back immediately: "I respectfully suggest that the only possible way to defeat Steele's movement is to whip the enemy now in the heart of the Red River Valley." He then accused Smith of renouncing his stated objective. "To decline concentration when we have the means, and when the enemy is already in the vitals of the department," he scoffed, "is a policy I am too obtuse to understand." [29]

At department headquarters, Smith took a different view of the situation than Taylor at the front. His perception of the campaign had been influenced by the arrival at Shreveport of his close friend and confidant, Dr. Sol Smith. William Boggs, Smith's chief of staff, noted a marked transformation in his commanding officer's handling of the campaign and attributed the shift to Dr. Smith. Boggs observed, "As the troops began to arrive from Arkansas Dr Sol Smith also arrived from Alexandria, and now began a change of movement, which I have always held him responsible for." Boggs charged that although the Arkansas reinforcements had been detained at Shreveport "ostensibly to be equipped," the actual reason "was that Dr. Smith disliked General Taylor as much as he liked General Smith."[30]

Smith understood that to reinforce Taylor at a time when Steele's column appeared vulnerable would jeopardize his own unofficial proclamation of 1864 as the "summer for the recovery of the Arkansas Valley." Still, Smith could not simply abandon Louisiana to the Federals, nor could he ignore the fact that Banks posed a greater threat than Steele. To address this dilemma, according to Boggs, Smith and Dr. Smith devised a plan: "Taylor was to harass Banks up to the last moment and then General Smith was to move down with additional troops, take command, and carry off the glory of the pitched battle." This scheme would enable Smith to reap accolades as the savior of Louisiana before turning the resources of the department to a campaign in Arkansas. Smith kept the plan from Taylor and ordered him to continue the retreat and to "examine the country . . . with reference to its susceptibility of defense." "In the meantime," noted Boggs derisively, "we at departmental headquarters, were having reviews, balls and a gay time generally."[31]

Dr. Smith exerted considerable influence over General Smith, who described him as a man possessing a "clear head and sound judgment." A devoted friend of the Kirby-Smith clan, he had served as the general's surgeon since the opening days of the war. He and Boggs just barely tolerated one another and had been at odds ever since the latter joined Smith's staff in Kentucky. Boggs, a contentious professional soldier, believed that during the Kentucky campaign Dr. Smith had persuaded the general to adopt an overly cautious approach once the army reached Lexington. He held the doctor responsible for Smith's failure to remain on the offensive, which he characterized as a "grand opportunity lost."[32]

The animosity between Boggs and Dr. Smith carried over into Louisiana. In January 1864 Smith attempted to replace Boggs with the doctor as chief of staff. In a letter to the president Smith complained that he was not "ably supported" by Boggs and requested that he be reassigned to "a position in the field." In the same correspondence Smith suggested a promotion to brigadier for Dr. Smith and urged Davis to award him the chief-of-staff position. Smith described his friend as a citizen of "spotless integrity," with "comprehensive ideas, with capacity, head, and administrative abilities of a high order." Davis refused to reassign Boggs or to promote Dr. Smith. Nevertheless, the doctor remained one of Smith's most trusted advisers throughout the Red River campaign, to the consternation of Boggs and the frustration of Taylor.[33]

The detention of the reinforcements in Shreveport was not the only piece of disturbing news in Kenner's March 26 letter to Taylor. The congressman also reported a rumor circulating at Smith's headquarters that Taylor was to blame for allowing the Federals to advance uncontested into the Red River Valley. Moreover, Kenner revealed that Smith was under the impression that Taylor neither wanted nor needed reinforcements. He recounted his meeting with Smith: "I called General Smith's attention to the great importance of sending you re-enforcements immediately. What was my astonishment when he replied that you did not desire any re-enforcements. I exclaimed that that was impossible. He said that you had so written, and called for your last letter which he handed me, calling my attention to that passage." Taylor was appalled by this disclosure, and by Smith's bizarre misinterpretation: "I certainly would have been the first commander possessing ordinary sense who voluntarily declined re-enforcements while retreating before a superior force."[34]

Taylor was not yet aware that Smith planned to ride down and "carry off the glory" in the battle for Louisiana, or that, as Boggs suspected, his orders to retreat positioned him to be the scapegoat for the state's destruction. He nonetheless had ample cause for outrage. His home state had been destroyed, his army was in retreat, and he was powerless to mount a defense against the invasion. His patience with Smith had run out, and he prepared to launch a personal attack. In an angry letter to headquarters dated March 28, Taylor protested that Smith had misconstrued his earlier correspondence. Referring to his letter of March 23, Taylor explained, "My language was 'As soon as Green joins me I shall assume the offensive, and hope to be able to do so without the assistance of General Price.' I can scarcely conceive how this could be interpreted into a declaration that I did not want re-enforcements." His willingness to turn and fight even under these circumstances did not mean that he had no need for additional troops: "I only desired to assure the lieutenant general commanding that I would do all in my power without Price's troops in case they could not be sent." He blamed the retreat along the Red River on Smith's failure to deliver reinforcements and charged, "It is most unfortunate that my desire to relieve the lieutenant-general commanding from any embarrassment should involve a delay in sending re-enforcements to this army." Taylor ended his letter on a clear note of contempt: "When Green joins me, I repeat, I shall fight a battle for Louisiana." [35]

Taken aback by Taylor's overt hostility, Smith responded sharply. "I object to the tone of your letter," he complained on March 31. "It certainly was not justi-fied by anything said or felt by myself." Although Smith did not deny that he had misconstrued Taylor's earlier letters, he refused to take responsibility for the misunderstanding. Instead, he tried to shift the blame to Kenner, whom he ac-cused of having blurred the lines between civil and military authority. In divulg-ing the substance of their meeting, Smith complained, Kenner had betrayed a professional trust. He closed the letter by urging Taylor not to let the unfortunate disagreement "interrupt the harmony and good understanding" that characterized their official relations. [36]

The letter typified Smith's way of responding to complaints from subordi-nates: denying accountability, casting himself as the victim, and then attempting to soothe his subordinate's feelings. He had done precisely the same with Holmes. Unlike his association with Holmes, however, Smith's relationship with Taylor had never been harmonious. Since taking command of the department, he had argued with Taylor over everything from black troops to troop deployments. This latest quarrel over reinforcements was merely a continuation of their larger dis-agreement on how to prosecute the war in the Trans-Mississippi.

Unmoved by Smith's attempt to appease him, Taylor lashed back in a letter dated April 3. Insisting that he could "find nothing disrespectful or improper" in his letter of the twenty-eighth, he refused to back down from the issue of account-ability for the Federal advance. He pointed to Dr. Smith as the source of the gossip that held him responsible for the enemy's gains in Louisiana since 1863. Taylor also accused the doctor of circulating the rumor that he did not want reinforce-ments. Since the doctor was reputed to be the general's closest confidant in the department, Taylor said, he assumed that Smith too held him responsible for the Confederate failure to stop the incursion into Louisiana. "I am not desirous to escape any just responsibility," he persisted, but indicated that a substantial por-tion of the blame for the invasion lay outside his district, apparently at department headquarters. He concluded by saying that he was "fully impressed with what is due from a subordinate to his military superior," yet his threat to disobey orders and offer battle to the Federals once Green arrived still stood. [37]

Taylor had thrown down the gauntlet. His allegations about Dr. Smith corroborate those leveled by Boggs. The doctor did indeed wield considerable influence over Smith. Smith's preoccupation with glory made him receptive to the doctor's counsel, biased as it was by concern for the general's personal achievements. Moreover, Smith was under political pressure from Price and Governor Thomas Reynolds to focus on the recovery of Arkansas and Missouri, and thus to alter his strategy of concentration in the Red River campaign. Smith's departure from this strategy came at an inopportune time for Taylor. Despite the presence of four thousand reinforcements at Shreveport, Smith refused to concentrate against the Federal column pushing Taylor back through the Louisiana heartland. Military theory demanded that Smith move to support Taylor. Personal and political considerations dictated that he turn to Arkansas.[38]

Notwithstanding Smith's change in plan, Taylor's threat to turn and strike the Federals in Louisiana without orders approached insubordination. Even with reinforcements from Green, Taylor's army would number less than nine thousand soldiers. His chance of success against the massive Federal ground force, protected by naval firepower, was remote at best. Smith had offered Taylor a succinct analysis of the situation on March 31: the defeat of either Price's army or the army in Louisiana "would be fatal to the whole cause and to the department."[39]

Like Smith, Taylor was subject to nonmilitary pressures. Relatives, friends, and politicians in his district depended upon him as a native son to halt the Federal aggression against their state. Perhaps only Robert E. Lee, under pressure from Virginians, felt such a burden of responsibility. Taylor's anguish was acute: "The fairest and richest portion of the Confederacy is now a waste. . . . [Louisiana's] children are exiles; her labor system is destroyed." For the moment, however, he had little choice but to obey orders, fall back toward Shreveport, and await reinforcements and the Federal advance.[40]

6

To Whip the Scoundrels Here

By April 3, Richard Taylor's retreat had carried him to the crossroads town of Mansfield, Louisiana, just a few miles beyond Pleasant Hill. The crucial importance of the town became apparent at once. From Mansfield, roads to the east allowed the Confederates to monitor Federal movements on the Red River, while roads to the west gave Texas troops across the Sabine River a direct path to Taylor's army. Taylor resolved to use the town as a staging ground for an offensive as soon as sufficient reinforcements arrived.[1]

Despite instructions from Edmund Kirby Smith to the contrary, Taylor clung stubbornly to the idea of striking the Federal column at Natchitoches. The dispute between the generals and the situation on Taylor's front compelled Smith to qualify his assessment of Arkansas as the preeminent theater of operations. In a return to his original position, Smith assured Taylor on April 1, "Further developments of the enemy's movements will determine the column upon which the concentration will be made." The restoration of the strategy came too late for Taylor. As reinforcements from Texas began to arrive in larger numbers, he resolved to take the initiative against Nathaniel P. Banks. He apprised Smith that he had "offered battle to the enemy" on April 3. Although the fighting amounted to only a skirmish, Taylor declared positively that the problem now was "how to take the offensive." Ignoring Smith's call for restraint, Taylor threatened to usurp the authority of the commanding general and unilaterally seek concentration below Shreveport.[2]

Reports of growing Federal numbers in Louisiana and Arkansas signaled to Smith that both claws of the Federal pincer were closing on the Trans-Mississippi capital. As the defiant tone of Taylor's messages made clear, Smith needed desperately to rein in his lieutenant. At the outset of the campaign he had confided to Arkansas congressman R. W. Johnson, "Taylor is the only district commander in whom I can rely . . . [if] only he could forget his habits and training as a politician." He considered Taylor "a good soldier and a man of ability." The urgency of the situation demanded that Smith try to mend their working relationship.[3]

Disregarding his subordinate's recent complaints, Smith sent Taylor details of the recent news from Sterling Price. The Missourian's report indicated that Frederick Steele was advancing in force and the cavalry could do little to stop him. "A decision must now soon be taken upon which the fate of the department must rest," Smith admitted, and he asked for advice: "You have always cheerfully given me your support, and I feel that I can with confidence call upon you for your views and opinions before taking a step." While Smith certainly respected Taylor's military sense, his appeal for guidance played mainly to the Louisianan's pride. With the fate of the Trans-Mississippi hanging in the balance, Smith could not afford to make a mistake or allow Taylor to act rashly and put the security of the department at risk. Visions of glory aside, he certainly did not need Taylor to remind him of the peril. He needed Taylor to cooperate.[4]

Taylor's anger had not yet subsided. He responded to Smith on April 4 with caustic criticism of the Fabian strategy that had allowed Banks to move uncontested as far as Natchitoches. In addition, Taylor delivered a stinging personal attack that questioned Smith's resolve: "Like a man who has admitted the robber into his bed-chamber instead of resisting him at the door, our defense will be embarrassed by the cries of wives and children." The implication was that Smith's attempt to defend Louisiana was something less than manly. "Action, prompt, vigorous action, is required," Taylor admonished. "While we are deliberating, the enemy is marching."[5]

Taylor's temper cooled midway through his reply. In the second part of the response he addressed the intelligence in Price's dispatch and delivered an objective analysis of the situation. "Banks is cold, timid, easily foiled," he asserted, "Steele is bold, ardent, [and] vigorous." Moreover, Taylor recognized that Banks depended upon the river for support while Steele moved overland with his trains. The falling water line of the Red River meant that Banks might not be able to continue the expedition as planned. Taylor noted that he had ordered the steamship *Falls City* sunk ahead of the Federal fleet as a means of further slowing Admiral David D. Porter's progress. Steele, however, was advancing rapidly and unchecked except by Price's horsemen. "If [Steele] has anything like the force represented he will sweep Price from his path," Taylor predicted. Despite his personal stake in the defense of Louisiana, Taylor recommended that at this point in the campaign, the threat from Steele appeared to be "the most dangerous and should be met and overthrown at once." He offered to march his army to Arkansas for the good of the department.[6]

Before he received Taylor's letter, Smith took action to appease his lieutenant. Partially as a peace offering and partially because Steele's advance had not yet lived up to Price's ballyhoo, Smith decided to send the Arkansas and Missouri reinforcements to Keachi, a sparsely populated village midway between Shreveport and Mansfield. On April 3 he placed Thomas Churchill in command of the reinforcements, and the troops marched out of Shreveport that afternoon. Two days later Taylor acknowledged completion of the movement and, claiming operational control over the four thousand reinforcements, renewed his vow to take the offensive. "If I receive no orders to the contrary," he told Smith, "I shall order Churchill to join me in the morning and move at once on Natchitoches."[7]

After receiving Taylor's recommendations, Smith decided that a council of war was in order. On April 5 he notified Taylor that he would ride to Mansfield the following day to confer "clearly and unreservedly" on the issues at stake. The mixed messages in Taylor's letters had left Smith confused and concerned. Taylor seemed unpredictable, one moment threatening to strike Banks at Natchitoches and the next offering to fight Steele in Arkansas. His personal attacks and persistent threats to disobey orders grew closer to outright insubordination. Taylor's recent pledge, to order Churchill to the front, proved most troublesome. Smith needed to ensure that Taylor's posturing did not jeopardize his campaign strategy. Before leaving Shreveport, he issued instructions for Churchill to prepare to return to Arkansas.[8]

Smith arrived at Taylor's headquarters on the morning of April 6. He explained his strategy and insisted that the only hope for victory against the enemy's superior numbers was to concentrate at a central position. In response to Taylor's threat to move against Banks unilaterally, Smith cautioned that an untimely strike would jeopardize the advantage of interior lines. Should Louisiana's army suffer defeat while Steele's column still posed a threat from Arkansas, the enemy would annihilate Price, and the Federal vise would inevitably clamp shut on Shreveport.[9]

Smith's next suggestions, however, belied the strategy he had just outlined. First, he proposed withdrawing Taylor's army to Shreveport and forcing the Federals to lay siege to the city. Then, as an alternative to a siege, he proposed that Taylor abandon Louisiana entirely and retreat across the Sabine River into Texas. Both options horrified Taylor. He deplored the idea of a siege and reminded Smith that the inevitable loss of troops and supplies would never be offset. The idea of relinquishing his state to the enemy also infuriated Taylor, and he warned that Louisiana troops would desert rather than go to Texas. Taylor flatly rejected

Smith's ideas and reiterated his intention to fight Banks as soon as reinforcements arrived. The generals had reached a strategic standoff that, unless resolved quickly, could lead to the destruction of Louisiana and Arkansas and the fall of the Trans-Mississippi.[10]

Before noon, Churchill rode into Mansfield and joined the meeting. Although elements of his command had already begun to move toward Arkansas, Smith had asked him to attend the conference. Upon Churchill's arrival, Smith rescinded his orders for Arkansas and held the troops at Keachi. Smith realized that Keachi gave him four strategic options. From there the northwest road divided, with the main route continuing to Shreveport and the spur running west to Marshall, Texas. This would allow Smith either to order a general withdrawal to Texas or to fall back and stand siege at Shreveport. In addition, the Line Road, just northeast of town, provided a path to Camden, Arkansas, should concentration against Steele prove necessary. Finally, if Banks advanced on Shreveport through Mansfield, Taylor could fall back on Churchill's infantry for support. In this case, since Keachi was less than a day's ride from Shreveport, Smith would have ample time to reach the front and lead the army into battle. Thus, Keachi emerged as an essential element in Smith's strategy and gave him the flexibility he needed to stabilize the situation on the southern front and to pacify Taylor.[11]

Smith gave Taylor discretionary control over the infantry at Keachi. Churchill later insisted that if the Federals advanced toward Mansfield, Taylor had standing orders to draw Banks to Keachi and select a strong defensive position before offering battle. Yet Taylor believed that in such a case Smith would issue specific orders for a retreat from Mansfield to Keachi based on the precise disposition of the Federal movements. In either case, none of them believed that Banks would attempt to advance his entire army "across the barren country stretching between Natchitoches and Mansfield." Despite reports of numerous Federal cavalry probes toward Pleasant Hill, Smith predicted a decisive battle in Arkansas while Taylor clung to his plan to attack Banks at Natchitoches.[12]

Although he refused to do anything more than suggest a strategic retreat, Smith knew that Taylor wanted desperately to move against Banks. By giving him discretionary control over the troops at Keachi, he provided Taylor with the means to take action. Strengthened by Churchill's infantry and by the long awaited arrival of Tom Green's cavalry, Taylor's numbers would swell to nearly thirteen thousand in a few days. Smith's decision to hold Churchill at Keachi bolstered Taylor's confidence that he could indeed stop the invasion along the Red River. Thus, Smith fortuitously empowered his lieutenant to disobey his orders and bring on a general engagement. Taylor emphasized, "General Kirby Smith did not insist on the adoption of either his own suggestions, nor expressed an approval of mine." Certainly Taylor did not misconstrue Smith's orders as discretionary, but he remarked later, "When Mansfield was reached, a decision became necessary."[13]

By dusk, the council had ended. Taylor's determination to attack the enemy at Natchitoches remained unchanged and plans for Keachi were still ambiguous. A crucial decision by the Federal commander, however, rendered Taylor's plans moot. That evening, as Smith rode back to Shreveport, Banks marched his army away from Natchitoches and directly toward Mansfield. The decision changed both the external friction of the campaign and the internal dynamics between Smith and Taylor.[14]

Two river roads ran roughly parallel to the Red, along the eastern and western banks, from Natchitoches to Shreveport. An advance along either of these roads would allow Federal gunboats to provide support for the infantry. Banks, however, committed a fateful blunder. Although the march alongside the river was operationally sound, Federal maps indicated only two roads to Shreveport: the road along the eastern bank of the river and the inland stagecoach road. According to Banks's lieutenant William B. Franklin, the general commanding insisted that the need to reach Shreveport by April 10 gave him no time "to reconnoiter that river." Banks chose the most direct route to Shreveport. The stagecoach road, which ran through Pleasant Hill and Mansfield, placed him on a collision course with Taylor.[15]

On the afternoon of April 7 Taylor ordered Green, whose full contingent of cavalry had reached Mansfield the night before, to probe the Federal position between Pleasant Hill and Natchitoches. Within hours, Taylor, at his headquarters in town, heard the sounds of battle from that direction and hurried toward the gunfire. At Wilson's Farm, three miles northwest of Pleasant Hill, he found the Texans heavily engaged with advance elements of Banks's column. While Taylor watched the battle, Green's horsemen began to carve up the Federal cavalry and slice into the lead wagons of their train. After nearly two hours of furious fighting, the Federals brought up artillery and reinforcements to break the stubborn Rebel attack. As the outnumbered Confederates slowly fell back, Taylor and Green recognized that the enemy troops at Wilson's Farm were not a mere reconnaissance force but the vanguard of Banks's general advance. Accordingly, they realized that Banks was no longer marching on Shreveport by way of the river but rather had chosen to move along the road through Mansfield.[16]

As Taylor returned to Mansfield, Confederate cavalry established a makeshift defensive position at Carroll's Mill, twelve miles below the town. There they grappled with Federal pursuit for control of Ten Mile Bayou, the only supply of fresh water in the immediate area. At nightfall the fighting ceased, with Green's men in control of the stream. The Federals lay in line of battle just across the field and awaited the arrival of their infantry.[17]

The stiff Confederate resistance worried Albert Lee, the Federal cavalry commander. Up until Wilson's Farm, he had faced very little opposition. Lee expressed concern that once the Confederates contested the advance, he "might be overpowered . . . and compelled to fall back." He implored Banks to hurry infantry support to the front. Despite Lee's fears, many Federals did not think the Confederates capable of mounting a sustained defense. "We have too much powder for the game," boasted an Illinois captain. Another Federal soldier believed that Wilson's Farm had been the decisive battle of the campaign. "We will not be likely to have to fight them," he predicted, "The rebs did not get reinforcements and had to fall back." Yet some Federals felt uneasy about the situation. A New Englander perceived a change in the disposition of the Rebels, noting that the enemy "sent word out to our lines that they was going to stand us battle and told us to com[e] on." Indeed, the Confederates felt that Wilson's Farm signaled the end of their long retreat. "An engagement is expected in a few days," wrote a Louisianan late that evening, "and we are filled with hope." Taylor was filled with determination.[18]

Taylor was certain that Mansfield, not Keachi, held the key to the campaign. He recognized that the network of roads running through the town made control of the place a tactical necessity. Just beyond Mansfield lay three separate overland routes to Shreveport. One wound its way northwest through Keachi, another stretched north through Kingston, and the third wandered northeast to the river at Springfield Landing. If Banks occupied Mansfield, he could divide his army and advance each of his three self-contained infantry corps along a separate route, within supporting distance of one another. In addition, the Sabine Crossroads, which bisected Mansfield, ran east toward the maze of lakes and bayous that meandered alongside the Red River, and forked west before emptying into a tangle of country lanes and trails that led to various points along the Sabine. Control of this roadway would allow Banks to reestablish communications with the fleet and intercept Rebel reinforcements coming east from Texas. Taylor's assessment of Mansfield's strategic importance was not lost on his able lieutenant John G. Walker. Walker reasoned that "beyond Mansfield the enemy's advance could not be disputed with prudence short of the . . . suburbs of Shreveport, where the enemy's entire army would be reunited." Taylor resolved to confront the Federal invasion short of Mansfield, lest it continue to an assuredly calamitous finale at Shreveport.[19]

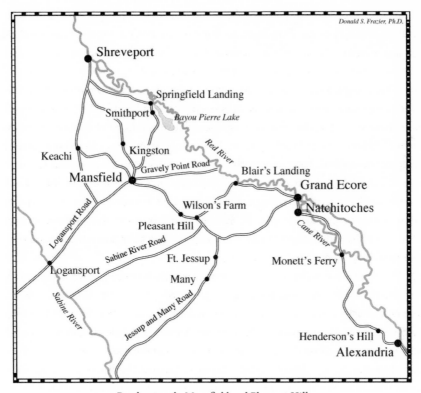

Donald S. Frazier, Ph.D.

Road network, Mansfield and Pleasant Hill

On his ride back to Mansfield from the front, Taylor crossed the Fincher farmstead and stopped at the adjacent property, the Moss plantation, an abandoned farm just three miles below town. At the southern edge of the Fincher farm, the road to Mansfield emerged from the pine forest and ran across two large pastures of green wheat not yet a foot high. A sparsely wooded, gently rising ridge known as Honeycutt Hill separated the fields, and a split-rail fence marked the property line. At the crest of Honeycutt Hill the road curved slightly to the right and descended gradually through the second field belonging to the Moss family and past the Moss farm road on the right before plunging back into piney woods. Taylor selected the northern edge of the woods beyond the latter pasture for the initial deployment of his forces. As he had practiced during the campaigns in Virginia, Taylor chose terrain that provided him with an effective position for either offense or defense. He reached Mansfield having already made the decision to fight Banks, regardless of Smith's orders.[20]

When Taylor arrived in camp, the soldiers quickly surmised that the time for battle had finally come. One Texan noted that the army received "orders to load up and be ready to march at a moments notice," while another recalled instructions to "cook one day's rations, and to be ready to leave . . . the following morning." That night Taylor designated a line of march, which, according to a field officer, "showed clearly that some action was contemplated." After several weeks of inglorious retreat, the men were anxious to turn and face the enemy. Louisiana colonel James H. Beard told his wife, "I do not have any fear of our being able to whip the scoundrels here, having the advantage of a good position and the army wants a fight." While attending a civilian gathering that evening in Mansfield, Taylor assured the panicked residents "that Banks would have to pass over his body before he got to Mansfield." He was "tired of running," noted Governor Henry Watkins Allen, and "Taylor was too much like his father, in temperament, not to be very soon wearied of retreat."[21]

That night Taylor summoned his lieutenants for a council of war to reconcile the dilemma of Banks's advance with Smith's orders for retreat. Seizing the initiative from Banks was no longer a strategic issue for Taylor. He had made this clear to Smith several days earlier. The question before the general and his lieutenants was one of a tactical nature. Although the Federal advance toward Mansfield did not preclude an offensive strike, Taylor's choice of the Moss plantation indicates that he favored a defensive posture. The wood line along the Confederate flanks and rear would conceal both the position and the strength of Taylor's army. Meanwhile, once the Federals emerged from the timber on Honeycutt Hill, they would have to funnel their advance into a confined area on ground that would leave them exposed on a clear field of converging fire. While discussing the situation at the council of war, Taylor received intelligence that Union general A. J. Smith had arrived at Natchitoches with the Sixteenth Corps. The presence of ten thousand additional troops would further strengthen the enemy grip on the Red River Valley. Taylor insisted that unless he stopped Banks below Mansfield, Shreveport would fall in a matter of days. Exercising his operational control over the reinforcements at Keachi, he sent instructions for Churchill to march to Mansfield at dawn.[22]

Throughout the day cavalry patrols had monitored Federal movements between Natchitoches and Pleasant Hill. Green explained that Banks's divisions marched along the stagecoach road as independent units, each supported by its own artillery, munitions, and supply train. The Federal column stretched well over twenty miles, which meant that the widely separated divisions would not be able to concentrate rapidly at the point of attack. Moreover, the thickly wooded pine forest that encroached upon the narrow stagecoach road would restrict the mobility of Banks's column. Soldiers on both sides understood the significance of the terrain. A Federal officer warned that the timber was so dense that it reduced the road to little more than a sunken footpath, hampering his progress. Wilson's Farm demonstrated that these conditions impaired Banks's ability to exploit his numerical superiority and hindered the efficient deployment of his troops for battle. One Confederate expressed what many in Taylor's army felt: "We can whip the enemy in these pine Woods if they advance." Taylor recognized the advantage that this terrain provided his small force against the lumbering Federal goliath. Green's report on the disposition of the Federal advance provided Taylor with the intelligence necessary to seize the tactical initiative from Banks and convert the campaign from one of retreat to one of attack.[23]

Taylor planned to draw the lead column of the Federal advance into the open area that he had selected earlier that day. There he would strike at the head and flanks of the column to drive the Federals back on their supply train. By successfully enveloping the flanks, the Confederates would gain access to the rear of the column. Continuing to press the issue from the flanks would also create the impression that Price had arrived and that the Confederates held a huge numerical advantage. The officers, particularly Louisianans Alfred Mouton and Henry Gray, endorsed the strategy. However, knowledge that Taylor's plan required Smith's approval tempered their enthusiasm. Should Taylor offer battle against orders, he would be guilty of insubordination. Further, the rumor that Smith planned to ride down from Shreveport and take command had finally reached Mansfield. The image of Smith as usurper stirred resentment among enlisted men and officers alike. As the meeting ended, Taylor's lieutenants realized that even if Smith endorsed the battle plans, victory would have a bittersweet taste, especially for the Louisianans. It was under orders from Smith that many had suffered the destruction of their homes and endured the humiliating surrender of the Red River Valley.[24]

Taylor faced a complex set of circumstances that reached well beyond battlefield strategy and tactics. The determination of his superior officer to avoid a general engagement was in direct conflict with the ardent desires of the men under his command and with Taylor's own philosophy of war. Despite his repeated threats to fight Banks, Taylor had used caution and restraint during the retreat to Mansfield. The unexpected movement by the Federals away from the river, however, had forced his hand and left him with two options: continue to retreat or stand and fight.

Later that night Taylor held an informal meeting with a few select officers. After deliberating with Green, Mouton, and Gray, he prepared a carefully worded dispatch to Smith. The message stated that at least four thousand Federals, "the forerunner of a positive advance on the part of the enemy," were moving toward the Confederate position at Mansfield. "I respectfully ask to know," Taylor wrote, "if it accords with the views of the lieutenant-general commanding that I should hazard a general engagement at this point." Taylor concluded the communication by requesting an answer before daylight. It was a clever ruse, for failure to receive a reply before daybreak on April 8 would release him from Smith's orders not to offer battle.[25]

Taylor disclosed in his memoirs, "A dispatch was sent to General Kirby Smith at Shreveport informing him that I had returned from the front, found the enemy advancing in force and would give battle on the following day, April 8, 1864, unless positive orders to the contrary were sent to me." While he did not present his case to Smith in such unequivocal terms at the time, Taylor understood the dispatch of April 7 to carry with it the implicit message that unless he received specific instructions, he would fight Banks at the Moss plantation. Indeed, Taylor had sent a similarly worded dispatch to Smith four days earlier, before learning of Banks's march toward Mansfield. In that message he assured Smith, "If I receive no orders to the contrary . . . I shall move at once on Natchitoches." That plan was contingent on Green's timely arrival, and since the Texan did not arrive for two days, Taylor's threat became moot. In his message of April 7, however, there were no contingencies other than Smith's instructions. Taylor arranged to send the dispatch at 9:00 P.M., to allow sufficient time for a courier to reach Shreveport, for Smith to issue a reply, and for a courier to return to Mansfield.[26]

Taylor could not risk a refusal from Smith. Should the general deny him permission to fight Banks, Taylor would be duty bound to stand by idly as little more than a witness to the destruction of Louisiana. During the late-night meeting, Taylor, Gray, and Mouton, whose shared love for Louisiana matched their dislike of Smith, developed a scheme to ensure that Smith would be unable to prevent the battle. Rather than assign the delivery of the dispatch to his own adjutant, Taylor gave the message to Captain Wilbur F. Blackman, Gray's adjutant. J. E. Sligh, a junior officer present at the April 7 council of war, recalled that Taylor and Gray enlisted Blackman in a conspiracy to prevent a timely delivery of the dispatch to

Smith's headquarters. Blackman, who had served under Taylor in Virginia, knew that both Taylor and Gray "did not want the courier to reach Smith in time." His course of action would determine the next move for Taylor and his army.[27]

Most of the soldiers in Gray's command were from the northwestern parishes of Louisiana and were thus familiar with the back roads from Mansfield to Shreveport. Blackman assigned the task of carrying the message to a courier who took a circuitous route from Mansfield to Shreveport. This strategy ensured that the letter would not reach Smith in time for him to forbid the engagement at Mansfield. Evidence suggests that twenty-seven-year-old William R. Kennedy of Claiborne Parish, who was a Partisan Ranger and thus immune from any official reprimand, carried the message to Shreveport. Taylor and Gray had made use of unofficial couriers throughout the campaign, primarily to avoid the Federals. At Mansfield, they employed the same method to confound Smith.[28]

Had Kennedy used the best roads, a round-trip ride from Mansfield to Shreveport would have taken a minimum of eight hours. A rider and horse could make the outbound trip in four hours only if the rider pushed the animal to the physical limits of its endurance. If the courier left at 9:00 P.M. and arrived at 1:00 A.M., there would have been only sixty minutes for Smith to receive the letter, digest the information, issue a reply, and still leave time for the courier to return to Taylor by 6:00 A.M. If the courier arrived past 1:00 A.M., Smith's opportunity to reply would be greatly reduced. Smith could not blame Taylor if a rider rested his horse, nor could he condemn a courier for getting lost. Taylor built these precautions into his scheme and timed the arrival of the message so as to put pressure on Smith to react immediately. He had taken the measure of Banks on the battlefield and now took the measure of Smith behind the lines.[29]

By the time Smith received Taylor's dispatch, the window of opportunity to issue a reply had nearly closed. Despite the urgency of the situation, however, the commanding general did not respond immediately. Instead, he chose to honor a decree issued by the Confederate Congress that proclaimed April 8 a national "day of fasting, humiliation and prayer." The provisions of the decree included a suspension of all military activities. Smith had decided weeks before to enforce a strict observance of the day throughout the department, and he clung to his literal interpretation of the decree despite the imminent danger to Confederate forces in Louisiana and Taylor's threat to disobey orders. He postponed drafting a reply to the message until after noon on April 8, effectively giving de facto approval to Taylor's battle plans.[30]

When the belated word from Smith arrived, the dispatch said what Taylor and his lieutenants had expected. Smith declined to give orders for the army at Mansfield to offer battle. "A general engagement now could not be given with our full force," Smith declared, explaining that even with the addition of Churchill's men, Taylor would not have sufficient strength to defeat the Federals. Smith also disclosed that while he would continue to make additional reinforcements available, he planned to concentrate every available soldier at the front before making a commitment to engage the enemy. The promise of reinforcements notwithstanding, Smith offered Taylor imprecise instructions for meeting Banks's advance: "I would compel the enemy to develop his intentions, selecting a position in rear where we can give him battle before he can occupy Shreveport." Smith concluded the letter by reminding Taylor, "Let me know as soon as you are convinced that a general advance is being made and I will come to the front."[31]

Smith had apparently not grasped the gravity of the situation. Taylor's letter had unambiguously confirmed that his army stood directly in the path of the Federal advance. The enemy had already developed his intentions—to move through Mansfield—and Taylor was soliciting instructions, not suggestions. But Smith did not consider Banks's inland advance dangerous enough to warrant immediate action, nor did he take seriously Taylor's vow to fight Banks once reinforcements arrived at Mansfield. Perhaps Smith had grown tired of his subordinate's constant saber rattling. Given the tone of Taylor's recent correspondence, Smith may have dismissed this latest dispatch as just another piece of bravado.[32]

Smith's reply also confirmed Taylor's suspicions that additional reinforcements were still available. Likewise, it corroborated rumors that Smith intended to ride down on the eve of battle so that the soldiers could "derive an element of morale" from his personal leadership "at the moment of action." As Duncan Kenner and William Boggs both suspected, Smith intended to delay permission for a battle until the last possible moment when he would swoop down upon the Federals with additional troops and "carry off the glory of the pitched battle." By the time Taylor received Smith's reply, however, it was too late. The battle of Mansfield was already under way.[33]

Richard Taylor
The Historical Society of Pennsylvania, Gratz
Collection, case 5, box 17

Alfred J. Mouton
The Historical Society of Pennsylvania, Gratz
Collection, case 5, box 15

Henry Gray
Valentine Richmond History Center, Cook
Collection #2967

Tom Green
The Historical Society of Pennsylvania, Gratz
Collection, case 5, box 13

William R. Boggs
The Historical Society of Pennsylvania, Gratz
Collection, case 5, box 11

Edmund Kirby Smith
The Historical Society of Pennsylvania, Gratz
Collection, case 5, box 16

Thomas J. Churchill
The Historical Society of Pennsylvania, Gratz
Collection, case 5, box 12

Hamilton P. Bee
Valentine Richmond History Center, Cook
Collection, #2728

St. John Liddell

*The Historical Society of Pennsylvania, Gratz
Collection, case 5, box 14*

Sterling Price

*The Historical Society of Pennsylvania, Gratz
Collection, case 5, box 15*

John G. Walker

*The Historical Society of Pennsylvania, Gratz
Collection, case 5, box 17*

Camille J. Polignac

Author's collection

Henry Watkins Allen
*The Historical Society of Pennsylvania, Gratz
Collection, case 5, box 11*

George Wythe Randolph
*The Historical Society of Pennsylvania, Gratz
Collection, case 3, box 13*

7
Too Late, Sir, the Battle Is Won

In the early-morning hours of April 8, as Edmund Kirby Smith pondered the correspondence from the front, Richard Taylor's Army of Western Louisiana began to move toward a battle below Mansfield. As the men passed through the town, crowds gathered to cheer them on. Ladies young and old cast flowers in the path of the marching soldiers and begged for protection from the Yankee invaders. Years later Texan James C. Carroll recalled, "I will never forget [how] with bands of music—colors flying, gun in hand . . . we turn[ed] back on the enemy and said you have come far enough."[1]

Throughout the morning Taylor deployed his troops at the Moss plantation. Along the northeastern edge of the woods, Alfred Mouton's division took a position behind the Moss farm road, his right flank buttressed against M. V. McMahan's battery astride the Mansfield road. John Walker's Texans extended the gray lines southwest through the woods, briars, and thickets. Interspersed with Mouton's brigades were three batteries, while Walker had the support of two. Cavalry chieftain Tom Green sent Hamilton Bee to anchor Walker's right flank while he rode with James Major to secure Mouton's left. Xavier DeBray's horsemen covered the center of the road. Over four thousand reinforcements from Keachi would arrive late that afternoon, but until then, just fifty-three hundred infantrymen, three thousand cavalry troopers, and five hundred artillerists stood between Nathaniel P. Banks and Mansfield. As Taylor rode along the lines he called out to General Camille Polignac, "Little Frenchman, I am going to fight Banks here if he has a million men."[2]

At 9:40 that morning, before deployment was complete, Taylor sent another dispatch to Smith. He explained that Banks's inland advance on Shreveport was well under way and that he considered the position below Mansfield "as favorable a point to engage him as any other." Taylor was hedging his bet. Hopeful that Banks would attack before Smith could reply, he followed protocol and gave the commanding general another opportunity to respond. Taylor recalled that his knowledge of enemy movements provided him with a strong measure of optimism.

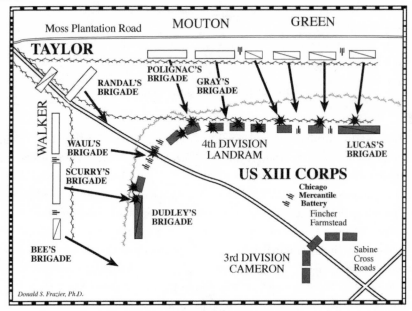

Battle of Mansfield, April 8, 1864 (first phase)

He also emphasized that personal insight into Banks's character, gained during previous campaigns in Virginia and along the Teche, gave him "confidence of success in the impending engagement." Governor Henry Watkins Allen described Taylor's mind-set at Mansfield as antagonistic and characterized his behavior as "imperious." Smith's failure to issue a timely response only served to embolden Taylor further.[3]

By noon, Taylor had still not received word from his commanding officer. Moreover, as the growing Federal lines frowned down from Honeycutt Hill, Banks showed no inclination to move against the Confederates. The lack of action on the part of the enemy was cause for concern, and Taylor began to worry that the Union Sixteenth Corps, recently arrived at Natchitoches, could advance southwest from the river to turn the Confederate position. Around 2:00 P.M., lead elements of Churchill's command began to arrive from Keachi, and Taylor sent them to hold the Gravely Point road connecting Springfield Landing with Mansfield. From this position Churchill could intercept a Federal turning movement or support the main Confederate body in the event of a breakthrough. In either case, as Churchill's men marched into town, they became the tactical reserve for Taylor's army.[4]

While the sounds of skirmishing echoed from the field, Taylor rode among Mouton's ranks to offer words of encouragement. He understood that the Louisiana troops were "already inflamed by outrages on their homes, as well as the camp rumors that it was intended to abandon their State with out a fight." Taylor met with Mouton in the pines behind the Confederate line to discuss the situation. As they spoke, a volley from Federal cavalry in pursuit of retreating skirmishers crackled through the woods and felled Taylor's horse, nearly spilling the general's blood. "Minie balls are dropping arround us like hail," declared one of the men stationed near the generals. The unsuspecting Union horsemen had raced to within twenty yards of the concealed Confederate position. Mouton barked, "Captain, those are Yankees!" and promptly ordered his men to return fire. The Louisianans scrambled to unleash a volley from the woods, then dashed onto the field and scattered the Federals back to Honeycutt Hill. "Louisiana has drawn the first blood to-day and the victory is ours," proclaimed Mouton as his men broke into a cheer before re-forming their lines. This time they took a position on the outer edge of the woods and used "a small fringe of bush . . . between [an] old worm fence and the road" to hide their true numbers.[5]

Despite Mouton's encounter, the Confederates retained the advantage of cover provided by the woods to conceal their flanks and disguise the actual disposition of the army. A Federal soldier recalled that Rebel "lines extended so far that [we] could not see the ends of either flank." The tactical use of the wooded terrain helped Taylor mislead the enemy with respect to Confederate troop strength and helped bait the trap for Banks near the Sabine Crossroads.[6]

Taylor's troop deployment accomplished his plan to deceive Banks even before the fighting had started. The Confederates could muster just eighty-eight hundred troops, but the Federals believed they faced a force of fifteen to twenty thousand. Union officers at the front assumed that Sterling Price had arrived from Arkansas. Because of their miscalculations, the Federals did not move immediately to attack the Confederate position. Their hesitancy frustrated Taylor's designs to lure the enemy forward, down from Honeycutt Hill, across the Moss fields, and toward the wood line where he had devised a deadly ambuscade. Taylor realized that the Federals intended to delay the attack to allow time for reinforcements to make their way to the front. He had expected that the relative lack of Confederate resistance during the campaign, and Banks's weak military acumen, would lead the Federals into a hasty decision to strike. The unexpected delay jeopardized his strategy. This consideration, combined with concern that a courier from Smith was on his way from Shreveport, prompted Taylor to take the offensive and launch an assault on Honeycutt Hill.[7]

In his memoirs Taylor detailed the military theory behind his shift in tactics. Initiative in warfare, he insisted, "surpasses in power mere accession of numbers, as it requires neither transport nor commissariat. Holding it, a commander lays his plans deliberately, and executes them at his own appointed time and in his own way." Taylor criticized the defensive posture as "weak, lowering morale of the army reduced to it, enforcing constant watchfulness lest threatened attacks become real, and keeping commander and troops in a state of anxious tension." This was the lesson he had learned from Stonewall Jackson during the Valley campaign in 1862, and the one he had attempted to use against the Federal advance on Bisland in 1863. On the afternoon of April 8, 1864, Taylor applied this principle to both Banks and Smith. He had taken the initiative with regard to Smith, forcing the commanding general to respond to the strategic situation at the front. Initially, in deference to Smith's original orders, Taylor had prepared to remain on the defensive. When Banks failed to inaugurate the battle, however, Taylor seized the initiative.[8]

At 3:30 P.M. Taylor observed blue-clad troops moving east to extend the Federal right across Honeycutt Hill. Believing that the shift signaled a flanking movement, he ordered Walker to send Horace Randal's brigade across the Mansfield road to bolster Mouton's right. At the same time, he directed Alexander W. Terrell's Texas cavalry to swing around in support of Major at the far left of the Confederate line. The entire left side of the army spilled forward as skirmishers, sent onto the field to cover the redeployment, advanced across the front toward the enemy. Since noon, Mouton and Green had been pressing Taylor to take the offensive before additional Federal reinforcements arrived. As the afternoon wore on, time increasingly became a factor. Taylor confessed that he grew "impatient at the delay of the enemy in developing his attack" and so ordered Mouton to advance. According to a staff officer, Mouton told his brigadiers that "suggestions had become an order." With that the division clamored over the fence, in lines four deep, and trotted across a half-mile of open ground toward the Federal guns. "The ardor of Mouton's troops," reported Taylor, "especially the Louisianans, could not be restrained."[9]

As Mouton's ranks emerged from the woods and streamed across the field, Taylor hurried to his command post along the Mansfield road behind the center of the Confederate lines. He sat on his coal black horse with one leg tossed across the saddle, as his father had done during battles in Mexico. Drawing a comparison some years later between Taylor and his father, Governor Allen insinuated that both tended to act on emotion and each lacked a "sufficient sense of subordination." Taylor clearly understood that the decision to give battle at Mansfield could be construed as deliberate insubordination if not outright mutiny. He lit a cigar and took a long, slow draw before blowing a plume of gray smoke into the sultry afternoon air. Turning to DeBray, Taylor confessed that he was fighting "with a rope around his neck."[10]

Henry Gray's brigade led the surge of Confederate soldiers as Mouton's men poured across the field under a firestorm of case and canister. The Federal right unleashed a searing volley into the Confederate lines and moved down from the crest of Honeycutt Hill to meet the advance. The Federals secured a strong position behind a split-rail fence just below the ridge, but within moments Mouton's booming voice reverberated across the field as he rallied his troops: "Throw down that fence, my boys, and charge across that field and drive the enemy away." When the charge staggered and began to falter less than a hundred yards short of the Union position, Captain Wilbur Blackman galloped to the front and seized the fallen colors. As Mouton cheered him on, Blackman reared back on his horse and rode directly toward the enemy lines, waving the flag, urging his men to follow. It remains unknown whether Blackman's charge was prompted by misgivings about the role he had played in the scheme to deceive Smith. After the battle one Federal prisoner claimed that "not less than two-hundred shots were fired at Blackman when he was not more than fifty yards distant," but the daring Confederate survived. Guided by their colors, the Louisianans stormed the hill, cascaded over the fence, and overwhelmed the enemy. "The charge made by Mouton across the open was magnificent," Taylor declared in his official report. "The field was crossed under murderous fire of artillery and musketry, the wood was reached, and our little line sprang with a yell on the foe."[11]

As the gray waves of Mouton's assault swept over the crest of Honeycutt Hill, a courier carrying a message from Smith raced down the Mansfield road toward Taylor. Upon the rider's approach, one witness reported, "Taylor's eye flashed, and he seemed to rise in his stirrups." Anxiously, he tore the message from the courier's hand and read aloud Smith's order not to hazard a general engagement.

From his location at the center of the Confederate lines, Taylor surveyed the battle-field. Mouton, joined by Major's cavalry, had begun to envelop the Federal right flank and threaten the enemy's control of the high ground at Honeycutt Hill. Taylor turned to the courier and snarled, as if he were addressing Smith, "Too late, sir, the battle is won!"[12]

The battle, however, was far from won. On the Confederate right, Walker began to push his skirmishers through the woods and "to feel the position of the enemy." Once the Texans began their advance, it became apparent that the gray lines extended well beyond the Federal left flank. The brigades closed quickly through a large field into a narrow skirt of timber six hundred yards from the enemy. Under heavy shelling from Federal artillery, Walker formed his battle lines and ordered the men to fix bayonets. "Aim low boys," he advised the troops, "and trust in God."[13]

The Texans rumbled across the field amid the sound of cheers that rose from the ranks above the bedlam. Walker expected support on his right, but Bee's dis-mounted cavalry became entangled in heavy underbrush and could not advance in concert. Walker's charge wavered briefly but continued to advance, drawing closer to the crest of the hill. Scores fell as the Confederates ascended the ridge and the bloody combat escalated into rifle fire at point-blank range and slaughter at the point of a bayonet. "At last," roared a Texan, "the fence is gained; over it our troops go, like an avalanche of fire." As the Federal lines crumbled, swarms of Texans mobbed an isolated battery and turned the guns on the enemy, raking them with the same deadly fire that moments before had been directed at them-selves. "Oh how we scattered the blues and captured flags, [and] killed men," recalled one of Walker's soldiers. Another described the triumphant crescendo of the fighting: "A loud prolonged Texas yell deafens the ear their cheers rise . . . over the noise of battle and [are] heard far down the lines to the left, where the Louisiana boys are at it."[14]

By 5:00 P.M., Taylor's Confederates controlled Honeycutt Hill. The men paused to survey the ground they had won and the cost in carnage. No division had suffered more than Mouton's. During the first thirty minutes of the charge, according to some veterans, Mouton's command sustained as many as seven hun-dred casualties out of twenty-two hundred men, a rate of nearly 32 percent. Gray's brigade suffered the heaviest losses, with his Consolidated Crescent regiment alone losing nearly two hundred men, including seven color bearers. By the time the Confederates took the hill, all three regiments in Gray's command had lost their colonels and half of their field officers. While the tenacity of the outnumbered Federal troops certainly played a role in the high casualties, Taylor must be held accountable for his battle plan, and his lieutenants for their execution of the commander's design.[15]

Although Taylor had skillfully devised a dual envelopment, he chose to initiate the battle with a frontal attack against the Union right, the strongest part of the enemy line. However, he did not launch his divisions in a coordinated assault. Mouton's command advanced first, and Walker did not receive orders to charge until at least thirty minutes after these troops were fully engaged. This delay allowed the Federals to concentrate on the attack against their right until Walker forced the issue on the Union left. T. E. G. Ransom, the Federal brigadier in Mouton's front, reported, "I felt confident that [the right] portion of our line could not be broken." Only after Walker broke through on the left did Ransom acknowledge that the position was hopeless and pull his men out.[16]

The decision to order a frontal attack against the Union right was itself dubious. The enemy position was more vulnerable near a point of timber where the Mansfield road crossed Honeycutt Hill. Here the Federal line, which extended roughly east to west across the ridge to the Mansfield road, bent back on itself at a ninety-degree angle and formed a salient. The position left its defenders exposed to converging fire from three directions and was thus virtually indefensible. Had Taylor attacked down the Mansfield road and threatened the salient with a coordinated blow, he would have forced the Federals to weaken both ends of their line so as to hold the angle. With the Union flanks undermanned, Confederate cavalry would have had a clear path to the Federal rear. This is ultimately what happened, but not until after Mouton was fully engaged on the left.[17]

Before the battle began, Taylor had expressed concern that enemy troop deployments signaled an attempt to turn his left. Accordingly, his attention remained fixed on that section of the field. The result was Mouton's charge and an excessive loss southern blood. With an attack against the salient to open the battle, Taylor could have splintered the blue lines immediately and driven a wedge between the Union wings. Then, with continuing pressure from the flanks, the Confederates could have annihilated each portion of the enemy force in detail. Further, Confederate cavalry would have encountered scant resistance in their efforts to envelop the enemy position, secure control of the Mansfield road, and sever the main artery of Federal support and supply—all of this with far fewer Confederate casualties. Five days before the battle, Taylor had told Smith that the issue had ceased to be whether or not to take the offensive; rather, the problem was "how to take the offensive." Upon delivery of the butcher's bill at Mansfield, it became apparent that Taylor and his lieutenants did not have an answer.[18]

Among the casualties sustained during the opening phase at Mansfield, none was as costly to Taylor as the loss of Mouton. The Louisianan fell as the Confederate left flank swept the Federals from the ridge. Even before this stage of the battle had ended, conflicting reports of the popular general's death raced through the Confederate ranks. On the right, Joseph P. Blessington recorded that Federal marksmen shot Mouton prior to Walker's advance. According to Louisianan J. E. Sligh, the enemy killed Mouton after the fighting on the left had nearly ceased. Another member of Gray's command, O. W. Wells, described the circumstances surrounding Mouton's death in a letter to his sister, written just four days after the battle: "When [Mouton] was killed he had just taken . . . prisoners who surrendered. At the same time he told them to surrender their arms however, six shot him and he took the balls in the chest."[19]

Numerous contemporary accounts of the incident support Wells's claim that an act of treachery played a role in Mouton's death. However, in a postwar report to the Historical Committee of the United Confederate Veterans, Frank L. Richardson claimed that Mouton's death was the result of his own carelessness. A veteran of the Second Louisiana Cavalry, on Mouton's left, Richardson recalled that the brigadier believed that a group of Federals had surrendered when in fact they were still actively engaged. Regardless of the circumstances, the perception among the Confederates that the enemy had violated the protocol of surrender spread throughout the ranks and influenced the demeanor of Taylor and his men. "At this our blood was brought to a boiling heat," recalled one Texan. Louisiana soldiers who witnessed the act cried out for vengeance and executed the Federals responsible before Confederate field officers could intercede. Sligh claimed that an enemy captain whom he had taken prisoner begged for protection from reprisals, while Blessington acknowledged that some of the Louisianans "threw themselves in wild grief on the ground, weeping scalding tears in their bitter sorrow" when they learned of Mouton's death. At his campfire after the battle Taylor confessed, "Above all, the death of gallant Mouton affected me. I thought of his wife and children." All the Confederates, particularly Taylor, would sorely miss Mouton's leadership skills in the coming days.[20]

Taylor's sorrow was more than personal. Mouton had played a significant role in the planning and execution of Taylor's covert strategy to disobey Smith's orders.

Sligh, a member of Gray's staff, revealed that Green and Mouton were the only two division commanders present at the council of war held the night before the battle. While it is unlikely that Taylor would have excluded Walker from an official strategy session, Sligh's comments indicate that Taylor met privately with Mouton and Green sometime after the conclusion of the formal council of war. Consequently, Walker was not privy to the clandestine plan of attack developed by Taylor, Green, and Mouton on the night of April 7. By excluding Walker from the conspiracy, Taylor protected his subordinate from any official repercussions that might have ensued. Further, Taylor's relationship with Green and Mouton, the former his cousin and the latter a fellow Louisiana aristocrat, ensured support for the unauthorized battle plan and reduced the chance of an internal security breach.[21]

Walker's exclusion from the inner circle explains his contention that Mouton "advanced without orders," and that until Mouton attacked, Taylor "was undecided as to the propriety of bringing on a general engagement." Walker vigorously defended his commander's decision to initiate the fighting and stressed that "Taylor did not intend to disobey [Smith's] instructions" to avoid a pitched battle. He also insisted that Green, not Mouton, unilaterally opened the assault against the Federal right flank and that Mouton advanced only to support the attack.[22]

From his position on the Confederate right flank, several hundred yards away, Walker could not have determined which regiments moved first. A battlefield meeting between the generals on April 8, however, helped shape Walker's conclusion. Around noon, a corporal assigned to Brigadier General William R. Scurry's staff spotted Green, Mouton, and Taylor riding behind Walker's lines. Taylor and his lieutenants located Walker and, according to the corporal, began a "deep consultation." Taylor apparently advised Walker of their intent to take the offensive if the Federals did not accept the offer of battle. Hours later, just before Mouton launched the assault, the corporal again noticed Taylor engaged in somber discussion with Walker. "The two generals converse[d] together some twenty minutes," he recalled, and then Taylor rode back toward Mouton's division "going a little quicker than he advanced." The Texan attributed Taylor's hasty departure to the news that "flashed along the line that the division of General Mouton had attacked." Taylor's location on the right flank and his hurried departure at the sounds of battle gave the impression to some in Walker's division that the Confederate left had moved forward without orders.[23]

It is doubtful that Confederate soldiers charged into the fangs of the Federal lines without explicit instructions from their commanding officer. The origin of the order to attack, however, came into further dispute, with two of Green's staff officers providing conflicting explanations. Joseph H. Beck claimed that Taylor deliberately violated Smith's instructions and ordered an assault "contrary to the advice of many officers." Beck insinuated that Green argued against the plan, only to have Taylor overrule him and send Mouton forward. However, John A. Green, the brother of the Texas general, insisted that Green and Taylor concurred on the need to give battle despite Smith's admonitions. According to John Green, Taylor gave the cavalry commander discretionary orders to escalate the fighting from a skirmish to a battle. Moreover, he claimed that it was Green, not Taylor, who gave the order to Mouton for a general advance of the Confederate left. This would explain Walker's assertion that Green had opened the assault. After the battle, Green reportedly took responsibility for his actions and Taylor reassured him, "You did as I intended you should have done."[24]

Ten days later, Taylor reported that he had issued direct orders for Mouton to open the attack at Mansfield. He explained earlier movements on the Confederate left as part of troop redeployments along the entire line, and absolved Mouton and Green of accountability. Mouton's brigadier Camille Polignac supported Taylor's claim and emphasized, "Our line was ordered to charge by Gl. R. Taylor." Nevertheless, Walker's version of events gained acceptance throughout the department. The pugnacious Louisiana general St. John R. Liddell, whose command was east of the Red River at the time of the battle, charged, "Generals Mouton and Thomas Green, I have been credibly informed, precipitated the fight at Mansfield, drawing Taylor into it." One of Smith's aides concurred: "General Mouton, without order or knowledge of General Taylor, attacked and repulsed the enemy." Smith personally defended Taylor's actions and insisted, "The battle of Mansfield was not an intentional violation of my instructions on General Taylor's part." He assured President Davis that "the rare intrepidity of Mouton's division" unexpectedly precipitated the battle at Mansfield. Regardless of the controversy surrounding Mansfield, the Confederates had won a convincing victory in the first phase of the battle, and Taylor had made good on his promise to strike Banks even without orders.[25]

After a momentary pause on top of Honeycutt Hill, the Confederates resumed the attack, and the battle raged for four more hours. Blue lines re-formed twice, and each time Taylor's army pushed them back toward Pleasant Hill. If not for dusk, moaned one exhausted Federal, "the rebs would of took nearly all of us for they was following us up right to our heels . . . hallowing halt at the boys that was trying to get away." As night fell, Union reinforcements took up a position on a ridge running across the Chapman farm. There they dealt the Rebels a sharp blow in the peach orchard just beyond Chapman's Bayou. In the final moments of the battle the enemy line was, in the words of one Texan, a "sheet of flame from end to end." A weary New Englander recalled, "We stood our ground and . . . mode them down like hay." With the field cloaked by darkness and the Confederates in control of the area's only source of fresh water, Taylor broke off the pursuit. At the end of the day, the Confederates had suffered over 1,000 casualties but had captured 20 pieces of artillery, 1,000 horses and mules, and nearly 250 wagons loaded with provisions. A shaken Federal explained, "The rebs got the batterys and the train and the ambalences and the napsacks and the guns and everything they wanted." As he had done in the Shenandoah in 1862 and in the Lafourche in 1863, Taylor had turned Banks into a commissary for the Confederacy.[26]

Taylor's attack had succeeded beyond all expectations. During the battle enemy supply trains clogged the road from Pleasant Hill, preventing reinforcements from reaching the front and fleeing Federals from reaching the rear. "We could not get at them only by a narrow wood road filled with baggage traines," chafed a Federal. An Iowan brooded, "I never knew what it was like to see a stampeed until that. The teams and ambalences was all mixed up together. The ground was all covered with napsacks and guns and all sorts of things. Men running and trying to get away." A Philadelphia newspaperman accompanying the invasion reported that Banks and his generals had tried valiantly to stem the fierce current of retreat. Nevertheless, a Federal soldier blamed the debacle on "the played out Potomac Genl named Franklin" and emphasized that the rout was "an everlasting disgrace to Banks." Taylor's army inflicted twenty-five hundred casualties on the enemy and reduced the Federal juggernaut to "a disorganized mob of screaming, sobbing, hysterical, pale, terror-stricken men."[27]

The Confederates were giddy at having reversed the ill fortunes of their re-treat. A Missourian who arrived shortly after nightfall remarked that the troops at Mansfield "were in fine spirits." He may have meant that literally, as the captured wares included a large stock of liquor. One of Randal's men recalled that his regiment spied a group of northern Zouave prisoners "dressed in red flannel trousers, looking somwhat like the ladies bloomers . . . [and] dainty red caps with tassels." Some of the southerners mocked the prisoners as they filed past, throwing down their guns and swearing that "if they were to fight any more women they would go home." The Texans had a particular reason to be derisive: captured wagons bore makeshift signs that read Austin, San Antonio, Houston, and Galveston.[28]

Taylor joined in the sport by sending a message across enemy lines requesting instructions on what to do with the dress-white paper collars that the Confederates found among the captured supplies. "[We have] baked them, boiled them, fried them, and stewed them, and found them of no use, and would like to exchange them for hard bread," he taunted Banks. A fatigued Texan, however, characterized his experience following the battle as horrific rather than joyous. "The enemy had left on the ground dying and dead . . . all through the woods and along the road," he recalled. "Horses and men by the hundreds, rolled down together; the road is red with their blood." A southern cavalry officer described feelings of melancholy and confessed, "Hardened as my heart is to scenes of suffering and misery, the silent tear started unbidden from eyes unused to weeping, as I passed among the maimed and wounded." And so the night passed with the victorious Confederates in various stages of celebration and mourning while the shattered Federals crouched warily in a defensive position between Chapman's Orchard and Pleasant Hill. Still there had been no further word from Smith at Shreveport.[29]

At 4:00 A.M. on April 9 a courier woke Smith with the first of three dispatches from Taylor, breaking the news of a battle at Mansfield. The message notified the commanding general that a midafternoon skirmish between Confederate forces and elements of the Federal Thirteenth Corps had, within two hours, escalated into a general engagement. Taylor had sent the dispatch at 6:00 P.M., just before the second phase of the fighting, and offered Smith an enthusiastic assessment of the battle. He announced that the army had driven the Federals back three miles and had initiated a torrid pursuit. The communication implied that Confederate troops had converted a defensive response into an offensive action. Taylor pledged to continue the fighting and to "push the enemy to the utmost."[30]

A second correspondence, sent at 7:30 P.M., reported the capture of "hundreds of wagons, many guns, caissons, ordnance wagons &c." Seizure of the large Federal train and the much-needed supplies gave added importance to the day's fighting. Taylor also affirmed that he had driven the Federals back an additional three miles and emphasized that the fighting still raged. Finally, at 10:30 P.M., Taylor notified Smith that the contest had closed with a sweeping Confederate victory. He reported that the army had engaged the Federal Thirteenth and Nineteenth Corps in severe fighting and had suffered heavy losses, particularly among the ranks of his officers. "Send all the medical assistance and medical stores you can," he implored. He took the opportunity to renew his plea for additional troops: "If you have any re-enforcements hurry them down. Churchill's and Parsons' divisions . . . have been ordered to the front before daylight to-morrow morning." Taylor also used the victory at Mansfield to underscore his earlier vow to fight rather than retreat, adding that in the morning he would "push the enemy with the utmost vigor."[31]

Upon receipt of the messages, Smith concluded that Taylor had met only the lead elements of the Federal advance and that a decisive battle still loomed somewhere below Shreveport. Accompanied by his aides, he left for the front immediately. Smith expected Taylor to meet him in Mansfield on the afternoon of April 9, but upon his arrival "he found only the wounded and prisoners." As he rode through Mansfield, the truth began to dawn on him. Contrary to orders issued on April 8, which instructed Taylor to "fall back" and "select a position to the rear," his subordinate had initiated a pursuit of Banks. Not until late that night, when Smith arrived at Pleasant Hill, did he learn that Taylor had fought a second major battle. The battle at Pleasant Hill had also resulted in success for Taylor's army, although the triumph was "not as brilliant" as that of the previous day.[32]

Guided by the eerie light of the campfires, Smith made his way through the grotesque scene. Mangled corpses covered the fields for nearly a mile around the Confederate campsite. The wounded could be heard crying out from the woods where they had taken refuge, pleading for salvation and "for someone to come out and get them." Upon entering the encampment, Smith learned that Taylor was with Green's men. The cavalry had suffered terribly in the fight, and as Smith continued to search for Taylor, he passed "the ghastly forms of the dead piled in all shapes . . . maimed horses [lying] about, some still plunging and endeavoring to drag their broken limbs after them." A celebratory atmosphere had permeated the victory at Mansfield, but the scene at Pleasant Hill was one of pure horror.[33]

"Bad business, bad business, General," grumbled Smith when he finally found Taylor, along with Henry Gray, resting at Hamilton Bee's campfire. "Banks will be on you at first daylight to-morrow with his whole army." Taylor took his time responding. "I don't know, General," he offered, slowly sipping his coffee. "If you will listen, you will hear Banks' artillery moving out now on their retreat." Taylor was right, as several stragglers from the front soon confirmed. Despite a narrow tactical victory by the Federals at Pleasant Hill, Banks had chosen to withdraw his army to the protection of Federal gunboats, thus giving Taylor a strategic win.[34]

The news of Pleasant Hill and the Federal retreat left Smith stunned. His chief of staff William Boggs disclosed that before the general arrived at Pleasant Hill he was still "of the opinion that Taylor had engaged only the advance guard and the battle was still to be fought" between Mansfield and Shreveport. Smith thus expected that he would still have a chance to lead the troops into battle. Xavier DeBray corroborated this claim, alleging that Taylor disregarded "orders to fall back on Keachi . . . where the General commanding the Trans Mississippi Department intended to offer battle." Indeed, the statements of Boggs and DeBray support Churchill's charge that Taylor acted in defiance of Smith's wish to use Keachi as a defensive staging area to concentrate his forces and offer battle. Instead, Taylor ordered up the disposable infantry, took the offensive at Mansfield, pursued the enemy to Pleasant Hill, and initiated a second major engagement, all without orders from the department commander. His actions mocked the spirit, if not the letter, of Smith's instructions and wrecked the cautiously crafted strategy of concentration that Smith had nurtured since the beginning of the campaign.[35]

Smith did not appreciate the strategic value of Taylor's pursuit of a defeated foe, something very few commanders undertook in any theater of the Civil War. While he refrained from criticizing Taylor in his official report, Smith later challenged his lieutenant's decision to fight at Pleasant Hill. "Our repulse at Pleasant Hill was so complete and our command was so disorganized," he declared, "that had Banks followed up his success vigorously he would have met but feeble opposition to his advance on Shreveport." Edward Cunningham, an aide who accompanied Smith to Pleasant Hill, agreed and deemed that Taylor's army "had been beaten, demoralized, [and] paralyzed in the fight of the 9th."[36]

Smith's assessment disregarded the slim margin of tactical victory that Banks had secured at Pleasant Hill. Further, it did not take into account Taylor's intimate knowledge of the enemy commander's habits and tendencies on the battlefield. Smith's criticism of Banks for failing to follow up at Pleasant Hill appeared disingenuous, particularly in view of his criticism of Taylor's decision to follow up at Mansfield. Although his contention that the Confederates "were completely paralyzed and disorganized" was to some extent accurate, Smith failed to consider the larger implications of Mansfield and Pleasant Hill. Rather than acknowledge that the Confederates had just broken the first arm of the Federal pincer movement, he denigrated Banks and reprimanded Taylor. Astonished by Banks's decision to retreat, Smith ordered Taylor to return to Mansfield for an inquiry into the turn of events and to map out a strategy for the rest of the campaign.[37]

On April 10, back at Mansfield, Taylor defended his decision to follow up the victory at the Moss plantation and articulated the need to crush Banks before the Federals could link up with Porter on the Red River. First, he described the situation along the Sabine Crossroads. He assumed full responsibility for initiating the fight and insisted that strategically, "the importance of pushing Banks beyond Pleasant Hill could not be overestimated." Next, Taylor took partial blame for the failure to destroy the enemy at Pleasant Hill and confessed that confusion among his subordinates had prevented proper troop deployment. He then proceeded to explain the particulars of Pleasant Hill to his commanding officer.[38]

Taylor had made clear his intention to continue the offensive in the April 8 dispatches sent to Smith during the battle at Mansfield. In that correspondence he had revealed plans to "push the enemy with Churchill's fresh troops in the morning." With his army reinforced, Taylor hoped to strike Banks before the Federals could recover from their crushing defeat at Mansfield.[39]

In the predawn hours of April 9, Taylor believed that the enemy held a position four or five miles beyond Chapman's Bayou, about twelve miles from Pleasant Hill. He ordered Churchill to assault the enemy lines "at early dawn," with the Arkansas division, under James C. Tappan, on the right wing and a Missouri contingent under Mosby M. Parsons on the left. Taylor planned to direct the attack personally and ordered Churchill to prepare his command to march at 3:00 A.M. Taylor also instructed Green to send cavalry to "occupy the road from Pleasant Hill to Blair's Landing as this road is the shortest for the enemy to reenforce." At this point Taylor still did not know the whereabouts of the Federal Sixteenth Corps and, believing them to be on the river, did not want to allow them uncontested access to Banks's wounded army. In a letter to Walker written at 1:30 A.M., Taylor stressed that only the Federal Nineteenth Corps held the front and, "should the enemy have disappeared in the morning, which is entirely possible, the cavalry must take an active pursuit."[40]

Taylor joined the infantry advance at 3:30 A.M. and soon discovered that the Federals had indeed fled toward Pleasant Hill during the night. He quickly summoned cavalry to take up the pursuit ahead of Churchill's advance. Riding in front with Green, Taylor surmised that Banks was in full retreat and would not stop until he reached Natchitoches. Horseman Hamilton Bee confirmed that this "opinion would seem to have been justly formed. . . . [The] burning wagons, scattered material of war, the capture of prisoners along the road . . . all told of a defeated and demoralized army." At 9:00 A.M. the cavalry found Banks drawn up in line of battle in front of Pleasant Hill. With Confederate infantry several hours behind, Taylor instructed Green to launch a series of feints against the flanks to determine the enemy's strength and position.[41]

As the cavalry probed the Federal lines, Taylor began to adapt his plan of attack to suit fresh intelligence from the cavalry. Instead of launching a frontal assault, Taylor adjusted his earlier battle plan and devised a strategy to encircle the enemy. He ordered Churchill to move to the right and march to the Jessup road, where he would wheel left. From there Churchill would envelop the enemy and sever the line of retreat on the Jessup road toward Natchitoches. Once Churchill was engaged, Walker was to strike the center while Green, on the left, would move to secure the town of Pleasant Hill and cut off Federal access to the Blair's Landing road, a potential escape route should Banks decide to fall back to the river along this line. It was a bold plan, reminiscent of Hannibal's deployment of his outnumbered forces at Cannae, but if it succeeded, Taylor could bag Banks's army and leave Porter's fleet isolated and at his mercy.[42]

Apparently, though, Confederate reconnaissance did not detect the presence of A. J. Smith's Sixteenth Corps, which had arrived at Pleasant Hill late on April 8. Now, on April 9, Banks held these troops as his tactical reserve in a position concealed from the prying eyes of Confederate cavalry. According to Walker, Taylor did not realize that he faced Banks's entire force, but remained convinced that the Confederates confronted "an inconsiderable rear guard of cavalry." Bee concurred and claimed that intelligence reports had led Taylor to conclude that the Federal resistance at Pleasant Hill "was a mere feint to cover the retreat . . . [and] on this hypothesis, he formed his plan of attack." These pronouncement are somewhat suspect. Although Taylor may not have known about the Sixteenth Corps, his actions were consistent with preparations to attack a large body of infantry. Had he believed that all he faced was rear-guard cavalry, Taylor would have sent Green to sweep them aside and pushed the infantry after Banks's main body. Nevertheless, this intelligence failure, along with the mistakes of two key subordinates, would prove costly for Taylor's Confederates.[43]

Upon Churchill's arrival at the front just after midday, Taylor took note of the infantry's jaded condition. The troops had covered forty-five miles in thirty-six hours, and Taylor delayed deployment for two hours to allow the men to rest. This delay also gave the Sixteenth Corps time to move into position in support of Banks's left. Taylor put the Army of Western Louisiana in motion at 3:00 P.M. and began shelling the center of the enemy lines at 4:30. Southern batteries exacted a heavy toll on the enemy guns, and at 5:00 P.M. Confederate infantry opened the attack against the Federal left. At the sound of firing from Churchill's direction, Walker advanced, and the fighting spread across a mile-and-a-half-wide front.[44]

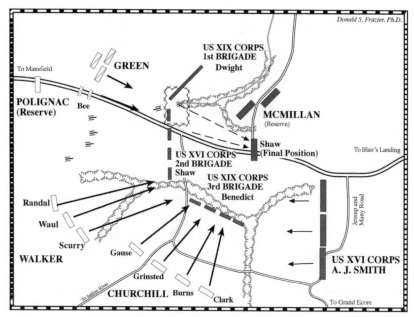

Battle of Pleasant Hill, April 9, 1864

Unfortunately for the Confederates, Churchill had failed to reconnoiter his position sufficiently and became confused by the road system that led to Pleasant Hill. Ordered to march to the Jessup road, which would have put him at a near 45-degree angle above the Federal left, Churchill and his guide, a local sheriff, turned prematurely and advanced along the old river road. Rather than moving on the Federal flank and rear, Churchill had come to a position closer to the center. Writing after the war, Churchill complained bitterly about the guide's miscalculation: "He did not know the ground and I was misled in forming my line, . . . believing that his information was correct, which it was not." The error left the Confederate right in the air, exposed to enemy fire, and rendered any gains untenable.[45]

Upon reaching the edge of a clearing, Churchill's Confederates met a brigade of Federals from the Nineteenth Corps dug in along a ravine to their front. Still unaware of their exposed position, the Arkansas and Missouri troops rushed forward through a tangle of brambles and thickets and drove the enemy back beyond a wooded ridge just outside the town. As the men continued to advance, however, Churchill discovered the Union Sixteenth Corps assembled on his right. Their artillery poured deadly fire into Churchill's lines, and moments later thousands of blue-clad troops swept down on his command and slammed into the Confederate right flank. A Federal described the scene in a letter home: "We advanced on them and drove them back through the little woods that was there mowing them down by the wholesail the ground was covered with gray backs." Churchill's flank soon melted away under the fire of the raging counterattack.[46]

As the Federals rolled up the Confederate right, Churchill's stumbling division collided with elements of Walker's Texans who were engaged along the Mansfield road. Walker had enjoyed success until now and had driven the center of the enemy line back into Pleasant Hill. But suddenly Churchill staggered into the Texas division and fractured the cohesion of the Confederate attack. One of Walker's infantry reported, "The enemy were flying in wild disorder, but suddenly our right is masked and overrun by our retreating troops." Churchill's collapse threw Walker's advance into confusion and forced the Texans to fall back grudgingly toward their original position.[47]

Meanwhile, on the Confederate left, Green had moved too quickly and charged ahead of Walker's advance. The cavalry found itself ensnared in grisly close-range combat, cut off from the main body of Confederate infantry. A Federal captain recalled Green's assault: "They moved forward at a rapid pace, sweeping across the field in one of the most perfect cavalry charges the late war produced, and its reception was as fatal as ever befell a charging column." In the words of Texan John Stark, the Federal fire "mowed down our men like grain before the reaper." Facing obliteration, Green's cavalry retreated with heavy casualties. The men regrouped and advanced again, this time dismounted. The fighting swayed back and forth as the Texans fought a losing struggle to hold their ground. To prevent the battle from becoming a rout, Taylor threw elements of Polignac's depleted division into the heart of the fighting. The tattered brigades fought savagely and repulsed the Federal onslaught, forcing the enemy back toward Pleasant Hill. As darkness encroached on the field, chaos and confusion beset the jumbled gray lines. Numerous units fell victim to incidents of friendly fire and scattered into the woods for safety. As the battle ended, each army clung to the ground upon which it had opened the day's slaughter.[48]

While some Federals maintained that Pleasant Hill was a "complete victory," others were not as certain. Taylor's audacity and the tenacity of the Confederate fight shook the confidence of many in the Federal command. "The rebs done good fighting" wrote Iowan George D. Patten to his family. "I tell you we was glad to get out of it." That night, at a council of war, Banks ordered a strategic retreat to the river. One Union soldier articulated the bitter sentiments held by some of his comrades: "A great victory was achieved by our forces, with all the results of a great defeat." Another Federal accepted the decision reluctantly, remarking, "Such is the fortunes of war. The wind sighs a mournful requeme."[49]

The Confederates acknowledged that their achievements at Pleasant Hill had come at a high cost. One of Walker's men called the battle "the bloodiest tragedy ever enacted in the Trans-Mississippi Department." Louisianan Felix Poche recalled the extraordinary number of dead on the field, "the greater number of whom were mutilated, some without heads, the faces of others completely mangled." Churchill's surgeon William McPheeters took a pragmatic view of the Federal casualties: "They came here to butcher our people and got butchered themselves." Others were clearly shaken by the carnage. "I know the Lord was with us or every one of us would have been killed," confessed one of Green's cavalrymen in a letter home. Another Texan, writing just after the battle, observed somberly, "Night has closed her curtains, as if in humanity, on the bloody scene."[50]

Many Confederates expressed a degree of satisfaction that in two successive battles they had beaten the enemy back. Hours before the fight at Pleasant Hill, a Missourian predicted, "I think we will make them sorry they have not let us alone." His prediction came true, though at a horrifying cost. Taylor had 12,500 troops on the field and suffered 1,600 casualties while the Confederates inflicted 1,300 casualties on Banks's 12,500 effectives. Despite the effusion of blood, Taylor had put a halt to the Federal invasion. McPheeters articulated the mood on Churchill's staff following Pleasant Hill: "The Yankees, not knowing the advantage they gained over us the evening before, had retreated . . . so instead of being badly routed we have all the advantages of a substantial victory." Nevertheless, the high casualties and the failure to annihilate the Federals at Pleasant Hill left some with the feeling that the victory of April 9 was tarnished.[51]

Immediately following the battle, Taylor recalled that Churchill "seemed much depressed," and he expressed sympathy rather than anger toward the crestfallen officer. Churchill "did all in his power," reported Taylor days after the battle. "A worthy and gallant gentleman, General Churchill," he affirmed later, "but not fortunate in war." Although Taylor had leveled blame at his lieutenants for earlier Confederate defeats, he assumed responsibility for the failure at Pleasant Hill: "Instead of intrusting the important attack by my right to a subordinate, I should have conducted it myself and taken Polignac's division to sustain it."[52]

Despondent over his misfortune on the battlefield, Churchill nevertheless refused to accept any degree of responsibility. Instead, he blamed Taylor and charged him with negligence. "Gen. Taylor never did the Arkansas troops justice in that engagement," he complained. "Our failure was entirely owing to the ignorance of the guide whom he furnished me." Churchill was still smarting from his orders to move down from Keachi and from the fact that Taylor had held him in reserve at Mansfield. He accused Taylor of blatant disregard for Smith's plans to offer battle above Mansfield. Churchill contended, "If Taylor had drawn Banks as high as Keachi where my command was—[Banks] would have been crushed." Once Churchill reached Pleasant Hill, however, Taylor's strategic decision was no longer an issue. The army was committed to fight, and Churchill needed to focus on the task at hand.[53]

Churchill did not demonstrate exceptional leadership skills on the field at Pleasant Hill. First, he relinquished responsibility for placement of his command to a civilian and then blamed Taylor for the guide's error. Even before the battle opened there were indications that the Confederate right wing was not in position. Sporadic fire from the right caused concern within the gray ranks, and yet despite attempts to extend the flank, the troops drifted repeatedly back toward the center. Taylor had assigned Colonel William P. Hardeman to direct the cavalry troopers on Churchill's right. When Hardeman arrived on the flank, he realized that the infantry was out of position and implored Parsons to redeploy. Parsons rejected the suggestion and told the colonel, "These troops are placed here by Gn'l Churchill and as he placed them they will be fought." As the fire on his right increased, Parsons decided to notify Churchill of Hardeman's judgment. Churchill, however, did not issue a reply. Thus, both Parsons and Churchill refused to heed the advice of a subordinate, and as a result, Confederate cavalry could not operate effectively against the Union left. Had Churchill followed Hardeman's recommendation and utilized the cavalry in accordance with Taylor's wishes, he would have relieved the pressure on the right and allowed the infantry a chance to secure the flank. While Taylor deserved a share of the blame, Churchill's failure to adjust to the conditions of battle proved the determining factor in the defeat.[54]

Taylor's "blunder at Pleasant Hill" was more an error of omission than of commission. At Pleasant Hill, as at Milliken's Bend in the summer of 1863, Taylor allowed his lieutenants to establish the tactical line of advance. At Mansfield, Taylor inspected the ground personally and positioned his troops according to his own reconnaissance. His direct involvement and adroit troop deployment at the Moss plantation played a crucial role in determining the outcome of the battle. Taylor's conduct at Mansfield was consistent with the custom he had adopted earlier in the war of personally examining "adjacent roads and paths . . . as well as general topography." Circumstances following the battle of Mansfield, however, and the presence of the Union army at Pleasant Hill made it nearly impossible for him to examine the ground before he designed a plan of attack on April 9. Indeed, an attempt to reconnoiter ground held by the enemy had cost Stonewall Jackson his life at Chancellorsville.[55]

Yet Taylor had been at Mansfield for several days before the Federal march along the stagecoach road and had ample opportunity to reconnoiter the terrain near Pleasant Hill. Since he had vowed to fight the Federals at the first opportunity, such reconnaissance would have been prudent. Taylor readily acknowledged his failure to direct operations at Pleasant Hill. "This flashed upon me the instant I learned of the disorder on my right," he confessed. "Herein lies the vast difference between genius and commonplace: one anticipates errors, the other discovers them too late."[56]

After the war, two of Taylor's lieutenants criticized the judgment he had shown at Pleasant Hill. Walker claimed that Taylor was "rendered incautious . . . by the brilliant results of the audacity of [Mansfield]." According to Walker's assessment, Taylor "was determined to strike a blow before . . . ascertaining the enemy's position and strength." Bee agreed, writing that Taylor was swept up in the euphoria of Mansfield and had not personally reconnoitered the "superb" enemy battle line at Pleasant Hill. This criticism, though somewhat consistent with Taylor's own analysis, neglected several other important factors that played a role at Pleasant Hill.[57]

First, the element of surprise demanded that the Confederates strike an immediate blow against the Federals. In the Shenandoah, Jackson instilled this theory in his lieutenants: "Always mystify, mislead, and surprise the enemy." Until Mansfield, Banks did not think the Confederates would put up a fight before reaching Shreveport. After Mansfield, while ensconced at Pleasant Hill, the Federals anticipated having time to recover from their defeat before resuming the march to Shreveport. Taylor's decision to strike a disorganized and dispirited enemy at Pleasant Hill adhered strictly to Jackson's philosophy. Had Taylor allowed the Federals time to recover from their beating at Mansfield, Banks might have learned from the mistake of marching the army along a narrow road as independent units. A modified order of march by the Federals, one that allowed rapid concentration, would have posed an even greater threat to Taylor's army and to the security of Shreveport. In addition, Banks would have surely received succor from the river. Given the condition of the Federal army and the stakes that Taylor played for at Mansfield, the decision to attack Banks at Pleasant Hill was strategically sound.[58]

Tactically, however, Green's actions on the Confederate left undermined Taylor's battle plans. The initial sounds of fighting on Churchill's flank confused Green and prompted him to advance prematurely. Taylor did not castigate Green but instead attributed the error to the fog of war. Polignac, however, claimed that Green had been drunk and that his intemperate condition had caused a "great deal of confusion" all along the lines. Had Green followed Taylor's instructions and delivered a timely flank attack, Walker would have stood a better chance of holding his ground and stemming Churchill's collapse. By ordering his cavalry to advance before Walker and Churchill were fully engaged, Green undermined the internal cohesion of the Confederate lines that Taylor had organized. The early repulse of Green's division diminished the threat to the Federal right and allowed the enemy to converge on Walker.[59]

Walker offered a radically different explanation for what he called Green's "blundering charge." He found nothing to criticize in Green's conduct or condition but blamed Taylor for ordering the cavalry forward in advance of the infantry. "Green attempted to carry out his instructions," asserted Walker, "the result of which was that in an instant his whole cavalry force was exposed to the fire of the whole federal right wing, laying, as it were, in ambuscade along the ravine." Walker argued that Taylor's failure to reconnoiter the ground led to the bloody error and ultimately cost the Confederates a tactical victory at Pleasant Hill.[60]

Tactical mistakes by Green and Churchill aside, another reason for the failure at Pleasant Hill surfaced during the April 10 meeting at Mansfield between Taylor and Smith. While conducting the interview, Smith noticed that Taylor seemed ill. The Louisianan had suffered another attack of rheumatoid arthritis after the battle at Mansfield, and he might have been physically unable to direct his troops at Pleasant Hill. Smith noted that Taylor was in "ill-health" and that he had apologized for his "irritability of disposition." Two weeks later, on April 27, Taylor acknowledged a steady deterioration of his physical condition. "I regret to report that my health is not good," he disclosed to S. S. Anderson, Smith's adjutant. "A low fever has much prostrated me, but I have been able to keep in the saddle." Less than one month later, Taylor notified Smith that because of "the condition of my health . . . I scarcely believe I will be able for some time to come to conduct the affairs of my present command." A letter written by Taylor to Walker on April 9, at 1:30 A.M., reveals a dramatic difference in his handwriting from earlier correspondences. The handwriting sample indicates a symptomatic lack of muscular control in the general's hands and arms. The pressures of a battle crucial to the success of his army and the security of his state, combined with the stress of fighting without orders, would have been sufficient to trigger Taylor's relapse.[61]

Despite his ill health, the April 9 letter to Walker affirmed Taylor's plans for immediate pursuit of the enemy. If Banks reached Natchitoches, he would take on reinforcements and fresh supplies. This made it imperative to strike the Federals at once. "The enemy cannot receive anything from the river until late in the day tomorrow," Taylor emphasized, "so it is all important to finish him vigorously." He also expressed confidence that Banks would mount little resistance to a renewed attack: "He has nothing in our front but the troops we beat today and the 19th Corp all Yankees whom we have . . . whipped."[62]

Taylor instructed Walker to deliver the letter to Green with orders to send a brigade of cavalry, "with artillery, to Blair's Landing, on the Red River, to attack [Porter's] gunboats." He hoped that operations along the road between Banks's army and Porter's ships would keep the Federal forces divided until Confederate infantry could come up to attack each in detail. "We had but to strike vigorously," Taylor affirmed, "to capture or destroy both." At 10:40 A.M. on April 9, five hours before the battle at Pleasant Hill, he notified Smith of the decision to post cavalry along the Blair's Landing road. The instructions to Walker and Green and the subsequent troop deployments for infantry and cavalry indicated that Taylor's objective had become more than merely stopping the Federal invasion. He now wanted to destroy Banks. The results of Pleasant Hill had done nothing to change that. To the contrary, Banks's retreat served to embolden Taylor even further. On April 10, confident that his plans would meet with the commanding general's approval, Taylor outlined this strategy to Smith.[63]

8

The Fruit of Your Victory

With the Confederates already massed in Louisiana, Taylor's plan to pursue Banks was consistent with Smith's strategy for concentration to destroy "one or the other of the enemy's column[s]." Intelligence reports indicating that Frederick Steele continued to move toward Shreveport, however, turned Smith's attention away from Banks, whom he no longer considered a threat, and toward Arkansas. "I deemed it imprudent to follow Banks below Grand Ecore with my whole force," Smith wrote, "and leave Steele so near Shreveport." A member of the commanding general's staff, Lieutenant Edward Cunningham, conveyed details of Smith's rationale in a letter home. Cunningham maintained that recovering the Arkansas Valley and "breaking up . . . the Yankee State government, as well as having the route to Missouri open, were considerations of great importance." While Taylor had stopped Banks in Louisiana, his success also served to breathe new life into Smith's plans for conquest in Arkansas.[1]

During the April 10 meeting at Mansfield, Taylor argued against the strategy. He reminded Smith that despite Steele's progress, the Federals in Arkansas remained farther from Shreveport than did Banks. In addition, Taylor insisted that once Steele learned of Mansfield and Pleasant Hill, he would abandon the campaign and return to Little Rock. Taylor reasoned that the decisive defeat of the Federals in Louisiana would secure a successful campaign. Walker concurred: "Doubtless it was to have been expected that the whole Confederate force would have thrown itself upon the track of [Banks's] army." [2]

Smith disagreed with Taylor's evaluation. He warned that despite the distance from Shreveport, Steele was in position to destroy the Confederate center of gravity in the Trans-Mississippi. Smith reiterated his plan to shift concentration by use of interior lines and reminded Taylor that the strategy had succeeded thus far in the campaign. He also stressed that "the country below Natchitoches had been completely desolated and stripped of supplies." Consequently, Taylor would be unable to sustain his army for an extended campaign against Banks. Determined to concentrate against Steele, Smith ordered Taylor to pull the bulk of his forces back from Pleasant Hill and prepare for a campaign in Arkansas. With the meeting ended and the issue decided, Smith returned to Shreveport.[3]

While Banks teetered on the edge of annihilation, Taylor remained skeptical about plans to strike Steele. On April 11, Smith received a note from Taylor that restated the argument for continuing the campaign in Louisiana: "Steele will no doubt commence retreating as soon as he hears the news from this quarter. If he is retreating . . . let me push my whole force south as rapidly as possible, to follow and prevent the escape of the enemy." He offered to take responsibility for the decision and declared, "Should the remnants of Banks's army escape me I shall deserve to wear the fool's cap for a helmet." He implored Smith to let him know the latest news from Arkansas.[4]

Taylor believed that the destruction of Banks's army would encourage Confederate enlistment throughout the state's lower parishes. He offered to revive his plans for New Orleans if Smith would allow the pursuit. Despite the prospect of replenishing the ranks, Taylor's proposal to shift the campaign even farther away from Arkansas did not appeal to Smith. During the early months of his tenure as department commander, Smith had flatly rejected Taylor's strategy to strike toward New Orleans. Further, Smith planned his own recruitment drive while campaigning in Arkansas. If anything, the suggestion raised suspicions about Taylor's true objectives and galvanized Smith's resolve to assert operational control over all Confederate forces in the Trans-Mississippi for a move against Steele.[5]

Smith immediately issued a detailed response to Taylor's plea. In a letter dated April 12 he again denied the request for continued concentration in Louisiana and supported his decision by enclosing a correspondence from Sterling Price in Arkansas. Price corroborated Smith's assessment of Steele's threat to Shreveport. The Confederates in Arkansas had only five thousand cavalrymen, and Price estimated the enemy troop strength at twelve thousand. He assured Smith that the cavalry would continue to fall back and endeavor to draw Steele so far from his base that once the commanding general arrived with reinforcements, destruction of the enemy column was certain. Even though Smith did not think highly of Price's military skills, he overlooked the Missourian's faults in the interest of his own personal aspirations. The prospect of victory in Arkansas continued to entice Smith, even at the expense of Taylor's success in Louisiana.[6]

Turning back Steele's column, Smith pledged to Taylor, would carry with it great results for the Confederacy. "Arkansas will be saved politically," he promised, and the "road opened to Missouri." The campaign in Louisiana did not, he reasoned, "offer the permanent results that would follow the defeat of Steele." Smith acknowledged the political importance that the possession of New Orleans afforded the Confederacy but concluded that Federal control of the Mississippi River made the mission impracticable. Either the recapture of New Orleans or a strike toward St. Louis presented monumental problems for the Confederates. Yet Smith's political justification for a campaign in Arkansas meant that Taylor would sacrifice his hard-fought military advantage in Louisiana.[7]

The explanation also provided Smith with another opportunity to justify his decision on military grounds. He rejected Taylor's contention that the Federals in Arkansas would abandon the campaign as soon as news of Banks's defeat reached them. He insisted that "Steele is bold to rashness" and predicted that the Federals would continue to advance from Arkansas "without thought or circumspection." Smith maintained that to win the Red River campaign, the Confederates must defeat both Banks's army and Steele's column in the field. He cautioned that if the Confederates moved against Banks while Steele reached Shreveport, they would be not only disgraced but "irreparably deprived" of all their means and resources. The rationale was prudent. Believing that Banks was so demoralized that he would not resume the offensive, Smith concluded that the Confederates had to stop Steele's advance to protect the military-industrial complex around Shreveport. Further, he reasoned that a campaign through Arkansas would add five thousand recruits to the army. The addition of these men would help pave the way for Smith to launch his Missouri campaign. "Prepare your command and organize your trains for rapid movement," he instructed Taylor. "The patient, uncomplaining spirit manifested by Arkansas, the prompt and unselfish behavior of Price in pushing on his whole infantry force to your support, merits a return." [8]

Not content with his written rejoinder, Smith returned to Mansfield on April 13 to continue talks with Taylor on strategy. In a letter to his wife written on the eve of his departure, Smith enthusiastically summed up the status of the campaign. "[With] Banks being checked, Steele will I trust, be easily disposed of," he told her, without mentioning any option other than the pursuit of Steele. He alluded to the imminent launch of the Arkansas campaign and announced, "I shall leave at daylight for Mansfield to arrange with Taylor for future operations." [9]

Upon his arrival at Taylor's headquarters, Smith ordered his subordinate to send Walker's division to Shreveport along with Churchill's command, including Parsons's contingent of Missourians. The combined infantry force of over eight thousand would prepare for operations against the northern arm of the Federal pincer. Smith allowed Taylor to retain Green's cavalry, already stationed along the river roads from Pleasant Hill to Blair's Landing, and keep the battered remnants of Polignac's division for operations against Banks and Porter along the Red River. Taylor's forces numbered less than five thousand, while the aggregate Federal ground force in Louisiana consisted of over twenty-five thousand infantry and cavalry augmented by Porter's powerful fleet.[10]

According to Smith, Taylor "distinctly expressed [his] approval of the movement" against Steele and offered to accompany the main body of infantry and serve under Price in Arkansas. Taylor based his offer of support on a remark contained in the April 12 correspondence from Smith, in which the commanding general stated that "were Steele in retreat the prompt pursuit of Banks would be wise." Although Taylor endorsed the Arkansas expedition and agreed to serve under Price, he believed "that Steele would receive intelligence of Banks' defeat and immediately beat a hasty retreat." In fact, Taylor suggested this scenario to Smith during the meeting between the generals following the battle at Pleasant Hill. Thus, Taylor considered his support for the Arkansas campaign conditional. Steele's retreat, which he thought inevitable, would nullify Smith's planned campaign and allow renewed concentration against Banks with the full force of the army.[11]

At daybreak on April 14, Walker, Churchill, and Parsons marched their divisions north along the roads toward Shreveport. An excited Arkansan crowed, "Gen Churchill told us when we came here that he would take us back to Ark. if we run the Feds. back. This has been done. . . . Our army now think it can whip anything." Confident that Steele would soon retreat and Smith would soon countermand the orders, Taylor noted specifically that the infantry was "prepared for an active and vigorous campaign."[12]

The forty-mile march between Shreveport and Mansfield would take the infantry two days to complete. Along the way, talk of an imminent battle against Steele churned the ranks. Many welcomed Smith's decision to concentrate in Arkansas, and some worried they would not arrive in time to prevent the Federals from reaching Shreveport. Reports of Price falling back toward Louisiana and fears that "General Steel might prove too strong for the cavalry under General Price to handle" gave the men an added sense of urgency. Missourian William McPheeters shared Smith's point of view and reasoned, "Having whipped the Yankees in La. and driven back and defeated Banks' grand expedition we will now turn our attention to Gen. Steele in Ark." A soldier in Parsons's infantry carried the idea even further: "I think if we can run Steels Army out of Ark we will proceed to Mo immediately." [13]

Taylor did not accompany the march to Shreveport. Instead, he remained behind at Mansfield ostensibly to confer with Polignac before the Frenchman's division joined Green at Grand Ecore. From there the troops would conduct operations against Banks and Porter. Taylor left for Shreveport just before noon on April 15 and timed his arrival to coincide with that of the infantry's advance columns. The slight delay also allowed additional time for information on Steele's movements in Arkansas to reach Smith. [14]

When he reached department headquarters that evening, Taylor learned that Steele had already begun to retreat. Taylor was delighted by the news and took it to mean that he could countermand the movement to Arkansas, assume operational command of the disposable infantry, and resume the campaign against Banks. His mood changed quickly, however, when he received word that despite the Federal retreat, Smith still planned to follow through with the campaign into Arkansas. With news of Steele's retreat, Smith had revised his strategy from a defensive plan to protect Shreveport to an offensive pursuit of the Federal army in Arkansas. He informed Taylor that only if Steele escaped across the Ouachita River would he return the infantry to Louisiana for concentration against Banks. [15]

Unbeknownst to Taylor, Smith had already taken steps to prevent Steele from crossing the Ouachita. Upon his return from the April 13 meeting with Taylor, Smith received information from Price indicating that Steele had turned away from Washington and begun a retrograde movement eastward toward Camden. Despite the understanding reached with Taylor earlier in the day, Smith hastily began to alter his strategy. He feared that if the Federals occupied Camden, a strategically vital town, Steele could replenish his dwindling supplies and establish communications with Banks. Of equal concern was the possibility that Steele would simply call off the campaign and return to Little Rock. Smith wanted to strike Steele before either of these contingencies occurred. Thus, just before midnight on April 14 he ordered Price to impede Steele's movement toward Camden. Should Steele reach the town, Price was to throw a cavalry force across the Ouachita and cut off enemy communications in the rear. [16]

Later that same night Smith sent Price another dispatch and reiterated his desire to stop Steele from reaching Camden. Smith was of two minds. He believed that Banks's "terribly crippled and much demoralized" army would soon fall back to Alexandria. Yet he also warned Price that Steele's retreat might signal an attempt by the Federal columns to concentrate. The concerns were mutually exclusive. Banks could not possibly move toward Alexandria and Camden at the same time. If he did move toward Arkansas, he faced a journey of nearly two hundred miles.[17]

The continued presence of a large Federal force along the Red River, however, was a legitimate cause for anxiety in Shreveport. With Steele in retreat, Smith could have returned the infantry to Louisiana, as he had indicated he would do, and allowed Taylor to concentrate against Banks. This would have discouraged the Federals from renewing their march on Shreveport and ensured that Banks could not move north to join forces with Steele. Further, if Steele had unilaterally resumed his advance on Shreveport, Smith could again detach infantry from Taylor's command and march the troops to meet the threat. Instead, he assured Price that three divisions of infantry were on the way to support the pursuit of Steele. Smith's ardent desire to lead the Confederates into Arkansas clouded his judgment at this critical juncture of the campaign.[18]

On the morning of April 15, the day Taylor arrived at Shreveport, Smith sent a third dispatch to Price with additional recommendations and revised instructions. He suggested that the Missourian seize Camden before Steele's army reached the town. This would not only prevent the Federals from taking advantage of Camden's supplies and fortifications but also put the enemy columns directly between Price's cavalry and Smith's advancing infantry. Despite his low opinion of Price's military skills, Smith did not order the occupation of Camden. Rather, he urged Price to exercise his own judgment and cautioned him against risking a general engagement before infantry support arrived. Infantry support was, by Smith's estimation, six days away from Camden. He implored Price to take any measures, short of the destruction of his command, to hamper Steele's retreat. "It is of the utmost possible importance that the enemy be delayed until the infantry reach him," he counseled. Taylor was unaware of these developments and on the afternoon of April 15 rode to Smith's headquarters confident that Steele's retreat would open the door for a renewed assault against Banks. At the same time, Smith hurried his preparations to lead the Confederates against Steele.[19]

During a brief interview at headquarters, Smith apprised Taylor of the situation and advised him that his leadership was no longer needed on the Arkansas expedition. Smith revealed that he would lead the campaign himself. He directed Taylor to assume nominal command of the department at Shreveport and suggested that Taylor could, at his own discretion, return to the field and oversee operations against Banks. Taylor took the news as a stinging personal insult. He recalled that Smith announced the sudden change of plans "with the curt manner of a superior to a subordinate, as if fearing remonstrance." [20]

While Smith advanced the army toward Arkansas, Taylor lingered in Shreveport, nursing his wounded pride. For three days he immersed himself in writing reports and directing supplies to the Confederates near Grand Ecore. However haughtily Smith may have treated Taylor, he realized that the Louisianan was his most reliable lieutenant. Before embarking on his campaign, Smith wrote to Jefferson Davis about leadership in the Trans-Mississippi. "Should the contingency arise whereby the command of the Trans-Mississippi Department might devolve to another," Smith told the president, Taylor was the only general officer "suited to take charge." [21]

Smith was justifiably optimistic about his crusade against Steele. The Federal column was weary from weeks of hard marching along muddy roads through barren prairies, as well as from the constant harassment delivered by Price's cavalry. Dangerously low on supplies, Steele had turned his army away from its objective and moved toward Camden to await reinforcements and resupply from Little Rock. "If [Steele's] half starved men do not quickly retreat," Smith wrote his wife, "I have strong hopes of capturing his command." On April 16 Smith rode out of Shreveport toward Arkansas at the head of Parsons's Missouri division. He spoke freely to the soldiers, offering words of encouragement and dispelling rumors that Steele was moving on Monroe. Smith also alluded to the possibility of expanding the campaign to encompass the liberation of Missouri. That night a Missourian confided to his diary, "We expect to meet Gnl Steels army at once near Camden. Our troops are in fine spirits. We now think we can whip Steel—easy—then all expect to go north." On the same day, Steele marched his army into Camden.[22]

On April 3, less than two weeks earlier, Smith had declared that Camden was "entirely out of the sphere of operations." He had instructed Price to evacuate the town and take up a defensive position closer to Washington. This put the cavalry in a better location from which to contest the Union advance. At the time, Smith's decision seemed reasonable. On April 12, however, when Steele turned his column away from Washington toward Camden, Price was not in position to offer a substantial challenge. Confederate cavalry units under John S. Marmaduke and Thomas P. Dockery attempted to slow the enemy until Price could bring his entire force to bear, but the Federals proved too strong. Smith was dismayed by the turn of events. Although he had explicitly instructed Price to abandon the town, he now held Price responsible for its loss. "Price let [Steele] by without opposition," he complained in a letter to his wife. Earlier, Smith had affirmed that should Steele escape before the Confederates could concentrate, he would return to Shreveport. The Federal occupation of Camden posed a serious obstacle to Smith's plans to fight in Arkansas. [23]

Smith arrived at his field headquarters in Calhoun, Arkansas, on April 19 and evaluated circumstances along both fronts. As long as Banks and Steele continued to hold their positions, the combined Federal threat against Shreveport remained potent. Although he declared that Steele's "dislodgment was an absolute necessity," Smith dared not attack the Federals in a heavily fortified position. Similarly, Banks remained at Grand Ecore, along the Red River, and had not begun a full retreat toward Alexandria. Further complicating the situation in Louisiana, Taylor had far fewer troops to contest a renewed advance. Fearing that Banks would resume his move on Shreveport, Smith ordered Walker to hold his division near Minden, sixty-six miles from Camden and forty-eight miles from Shreveport. From this position Smith could send the Texans against either Banks or Steele, depending on which column presented the more immediate threat. On April 20 Smith notified Taylor of his intentions and suggested that he might order Walker to Campti, which would return operational control of the division to Taylor. A response arrived the following day. "Be pleased to order it there at once," Taylor replied, and he reported that Banks had begun to withdraw from Grand Ecore.[24]

News that the Federals at Grand Ecore had started to retreat down the Red River alleviated Smith's worry about a renewed threat on the southern front. With the danger from Banks diminished, Smith directed Walker to continue his advance through southwestern Arkansas and move to join Price at Camden. In a candid letter to Taylor, dated April 22, Smith offered a spirited defense of his decision to retain Walker for operations in Arkansas. "Steele cannot be left in his present position," he argued, "without endangering the fruit of your victories [at Mansfield and Pleasant Hill]." Steele would either advance on Shreveport or retreat to Little Rock, Smith insisted, and in either case the presence of Walker's division would assure success. Smith recognized that his decision to retain Walker would disrupt Taylor's plans for the continued pursuit of Banks. Accordingly, he urged Taylor to leave command of the forces in Louisiana to a subordinate and join the campaign in Arkansas. [25]

Adding to Smith's woes, Price had neglected to follow earlier instructions for troop deployment along the Ouachita River. His failure allowed Steele to receive a large train of stores from Pine Bluff. On April 19 the Missouri general rode down from his headquarters at Woodlawn, sixteen miles southwest of Camden, to confer with Smith at Calhoun. Smith addressed the problem by issuing orders for James F. Fagan to take four thousand cavalrymen north and east of the river. Fagan's mission was to sack Federal supply depots, disrupt Steele's communications, and, most important, to establish a position between the enemy and Little Rock. With troops aligned along the road from Camden to Little Rock, Smith hoped to catch the retreating Federals between his infantry and Fagan's cavalry. According to a member of Smith's staff, Fagan received a promise of promotion if he succeeded in his mission. Yet despite the urgency of the situation, three days elapsed before Fagan began operations. It was not until April 24 that his cavalry finally crossed the Ouachita at El Dorado Landing and rode for enemy depots at Pine Bluff, Little Rock, and DeVall's Bluff. [26]

Two days before meeting with Smith, Price had submitted a proposal to attack a large enemy forage expedition moving slowly west from Camden. The operation met with Smith's approval, and by the time he reached Calhoun, Confederate cavalry under Samuel B. Maxey had already dealt a devastating blow to Steele's hopes for resupply. Maxey commanded three thousand troops including a brigade of Choctaw Indians and a brigade of Marmaduke's ferocious Missouri cavalry. The Confederates destroyed the Federal supply train fifteen miles outside Camden in a lopsided affair at Poison Spring. Maxey's troops suffered just over one hundred casualties in bloody fighting that lasted approximately two hours. The Federals lost two hundred supply-laden wagons, and suffered over three hundred casualties out of the nearly one thousand troops engaged. Deprived of the much-needed supplies and disillusioned by the thrashing suffered at the hands of the ragged Rebel horsemen, the Federals at Camden began to consider a retreat to Little Rock. [27]

The mood of the Federals darkened further amid persistent rumors that Banks had abandoned the campaign and retreated downriver toward Alexandria. Steele feared that Banks's withdrawal would enable Smith to concentrate the resources of the Trans-Mississippi against his columns. After receiving confirmation of Banks's retreat, Steele disclosed that he "did not expect to meet successfully" the force that Smith would send against him. The Confederates in Arkansas seemed revitalized, and Steele attributed the development to reports of Taylor's success against Banks in Louisiana. [28]

To augment the Federal miseries, the supply train that had brought provisions into Camden from Pine Bluff met with disaster during the return trip. On

April 25 Fagan intercepted the wagons eight miles west of the Saline River at Marks' Mills. In the five-hour battle that ensued, Fagan's troops overpowered sixteen hundred Federals and took thirteen hundred prisoners. The determined resistance cost Fagan a casualty rate close to 20 percent of the twenty-five hundred men engaged. Strategically, the Confederates paid an even higher cost for Fagan's decision to strike the train on the road to Pine Bluff. Marks' Mills was west of the Saline River, and Fagan had chosen to move south. His orders were to block the path of Steele's retreat by establishing a defensive line east of the river, on the road from Camden to Little Rock. [29]

The action at Marks' Mills and the intelligence that Banks's army was in flight had convinced Steele that his army was in great danger. At a council of war on the night of the Marks' Mills affair, Steele and his lieutenants decided to evacuate Camden, abandon the campaign, and return to Little Rock as quickly as possible. On April 26, under cover of night, the Union forces began their withdrawal across the Ouachita River. [30]

During his April 16 meeting with Taylor, Smith had pledged to call a halt to his pursuit of Steele if the Federals crossed the Ouachita. On April 27, when he learned of the enemy's escape, he called a meeting to discuss his options. Chief of staff William Boggs recalled that Smith engaged in lengthy deliberations about the propriety of following Steele. According to Boggs, Smith "knew that he ought not to fight except under the most favorable circumstances and if he followed at all he must follow rapidly, [or give] Steele the advantage of selecting his own ground to receive him and to force a fight that he wished to avoid." With Confederate forces concentrated outside Camden, Smith resolved to take the offensive and "issued orders for the troops to pursue Steele to his fortifications at Little Rock." Amid spring rains and along mud-choked Arkansas roads, he resumed pursuit on April 28, almost a full day behind the Union army. [31]

The decision to chase Steele came despite information that Fagan's cavalry was not in position to challenge the Federal retreat. Smith's orders to establish a line across Steele's projected route went to Price on April 14 and to Fagan five days later. The instructions apparently befuddled both subordinates, and neither officer complied fully. Part of the confusion stemmed from their strict adherence to Smith's departmental command protocol. Although Smith personally organized the mission with Fagan and Price on April 19, he did not officially assume control of the Army of Arkansas until April 26. Thus, Fagan's written orders came directly from Price and the District of Arkansas headquarters. When Price issued the orders, his instructions differed from those given verbally by Smith. Price indicated that Fagan should "attack and cut off all trains of the enemy" east of the river. While this was consistent with Smith's wishes, the commanding general emphasized that Fagan's primary responsibility was to "throw himself between the enemy and Little Rock." Furthermore, Price claimed that he issued the orders on April 19, immediately following the meeting. However, Fagan reported that he did not advance his division until April 22, "in accordance with instructions from district headquarters." Thus, despite Smith's admonition to "move rapidly and stop for nothing," Price's orders gave Fagan too much leeway and did not convey the urgency of the mission. As a result, the absence of Confederate cavalry along the Saline River road, which ran northeast from Camden through Jenkins' Ferry and on to Little Rock, gave the enemy a clear path of retreat. [32]

From the news that Fagan's men had engaged the blue coats at Marks' Mills, Smith knew that the cavalry was not athwart the road to Little Rock. He dispatched aides to scour the countryside, find Fagan, and order him to "throw himself in front of Steele," but no one could locate the wayward cavalry. "It is to the failure of this officer to receive these instructions . . . ," claimed Walker, "that Steele owes the escape of his army." As Fagan moved north from Marks' Mills on April 26, he found the Saline swollen from heavy spring rains and was unable to locate a crossing. In desperation, he pushed his horsemen along the west bank of the river toward Benton. A courier carrying details of the cavalry's predicament rode to Smith's headquarters on April 27, but the general did not issue an immediate response. Out of contact with the high command, Fagan still did not know that Steele's army was moving rapidly in his direction. Consequently, his cavalry wandered farther away from the true line of operations. Fagan's failure to hold a position along Steele's escape route drastically compromised Smith's plans, but the commanding general refused to acknowledge that his strategy was in disarray. [33]

In an attempt to compensate for the breakdown, Smith devised a contingency plan to impede the Federal retreat. On April 27 he ordered Colonel Colton Greene's small brigade of Missouri cavalry to join Marmaduke and ford the Ouachita. The cavalry would swing northeast of the Federal column and cut off the retreat at Princeton. All went well until the gray riders reached Princeton, where they found the enemy's rear guard rather than advance units. Marmaduke decided to divide the cavalry into two columns, one to harass the Federal rear and the other to continue around the enemy flank and establish a position along the Saline. It was a desperate maneuver, but Marmaduke had little choice. Missouri cavalryman

John Newman Edwards blamed Smith for the difficulties and called the entire operation "an utter impossibility." Edwards considered it just one more debacle in "a series of enormous blunders" committed by Smith and his lieutenants. Even if the cavalry could engage Steele, he scoffed, the "force was too light to have seriously checked the advance of the Federal column." [34]

Several other problematic decisions worked against Smith's plan. The most glaring was his failure to provide the infantry with a pontoon to ensure that the troops could cross the Ouachita or Saline. The army had originally traveled with a pontoon, but on April 19 Smith ordered the train returned to Shreveport for use by Taylor. Smith's aide Edward Cunningham complained that a "misconception of orders" caused the pontoon intended for the campaign in Arkansas to be diverted to Louisiana. Taylor claimed that Smith sent the train to Louisiana as recompense for his having taken Walker's division to Arkansas. Whatever the reason, the lack of a pontoon at Camden delayed Confederate pursuit until the construction of a raft-bridge enabled the infantry to cross the Ouachita. Ironically, the pontoon arrived in Louisiana too late to assist Taylor in the pursuit of Banks, and its absence in Arkansas prevented Smith's timely pursuit of Steele. [35]

Another questionable measure was Smith's decision on April 28 to order Maxey's command back to Indian Territory. The division totaled nearly fifteen hundred effectives, including Richard Gano's Texans and a brigade of Choctaws under Tandy Walker. The troops had fought fiercely at Poison Spring, but Smith expressed concern about the security of Indian Territory. Still, the reduction in troop strength at such a crucial juncture of the Arkansas campaign belied Smith's assertion that it was necessary to concentrate every available soldier for the campaign against Steele. If Smith could spare fifteen hundred troops from the campaign, surely Taylor's operations against Banks ranked as a higher priority than operations in Indian Territory. Nevertheless, on April 28, the day that Smith's infantry marched after Steele, Maxey's brigades turned and marched in the opposite direction. [36]

Fagan's whereabouts remained Smith's biggest concern. Confederate couriers continued their fruitless search for the missing cavalry as the infantry crossed the Ouachita. Likewise, Fagan still did not know the location of the enemy, nor did he realize that Smith was moving along the road to Jenkins' Ferry. From his camp near Tulip, some thirty miles northeast of Camden, Fagan sent a battalion of cavalry on a reconnaissance mission to ascertain Steele's position. Above Princeton, seven miles south of Tulip, the cavalry skirmished with lead elements of the Federal retreat, less than twenty miles from the Saline River. Although they did not know it, Marmaduke was closing on the Federal rear at the same moment. For Fagan's reconnaissance team, the encounter near Princeton established conclusively that Steele's army was marching toward a river crossing at Jenkins' Ferry rather than at Mount Elba, farther south along the road to Pine Bluff. The gray horsemen raced back to deliver the news, but they failed to locate Fagan's main force at Pratt's Ferry, the appointed rendezvous point. Thus, the intelligence that Fagan needed to slow the Union advance went undelivered. [37]

Smith already knew that the enemy was moving on the road from Camden to Little Rock, and Steele reached the banks of the Saline on April 29. From his position at the Jenkins' Ferry crossing, Union brigadier E. A. Carr reported that less than twenty-four hours earlier Fagan's force had marched across the same road that carried the Federals toward the river. Had Fagan been in contact with Smith, the cavalry could have secured Jenkins' Ferry and established a position in front of the enemy advance. Instead, the cavalry stumbled blindly along the network of roads running through the Saline bottomland. Exhausted, without subsistence or forage, and completely unaware of the developments between Camden and the Saline, Fagan turned his horsemen away from the river on April 29 and marched west toward supplies at Arkadelphia. Days later, a resentful member of the Eleventh Missouri Infantry complained, "Our cavalry was as usual at the rong place." [38]

Fagan's failure to carry out orders was not Smith's fault. The lack of communication between cavalry and infantry, however, indicated that the commanding general was leaving too much to chance. At this point in the campaign Smith did not know the location of his cavalry, but he still believed that Fagan would block Steele's retreat. With Fagan heading for Arkadelphia, however, the character of the Confederate pursuit changed. Although Smith did not know it, the speed of his infantry became the key element for success or failure. Instead of trapping Steele between two Confederate forces, the chase became a contest to reach the Saline and a race to Little Rock.

Once across the Ouachita, the vanguard of the Confederate infantry moved quickly in pursuit of Steele's fleeing army. The quantity of accouterments that littered the track of retreat affirmed that the Federals knew they were running for their lives. Indeed, the enemy destroyed anything that could slow them down or that could fall into the hands of their pursuers. William N. Hoskin of the Missouri State Guard described the spectacle: "Ded mules and horses are lieing thick. . . . The road has bin strone thick with the spoils of the enemy—they have torne and burned there clothing all along the road—the road is allmost carpeted with coats—pants—jackets and blankets of the enemy." Only an opportunity to seize food from civilians unlucky enough to live in the path of the retreat seemed to slow the Union men. Hoskin charged that "every family on the road is rob[b]ed by the enemy as they pas—their bacon—flour & even their chickens corn & grain wheat. . . . women & children are left to starve or go a begging." [39]

Churchill and Parsons reached Tulip on April 29, having covered a distance of forty-four miles in two days. By contrast, Walker's division, bringing up the rear, advanced just thirty-four miles and barely made Princeton before nightfall. This discrepancy meant that the army would not arrive at the Saline as a single unit but as separate divisions. On the same night, Smith realized that the Federals had reached Jenkins' Ferry. He called a council of war to examine the situation. During the meeting the commanders received word from Fagan that the cavalry had not crossed the Saline but had gone instead to Arkadelphia for supplies. The intelligence left Smith crestfallen. Until the receipt of Fagan's message, Smith believed that he had snared Steele's army between Confederate infantry and cavalry. The new circumstances required a change in strategy. [40]

Smith did not want to fight at Jenkins' Ferry. The Saline bottomland was a quagmire three miles in width that stretched along five miles of riverbank. Moving toward the river, the road descended the ridge and ran through nearly one hundred yards of gnarled woods, choked scrub, and bristling thickets until reaching a large cotton field at the Jiles farm. Beyond the field, three hundred yards of timber separated the Jiles land from the Cooper field. The road continued east through another six-hundred-yard expanse of woods and led to a third clearing on the Kelly property. The river lay nearly two miles beyond Kelly's field. All three fields were south of the road, and with good reason. Directly to the north, a plodding bayou restricted access to the ground. South of the fields, however, an impenetrable swamp hemmed in the farmland. The location was ideal for a defensive stand. An attacker would have to enter the field via a single route and deploy across a narrow front. The ground would disrupt an infantry advance, and the muddy conditions would limit the use of artillery. In fact, Steele had no choice but to defend the ground in front of the crossing. It was a great stroke of luck—the first he had experienced since the campaign began. [41]

The Federals established a defensive perimeter astride the Little Rock road on the marshy ground around Jenkins' Ferry. A portion of the blue army soon crossed the river to occupy the high ground on the eastern bank, the same ground that

Fagan would have secured had he not become disoriented. Smith recognized the strength of the Federal position and knew that even with a pontoon he could not pursue the enemy across the river. Disheartened, he had either to abandon the campaign or to risk his army in battle. Rather than allow Steele to escape without a fight, Smith vowed to push forward "in a vague hope of being able to overtake the enemy's rear guard." He issued orders for the infantry to step up its advance, knowing that his quarry manned a formidable defensive alignment along the river just a few miles to his front. [42]

A torrential downpour that had begun the previous day continued to pelt the soldiers throughout the morning of April 30. They marched along flooded roads thick with mud that was often knee-deep. While the weather hindered the Confederate advance, it also slowed Steele's retreat. Aware that Smith's army was closing in from the southwest, and with no pressure from the east, the Federals worked tirelessly to complete the crossing before Confederate infantry arrived. Marmaduke's cavalry kept up a constant skirmish with elements of two Federal divisions that still languished west of the river. Confronted by over four thousand enemy troops along the Saline Bottoms, Marmaduke faced much more than the rear guard that Smith had anticipated. [43]

As Churchill approached, Smith realized that something was amiss. Price had ordered Churchill's division, closest to the front, to advance at midnight. Two miles to the rear, Parsons's men took to the road one hour later, while Walker's Texans, the farthest from the front, did not leave until after 2:00 A.M. Smith should have issued orders for Price to start the divisions at the same time. Instead, he left the logistics up to Price, who chose to stagger the advance. Troop movements were already slowed by rain and mud, and the uncoordinated sequence of march prevented Smith from achieving tactical concentration at Jenkins' Ferry. The mistake would prove calamitous. [44]

When Churchill's men arrived on the field, Smith found them fatigued from their forced march. He could have allowed the Arkansans to rest and regain their strength, as Taylor had done at Pleasant Hill. A tactical delay would have benefited the Confederates in two ways. First, the respite would have given Parsons's division time to catch up with Churchill. This would have reunited Price's infantry at the outset of the battle and, in doing so, doubled Confederate troop strength and given Smith superior numbers at the point of attack. Second, a pause would have allowed Smith time to reconnoiter the battlefield. Price described the terrain in front of Jenkins' Ferry as "swampy, with dense woods and undergrowth [that] rendered the movements of the troops very difficult." Despite these factors, Smith did not want to risk letting Steele slip away without a fight. He knew that the Confederates had "hurried" to the field and that Federals were "posted most advantageously." Still, at 8:00 A.M., Smith ordered Churchill to open the attack. [45]

Smith's failure to analyze the strength of the Federal position thoroughly compromised Churchill's assault. Union field general Frederick Salomon had arranged his men in a strong defensive position on a field that forced the Confederates to funnel their troops into a narrow killing zone. Brigadier General John B. Clark of Parsons's division described the enemy's alignment as "beyond an open field, concealed behind logs and underbrush." Thomas N. Waul, one of Walker's brigadiers, concurred with Clark's assessment and added that the Federals held formidable positions on either flank: "They had also a strong force nearly at right angles with the right of their main line . . . enfilading any force that might enter the field in front of the main line." The Federal left, according to Waul, extended far beyond the field and threatened to envelop the right flank of a frontal attack. "[The enemy] position was a strong one," a Texas infantryman admitted, "thickly timbered

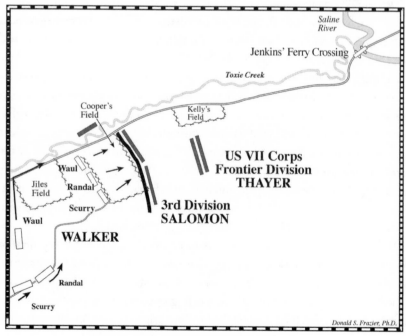

Battle of Jenkins' Ferry, April 30, 1864 (third phase)

bottom, and the ground was covered with water, from ankle to knee." But the conditions on the field did not matter to Smith. The enemy's alignment did not worry him, either. He had finally cornered the prey he had stalked for weeks. Firmly entrenched, with their backs to the river, the Federals prepared to receive the Confederate assault across a narrow, marshy field in front of the crossing at Jenkins' Ferry. [46]

Smith gave Price tactical control of troops on the battlefield, and in rapid succession the latter issued three sets of contradictory orders for Churchill's deployment. After a series of false starts, elements of James C. Tappan's brigade lurched forward. "The line was formed," reported Price, "and under all obstacles moved with spirit and alacrity to the attack." Under heavy fire, the Confederates crossed the Jiles field and drove the Federals out of the woods. Upon entering the Cooper field, however, the Arkansans found themselves facing a much larger force than anticipated. Undeterred, they pushed ahead into the maw of the Federal guns. As Tappan's men struggled across the mire, Churchill sent Alexander T. Hawthorne's brigade onto the field. The battle raged over "boggy ground [that] was almost impassable," reported Price. Churchill described the struggle as "desperate beyond description." Upon his arrival at the front, Smith ordered an attack against the right flank. The Confederates drove the Federal right back on itself, yet the enemy refused to break. Churchill's men fought doggedly for two hours but yielded the ground to the Federals. [47]

As the exhausted Arkansas troops began to retire, Parsons's Missourians descended into the Saline basin. Joined by Marmaduke's cavalry and Churchill's reserves, under Lucien C. Gause, the Confederates renewed the assault. The battle soon became a melee, and confusion reigned on both sides of the field. Gause reported, "Churchill dismounted, seized a rifle, and rallied the remnant of the brigade around him under a heavy fire." The enemy right again presented a deadly problem as it poured withering fire into the Confederate advance. Unable to maintain control of the ground, the Confederates fell back and by 11:30 A.M. had begun to withdraw from the field. [48]

The repulse of Price's command convinced Smith that it would be futile to order a third frontal attack against enemy entrenchments. Having failed to turn the Federal right, he decided to try his luck against the left. As Walker drew closer to the field, Smith ordered him to take two brigades along a narrow farm road toward the Federal left flank. Meanwhile, his third brigade was to attack the Federal center. Smith also instructed Churchill and Parsons to regroup and prepare to support Walker. [49]

As the rain intensified and mist shrouded the field, Walker's men pitched forward into the fray. Smith hoped the muddy road would carry the Confederates beyond the Federal flank. Unfortunately, it deposited Walker's men directly across the Federal front. Undeterred, the Texans "dashed onto the field with a shout that seemed to shake the very earth." A Confederate marveled, "The tide of battle ebbed and flowed[,] now advancing, then receding; but at no time did the ground fought over vary more than two hundred and fifty yards." Smith rode to the front lines and cheered on his troops. One of Walker's men recalled that Smith joined the fight and rallied the troops: "Dismounting from his horse, and, taking a gun from one of the soldiers, he took his place in the ranks as a private [during] the thickest of the conflict." [50]

"The contest now raged in a great violence," recalled Price. Shortly after the Confederates drove back a flanking movement on their left, the Texans pushed forward. In the charge against the center, Waul suffered a serious wound but remained in the field. On the right, however, Generals William R. Scurry and Horace B. Randal fell, mortally wounded, and the attack stalled. Disorganized and demoralized by the loss of their brigadiers, Walker's right fell back in disarray. Unsupported on his flank, Waul determined that the position was untenable and ordered a retreat. At 12:30 P.M. the fighting along the lines ceased. During the ensuing lull the Federals withdrew and abandoned the field to the Confederates. [51]

Both Smith and Steele expected another assault, and each general planned accordingly. Concern that Confederate reinforcements were still arriving at the front prompted the Federals to shorten their lines and shift their defensive position closer to the river. Steele also stepped up the pace of his retreat across the Saline. Smith took the withdrawal as a sign of victory. He ordered Churchill to probe the new Federal position and personally readied Waul's brigade for another attack. By the time Churchill's men reached the Saline, around 4:00 P.M., the Federals had crossed the river and destroyed the pontoon. At the same time, Fagan arrived on the field. In the early-morning hours a courier had at last found the cavalry thirty-four miles west of Jenkins' Ferry and alerted Fagan to Steele's movement. The horsemen rode hard to reach the front but arrived too late for the fight. Fagan and his officers begged Smith to "allow their command to swim the river in pursuit of Steele's army," but he refused. "As it was," wrote one of Walker's Texans, "[Smith] was satisfied with the laurels already won [and] consequently he allowed Steele's army to return to Little Rock . . . unmolested." The Federal column reached the safety of their base on May 3. Smith's boast that he would pursue Steele all the way to Little Rock echoed along the Saline like the rattling of a tarnished saber. [52]

The mediocre results at Jenkins' Ferry and the disappointing outcome of the campaign in Arkansas left Smith open to criticism. The day after the battle, Missourian John P. Quesenberry recorded a stinging analysis in his diary: "From what I know of this expedition, I think it has been badly managed. No preparation made to cross the River at Camden spe[e]dily . . . and when the fight came off the cavalry was still on scout. The Abbs [abolitionists] had the advantage of position and consequently we suffered much." Before Jenkins' Ferry, many in Walker's division spoke of an "implicit confidence" that the commanding general would not permit "any useless sacrifice of life in the forthcoming battle." In the aftermath, Texan Joseph P. Blessington expressed a feeling of betrayal and asserted that Smith had done nothing at Jenkins' Ferry but cause the death of Randal, Scurry, and nearly one thousand other Confederate soldiers. R. S. Wilson, a member Randal's brigade, agreed: "It was a bloody little fight for us and nothing accomplished and I could never figure out why our commander ran up against such a hard proposition." Jenkins' Ferry, Blessington declared, left Walker's division "broken down in spirits." [53]

Walker bitterly criticized Smith's performance on the battlefield. He condemned the general for failing to reconnoiter unfamiliar ground before committing troops to the assault, a lapse he compared with Taylor's oversight at Pleasant Hill: "The same fatal blunder was committed as at Pl Hill, and the enemy was attacked before any information was gained." In addition, Walker complained about the sluggish manner in which Smith sent troops onto the battlefield and concluded, "No wonder that the attack was feeble and easily repulsed." While Walker's accusations were well grounded, he did not acknowledge certain extenuating circumstances. The Confederates at Jenkins' Ferry enjoyed less time to reconnoiter unfamiliar ground than did Taylor at the familiar site of Pleasant Hill. Moreover, the ground was a morass of muck and ooze made even worse by dreadful weather conditions. Nevertheless, both Smith and Taylor displayed a clear lack of resourcefulness with respect to battlefield tactics. The generals deployed their brigades unevenly and committed their troops in piecemeal fashion. These mistakes allowed the enemy to shift regiments along tactical interior lines where needed, resulting in high Confederate casualties at each battle. [54]

At Jenkins' Ferry, each side suffered a casualty rate of approximately 17 percent, with Smith losing one thousand of his six thousand soldiers and the Federals losing seven hundred of their four thousand. Strategically, Steele made good his retreat while Smith gained very little. Taylor had predicted that Steele would retreat from the Arkansas claw of the pincer once the Federals learned of Banks's defeat in Louisiana. In Taylor's view, Banks's repulse had already prevented concentration of the Federal columns at Shreveport three weeks before a single drop of southern blood spilled onto the banks of the Saline at Jenkins' Ferry. [55]

Yet until Steele began his retreat, Smith could not risk leaving such a large Federal force prowling southwestern Arkansas. Edward Cunningham, Smith's aide, summarized his commander's strategic rationale: "Steele, with 11,000 men, was moving on Camden . . . at which point he could, in perfect security from our cavalry, watch our operations, and if an opportunity offered, strike at Jefferson, Marshall, or Shreveport. To leave him in this position . . . would be to jeopardize our very salvation." Once Steele evacuated Camden, however, there was no longer a viable military reason for Smith to take the infantry to Arkansas. Smith had contended that the destruction of Steele would open Arkansas to Confederate control and pave the way into Missouri—not entirely implausible, but a remote possibility even under ideal circumstances. The annihilation of Banks's army in Louisiana and the destruction of Porter's fleet were far more attainable goals than securing Arkansas. In a practical sense, dividends from the defeat of Banks outweighed any tangible benefits from the overthrow of Steele. And no matter how important the capture of St. Louis was to Smith, the battle of Jenkins' Ferry did not contribute to that end. Ultimately, Banks's defeat at Mansfield and the Federal decision to retreat from Pleasant Hill greatly reduced the strategic importance of the Arkansas campaign. [56]

Similarly, Taylor's hopes for the liberation of New Orleans were, by this stage of the war, unrealistic. His strategy to destroy Banks and Porter, however, remained feasible. Smith's decision to use two-thirds of Taylor's command in Arkansas rather than Louisiana became the principal factor affecting Taylor's operations against Banks. Walker, whose division remained caught between Smith and Taylor, offered a harsh assessment of Smith: "Unfortunately for the Confederates . . . " Smith ignored the "advice of his principal subordinates [and] unwisely determined to leave the pursuit of Banks to Gen. Taylor" with a greatly depleted force while the rest of the army marched to Arkansas. Chief of staff Boggs concurred with Walker's judgment. He recalled that Smith, after learning of Steele's flight from Camden on April 27, considered returning the infantry to Taylor but rejected the idea and chose to effect concentration in Arkansas. Boggs later criticized his commanding officer for this decision, charging that Smith knew the army should have marched to aid Taylor in Louisiana but refused to relinquish his ambitions in Arkansas. While Smith hunted Steele to the edge of the Saline, Taylor continued his struggle against Banks along the Red River. Smith's decision to prosecute a campaign in Arkansas had, in Taylor's bitter estimation, destroyed the last hope for the Confederate cause in the Trans-Mississippi. [57]

9
The Path of Glory

"I have just passed through the most brilliant and successful campaign of the war," Edmund Kirby Smith wrote to his mother on May 5, 1864. The letter proudly traced his recently concluded exploits in Arkansas and alluded to Richard Taylor's ongoing Louisiana adventures. Smith boasted, "The enemy moved upon us with 50,000 men . . . [and] with only 22,000 men at my disposal, by rapid marching and concentration we whipped the enemy in detail." The same day, Smith sent another letter to Jefferson Davis and complained bluntly that despite the Confederate successes in Arkansas and Louisiana, the Trans-Mississippi Department was in disarray.[1]

Smith suggested that Davis replace the current leadership in Arkansas, Louisiana, and Texas. Announcing that the department was "greatly in want of good subordinates," he begged Richmond for prompt assistance to better sustain his administration. Although he did not single out Taylor or Magruder, Smith intimated that a "change in the command of those districts [was] demanded by the best interests of the country." He did, however, level harsh criticism at Price, the district head who had supported the Smith administration since the commanding general arrived in the Trans-Mississippi. Smith maintained that Price was "neither capable of organizing, disciplining, nor operating an army [and] should not be left in command of the district [or] of an army in the field." He downplayed the contention that "Price's name and popularity would [provide] a strong element of success in an advance on Missouri" and argued that a change in command in Arkansas would aid the Confederate cause dramatically.[2]

Much of his disdain for Price's military skill sprang from the Missourian's failure to follow orders to secure Camden and cut off the Federal retreat. Price's lackluster tactical performance at Jenkins' Ferry seemingly did not bother Smith. Yet in a detailed report to Davis filed after the close of the campaign, he indicated that Price's command bore sole responsibility for Steele's escape. He complained that "Price had not crossed any cavalry to the north side of the Arkansas river, as directed," and insisted that had the cavalry "thrown itself on the enemy's front on his march from Camden, Steele would have been . . . utterly destroyed."[3]

Rumors of a growing rift between Smith and Price began to surface in Confederate cities east of the Mississippi. Thomas Snead, Price's adjutant during the campaign, told Price that he had heard rumors in Richmond and Mobile that Smith held him responsible for the failure to stop Steele's retreat. "I have heard the same charge made again and again," Snead lamented, and the allegations, he reported, were coming from friends of Smith. With his army in Arkansas bloodied and his elusive foe racing toward Little Rock, Smith had once again dealt with failure by blaming a fellow officer. Faced with the knowledge that the only remaining threat to the department lay at Taylor's front, he resolved to return the infantry to Louisiana. Three days after the battle of Jenkins' Ferry, Churchill, Parsons, and Walker received instructions to prepare their troops to rejoin Taylor.[4]

The engagement at Jenkins' Ferry had left the men dispirited, despite their belief that they had carried the day. Before taking up their line of march, the mangled divisions assembled on dress parade to receive a congratulatory message from Smith. "The campaign inaugurated at Mansfield," Smith assured the assembly on the eve of their departure, "has, under Providence, been crowned with the most glorious and brilliant success [at Jenkins' Ferry]," and he reminded the men that "The path of glory is still open to you." Joseph Blessington, one of Walker's men, listened cynically, with his thoughts turned toward his recently fallen comrades. "The path of glory," he sneered, "leads but to the grave."[5]

On May 12 Smith notified Taylor that reinforcements from Arkansas were finally on the way to Louisiana. Smith also took the opportunity to extend the same advice he had offered before the battle at Mansfield. "I do not wish to restrain you in operations," he insisted, but he warned Taylor, "You cannot exercise too much caution in risking a general engagement or in too far committing your whole force to a position . . . beyond the power of retreat in the event of a disaster." Considering his decision to detach the bulk of Taylor's infantry after Pleasant Hill for the pursuit of Steele, Smith's claim that he did not wish to restrain Taylor's operations seems disingenuous. Smith's urging of caution appears to have been less a strategic concern than a reactionary response to the miscarriage of the campaign in Arkansas.[6]

Five days later Smith informed Taylor that only Walker's Greyhounds were still on the move to Alexandria. In a disconcerting letter, he announced that the rest of the infantry was returning to Camden. Smith explained that once Banks completed his withdrawal, Arkansas and Missouri would again become the "true field of operations." He revealed that preparations for a general advance into Arkansas and ultimately Missouri were already under way and that Price would lead the expedition. Further, Smith issued instructions for Taylor to prepare the remainder of his command to join the campaign and insisted that he accompany the Louisiana column to "add to its efficiency and increase the prospects of success."[7]

The timing of Smith's decision to renew campaigning in Arkansas was suspect. Smith put the plans into motion less than three weeks after he dispersed the army, already concentrated at Jenkins' Ferry, and abandoned his pursuit of Steele. At this juncture of the Red River campaign, Banks still occupied territory in Taylor's district and thus posed a greater potential threat to the department's overall security than did Steele. Reluctantly, Smith followed through on his commitment to Taylor and ordered the infantry to Louisiana. The continued movement of Walker's division toward Alexandria, even after the decision to launch a new campaign in Arkansas, suggests that Smith still harbored a significant degree of concern over the presence of Federal troops in Taylor's district. Had Smith not considered Banks a threat, Walker would have joined the march to Camden rather than continue to push on toward Taylor in Alexandria.[8]

Yet it may have been Taylor rather than Banks who most worried Smith. In the event that Banks successfully crossed into eastern Louisiana, as Taylor and Smith both fully expected, Taylor had devised plans to place batteries along the Mississippi River and to reoccupy and hold the Lafourche region. Smith was aware of his subordinate's determination to shift operations into the Lafourche. As recently as April 11, just two days after Pleasant Hill, Taylor had suggested a strike toward New Orleans or Algiers. This strategy, however, was diametrically opposed to Smith's design for the conquest of Arkansas and Missouri. His decision to send only Walker and to countermand Churchill and Parsons appears to have been a preemptive strike against Taylor's plans to campaign in the Lafourche. Meanwhile, in his eagerness to initiate a summer campaign through Arkansas and Missouri, Smith chose to rely on Price, an officer whose recent performance had prompted him to petition Richmond for his removal. Smith had once again allowed his desire for the conquest of Arkansas and Missouri to override all other concerns, including the security of the department and the caliber of the officers running the campaign.[9]

On May 19, the same day Walker's men reached the outskirts of Alexandria, the final remnants of Banks's invasion force escaped to safety across the Atchafa-

138/ A CRISIS IN CONFEDERATE COMMAND

laya River. Smith later asserted, "Taylor's force was too weak to warrant the hope that he could successfully impede the march of Banks' column." He shouldered none of the blame for the Federals' escape, a fiasco to which his own orders for the reduction of Taylor's troop strength and the pursuit of Steele's fleeing column had largely contributed.[10]

The Federal retreat down the Red River had taken forty days. During this time, while Smith chased Steele across Arkansas, Taylor's small force had several chances to trap Banks's army and Porter's fleet. With insufficient manpower to capitalize on these opportunities, however, Taylor could do little more than harass the enemy.

Taylor began pursuit on April 10, when Confederate troops stopped Porter's advance at Loggy Bayou, about one hundred miles equidistant from Shreveport to the northwest and Grand Ecore to the south. Porter stated that the Rebels "had gotten that huge steamer, *New Falls City*, across Red River . . . 15 feet of her on shore on each side, the boat broken down in the middle, and a sand bar making below her." The position of the ship made it impossible for Porter to continue without spending hours to clear the wreck. "It was the smartest thing I ever knew the rebels to do," he later told General William T. Sherman. The idea was part of Smith's defensive plan for the river, and Taylor had executed his instructions impeccably. Proud of their accomplishment, some of Taylor's men left a taunting message scrawled across the wreckage inviting Porter's sailors to a ball that night in Shreveport. Porter began immediate preparations to remove the scuttled steamer, but before the Federals could clear the obstruction from their path, a courier thundered down the road from Pleasant Hill with news of Banks's defeat. The army was withdrawing to Grand Ecore, and Banks urged the fleet do the same. Porter turned his ships around and began the treacherous navigation back down the river to rejoin the army.[11]

From his headquarters in Mansfield, Taylor continued to petition Smith for concentration against Banks. In addition, he requested the use of a pontoon train to assist in operations along the river. The lack of a pontoon had already disrupted Taylor's plans for Porter. After Pleasant Hill, he anticipated that the Federals would attempt to reestablish the link between army and navy. Accordingly, Taylor ordered Arthur P. Bagby's horsemen to ride northeast to Grand Bayou and sent Tom Green due east to Blair's Landing. He hoped to trap Porter between the two forces before the Federal infantry reached the river. The pontoon, however, was scheduled to accompany Smith to Arkansas. By the time Bagby crossed the Bayou Pierre, the fleet had steamed past and Green was left to contest Porter's retreat on his own.[12]

On April 12 Green's cavalry secured a position ahead of the fleet along the bluffs at Blair's Landing. Just before 3:00 P.M., Confederate guns opened fire on the warships. Several of the ships had difficulty navigating a sharp bend in the river, and as the fleet steamed past the gray gauntlet, two ran aground. Federal sailors scrambled to free the vessels and drew what Union naval commander Thomas O. Selfridge claimed was "the heaviest and most concentrated fire of musketry" he had ever witnessed. For nearly two hours the Confederates continued to pour fire into the hapless ships. Astride his white horse, Green rode along the lines to encourage his men. The move was rash and left him exposed to enemy fire. Late in the day, one of the gunships broke free and turned her 11-inch guns on the Rebels. A Federal shell tore through the lines and decapitated Green. As word of their leader's gruesome death spread through the ranks, the Texans became disorganized and fell back while the Federals proceeded to wind their way south to Grand Ecore. "Losing General Green has paralyzed them," noted Porter. "He was worth 5,000 men to them."[13]

Soldiers throughout Taylor's command mourned the loss of Green. "This dreadful casualty has thrown a sad gloom over our otherwise elated army," lamented cavalryman H. C. Medford. "I feel myself entirely unable to write a eulogy of so great a man." Taylor eulogized Green in his memoirs: "To me he was a tried and devoted friend. . . . His men adored him, and would follow him where ever he led." The diary entry of a Louisianan stated simply, "In my opinion we could better have lost *any* other man in the Department than Gen. Green." Within four days, Taylor had suffered the loss of two trusted subordinates. Mouton's death at Mansfield and Green's death at Blair's Landing deprived Taylor's army of its most reliable general officers at a crucial time in the campaign. Combined with Smith's decision to send two-thirds of the army in Louisiana to Arkansas, the loss of Taylor's lieutenants threatened to leave him bereft of experienced officers and stripped the district of human resources.[14]

On April 13, the day after Green's death, Taylor received more bad news from two fronts. First, Porter's escape at Blair's Landing had enabled the Federal columns to reunite at Grand Ecore. Under the protection of naval guns, Banks's wounded army could regain its balance and again pose a potential threat to Shreveport. Second, Smith arrived in Mansfield and unreservedly rejected Taylor's plea for continued concentration against Banks. The army would concentrate against the Federals in Arkansas, and Taylor was to join the campaign. Taylor reacted angrily and accused Smith of implementing "a policy that would fail to reap . . . the legitimate fruits of those victories" at Mansfield and Pleasant Hill. "It was for this that Green and Mouton and other gallant spirits fell," he later fumed. Downhearted but undeterred by Smith's decision, Taylor vowed to avenge the deaths of his lieutenants. "The fall of these heroes shall not be in vain," he proclaimed.[15]

Two days later, as he made his way toward Shreveport, Taylor clung to the hope that Smith's Arkansas campaign would never leave Louisiana and that his troops would return in a matter of days. During the April 15 meeting with Smith, however, he learned otherwise. Even with news that Steele was in retreat, Smith refused to endorse renewed concentration against Banks and insisted that the march to Arkansas proceed. He ordered Taylor to remain with a small force in Louisiana and, perhaps by way of recompense, promoted his subordinate to lieutenant general. Taylor's "past services and eminent qualifications," he explained to Richmond, entitled him to the elevation of grade. Smith also ordered the pontoon train held for Taylor's use against Banks and Porter. But neither the promotion nor the pontoon could compensate Taylor for the loss of Walker and Churchill. Including the various Texas cavalry units, Camille Polignac's division, and a small brigade east of the river, Taylor controlled fewer than five thousand troops for operations against Banks's army of over twenty-five thousand and Porter's fleet of warships.[16]

Three days after Smith left for Arkansas, John A. Wharton, a veteran cavalryman from the Army of Tennessee, arrived at headquarters to take command of Green's division. He and Taylor left Shreveport on April 19 and rode southeast toward the Confederate positions along the Red River. They reached Polignac's infantry outside of Grand Ecore on April 21. The depleted division could muster only sixteen hundred arms, yet they had effectively pinned the Federals against the river. Polignac claimed that his own skilled deployment of troops had unnerved the Federals, and perhaps it had. Banks's initial thoughts of renewing the campaign gave way to fears that Taylor had massed twenty-five thousand men against him. A Confederate prisoner of war held at Grand Ecore supported Polignac's assessment and noted in his diary, "Banks' army is here completely whipped out and demoralized."[17]

Another Confederate prisoner at Grand Ecore was David French Boyd, a member of Taylor's staff who had served with the general since the beginning of the war. Boyd managed to get a message through the lines and implored Taylor to concentrate on reducing Porter's armada. "If the fleet is lost, General Banks considers himself ruined. He has been heard to say so," Boyd disclosed. He reminded

Taylor that the river was falling rapidly and begged him to "move heaven and earth to close up." When Boyd wrote the message, he was unaware of Smith's decision to detach two-thirds of the infantry for a campaign in Arkansas. Although the letter did not reach Taylor at the front, Boyd had articulated what would become the key strategic consideration for the Louisiana Confederates during the next phase of the campaign. Banks's army and Porter's navy were dependent upon one another, and if Taylor could disable one, he might be able to destroy the other. If Boyd understood this, certainly Taylor understood it as well.[18]

Taylor assessed the situation at Grand Ecore and dismissed any notion that the Federals would resume their advance on Shreveport. He interpreted enemy forays toward the Confederate position as a screen intended to cover the withdrawal to Alexandria, nearly seventy miles downriver. Indeed, Banks had opted to abandon the campaign on April 19, the same day Taylor left Shreveport for the front. On the day Taylor arrived, the Federals began their retreat.[19]

Just below Grand Ecore, the line of retreat carried Banks south along the Alexandria road and onto an island created by the confluence of the Cane and Red rivers. The Cane branched off to the southwest, and the rivers continued to flow roughly parallel to each other. The Alexandria road hugged the eastern banks of the Cane River for nearly forty-five miles until it reached a crossing at Monett's Ferry. Here the road continued south while the Cane meandered southeast and rejoined the Red at Calhoun's Landing. This unusual quirk of topography placed the Federal army on an island roughly forty-five miles in length and no more than seven miles wide. Taylor recognized that the Federal columns would be vulnerable as Banks moved his twenty-five thousand men across the narrow island. Banks's perilous situation gave Taylor an opportunity to take the initiative. Despite the disparity in numbers, he developed a plan to trap the Federals between the Cane and the Red and force Banks to fight his way off the island or surrender his army.[20]

Hamilton Bee received orders to take his four small brigades of cavalry along with four batteries and occupy a position south of the Cane on the wooded bluffs overlooking Monett's Ferry. From this point Bee's two thousand Confederates could maintain control of the Alexandria road and prevent the Federal column from crossing the Cane. To apply pressure to the enemy from the north, Taylor directed Wharton's cavalry to harass Banks's rear guard. Meanwhile, Polignac moved his division along the west bank of the Cane toward a crossing at Cloutierville, a small island town five miles north of Monett's Ferry. Simultaneously,

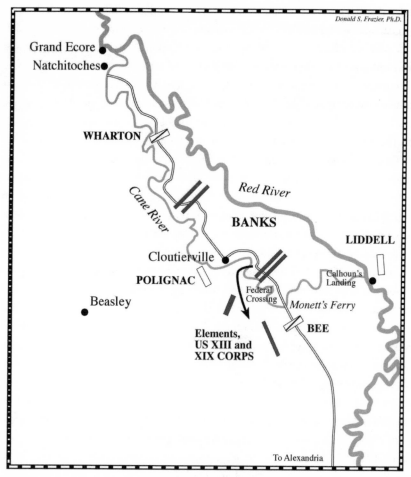

Monett's Ferry, 1864

St. John Liddell's cavalry, stationed east of the Red River, held the ford at Calhoun's near the southern confluence of the Cane and the Red. The troop deployment encircled the Federals completely. By covering the strategic crossings and driving the enemy's rear, Taylor would slowly tighten the coils around Banks's legions.[21]

Taylor's plan to divide his modest army in the face of a superior foe carried with it a serious risk. Should Banks concentrate his forces against any one of Taylor's positions, the massive Federal firepower would eventually overwhelm Confederate resistance. According to Taylor, however, his strategy would succeed if the Confederates executed their instructions and held firmly to their strong defensive positions. Taylor based his optimism on the demoralized state of the Federal forces and on Banks's poor performance at Mansfield and Pleasant Hill. Significantly, Smith's decision to detach two-thirds of Taylor's command left very few alternatives for the pursuit and destruction of Banks's command.[22]

Before he had completed arrangements for the Cane River Valley, Taylor received a letter from Liddell that outlined an alternative strategy. Liddell suggested that "Taylor should move rapidly to Alexandria, and occupy that place with the whole of his infantry" and leave the cavalry to operate against Banks's rear. The occupation of Alexandria would sever Federal communications, prevent reinforcements from coming to Banks's assistance, and replenish dwindling Confederate provisions with captured Union supplies. "All must end in our capturing or destroying the fleet and disintegrating Banks' army," Liddell reasoned. The strategy was similar to Smith's plan to thwart Steele's retreat in Arkansas by occupying Camden ahead of the Federals. Taylor did not issue an immediate reply to Liddell's proposition. Instead, he turned his attention to Bee at Monett's Ferry and underscored "the importance of holding the position to the last extremity." He called the position "the strongest in the State."[23]

Taylor's Cane River gambit failed at Monett's Ferry on April 23. Bee's two thousand men found themselves in front of twenty-five thousand advancing Federals "spread over the valley of the Cane River as far as the eye could reach." Bee, who had arrived at Monett's the night before, apparently misunderstood Taylor's instructions. It was not until the morning of April 23, when Banks's entire force approached the ferry, that the "importance of holding the position became apparent" to the officer entrusted with holding the strategic heights. The low water level of the Cane also compromised Bee's stand and allowed Banks to divide his force and cross several thousand troops at an abandoned ford two miles above Monett's Ferry. As a fierce fight developed on the Confederate left flank, Bee became confused by a Union feint to his right and thus failed to reinforce the troops engaged on his left. Fearing that both of his flanks had been turned, Bee abandoned the heights at Monett's Ferry after holding the Federals back for seven hours. The withdrawal left a clear path for Banks across the Cane and on to Alexandria. By midafternoon on April 24, the last elements of Banks's army had crossed the river and escaped Taylor's trap.[24]

Bee's decision to disengage at Monett's Ferry wrecked the strategy to snare Banks. Taylor was incensed. "If Bee stood firm at Monette's we were in a position to make Banks unhappy," he seethed. In an after-action report to Smith, Taylor analyzed the circumstances and accused Bee of neglecting to fortify his position and of improperly aligning his troops: "[Bee] concentrated his forces to protect the center, the strongest [and] most impregnable point on his line." In doing so, he permitted the Federals to flank his position. Taylor concluded that the Texan had "displayed great personal gallantry, but no generalship." Taylor was enraged not only by Bee's withdrawal from the field but also by the line of retreat he chose, which allowed Banks to proceed toward Alexandria unmolested: "Instead of falling back to the pine woods . . . and harassing the enemy on his disorderly march, attacking his trains and inflicting punishment on him, Gnl. Bee fell back at once to Beasley's," a nearby forage depot.[25]

Bee insisted that he had failed "because success was impossible" and explained that he had fallen back to Beasley's because his men were starving. Taylor rejected the rationalization and relieved Bee from command, stating, "You were in a position to annihilate the enemy. You accomplished nothing." Taylor continued his caustic tirade by accusing Bee of incompetence: "Had you done your duty I would have sung your praises [but] you have shown yourself wanting in ability to conduct operations [and] were I to have you in a position to ruin my plan again, I would be responsible [for the] errors."[26]

Weeks after Bee's removal, a debate arose among the general officers of the department regarding the allegations of incompetence. Wharton came to Bee's defense and offered to publicly defend the decision to withdraw from Monett's Ferry. He considered Bee a friend and enlisted the support of other cavalry officers present at Monett's Ferry to speak in Bee's behalf. Wharton also promised to provide a written statement that Bee had done his duty and remained in position as long as practicable. In a report to Smith, Joseph L. Brent, Taylor's artillery chief, offered support for Bee's decision to fall back on Beasley's. He revealed that "for four days the horses did not have a grain of corn and for two days the men were without rations." Brent emphasized that once Bee's men secured rations, they were eager to return to the front.[27]

Walker, who was in Arkansas during the battle at Monett's Ferry, openly supported Taylor's decision to relieve Bee. He candidly informed Smith that he would "regard it as a public calamity to know of [Bee] being assigned to an important command." Walker based his harsh assessment on Bee's lackluster performance at Mansfield and Pleasant Hill and provided Smith with a detailed critique of the brigadier's failures. Later, Walker tempered his criticism and acknowledged that "Bee's force [at Monett's Ferry] was entirely insufficient to bar the passage of a retreating army." He reaffirmed Taylor's contention, however, that "the position itself was so advantageous that with a more skillful handling of his troops, and a more vigorous resistance[,] the Federal army would have found it extremely difficult to dislodge their enemy and to force a passage." Unfortunately, by the time the Federals reached Monett's Ferry, most of Taylor's skilled generals were either dead or with Smith in Arkansas.[28]

While the officers squabbled amongst themselves, Bee petitioned Smith for a court of inquiry into the allegations against him. He asserted that his own support for Smith's strategy of concentration against Steele, rather than the defeat at Monett's Ferry, had motivated Taylor to relieve him from duty. Smith concurred that Bee's performance at Monett's Ferry "was that of a brave and gallant soldier" and characterized Taylor's plan to trap Banks as "impracticable." He reasoned that if Bee had continued to hold the position at Monett's, he "would have endangered the safety" of every soldier on the bluffs. Smith agreed to open an official investigation into the incident if Bee insisted. Instead, Bee accepted Smith's offer for assignment to Samuel Maxey's command in Indian Territory.[29]

Bee was not entirely to blame for the failure at Monett's Ferry. Taylor conceded in his memoirs that although Bee had performed valiantly during the Red River campaign, he had insufficient combat experience to prevent Banks's escape across the Cane River. Having by his own admission assigned an inexperienced officer to a position vital to the success of the strategy, Taylor himself must bear some of the blame for the results. Yet Taylor's options on the field were limited. Smith's removal of three infantry divisions for the Arkansas expedition not only reduced the manpower available to Taylor but also depleted his officer corps. Originally Taylor had planned to deploy Polignac on the bluffs commanding Monett's Ferry and hoped to use Walker to pressure the Federal rear. This plan was contingent upon Smith countermarching the Texas infantry and returning it to Louisiana. Two days before the battle, Taylor implored Smith to send him both the pontoon and Walker's division. Taylor waited until the last possible moment for word from Smith before ordering Bee to Monett's Ferry and shifting Polignac to Cloutierville. Consequently, Bee arrived on the scene just hours before the Federals and did not possess a thorough understanding of the terrain or of Taylor's strategy. Had Polignac's division held the high ground opposite Banks and had Walker been engaged on the floor of the Cane River Valley, the Federals would have found the crossing at Monett's Ferry far more hazardous.[30]

Wharton and Polignac did not dispute Taylor's plan for defeating Banks before the Federals reached Alexandria. However, Taylor's insistence on the strategy angered Liddell. Following Banks's escape across the Cane, Taylor sent a message to Liddell in which he pledged to "drive the enemy into and out of Alexandria." Taylor's letter served to incite rather than inspire his subordinate. Liddell remained convinced that Taylor had made a mistake in trying to thwart the Federals at Monett's Ferry when the Confederates could have easily captured Alexandria. He alleged that Taylor had taken his suggestion to move the army below Banks as a repudiation of the Cane River strategy. Liddell interpreted Taylor's failure to adopt his proposal as a personal insult and charged, "My temerity in presuming to send him a suggestion had incurred his enmity." The strategy to drive Banks into and out of Alexandria drew acrimonious criticism from Liddell. Referring to Taylor's complaints of reduced troop strength, he asked, "If [Taylor] could drive the enemy before him what need had he for more [troops]?" Yet Smith's decision to take the infantry to Arkansas was precisely the reason that Taylor had scant opportunity to follow Liddell's plan. Unless Banks stumbled, the reduced Confederate troop strength would force Taylor to gamble in the Cane River Valley. His only other alternative was to let Banks go.[31]

Advance elements of Banks's army reached Alexandria on the evening of April 24, and the Federal columns extended back across the Cane as far as Cloutierville, twenty-five miles away. Some units became lost along the march while others used the retreat as an opportunity to wage war against Louisiana's citizenry. "From the Cane River to Alexandria the country was in ruins" recalled a Federal. "It was a picture, whose equal the men had never seen before." Another Yankee admitted, "It was a grand sight to see such fires. . . . I want to see their country desalated. . . . A feeling of reaevenge took hold of me and if it was in my power I would not leave one brick on top of another or an eare of corn for the Deavls to subsist on." Taylor corroborated the accounts of warfare against civilians. "The destruction of this country by the enemy exceeds anything in history," he noted sharply in his report to Smith. "For many miles every dwellinghouse, every negro cabin, every cotton-gin, every corn crib, and even chicken houses have been burned to the ground . . . hundreds of persons are utterly without shelter." Stunned by the devastation, a Confederate pointed to "clouds of smoke by day and pillars of fire by night [that] marked the progress" of Banks's retreat. Taylor's only hope of avenging the destruction was to destroy the Federals at Alexandria.[32]

On April 25 Taylor reported that Porter's fleet of warships and transports had begun to crowd above the Alexandria falls. Since beginning its descent from Loggy Bayou, the fleet had endured relentless fire from Confederates along the river. A

Federal soldier who watched the ships steam into Alexandria described the fleet as being in a "speckled condition from bullet shots." Another declared that "the transport *Blackhawk* looked like a monster pepper box." Despite the relative safety Alexandria provided the infantry, the Federal fleet was in deep trouble. Above the rapids, the water line had fallen as low as forty inches, less than half the depth required for ten of Porter's most prized warships to descend into the lower channel of the river. In an extraordinary reversal of roles, Porter found his naval force in dire need of protection from the infantry. Banks agreed to keep his army in Alexandria until the fleet could cross the rapids, a decision that gave Taylor one more opportunity to destroy the Federals.[33]

Taylor continued to plan his operations against the joint Federal forces based on assurances from Smith that Walker would return to Louisiana once Steele began his retreat. Before committing the division to the campaign in Arkansas, Smith held Walker below the state line at Minden. From there Walker could operate along interior lines to support either Smith or Taylor, depending upon enemy movements on either front. Smith notified Taylor of the decision on April 20 and requested information on the roads to Campti, a town just ten miles north of Natchitoches. On the morning of April 23, the day the main Federal force arrived in Alexandria, Taylor received an encouraging dispatch from S. S. Anderson, Smith's adjutant. Anderson disclosed that Walker had begun preparations to undertake the march to Campti. The news strengthened Taylor's resolve, and for a few hours the ruin of Banks and Porter seemed within reach. However, by 5:00 P.M. Smith had countermanded the orders and directed Walker to "proceed to Arkansas without delay."[34]

The news frustrated Taylor and left him "disheartened." With both Banks and Porter trapped above the rapids in Alexandria, the decision to withhold Walker could not have come at a worse time. In a message to Smith, Taylor argued that Walker was a part of his command and that he needed the division to secure the destruction of Porter and Banks. According to Taylor, on the day Smith left Shreveport for Arkansas, he had received assurances from the commander that Walker's division "would not be taken" from his command and that "the expedition in which it was engaged would occupy but a few days," whereupon it would be returned to him. Taylor proceeded to direct the actions at Monett's Ferry and to formulate a strategy for Alexandria expecting Walker's imminent return. "My plans for following and driving the enemy were to a great extent based upon the assurance that Walker's Div would be kept at my disposal," he reminded Smith sternly.[35]

Taylor accused Smith of meddling in the affairs of his district. He referred not only to the situation with Walker but also to a directive sent from department headquarters to Liddell, east of the Red River. Without notifying Taylor, Smith had requisitioned several guns and a portion of Liddell's force for the campaign in Arkansas. Insisting that the "limited means" placed at his disposal had already hindered his operations, Taylor argued that Liddell's command was "highly important" to the success of his strategy. During the Arkansas campaign Smith had followed protocol to the letter by having Price issue the orders for Fagan's ride, but in this case he had sidestepped departmental procedure. It was improper, Taylor insisted, for Smith to issue orders to officers under his immediate command: "[Such orders] conflict with my arrangements and render my plans for the future so uncertain."[36]

Unable to assault the Federals at Alexandria, Taylor watched the remainder of the enemy fleet, battered from running the gauntlet of sharpshooters that lined the Red River, steam into port. Yet even without Walker, he remained optimistic about his prospects for success. "I have every reason to think," Taylor wrote on April 26, "that the low stage of the river will enable me to capture or make [Porter] destroy a large portion of his fleet which now lies stuck by the falls above Alexandria." On that same day, Porter scuttled the hulking ironclad *Eastport*, which had become inextricably snared in a tangle of rocks and driftwood and been left exposed by the rapidly falling water line.[37]

The lack of manpower motivated Taylor to use psychological warfare against the Federals. According to the recollections of one Louisianan, Taylor ordered "fires built up around at great distances, to simulate campfires; he put drummers and buglers on horseback, and made them sound the calls in every direction, for miles around. He had six thousand; the Federals said he had seventy-five thousand." When Union foraging parties ventured beyond the town, the thinly stretched gray lines greeted them with stiff resistance. "Guerillas are said to be all about us," complained a Federal officer in his diary. In a letter home, a Federal soldier complained that conditions at Alexandria were claustrophobic: "The Rebs closed in all around us so that we could not go out more than a few miles in any direction without meeting them. . . . Thus we were completely cut off from the rest of the world." Taylor reported, "We have a continuous line of pickets enclosing Banks' army and Porter's fleet, and they are as closely besieged as Vicksburg."[38]

With the Federals held hostage by the river and by the Confederates who ringed Alexandria, Taylor renewed his hope that Walker's division would return in time to seal the fate of Banks and Porter. "Day after day we strained our eyes to see the dust of our approaching comrades arise," he reported. In a letter to Walker, Taylor's assistant adjutant Eustace Surget echoed the general's sentiments: "I wish to God you and your Division had been with us and Banks' army would never have reached Alexandria."[39]

While waiting anxiously for Walker, Taylor received a copy of General Order 18, issued by Smith on April 19. The order offered congratulations to the army for the victories at Mansfield and Pleasant Hill. The order read, in part, "The commanding general finds it an appropriate occasion to pay a well-merited tribute to the endurance and valor of the troops engaged in these battles." Yet Smith failed to mention Taylor's role or to congratulate his lieutenant. The order, received on April 27, left Taylor dumbfounded. "This is the only instance within my recollection in which the officer commanding an army was entirely ignored in an order of the kind," he protested to Smith. "I note this because it is singular in itself and in keeping with the treatment I have lately experienced from the general commanding this department." Taylor took this breach of decorum personally, coming as it did on the heels of Smith's seemingly cavalier decision to detach Walker. He resolved to persevere against Banks regardless of the way Smith mishandled the affairs of the department or mistreated his subordinates. "No injustice, no unkindness, even from a quarter whence I had some reason to expect the reverse, will turn me from the great work before me," he pledged. Accustomed to attacks from the Federals, Taylor would not stand for what he perceived to be personal insults from his commanding officer.[40]

The following day, Taylor received another startling letter from Smith. Writing on April 22, less than twenty-four hours before he countermarched Walker, Smith attempted to explain and defend his decision not to aid Louisiana. "Finding that Banks was rapidly retreating," Smith declared, "I ordered Walker to move up to Price's support." The characterization of Bank's retreat as "rapid" indicated that Smith had not based his decision on intelligence from the Louisiana front. Dispatches had emphasized that the enemy was retreating "gradually," and on April 21 Taylor had reported that he planned to attack the Federals to slow their withdrawal from Grand Ecore. Further, on April 20, the day after Banks had begun preparations for his retreat from Grand Ecore, Smith had asked for information from Taylor about the roads from Minden to Campti. The request indicated that Smith sensed an opportunity on the Red River. Thus, Walker prepared to march his infantry to Campti on the same day that Banks fought his way across Monett's Ferry. As the battle raged along the Cane River, Smith changed his mind and ordered Walker to Arkansas. He reasoned that "Walker was too far off to join [Taylor] before the enemy reached Alexandria." Yet the distance from Minden to Alexandria was only twenty-five miles more than that from Minden to Price's position northwest of Camden.[41]

Smith shifted the argument from Louisiana to Arkansas. "Steele had taken a position in Price's front at Camden," he explained, and could not be allowed to hold the town. He further asserted that unless compelled to withdraw, the Federals would reinforce, resupply, and fortify the position. Curiously, Smith failed to explain how the Federals would be resupplied, particularly since he had instructed Fagan's cavalry to cut enemy lines of communications between Camden and Little Rock. If Fagan succeeded, resupply was impossible.[42]

The letter also revealed that the commanding general was unsure of Walker's precise location. Initially Smith announced that the division was forty miles below Camden, but he later wondered whether Walker had already left Minden for Alexandria. He implied that if Walker was en route to Alexandria, then Taylor should countermarch the troops for "important military operations" against Steele. "In both a political and military point of view," Smith insisted, "everything is to be gained for the department" by concentration in Arkansas. Smith acknowledged Taylor's eagerness to pursue Banks toward New Orleans but belittled the idea by suggesting that Polignac or Wharton could handle the operation. In closing, Smith extended an invitation for Taylor to join the Arkansas campaign. "I can place you on duty with your increased rank," he offered, "and would feel that I had left the conduct of operations in safe hands."[43]

Unmoved by the patronizing invitation to serve in Arkansas, Taylor issued a searing rebuttal of Smith's strategy. In a long and emotionally charged letter dated April 28 he condemned Smith's decision to remove Walker's division after the victories at Mansfield and Pleasant Hill, only to hold them at Minden, "a useless position," seventy miles from the front. Taylor accused Smith of using Walker's position at Minden as a pretext for taking the division to Arkansas rather than sending it to Alexandria. Incensed, he charged that these actions not only failed to take into account the strategic situation along the Red River but also betrayed the Shreveport agreement that would have returned Walker to Louisiana.[44]

Without Walker, Taylor's strategy for crushing Banks and capturing Porter's fleet lay in ruins. After seven weeks of campaigning, his health too had begun to fail. Still, Taylor clung tenaciously to his strategic position. Unwilling to admit defeat, he conceded nothing to Smith's assertion that Louisiana was the secondary theater of operations. He challenged the logic of Smith's assumption that Steele, "who had already retreated over 100 miles and been completely foiled in his plans by General Price," would still consider a move on Shreveport. "If such a purpose could be rationally entertained," Taylor persisted, "why not suppose that Banks would advance again from Alexandria?" He reminded Smith that Banks's force far outnumbered Steele's and derided the commander's reluctance to support operations in Louisiana.[45]

The protest was a mere skirmish, and Taylor proceeded to denounce the policies Smith had pursued throughout the campaign. He questioned the "inscrutable purpose" that had first prevented him from following up battlefield victories and then lured him to Shreveport, where he had been "unexpectedly deprived of the bulk of my army." Citing the most recent correspondence, he declared, "I cannot conceive what 'political and military points of view' are to be obtained for the Confederacy by abandoning the certain destruction of an army of 30,000 men, backed by a huge fleet, to chase after a force of 10,000 in full retreat with over 100 miles the start."[46]

Smith's handling of matters before the battle of Mansfield provided still more fodder for Taylor's caustic analysis of the campaign. He accused Smith of having failed to act expeditiously despite the desperate need for troops to meet Banks's advance. It should have taken a mere two hours to distribute ammunition, Taylor claimed, not the twelve days that Churchill and Parsons had spent waiting in Shreveport under the pretext of resupply. Taylor also detailed Smith's systematic bleeding of his command for soldiers to perform noncombat duties at department headquarters. After Pleasant Hill, Smith had ordered the soldiers from Walker's division who staffed department headquarters to return to active duty for the Arkansas campaign. Those from Polignac's command, however, remained mired in the Shreveport bureaucracy. Taylor charged that Smith continually siphoned off troops from Louisiana for the campaign in Arkansas "without even the usual official courtesy of sending the order through my hands."[47]

Smith's decisions and deployments suggested that he did not trust Taylor. Since Pleasant Hill, he had taken Churchill, Parsons, and Walker, surreptitiously detached troops from the District of Western Louisiana, refused to allow Taylor to accompany the Arkansas expedition, violated the Shreveport agreement, and failed to officially acknowledge Taylor's role on the battlefield. In light of these actions, Smith's latest proposal—that Taylor hasten to Arkansas and take the field against Steele—reeked of hypocrisy. "What has occurred since you removed the conduct of operations from my hands after Pleasant Hill," Taylor demanded, "to change your opinion of my capacity?" Indeed, the victory at Mansfield, the pursuit to Pleasant Hill, and the operations against Banks's retreat demonstrated that in leadership ability and grasp of the strategic situation, Taylor far surpassed any other general in the Trans-Mississippi, including Smith.[48]

Secure in the knowledge that Banks and Porter would remain trapped at Alexandria indefinitely, Taylor used their predicament as further ammunition to condemn Smith's enigmatic strategy. He unreservedly avowed that the Federal army and navy would have been destroyed or captured by late April had not Smith disrupted operations in Louisiana. From the hypothetical destruction of Banks and Porter, Taylor projected a scenario that fixed the Confederate position "near the gates of New Orleans." He then addressed the ramifications of this conjecture with respect to Smith's strategy for Arkansas: "I would have been on the way with the bulk of my army to join Price at Camden, enriched with captured spoils of a great army and fleet." Victory in Louisiana, Taylor insisted, would have ensured success for Smith's cherished dream of winning Arkansas and Missouri: "Steele would have been brushed from our path as a cobweb before the broom of a housemaid [and] we would have reached St. Louis, our objective point, by midsummer." Taylor emphasized that without exception, accolades for the campaign would have gone to Smith. "You might have had all the glory" he declared. "I would have been contented to do the work."[49]

Taylor next turned to the notion of glory and unleashed a barrage of personal attacks aimed at Smith and his staff. He accused the general of using the campaign to secure fame for himself and suggested that department headquarters had already begun a crusade to anoint Smith as the architect of the triumphs at Mansfield and Pleasant Hill. Throughout his sixteen months of service under Smith, Taylor claimed, he had desired neither fame nor glory, and he scolded the commander for scheming to take credit for successes that others had engineered: "Your confidential staff might have thrown the blame of every failure on me unrebuked, and claimed the credit of every success for you without contradiction." Taylor also sought to deflect any notion that he himself was interested in personal glory. "I have learned from my ancestors," he wrote, in a reference to his father, "that it is the duty of a soldier so to conduct himself as to dignify titles and not derive importance from them."[50]

Smith might have guessed where this lengthy catalog of grievances and accusations was heading, but Taylor's closing remarks still caught him off guard.

"For more than a year," Taylor reminded the general, "I have supported you, even when your policy was fatally wrong, for I believed it my duty." Circumstances, however, had changed: "Events of the past few weeks have so filled me with discouragement that I much fear I cannot do my whole duty under your command." The day before writing these words, Taylor had confessed that his health was not good, telling Smith that "a low fever has prostrated me" but that he was able to remain in the saddle and active along the front. Now, however, having reviewed Smith's April 22 message from Arkansas, Taylor felt that he could no longer continue to serve under his command: "I ask that you take steps to relieve me as soon as it can be done without injury to the service."[51]

Smith could not afford to lose Taylor. His popularity among the citizens of Louisiana, combined with their growing mistrust of the regime at Shreveport, made Taylor's continued service vital to the stability of the department. By the time Smith received the letter, the campaign in Arkansas was over. On May 8, the same day Walker's division marched out of Camden to rejoin the forces in Louisiana, Smith issued a terse response to Taylor's letter. "Respectfully returned to General Taylor," the message began. "This communication is not only improper but unjust. I cannot believe but that it was written in a moment of irritation or sickness." And so for the time being, Taylor remained in command. Smith proceeded to busy himself mopping up after operations in Arkansas, leaving Taylor with his hands full at Alexandria.[52]

10

This Fatal Blunder

Unfortunately for the Louisiana Confederates, Joseph Bailey, a Union officer from Wisconsin, devised a plan to free the ships trapped by the low water level above Alexandria. On May 2 nearly three thousand workers began a massive, round-the-clock project to build a series of dams across the river. The Federals needed to raise the water level at least six feet to free the fleet that Porter had once boasted could run "wherever the sand was damp." Taylor's forces south and west of Alexandria were unable to mount a concerted attack on the construction sites. On the northeastern bank, Liddell had better access to the labor details. Yet he failed to demonstrate effectively against the workers, and the Federals completed the dams in one week. On May 13 the last of Porter's fleet slipped past the falls and steamed into the lower Red River as the Federal infantry prepared to leave Alexandria.[1]

Although Taylor did not possess the strength to prevent construction of the dams, he hoped his sharpshooters could delay the progress long enough for reinforcements to arrive. A wary Federal noted that the Rebels dug "rifle pits along the shore for 3 miles [where] the infantry could pick off the pilots and boatmen." As Union infantry sought to push the perimeter beyond the range of Taylor's firepower, Confederate skirmishers drove them back into their works along the riverbanks. A Confederate officer west of Alexandria contended that if Liddell had attacked from the east side of the river, which was densely wooded and lined with bluffs, the Federals "would never have gotten away." Taylor immediately assigned Smith the blame for the Federal escape from Alexandria.[2]

Taylor accused Smith of insisting on a strategy that threw "a protecting shield around the Federal army and fleet." During the aborted Alexandria siege, numerous couriers and staff officers raced north from Taylor's camp to advise Smith of conditions along the river. The Federal work details toiled in the open while the navy relied on Banks's unnerved infantry for protection. "The enemy was daily attacked," reported Taylor, "and confined closely to his lines around Alexandria." He hoped Smith would hurry reinforcements to help delay construction until troops from the Arkansas campaign could reach Alexandria to contest the Federal flight. "Not a man was sent to me," Taylor fumed, and he condemned Smith for having reduced his strength in Louisiana at a time when the enemy was most vulnerable.[3]

Alleged incompetence on the part of his commanding officer did not stop Taylor from assigning tactical blame for the failure at Alexandria to Liddell. Taylor reprimanded the brigadier for his reluctance to attack enemy outposts east of the river and for refusing to disrupt construction crews. On May 8, five days before Porter made good his escape, Taylor had ordered Liddell to "harass the enemy at Pineville, and at their works on the falls." He also warned that failure to carry out those instructions "would necessitate a change in the command." Already upset with Taylor for rejecting his proposal to occupy Alexandria ahead of the Federal retreat, Liddell balked at committing his troops to this latest plan. The following day Liddell received instructions to divide his command and leave a detachment near Pineville while the majority of his force moved to a position below Alexandria. The instructions left him confused and irritated. "I could not reconcile the conflicting orders, accompanied particularly with a gratuitous threat," he grumbled. Flustered, Liddell left a small force to monitor the Federals at Pineville and marched the remainder of his brigade south of Alexandria. Despite the redeployment, neither the dam nor the Pineville outpost came under attack, and the fleet evacuated Alexandria relatively unscathed. Liddell did not wait for Taylor to remove him from command. He requested to be relieved from duty even before Porter completed his escape. Taylor complied, and Liddell, leaving his brigade below Alexandria, rode to Shreveport.[4]

Upon his arrival at department headquarters, Liddell requested a conference with Smith, who had just returned from Arkansas. Aware of the increasingly strained relations between Taylor and Smith, Liddell sought a sympathetic forum in which to present his grievances against Taylor and to solicit redress. Liddell had disliked Taylor since their initial meeting in January 1864. He had found Taylor to be a "very self-important and self-opinionated" individual who ruled Louisiana like a despot. Now, four months after that first meeting, he found himself on the receiving end of Taylor's "arbitrary will" following an operation that Liddell considered a "wretchedly mismanaged business under the guidance of a foolish man." Liddell was also aware of Taylor's tendency to blame subordinates for battlefield failures and to go into "paroxysms of passionate abuse of his officers for not repairing faults which he himself had committed." A consultation with

Smith was Liddell's opportunity to set the record straight and turn the tables on his nemesis.[5]

At the meeting, Liddell criticized Taylor for failing to strike the Federals at Alexandria from the west bank. He described Taylor's location as "equally, if not more convenient to the enemy's works" than his own position east of the river. Liddell claimed, mistakenly, that Taylor had crippled his operational capacity by sending the artillery east of the river to join Smith's campaign in Arkansas. The general also complained that his force consisted of fewer than six hundred soldiers, while Taylor had ten times that number of troops and at least fifty guns.[6]

Although Taylor was partially to blame, Liddell's argument had little merit. Outnumbered and in an inferior position, Taylor had mounted a capable, albeit uncoordinated, effort to slow the construction of the dams. According to Xavier DeBray, a cavalry officer stationed west of Alexandria, "The standing order was to attack every day and annoy the enemy by every possible means." In fact, the fire from Confederate guns grew so fierce at times that some Federals anticipated an assault on their works and slept in line of battle. "The rebels seem bent on giving us no rest," complained a fatigued Federal. The Confederate troops expended so much powder and ordnance that on May 4, Taylor warned department headquarters of the impending supply problem and on May 7 withdrew many of his guns "for want of ammunition."[7]

Taylor's plan relied heavily on Liddell to take the initiative east of the river. Liddell had operated independently throughout the Red River campaign, and Taylor praised him for making a swift dash into Pineville and securing the area beyond the town. Taylor counted on Liddell to remain aggressive and strike the enemy regardless of activity on the west bank. Liddell's troops were undisciplined, however, consisting primarily of conscripts and deserters, and because Taylor overestimated Liddell's capacity for independent command, he failed to reinforce the battalions with veteran troops. As a result, while the Confederates west of the river engaged the enemy around the clock, Liddell's sorties were sporadic and disjointed. The results were ruinous. "Liddell's force was operating but the energy which was expected was not displayed," Taylor reported. Moreover, Taylor left much to chance and failed to develop a plan of attack that coordinated actions on both sides of the river. As construction on the dams progressed, the Confederates forfeited an opportunity to foil Banks and Porter. In that sense the failure at Alexandria was similar to that at Monett's Ferry. In both instances Taylor relied on a general officer who was not able to exploit the situation at his front. From

Taylor's point of view, Smith's failure to return the infantry to Louisiana left him with no alternative.[8]

As their meeting continued, Smith listened calmly to Liddell's blistering attack on Taylor. When the brigadier alleged that Taylor had sent his artillery to Arkansas, however, Smith did not admit to having issued the order himself and let the error stand. Liddell presented a stack of communications from Taylor that he characterized as "exhibiting childishness and absurdities unbecoming an officer." At this, Smith stood up, grabbed the papers, and "threw them down abruptly on the table before him, saying, 'General Taylor's mind is affected from the paralysis he had some years since, and is hardly responsible.'" Liddell shot back, "General, he should not be in such a place, when so much is at stake for others. I will serve no more under such a man." Smith approved the request but left Liddell dumbfounded by his sympathetic attitude toward Taylor. "General Smith still continued to apologize for and mitigate Taylor's follies," marveled Liddell, "evidently influenced by the kindest feelings. He never gave me the slightest intimation of difference between them, though it had not only been common rumor but I had indications of misunderstandings from official endorsements of papers forwarded by me." Regardless of the accusations against Taylor, there was little Smith could do. The Federals still occupied much of Taylor's territory, and Walker's division was rushing to rejoin the campaign against Banks. "I have every confidence in your ability and judgment," he confided to Taylor after the meeting with Liddell.[9]

After Porter's warships and transports steamed away from Alexandria, Banks's army resumed its retreat. Before the Federal infantry left, however, General Andrew Jackson Smith, who commanded the detachment of troops from Sherman's army, instructed his men to fire the town. The Confederates on both riverbanks watched in horror as the atrocity unfolded. "Little boys and girls running . . . crying for their mothers and fathers; old men leaning on a staff for support to their trembling limbs, hurrying away from the suffocating heat . . . driven from their burning homes into the streets, leaving everything behind but the clothes they then wore," recalled a Federal who witnessed the act. A Confederate survivor testified that Union soldiers smeared houses, commercial structures, fencing, and outbuildings "with a mixture of turpentine and camphene, saying that they 'were preparing the place for Hell.'" As Alexandria burned, A. J. Smith rode through the streets waving his sword and encouraging his troops by shouting, "Hurrah, boys, this looks like war."[10]

By the time the Federals had gone and the Confederates entered the town, there were only two houses left standing in the main district. Arriving on the scene, General Polignac accused the enemy of "taking a wanton revenge for having been defeated . . . upon the non-combattants women, children, old men & even slaves whom in many instances they robbed of all they had accumulated, with the frantic madness of despair." With Porter's fleet gone and Banks's army marching to safety, Taylor's plans to save Louisiana were wrecked beyond repair. The wanton destruction of Alexandria left him embittered toward both the Federals and Smith. Taylor criticized Banks for having "lost authority over some of his troops" and condemned Smith for failing to capitalize on opportunities that "required no more than ordinary energy for [their] accomplishment."[11]

On May 14 Taylor notified Smith that the enemy had evacuated Alexandria and burned the town. He vowed to regroup his forces and pursue the Federals "to the bank of the Mississippi, and beyond if possible." Unlike the Cane River Valley, the terrain below Alexandria did not afford a strong position for the Confederates to contest the Federal retreat, and Taylor harbored no illusions of bringing on a general engagement. All that remained was the opportunity to harass the enemy and force Banks to destroy large quantities of supplies before he crossed the Mississippi.[12]

Bitterly, Taylor turned his attention to the disposal of Walker's division, still on the way to Alexandria. "The troops from above cannot reach me in time to begin this campaign," he lamented in a letter to Smith, and he offered to halt Walker at Campti to rest and reorganize the weary division. "[Walker's] presence here at the right time would have insured the most brilliant results," Taylor added pointedly, "but such opportunities never occur twice in the same campaign."[13]

Anticipating that Banks would successfully complete his escape, Taylor revived plans to lead his troops into the Lafourche. Unbeknownst to Smith, he had already sought to circumvent the authority of the commanding general and secure support for the campaign from outside the department. On May 12 Taylor apprised Texas district commander John B. Magruder that he had written to generals Leonidas Polk and Tom Taylor (no relation) in the Department of Alabama, Mississippi, and East Louisiana, "soliciting their cooperation . . . in a demonstration against New Orleans." The violation of military protocol, and the failure to mention the petitions to his commanding officer, meant that Taylor still considered the District of Western Louisiana an independent command and planned to move into the Lafourche with or without Smith's permission. Taylor suggested to Smith that the remainder of the department's resources make ready for a summer campaign into Missouri.[14]

Taylor continued to harass Banks's withdrawal as the Federal column snaked through the swamps and bayous that emerged at Marksville, a village on the Avoyelles prairie. Banks drove the stubborn Confederate cavalry beyond the town and occupied Marksville on May 15. From there he planned to march to Simmesport, a small town on the Atchafalaya River about twenty miles distant. From Simmesport he could cross the Atchafalaya into the relative safety of occupied eastern Louisiana. A bend in the Red River took the Federal line of march away from the river and put the column on an inland road that ran through the hamlet of Mansura, less than five miles south of Marksville. Here Taylor concentrated his forces and decided to contest the enemy retreat.[15]

To block the Federals, Taylor arrayed his troops across the Simmesport road on a sprawling meadow in front of Mansura. Arthur Bagby and James Major patrolled the right flank while DeBray's Texans and Polignac's infantry held the left. At daybreak on May 16 sporadic firing across the lines escalated into a fierce skirmish as Banks deployed his army and attempted to push the Rebels back. After two months of hard campaigning, the Federals were eager to bring the proceedings to a close as soon as possible. Henry C. Fike, an Illinois soldier in the Union Sixteenth Corps, experienced a feeling of anxious exhilaration as the Yankee brigades moved forward: "Our entire army was drawn up in line of battle stretching entirely across the plain south of Marksville and presented the most magnificent sight I ever saw, or ever expect to see. In my opinion nothing in the war of the kind has equalled it." But the opening phase of the fighting produced a sense of uneasiness among the blue ranks. As one Federal explained in a letter home, "The rebs would stand and fight like tigers for 1/2 hour or so then would retreat." The Confederate retreat was part of Taylor's plan. As the skirmishers fell back, they drew Banks into the open where Taylor's main force waited in line of battle.[16]

The position that Taylor had selected the night before gave his army a distinct advantage, one that compensated for the discrepancy in numbers. "The broad, open prairie, smooth as a billiard table, afforded an admirable field for artillery practice," Taylor later reported. The Confederates swiftly brought thirty-two guns to bear against Banks's army. Many of the artillery pieces were guns captured from the Federals during the battle of Mansfield. "Shot and shell flew in every direction," commented a Federal, adding, "The shells would strike the smooth grassy plaine and then rise again and shift from point to point until they were spent or exploded." The advance staggered under heavy fire, and the Federals fell back grudgingly. Banks ordered his batteries forward, and for the next four hours the blue and the gray engaged in a thunderous artillery duel described by one Federal as a game of "ball play." [17]

The overwhelming size of the Federal force enabled Banks to mass two corps against the Confederate left. While his artillery pounded the Confederate lines, Banks's infantry moved to turn Taylor's position and threaten his trains on the Evergreen road. Outnumbered on the flank by more than three to one, Taylor wisely determined not to risk a general engagement and abandoned the field to the enemy. After looting Mansura, Banks's men resumed their hurried retreat to Simmesport. For the remainder of the day the Union columns paused only to beat back Confederate cavalry thrusts and to wreck the small village of Evergreen, where, as one Federal admitted, "the soldiers ransacked every house and turned things upside down." As Confederate cavalry increased their pressure on the Federal flanks and rear, Taylor moved the remainder of his force into position near Simmesport. "The campaign here will close to-morrow," he reported to department headquarters. [18]

While he waited, Taylor requested information from Smith on the prospects for a Missouri campaign. At the same time, he took the opportunity to reiterate his plan to occupy the Lafourche. Taylor tied the movement of Walker's division to both theaters. Referring to his May 14 letter to Smith, Taylor declared, "I will await for a day or two the decision of department headquarters on my suggestion of a Missouri movement." Then, using the same stratagem he had employed to circumvent Smith's orders prohibiting a battle at Mansfield, Taylor added a condition: "Not hearing, I will order down Walker's division, throw myself into the Lafourche, confine the enemy to New Orleans, and close the navigation of the Mississippi." Thus, Taylor made control of Walker's infantry and a campaign toward New Orleans contingent on a timely reply from Smith. As his struggle with Banks in the field wound down, Taylor recommenced hostilities with Smith over operations in his district. [19]

Before receiving Taylor's May 16 letter, Smith issued a favorable reply to the suggested Missouri campaign. He pointed out that Price had already received orders to prepare for an advance into the Arkansas Valley and "ultimately on Missouri." The assertion was misleading. Smith did not issue the instructions to Price until May 19, two days after he responded to Taylor. However, in a May 17 correspondence to Price he had misrepresented the strategic situation in the department by taking remarks from Taylor's May 14 letter out of context. Smith advised Price, "Major-General Taylor reports that the Sixteenth and Seventeenth Army Corps will be sent up the river," and instructed him to prepare to attack the transports. In fact, Taylor merely stated that these troops would not accompany Banks to New Orleans. While Taylor had hoped this intelligence would bolster his argument for a campaign in the Lafourche, Smith twisted the information to strengthen his own case for a Missouri campaign. Moreover, he directed Price to restructure his command and make room for Taylor's arrival.[20]

To Taylor, Smith stressed the notion that once the Federals withdrew from western Louisiana, Arkansas and Missouri would become the "true field of operations" for the department's forces. Urging the Louisianan to join the campaign into Arkansas, Smith maintained that Taylor should assign a reliable force for the defense of western Louisiana and then prepare the remainder of his command for the march to Arkansas. He requested a personal interview with Taylor to discuss the strategy for the operations and offered to meet at any point between Shreveport and Alexandria at Taylor's convenience.[21]

Although Smith acknowledged that Walker's Texans were fast approaching Alexandria, he did not divulge his immediate plans for the division. The outline he presented for Arkansas and Missouri implied that Walker would not continue to move south for operations in the Lafourche. Upon the conclusion of the Red River campaign, Smith indicated that Taylor should accompany Walker's division on its march back to Arkansas. He ignored Taylor's contention that the Federals were vulnerable along the banks of the southern Mississippi and refused to address his strategy for the Lafourche. In later correspondence with Jefferson Davis, Smith would characterize Taylor's proposal as unduly hazardous and "barren of military results."[22]

On May 17, the day Smith sent his reply to Taylor, the Federals pressed their retreat along the Simmesport road. Passing through Moreauville and across the Yellow Bayou, a small, sluggish tributary of the Atchafalaya, Banks faced steady fire from Taylor's troopers. Butternut skirmishers further slowed the retreat until midafternoon, when the vanguard of Banks's army finally took possession of Simmesport, a mere ghost town at this point in the campaign. The following morning found most of the Federal army concentrated in and around the ruined village, but their escape would have to wait. Banks soon discovered, much to his consternation, that the Atchafalaya had crested and his troops could not cross even with Yankee-engineered pontoons. For the third time since they began their retreat, the Federals found themselves trapped between the Confederates and the river. Unlike the predicaments at Grand Ecore and Alexandria, however, Banks could not look to the fleet to help drive off Taylor's Confederates. Only the Federal rear guard, holding a tenuous position east of the Yellow Bayou, stood between Banks and Taylor.[23]

Banks again turned to Joseph Bailey, the officer whose engineering designs had freed the fleet at Alexandria. Bailey gathered all available boats and transports and lashed them together to span the raging Atchafalaya. He then ordered timber and boards laid across the boats to form a crude plank road over which Banks's hapless army could finally cross to safety. As Bailey proceeded with his project, the tactical situation to Banks's rear created a growing concern. Once the main Federal force began to cross to the east bank of the river, they would leave behind a progressively smaller force on the west bank to hold off Taylor's persistent attacks. To secure the retreat, Banks ordered the rear guard to recross the Yellow Bayou and drive the Confederates away.[24]

At midmorning a Federal force of forty-five hundred under James A. Mower crossed to the west bank of Yellow Bayou and began to dislodge the large gaggle of Confederate skirmishers. Three brigades of Union infantry pursued the Rebels for two miles across marshlands and through gnarled thickets. Along the Bayou De Glaise, Mower emerged from a belt of woods and discovered Taylor's entire force of five thousand in battle formation. In a troop deployment similar to that at Mansfield, Taylor used the woods along the edges of a sugarcane field on the Norwood plantation to conceal the alignment of his army. He ordered a frontal assault under cover of artillery, before the enemy could fully deploy. Simultaneously, Confederate horsemen closed in from the flanks and attempted a dual envelopment of the Federal lines. The Federals rushed forward to meet the attack, and the armies drew to "within twenty-five to forty yards of each other" before opening fire. One Texas horseman called the engagement "the hottest fight I ever experienced during the war." The battle raged back and forth for five hours under a broiling Louisiana sun with neither army able to hold the ground it gained. "Rebs attempted to charge 3 times but were swept down like a field of ripe wheat through which a tornado had past," affirmed a midwesterner in Union blue. Soldiers on both sides were wilting from the lack of potable water, and many fell from sunstroke. Late in the afternoon a wide expanse of dried underbrush caught fire from the exploding shells and burned out of control. The fire effectively separated the warring armies and gave the opposing commanders an opportunity to disengage. At dusk, the Federals withdrew to Simmesport and Taylor withdrew toward Moreauville.[25]

For Banks, the action at Yellow Bayou bought the time necessary for his army to cross the Atchafalaya. For Taylor, the fight accomplished little more than a needless loss of life. Confederate casualties exceeded 500 while the Federals lost 350 men. Some Confederate soldiers believed that the battle of Yellow Bayou taught the Federals a lesson. Others, however, considered the lesson a costly exercise in futility. According to a member of the Louisiana brigade, Polignac had argued against the attack and challenged the wisdom of "risking the lives of his men in an engagement that could not possibly result in any advantage." Xavier DeBray characterized Yellow Bayou as an "unfortunate and unnecessary affair." "The only result," he marveled, "was to delay the enemy in reaching the eastern side of the Atchafalaya, where we wanted him to go." Yet despite the prevailing opinion that the losses at Yellow Bayou were not commensurate with the strategic gains, few held Taylor responsible. Instead, John Wharton, to whom Taylor had assigned tactical control of operations from Alexandria to Simmesport, bore the ignominy of a pointless victory.[26]

Wharton's role on the field, however, does not exempt Taylor from criticism for a lapse in strategic judgment. On May 14, three days before the battle, Taylor announced his plans for driving Banks out of western Louisiana. "I have not the pretension to attempt to fight a general battle with my little force," he assured Smith. He planned to harass Banks until the Federals crossed the river and acknowledged that even without a general engagement the campaign would soon end. Yet Taylor reversed himself at Yellow Bayou and attacked the enemy with his entire force, despite the absence of a clearly defined strategic objective. The numerical strength of Banks's rear guard, roughly equal to Taylor's whole army, presented an enticing opportunity for the Confederates. However, even if Taylor had destroyed the Federal rear guard, the main body of Banks's army would still have crossed the Atchafalaya.[27]

The decision to attack a retreating enemy attempting to withdraw to safety across a river had more in common with Smith's strategy in Arkansas than with Stonewall Jackson's generalship in the Shenandoah. While Jackson touted the pursuit of a routed enemy, he also emphasized that a good commander must utilize the military principles of surprise and maneuver, particularly when pitted against a numerically superior force. Taylor neither surprised nor outmaneuvered Banks at Yellow Bayou. Instead, he ordered an attack against an enemy whose only objective was to delay pursuit of the main Federal column. This was precisely what Smith had done against Steele at Jenkins' Ferry. Yet Taylor leveled scathing criticism at Smith for "marching against a retreating foe" who would have retired even "if the fight [at Jenkins' Ferry had] never occurred." In both cases, all that was necessary to secure the withdrawal was pressure from cavalry. By the time of the battles at Jenkins' Ferry and Yellow Bayou, the opportunity to destroy the Federal invasion columns in Arkansas and Louisiana had already slipped out of the Confederates' reach. Smith and Taylor, however, insisted on committing infantry to the pursuit and in initiating pitched battles. The hollow victories at Jenkins' Ferry and Yellow Bayou neither secured the Federal withdrawal nor enhanced the condition of the Confederacy in the Trans-Mississippi.[28]

"The campaign may be considered closed here, where it opened on the 12th of last March," Taylor reported on May 19 from Moreauville. "It has been a most arduous one to me and this army." His command suffered forty-three hundred casualties during the two months of campaigning while inflicting fifty-four hundred on the Federal invasion force. By contrast, Smith lost twenty-three hundred in Arkansas while the enemy suffered nearly twenty-eight hundred killed, wounded, or captured. As the Red River campaign reached its military conclusion, Taylor renewed his criticism of Smith's strategy. "Nothing but the withdrawal of Walker's division from me has prevented the capture of Banks' army and the destruction of Porter's fleet," he complained. "I feel bitterly about this, because my army has been robbed of the just measure of its glory and the country of the most brilliant and complete success of the war." Walker concurred with Taylor's post-mortem analysis. "To this fatal blunder," he asserted, "Banks was indebted for his safety."[29]

Taylor returned to Alexandria to begin preparations for his Lafourche campaign. He ordered Confederate cavalry to cross the Atchafalaya and gather information on Federal troop disposition but notified Smith that the infantry, "utterly worn down with marching and fighting," would remain in Alexandria to rest and resupply. By insisting that Walker's and Polignac's divisions were too jaded to "engage in very active service in any quarter," Taylor accomplished three objectives. First, he gave the troops an opportunity to recover from the months of harsh campaigning. Second, he kept the infantry concentrated near Alexandria and in position for use in the Lafourche. Third, he reasserted operational control over Walker's division. Taylor's focus shifted quickly to an emphasis on resupply rather than resumption of military operations. Without immediate resupply, he argued on May 23, it would be "impossible to act on the defensive, much less upon the offensive." Outlining the desperate need for shoes, clothing, and animals, Taylor insisted that Shreveport had ignored his pleas for over twelve months. "I cannot too urgently impress upon department headquarters the vital importance of immediate action which will resupply my wants in this department."[30]

Taylor acknowledged receipt of Smith's May 17 letter, which urged him to prepare his command for operations in Arkansas and Missouri, but he did not respond directly to the suggestion. Instead, he complained of "suffering from sickness and exhaustion" and promised to respond as soon as his health allowed. The following day, May 24, Taylor was well enough to write a lengthy reply to Smith's proposals. Citing his failing health, Taylor balked at participating in the Missouri campaign. "I scarcely believe I will be able . . . to conduct the affairs of my present command," he predicted. Contrary to Smith's enthusiasm for a summer campaign, Taylor asserted that the fall presented a better opportunity for success and argued that the Confederates should spend the summer in preparation. Taylor thus directly contradicted the endorsement of a summer campaign he had made ten days earlier. On May 14 he had contended that twenty thousand troops could reach the Missouri River before the summer passed and secure Missouri for the Confederacy. "There can be no doubt that this is the last campaign of the war," Taylor had forecast, and he urged Smith to act.[31]

Upon receipt of Taylor's May 14 letter, Smith asked for a face-to-face strategy session. Rather than agree to the request, Taylor submitted a detailed outline for the conquest of Arkansas and Missouri. To lay the groundwork for the campaign, he insisted first that the bureaucratic labyrinth at Shreveport—"liberal in promise and utterly barren in performance"—undergo radical change. He also itemized several departmental modifications deemed imperative for efficient support of the campaign and presented a strategy for reorganizing the army and deploying troops. Taylor stressed that the Arkansas division required new leadership. He implored Smith to replace Thomas Churchill, who was "no soldier" and would "never succeed in the field." Taylor warned that Churchill's failure to tend to detail would doom any operation dependent upon his military abilities. "I regard the troops intrusted to his command as almost lost to the service," he declared. Certainly, Churchill's failure at Pleasant Hill and his mediocre performance at Jenkins' Ferry supported Taylor's evaluation, and the merit of the recommendation was not lost on Smith.[32]

Taylor's letters of May 14 and 24 supported many of the same objectives for a Missouri campaign that Smith had been attempting to secure since his arrival in the Trans-Mississippi. Taylor's real goal, however, was to resume operations in the Lafourche. While Smith managed the army's reorganization and prepared for the campaign in Missouri, Taylor intended to move troops toward New Orleans, ostensibly to gather supplies and recruits. Taylor's earlier resistance to a push into Missouri had sprung from a desire to defend Louisiana. The Red River campaign, however, had cleared the Federals from his district. With Confederate troops concentrated below Alexandria and Smith preparing to march into Arkansas, Taylor faced few impediments to a unilateral movement toward New Orleans. His support for the Missouri campaign notwithstanding, Taylor sought to reestablish the autonomy in western Louisiana that he had initially enjoyed upon taking command in 1862, and that Smith's authority had slowly eroded.[33]

To conclude his analysis of the proposed foray into Arkansas and Missouri, Taylor insisted that Confederate success depended entirely upon the reform of Smith's bureaucracy in Shreveport, which he compared to "a disproportionated garment—all ruffles and no shirt." Taylor singled out Smith's headquarters for particularly harsh criticism. The general staff, he declared, existed purely to serve its own interests rather than "to promote the efficiency of the little army." Taylor upbraided Smith for allowing the troops in the field to suffer while his personal staff grew to bloated proportions. "Requisitions for the most important articles upon which depend the fate of the campaign are lost in a mingled maze of red tape and circumlocution," he complained, and he assured Smith that these opinions were "shared by every intelligent officer of this army."[34]

There were indeed others in the department who agreed with Taylor's assessment of the administration at Shreveport. From inside headquarters, Smith's own chief of staff emerged as one of Taylor's allies. William Boggs witnessed first-hand the inefficiency of the department and acknowledged "that in a department capable of supplying Europe with beef, [Taylor's] district had received scarcely enough to supply his hospitals." After the war Boggs provided an explanation for the inefficiency. He alleged that Smith often filled positions in the bureaucracy on the basis of favoritism and personality rather than qualifications. Boggs characterized the department quartermaster as mediocre, the head of the Nitre and Mining Bureau as "impracticable," and the chief commissary officer as "entirely out of place [having] neither the education or ability to take in the work of the department." He also described three of Smith's personal aides as "unexceptional gentlemen in every respect" and complained that the general carried two personal surgeons on his staff, one "indolent and selfish" and the other having "no specific duties." Boggs indicated that the Smith regime seemed insulated from the hardships of war and claimed that until the battle of Mansfield, the staff at department headquarters frequently regaled themselves with dinner parties, dances, and reviews.[35]

The suspicion of incompetence at headquarters had a corrosive effect on the entire department. "Hydrocephalus at Shreveport produced atrophy elsewhere," Taylor noted in his memoirs, and he blamed Smith's management style for creating derelict conditions throughout the Trans-Mississippi. In Taylor's estimation, Smith was less concerned with the troops in the field than with the prominence of his department: "The commander of the Trans-Mississippi Department displayed much ardor in the establishment of bureaux, and on a scale proportioned rather to the extent of his territory than to the smallness of his force." If this assertion was true, and Taylor no doubt believed that it was, then conditions in the department would continue to deteriorate. During the Red River campaign Taylor's district had suffered while Smith manipulated the department's resources for personal gain. Furthermore, Smith had mismanaged the military with poor timing, clumsy campaigning, and a reckless disregard for his troops. This left Taylor two options. He could attempt to operate his district as an independent command, or he could resign.[36]

Taylor closed his May 24 letter to Smith with a reminder that his April 28 appeal still stood: "I repeat the request previously made, that I be relieved from duty in this department." Taylor had no doubt calculated that this latest denunciation of his commanding officer would hasten his own removal from command. Given his intelligence, his skill with words, and the strength of his desire to escape Smith's control, it is unlikely that his increasingly vitriolic letters represented spontaneous outbursts of rage. Rather, they were carefully crafted diatribes intended to secure his own release.[37]

In two letters, written ten days apart, Smith methodically addressed Taylor's criticisms and demands. In the first, written on May 26, Smith concerned himself with Taylor's April 28 letter. He chastised Taylor for the "objectionable and improper" tone of the correspondence, which he characterized as "most unjust." Throughout the remainder of the letter, Smith defended his use of Walker's Texans during the Red River campaign. Smith pointed out that "[although] you complain bitterly of the withdrawal of Walker's division and say it has robbed your army of the just measure of its glory," it was in fact Taylor who had selected Walker for the campaign. Further, he emphasized that Taylor had "distinctly expressed [his] approval of the movement" and had planned to accompany the Texans to Arkansas. Unlike Taylor, Smith did not use this letter as a platform for personal criticism.

In fact, he mentioned Taylor's ill health as a component in the deteriorating relationship between the generals. He also sought to deflect criticism of his strategy by detailing the circumstances that surrounded Walker's march to Arkansas. Notably absent from Smith's recollection of events, however, was his sudden decision to leave Taylor in Louisiana—the affront that had so bruised Taylor's pride that he still carried the resentment. Smith ended his letter with a remark that could do nothing but inflame Taylor further. "The complete success of the campaign was determined by the overthrow of Steele at Jenkins' Ferry," he insisted, and not by the defeat of Banks at Mansfield and Pleasant Hill.[38]

Having issued a defense of his Red River strategy, Smith spent the next week drafting a reply to Taylor's detailed letter of May 24. This time Taylor's trenchant remarks seem to have hit a nerve, for Smith's June 5 reply had an angry tone that had been absent from his previous communications with Taylor. "I shall no further reply to your letter than to call your attention to some of the inaccurate and unjust statements made therein," he bristled. Smith quoted each of Taylor's complaints before offering a response. In response to the accusation that the troops had lacked shoes, he insisted that they had otherwise been well equipped. To the charge that they had been "insufficiently supplied with food," he answered that the chief commissary stated there had been "abundant supplies." To the complaint that "there are no horses for the artillery," he replied that "arrangements recently made" would soon "meet all its wants." Smith disputed Taylor's contention that troop strength had "dwindled to nothing," and that the Conscript Department had failed to act, presenting statistics to refute both claims.[39]

These issue were impersonal, and Smith addressed them accordingly. Taylor's attack on Smith's character, however, evoked a more emotional response. Taylor had mocked Smith's organizational skills at Shreveport by claiming that "the number of bureaus ... [in the department] and the army of employees attached to them would do honor to St. Petersburg or Paris." Smith pointed to instructions from Richmond as justification and insisted that he had organized bureaus at department headquarters according to the advice of the Secretary of War: "They are but few in number and have but few employes." To support his claim, Smith provided Taylor with a list of agencies and enclosed a register of the men assigned to each. To Taylor's charge that the administrative "Shreveport Maelstrom" forcibly consumed some of his soldiers, Smith replied that the "large shops, arsenals, and depots of supplies required guards." He pressed this point and accused Taylor of failing to comply with orders to provide men for this purpose. Finally, Smith refused to address Taylor's charge that a "maze of red tape" had hampered the Confederates in the Red River campaign and would derail the proposed Missouri campaign. "This is such a general statement that I cannot answer it," he snapped, and with that the letter came to an abrupt end. Taylor had drawn battle lines, and Smith had chosen to cross them. Although he could have ignored Taylor's personal attacks, Smith elected to confront the charges with a defensive war of words.[40]

Upon receiving Smith's May 26 communiqué, Taylor fired off another lengthy tirade. "You are mistaken in supposing that my communications were intended as complaints," Taylor announced on June 5. "I have no complaints to make. My communications were statements of facts." He then raised the stakes. Declaring that truth was often "considered objectionable by superiors," Taylor pledged that he would continue to speak his mind. "From no man living have I ever begged an indulgence for my acts, whether personal or official," he warned Smith.[41]

Picking the scabs of wounds that had barely healed, Taylor now replayed his April 13 and 15 meetings with Smith. He rejected Smith's contention that he had endorsed the campaign against Steele and denied that he had willingly sent Walker to Arkansas. He insisted that Smith's irrational fear of Steele provided the basis for the Arkansas campaign and charged that the commander had refused to consider sound arguments for continued concentration against Banks. Moreover, Taylor implied that Smith had coerced him into endorsing the campaign by threatening to hand-pick the troops for Arkansas from Taylor's command. Taylor alleged that only after he recognized the intransigence of Smith's position did he sanction the campaign, select Walker, and offer to accompany the troops to Arkansas. Even then, he claimed to have understood "most distinctly" that should Steele begin to retreat, the Confederate "movement northward would stop at once."[42]

Accordingly, Taylor charged that on the eve of the Arkansas campaign Smith had violated their agreement and betrayed his trust. He revealed that information secured from the department's quartermaster confirmed that Smith had intended all along to take the field in Arkansas without him. He had deliberately misled Taylor. Taylor denounced Smith's conduct as an insulting breach of professional faith: "You permitted me to move 40 miles to Shreveport, leave my command, and make all arrangements for a campaign which you had determined I was not to make. From the 13th to the night of the 15th, I remained under this delusion, which you by a word, could have dispelled." Taylor also complained that Smith knew Steele was in retreat and yet had refused to honor his commitment to release Walker.

"I repeated the arguments against the movement, but was overruled," he reminded Smith. "In justification of your policy you observed that it was an affair of a few days, and in answer to my inquiry stated positively that Walker's division was not to be removed from my command."[43]

The Federal column in Arkansas had enjoyed a head start on Smith of over one hundred miles. Given this information, Smith could not have seriously believed that the campaign would take only a few days. While Smith slogged after Steele through the river bottoms of south-central Arkansas, Banks and Porter lay trapped at Alexandria and vulnerable to attack. Taylor had taken Smith at his word and waited in vain for Walker's return. Without Walker, he could do nothing—neither sustain an effective assault at Alexandria nor inflict significant damage during Banks's retreat. For this he would not forgive Smith. The situation was even more galling to Taylor in light of Smith's decision to exclude him from the Arkansas campaign. In so doing Smith may have hoped to head off a situation potentially rife with disagreement, but the decision backfired. Had Taylor accompanied the expedition, his difficulties with Banks and Porter might not have become such an obsession. But as matters stood, Taylor's exclusion had merely fostered more ill will. He perceived Smith's withdrawal of Walker's division as an unforgivable breach of faith.[44]

In an extraordinary written attack on a superior officer, Taylor's June 5 letter revealed the core of his quarrel with Smith. "You state that the fruits of the victory at Mansfield were secured by the march of the column against Steele," he recounted, "and that the complete success of the campaign was determined by his overthrow at Jenkins' Ferry. . . . Banks was driven into his works at Alexandria on April 28, two days before the fight at Jenkins' Ferry. . . . I am at a loss to conceive what connection the fruits of Mansfield have with the fight at Jenkins' Ferry." The most incriminating evidence Taylor presented to support this charge was the indecisive manner in which Smith had handled Walker's division during the campaign. Even before the division had reached Arkansas, Smith had contemplated returning it to Taylor. In addition, immediately following Jenkins' Ferry, Smith did not order a pursuit of Steele but rather ordered Walker back to Louisiana. Taylor charged that this strategy was telling: "Even in your opinion the Red River was the theater of events."[45]

Taylor extended his attack on Smith's abilities to include battlefield tactics. He alleged that piecemeal assaults at Jenkins' Ferry and the dearth of cavalry on the field were evidence that Smith had mishandled the army. Had Smith been better able to manage the Arkansas and Missouri divisions, Taylor argued, Walker could have remained in Louisiana. Taylor also reasoned that Jenkins' Ferry needlessly slowed Steele's retreat to Little Rock at a great cost in Confederate lives. The enemy "marched to Little Rock after the fight entirely unmolested. He would unquestionably have gone there had the fight never occurred." Taylor challenged Smith's claim that the Arkansas campaign had secured victory: "We do not to-day hold one foot more of Arkansas than if Jenkins' Ferry had never been, and we have a jaded army and 1,000 less soldiers. How, then, was the 'complete success of the campaign determined by Steele's overthrow at Jenkins' Ferry?'" Taylor characterized the Red River campaign as a "hideous failure" and charged that the "fruits of Mansfield [had] been turned to dust" by Smith's incompetence.[46]

Taylor next denounced the disastrous impact of Smith's grand strategy. In his April 28 letter he had lectured Smith about the devastating psychological effect the loss of Porter's fleet and the capitulation of Banks's army would have on the northern population. Now, five weeks later, Banks's men had swollen the ranks of the Federal armies in Virginia and Georgia where, Taylor worried, the increased troop strength might "turn the scale." Had Walker remained in Louisiana, Taylor insisted, Trans-Mississippi Federals never would have crossed the river. Citing Union reports, he argued that at Monett's Ferry and Alexandria, the Confederates could have crushed Banks's army and destroyed Porter's fleet. The escape of Banks and Porter was Smith's fault, and Taylor accused the commanding general of wasting a chance to aid the war effort across the Mississippi. Further, Taylor contended that the overthrow of Banks and Porter would have opened the road for him to take New Orleans and for Smith to move on St. Louis. But as matters now stood, Taylor complained, Smith's "strategy has riveted the fetters on both." He concluded that the opportunities of the Red River campaign "were all thrown away, to the utter destruction of the best interests of the country, and in their place we have Jenkins' Ferry."[47]

Having thoroughly vilified Smith's leadership abilities, Taylor might have paused at this point to extend an olive branch to his commanding officer. But he did not. Instead, he threatened to make their dispute public and pledged to continue to denounce Smith's policies however uncomfortable the outcome. "The grave errors you committed in the recent campaign may be repeated if the unhappy consequences are not kept before you," Taylor warned.[48]

The June 5 diatribe had crossed the line between remonstrance and insubordination. Taylor surely understood that the sheer number of his accusations and the ferocious manner in which he had delivered them made reconciliation all but impossible. The only alternative was for Smith to replace him as district commander, and Taylor closed his letter accordingly: "After the desire to serve my country I have none more ardent than to be relieved from longer serving under your command." It was more an ultimatum than a request.[49]

On June 10 Smith accommodated Taylor in Special Order 145, which removed him from command. He instructed the Louisianan to proceed to Natchitoches and remain there indefinitely. Ironically, Smith turned command of the district over to Walker. On the same day, the Confederate Congress passed a joint resolution that thanked Taylor for his "brilliant successes . . . over the enemy in Louisiana . . . and particularly for the victories at Mansfield and Pleasant Hill."[50]

In the interim between his June 5 letter and Smith's decision to relieve him from command, Taylor reconsidered his intransigence. His report to Smith's headquarters on June 8 verified rumors of a strong enemy force at Morganza, just east of the Mississippi and thirty miles north of Baton Rouge. Taylor suggested that the water level in the surrounding rivers and bayous made a Confederate foray into the region impracticable. Moreover, he indicated a willingness to abandon the proposed campaign into the Lafourche. He affirmed that the District of Western Louisiana was gradually recovering its strength and provided details of reinforcements, resupply, and troop disposition, all of which suggested that Taylor intended to remain in command. Concluding the letter, Taylor appealed to Smith's aspirations for a campaign into Missouri and pledged his full support. He announced, "I feel safe in asserting that this command will cheerfully encounter all the risks and hardships of a Missouri campaign," and guaranteed that his troops would be ready to march whenever Smith desired.[51]

In his memoirs Taylor asserted that he could achieve nothing under Smith after the close of the Red River campaign. Nevertheless, his June 8 analysis of the situation in the Trans-Mississippi suggests otherwise. Although it is unlikely that Taylor underestimated the viciousness of his written attacks on Smith, the commanding general had given no previous indication that he was inclined to take action. To the contrary, earlier tirades had gone unpunished. This gave Taylor a false sense of security that this latest firestorm between the generals would pass, particularly if he busied himself with preparations for a Missouri campaign. Taylor may also have realized that his family and his state could suffer even greater hardship if Smith dismissed him from command in Louisiana. While Taylor emphasized years later that he asked Smith several times to relieve him from duty, he made no such request in his letter of June 8. That letter was an attempt at reconciliation.[52]

By the time Smith received Taylor's outline for summer operations, he had already relieved him and turned the matter of misconduct over to Richmond. On June 11 Smith notified Davis of his decision. "I have relieved him from command until the pleasure of Your Excellency can be known," he announced. Smith explained that Taylor had committed a serious breach of military protocol by expressing his opinions to a civilian audience: "General Taylor has spoken publicly of me in an improper way [and] I am credibly informed he has read his letters inclosed to citizens and others." While Smith provided no evidence to support that allegation, he enclosed three recent letters from Taylor as proof of insubordination: Taylor's April 28 letter accusing Smith of putting his desire for personal glory ahead of all other considerations, the May 24 letter in which Taylor delivered a critical analysis of Smith's bureaucracy, and the June 5 denunciation of the campaign strategy. Smith confided to Davis, "I would have arrested General Taylor on the receipt of his first letter but acknowledging his merits as a soldier and feeling kindly disposed toward him, I passed it by."[53]

Although he expressed surprise at the "untruthfulness" of the April 28 letter, Smith admitted that he had initially attributed its harsh tone to a recurrence of Taylor's illness. Regarding the other two letters, however, Smith acknowledged that it had taken a great deal of self-control to keep from censuring Taylor immediately. Smith asserted that he declined to offer a direct response to Taylor out of a sense of professionalism and duty: "I would not commence a correspondence which was undignified, unbefitting my position, and could only result in recriminations." However, he denounced Taylor's letters as "improper and disrespectful" and implored the president to intercede in the matter.[54]

In his petition to Davis, Smith did not attempt to refute the specific charges leveled against him. Instead, he declared that the accusations were "untrue throughout" and would be "proved to be so by the simple narrative of events." Taylor's account of the campaign and his accusations of malfeasance had surely stung Smith's professional pride. The general had tried discreetly to contain the rift in hopes that Taylor would regain his composure in time for the Missouri campaign. Had Taylor's contempt for Smith not driven him to insubordination, Smith would have managed the matter internally. Between April 28 and June

5, however, the attacks escalated from harsh criticism to open defiance, leaving Smith no choice but to relieve Taylor, confine him to Natchitoches, and turn to Davis for a resolution.[55]

These actions carried with them substantial risk for Smith's career. The personal relationship between Davis and Taylor notwithstanding, the results of the Red River campaign tended to support Taylor's contention that Louisiana was the true theater of events. Accordingly, Smith suggested that the "public interest required" Davis to review the facts of the campaign and, if the evidence warranted, remove Taylor from command. Should the president determine that Taylor was correct, Smith pledged to tender his resignation: "I will willingly, and with no feeling of envy or abatement of interest in the service of my country, turn over my arduous duties and responsibilities to a successor."[56]

Despite Taylor's family ties with Davis, Smith was confident that the president would support him and reject the offer to resign. He sent Davis a comprehensive narrative of the campaign that emphasized Taylor's endorsement of the Arkansas expedition following the April 13 conference at Mansfield. The recounting of Taylor's endorsement deflected any contention that Smith had acted irresponsibly or unilaterally in his decision to withdraw Walker and pursue Steele. Smith also addressed a growing rumor that Taylor's supporters sought to damage his reputation. "I understand that efforts have been made in Richmond to have me relieved from command of the department," he admitted. "I know that facts will be misrepresented and distorted by certain parties in Louisiana who are waging a bitter war against me." While the letter did not disclose the identities of his enemies, Smith implied that the criticism came from army officers without a West Point background and from politicians. In restating his defense of the Red River strategy, Smith insisted that the operations were "founded on true military principles" and had produced greater results than could have been "achieved by a different course." The correspondence closed with Smith again offering to step down from command should Davis deem such a move necessary for the good of the Confederacy.[57]

Smith and Taylor were as disgusted with the results of the Red River campaign as they were with one another. Although each desired to serve his country in its fight for independence, both were ready to quit rather than continue struggling under the same conditions. Over the next several weeks both would resume the fight against the Federals, and against each other.

11

An Unfortunate Manner of Expression

S tripped of command and banished behind the lines, Taylor could do little more than gather his family and begin the trek to Natchitoches. On June 18, one week after Smith relieved him from duty, Taylor notified department headquarters that he had reached the old Spanish town and requested specific guidelines as to the limits of his confinement. The issue was problematic. Smith could have ordered him jailed, and given that he considered arresting Taylor several weeks earlier, imprisonment was certainly a possibility. Instead, Smith merely restricted Taylor to Natchitoches until Davis could resolve the dispute between the generals. In his postwar recollections Taylor wrote that he, his wife, and their two daughters "retired" to a "comfortable house" where they "remained for several weeks." While Taylor was not technically under house arrest, he was still not free to leave the town.[1]

During this time Taylor sought to recover his health and to redeem his reputation. He began writing a series of letters to friends and political allies discussing recent events. As a result, word of the strife between the generals spread rapidly across the Confederacy, with a decidedly pro-Taylor bias. The propaganda campaign could not have come as a surprise to Smith. Taylor claimed that he had earlier sought to deflect criticism of the Red River strategy away from department headquarters but indicated that he would no longer protect Smith from public outcry against official policies. "The same regard for duty which led me to throw myself between you and popular indignation and quietly take the blame for your errors," Taylor warned, "compels me to tell you the truth, however objectionable to you." As a result, Smith faced steadily mounting pressure from Taylor's supporters on both sides of the Mississippi.[2]

On July 4 Taylor wrote to Louisianan Braxton Bragg, Davis's military adviser and a man with whom he had enjoyed a long working relationship. Taylor implored Bragg to help him secure an assignment away from Smith's control. If there was no suitable position for him east of the river, he vowed to "retire into the ranks." The situation in the Trans-Mississippi had approached the crisis stage, Taylor declared, and he predicted that another campaign under Smith's direction would lead to the destruction of the department. He suggested that the only hope for the Confederacy west of the river was for Bragg to come to Louisiana and personally replace Smith.[3]

The next day Taylor expressed his dismay over conditions in the department in a personal letter to Joseph L. Brent, chief of artillery in Louisiana. Brent was a trusted subordinate who also enjoyed the confidence of several state officials. In the letter Taylor linked Smith's tenure in the Trans-Mississippi to the waning fortunes of the Confederacy in the East. He stated that Smith's failure to sustain concentration after Pleasant Hill had done more than simply allow Banks to escape Alexandria. Taylor believed that destruction of the Federals on the Red River would have been the first step in implementing a grand strategy to win the war west of the Mississippi. "By the end of May we would have been in Missouri," he speculated, and "results of immense magnitude in view of a peace announcement would have followed." During the Red River campaign, Taylor had discussed this scenario with others, including Smith, and he reminded Brent, "These are not after thoughts. You know they were my opinion at the time."[4]

Both Taylor and Brent maintained a strong relationship with Congressman Duncan F. Kenner, the chair of the House Ways and Means Committee. Upon learning of Taylor's plight, Kenner took the case to Richmond and appealed to Secretary of State Judah Benjamin, also a Louisianan. Kenner vilified Smith for neglect of duty and accused him of sacrificing the welfare of the army to personal interests. Kenner had toured the camps below Natchitoches and determined that the infantry was "idling away the time and becoming sick from inaction" while Smith used the hot weather as an excuse for inactivity. He accused Smith of instituting a policy that benefited the enemy and begged Benjamin to bring the matter to Davis's attention.[5]

As the nature of their dispute leaked to the public, each protagonist cultivated a legion of supporters, and each had a legion of detractors. Barthes Egan, a Louisiana judge, protested that Taylor's intimate knowledge of the state and his love for the people made the general irreplaceable. During the summer of 1864 Egan discussed the situation with former governor Thomas O. Moore. He admitted that he did "not pretend to know the merits of the difficulty between [Taylor] and General Smith" but concluded that the "people are greatly chagrined at the loss of General Taylor's services." Another influential citizen, M. C. Manning, implored Bragg to intervene on behalf of Taylor and the state. From Alexandria,

Manning claimed that the people of Louisiana clung to Taylor as "their salvation," and he entreated Bragg to remove Smith from command.[6]

Unlike Egan, Manning cited Smith's quest for glory as the cause of the discord. He alleged that Taylor had acted "almost against orders" to stop Banks while Smith remained at Shreveport "trembling for his depots and workshops," ready to abandon Louisiana and retreat into Texas. The "whispers" of Smith's personal staff, a group that Manning characterized as a pack of "parasites," influenced the departmental decisions, and Smith fretted that Taylor had "snatched glory from him at Mansfield." Despite Taylor's pleas for concentration against Banks and Porter, Smith sent the infantry in pursuit of Steele, hoping to surpass the accolades that his subordinate had won. Manning alleged that this showed "contemptuous disregard" for the service that Taylor had provided Louisiana and the Confederacy. Many Louisianans, including Manning, believed that Smith had thrown Taylor in irons, and he told Bragg that "gloom and despair . . . settled upon men's minds when news of this event became known." Manning begged Bragg to assist Louisiana by using his influence to secure Taylor's return and to rid the state of that "incubus at department headquarters," Smith.[7]

In Richmond, Louisiana congressman Charles M. Conrad received a fiery letter from E. Warren Moise, a powerful state magistrate. In Taylor's defense, Moise painted Jenkins' Ferry as "the pretended success of Genl. Smith" and complained that since the end of the Red River campaign "there has not been attempted a military operation of any kind in Arkansas, Louisiana, or Texas." Moise disclosed that, immediately following the campaign, Smith had gone to Texas to be with his wife for the birth of their daughter. "He has been nursing his wife who has been introducing a new 'Smith' into the world," Moise jeered, "as if Smiths new or old were very remarkable things." His low opinion of the Smith family heritage aside, Moise charged that urgent appeals from east of the Mississippi were going unanswered while Confederate soldiers and officers stood by in Louisiana, disheartened by their idleness and by the lack of leadership from Shreveport. "For more than two months . . . this Department has been kept in entire inactivity while the armies of Lee and Johnston were sorely pressed on the other side of the river," he affirmed.[8]

The quarrel between Smith and Taylor also became fodder for the gossip mill. Diarist Mary Chesnut, wife of South Carolina politician James Chesnut Jr., an adviser to the president, chronicled reactions to the dispute. "Mr. Kelly from New Orleans says Dick Taylor and Kirby Smith have quarreled," she wrote in July.

Weeks later Chesnut noted, "Dick Taylor does the work and Kirby Smith gets the credit of it."[9]

From the Smith camp flew accusations, equally swift and acerbic, denouncing Taylor's conduct. Missouri governor Thomas Reynolds, Smith's staunch political ally, wrote to members of the Confederate Congress in the general's behalf. To Arkansan Charles B. Mitchel he confided that Smith would not allow anyone to impugn his reputation and challenge his authority, while to Missourian Waldo P. Johnson he lauded the general's abilities "as a department commander and a strategist." His letter from the makeshift Missouri capital in Camden, Arkansas, implored Johnson to stand by Smith. In a thinly veiled reference to Taylor, Reynolds contended, "No general, however, great his merits, who resides in this department, can give satisfaction as its commander. State jealousies will occasion suspicions impairing his usefulness. . . . Gen. Smith may have committed errors, defeats; still I know of no one who would suit the Department as well, [or] better."[10]

In Shreveport, Smith's confidant Dr. Sol Smith churned out anti-Taylor propaganda. Sol Smith, along with his associate, Dr. David. W. Yandell, diverted attention away from Taylor's accusations and focused on the character of the men in question. Yandell stated unreservedly that "he had never met with a purer or more conscientious man than E. Kirby Smith, or a more ambitious and self-important one than R. Taylor." Sol Smith insisted that Taylor's opposition to the pursuit of Steele came only *after* Smith had refused to assign him operational command of the Arkansas campaign. He also maintained that Taylor had issued orders for Camille Polignac to retreat at Pleasant Hill and asserted, falsely, that Smith had countermanded the orders and in doing so secured the victory. From Texas, Smith's wife told relatives that Taylor had usurped Smith's authority at Mansfield and deprived her husband of his just glory on the battlefield.[11]

At department headquarters, Lieutenant Edward Cunningham, an aide-de-camp, penned an eloquent defense of Smith's conduct and strategy. He composed the commentary on June 27 as part of a lengthy correspondence to his uncle in Virginia. Before offering a description of affairs, Cunningham warned his family that Taylor's allies in Richmond would launch a malicious campaign to discredit Smith and attempt to have the general removed from command. "You cannot depend upon the truth of many statements you may hear," he cautioned. "General Taylor's friends will doubtless get their information from him and those around him here, among whom there is a disposition to criticize, misrepresent, and condemn everything done by or connected with General Smith." Cunningham disclosed that for over a year he had exercised great caution when expressing disapproval of Taylor's actions, implying that any criticism could easily make its way back to the general and lead to repercussions. Furthermore, he confided that "General Smith and some of his friends" shared these sentiments. Cunningham emphasized that he wrote not in a "partisan spirit" but with the intent of providing an accurate account of the situation during the Red River campaign. In fact, his opinion of Taylor delineated the factional nature of the dispute. Cunningham's judgment reflected the view of many on Smith's staff: "General Taylor is a very bad man."[12]

Cunningham's letter carefully chronicled events through the battle of Pleasant Hill and included an explanation of Smith's decision to move against Steele. Cunningham claimed that the lack of supplies and transportation below Mansfield, an area he described as a "howling wilderness," made pursuit of Banks impossible. Further, he insisted that the presence of the Federal fleet precluded any serious attempt to gain control of the Red River. Cunningham emphasized that if Taylor could not whip a portion of Banks's unsupported infantry in the open field, then he certainly could not annihilate an entrenched army under the protection of gunboats.[13]

Both arguments failed to take into account Taylor's accomplishments on the battlefield and his effective management of the district. The contention that the Confederates could not supply an army below Mansfield ignored the hundreds of Federal supply wagons and horses captured at Mansfield. In addition, Taylor was better acquainted with the network of roads and bayous and with the forage depots scattered throughout the district than was Smith or any member of his staff. The claim that Taylor could not have destroyed the Federals along the river disregarded the underlying cause of the dispute with Smith. Had Smith allowed Taylor to continue to concentrate against the Federals, the Confederates would have had a chance to secure a decisive victory on the Red River. It was, in Taylor's view, the removal of his infantry following Pleasant Hill that prevented the destruction of Banks and Porter. Confused, disorganized, and vulnerable, Banks was resigned to retreat. Taylor, flush from victory, was anxious to avenge the devastation of his homeland and continue the fight.[14]

Cunningham dismissed Taylor's plea for continued operations against Banks as irrational and characterized his persistent clamor for a campaign against New Orleans as "utter madness." He echoed Smith's contention that Arkansas and Missouri were "considerations of great importance." Turning his attention to the

Federal threat from Arkansas, Cunningham stressed that while Taylor argued for the pursuit of Banks, Steele was moving steadily toward Shreveport, Jefferson, and Marshall, all vitally important centers of supply and manufacturing. As a result, he asserted, defeat of the northern claw of the pincer was essential for the survival of the department, a priority that superseded Taylor's singular goal of reducing Banks and Porter. Further, Cunningham insisted that the defeat of Steele ensured recovery of Arkansas and opened a route to Missouri.[15]

The letter continued with a painstaking depiction of the Arkansas campaign. While Cunningham noted the piecemeal manner in which the Confederates had fought at Jenkins' Ferry, he refrained from criticizing Smith. Blame for the failure to achieve a decisive victory fell upon Walker, Churchill, and Parsons. According to Cunningham, the Texas troops had fought "in great disorder," and the officers under Churchill and Parsons had been "of no earthly account." He insisted that Smith would have accomplished his goals in Arkansas had cavalry under Price and Fagan cut off the enemy at the Saline.[16]

Aside from the conspicuous absence of any criticism of Smith, Cunningham's summary of the battle at Jenkins' Ferry and the Arkansas campaign was thorough. Cunningham claimed that poor roads and a lack of supplies had been Smith's reasons for not pursuing Steele across the Saline. These were the same reasons he had cited earlier for Smith's refusal to grant Taylor permission to follow Banks. "To campaign permanently beyond the Saline without the establishment of depots of supplies was utterly impossible," Cunningham argued. This claim, however, is inconsistent with his contention that Smith could have secured the entire Arkansas Valley by crushing Steele. Had Price and Fagan cut off the Federal retreat and had the Confederates destroyed the enemy and captured the depleted trains, Smith would have held fewer supplies than Taylor held after Mansfield. Yet Smith refused to allow Taylor to pursue Banks, ostensibly because of a lack of supplies. Cunningham also failed to recognize two key differences between Smith's situation after Jenkins' Ferry and Taylor's after Pleasant Hill. Without a pontoon, Smith had no way to cross the Saline and resume the pursuit of Steele. Taylor, however, had Banks and Porter pinned along the Red River and held control of the surrounding countryside. Moreover, the campaigning had left Smith discouraged while Taylor was eager to persevere.[17]

Cunningham's narrative returned briefly to the conclusion of events in Louisiana before renewing the criticism of Taylor. He issued another warning to his Virginia relatives: "It will doubtless be asserted in the East, as it already has been here, that the movement of troops from Louisiana to Arkansas . . . was against General Taylor's views and protests. On this point I need only say that General Smith told me immediately after our return from Mansfield, where the decision was made, that General Taylor approved of his plan of moving immediately against Steele." Cunningham insisted that Taylor had selected the troops from his command and planned to accompany them on the march to Arkansas. "I never heard a word of his disapproval of the movement until after he arrived at Shreveport on his way to Arkansas [April 15], and it was determined that he should remain in Louisiana." This affront to Taylor's pride, Cunningham contended, sparked the acrimonious critique of Smith and the condemnation of the campaign strategy: "I have not a shadow of a doubt that all the subsequent criticisms and complaints of [Taylor] and friends are entirely the result of pique."[18]

Taylor's own recollection of the April 15 incident tends to support Cunningham's understanding of the Louisianan's wounded ego. Yet Cunningham failed to examine, or was not privy to, the agreement between Smith and Taylor that promised the return of Walker to Louisiana once Steele began his retreat. Nevertheless, Cunningham maintained that the rationale behind the Arkansas movement was twofold. First, Steele's exposed column was far more vulnerable to attack than was Banks's entrenched army. Cunningham argued that Banks was in a "fortified position with a superior force" under the protection of gunboats while Steele moved "through an open pine country . . . with nothing to protect him from literally being devoured" by the Confederates. Second, Cunningham stressed that Smith could not risk continued concentration against Banks while Steele hovered near Shreveport. Had Taylor's Confederates "become seriously involved with Banks on the lower Red River, Steele might have advanced and seized Shreveport and Marshall before we could extricate ourselves to meet him," he explained.[19]

"I do not think General Smith's late campaign admits a well-grounded criticism," Cunningham professed. "All turns upon a comparison of the objects to be gained by operating against Banks or Steele after Pleasant Hill." To Cunningham as to Smith, the military and political advantages of concentration in Arkansas far outweighed the risk of continued concentration in Louisiana. Their argument carried significant weight in terms of Smith's responsibilities as commander of the Trans-Mississippi. Cunningham and Smith hoped that President Davis and the War Department would view the situation the same way.[20]

Despite the apparent urgency of events in Louisiana, Davis did not issue an immediate response to Smith's June 11 petition. Lee's struggle with Grant and

Sherman's Atlanta campaign each presented a more pressing threat to the Confederacy than did an intradepartmental squabble between Trans-Mississippi generals. Nevertheless, on July 18, one month after his arrival in Natchitoches, Taylor received news of his promotion to lieutenant general. This did not come as a complete surprise to either Smith or Taylor. Smith had recommended the advancement immediately after Mansfield and Pleasant Hill. Further, several Louisiana politicians had begun lobbying to secure a promotion for Taylor as early as December 1863. More surprising was word from Bragg that Taylor had been reassigned to replace Stephen D. Lee as commander of the Department of Alabama, Mississippi, and East Louisiana.[21]

Days before Taylor's promotion, Stephen D. Lee approached Smith regarding a transfer of troops from the Trans-Mississippi to assist in operations east of the river. The appeal was similar to an earlier directive by the War Department. Then, in February 1864, Richmond had instructed Smith to prepare eight regiments of Texas infantry and cavalry to cross the Mississippi and join Joseph E. Johnston in northwestern Georgia. In April, Smith replied that Federal control of the Mississippi made it impracticable to cross any significant number of troops. In his July 9 correspondence, Lee argued that a Federal campaign against Mobile made the troop movement vitally important. One week later he asserted that Davis wanted Smith to begin the transfer immediately. Four days after Taylor's promotion, Lee contacted Smith again, this time with a message from Bragg. "The President orders a prompt movement of Lieutenant-General Taylor and the infantry of his corps to cross the Mississippi," Bragg stated. "Such other infantry as can be spared by General Smith will follow as soon as possible." Lee reminded Smith that the "movement of troops ordered by the President should be executed with the least possible delay." Smith received the telegram on July 28 and returned Taylor to active duty on the same day.[22]

Smith ordered Taylor to move at once to Alexandria. From there Taylor would take Polignac's division along with Walker's former division, commanded temporarily by W. H. King, and cross the Mississippi "with as little delay as possible." He also gave Taylor permission to retain his staff officers. At the same time, Smith notified Walker of the movement and gave him the option of accompanying the Greyhounds across the Mississippi or remaining in Louisiana as district commander. Smith also instructed the department's chief engineer, H. T. Douglas, to develop a means for crossing the troops and assigned procedural control of the entire operation to Taylor. Yet Smith directed Douglas to report to Walker rather than Taylor. This undermined Taylor's ability to oversee the project. Further, Smith immediately interfered with Douglas's work by sending forty-two boats and a company of pontoniers to Walker with the suggestion that they ferry the troops across the river.[23]

As preparations got under way, Smith pledged that he would use every means at his disposal to secure the success of Taylor's mission. In a July 30 letter to Davis, however, he brooded that there were perilous consequences to the strategy. "The withdrawal of this force deprives the Trans-Mississippi Department of that portion of the troops upon which my dependence is placed for either offensive or defensive operations," he protested. Addressing the offensive, Smith complained that his projected Arkansas and Missouri campaign was the first casualty of Taylor's crossing. Since May he had worked with Price and Churchill to secure proper supply, intelligence, and troop organization in Arkansas. "Arrangements were perfected for offensive operations in Arkansas and Missouri," he declared. Disappointed and somewhat dispirited, Smith affirmed, "Since the withdrawal of Lieutenant-General Taylor and the infantry of his command, I will be too weak for prosecuting a campaign in the Arkansas Valley." The defense of the department was the second casualty of Taylor's movement across the river. "Should the enemy in force renew the campaign west of the Mississippi River, in the reduced condition of my command, I will be powerless to oppose his advance," Smith warned. Given the immediate crisis that faced Confederate armies in Virginia and Georgia, Smith's fears were relevant to Davis only for their impact on the war in the East.[24]

To underscore the urgency of the situation east of the Mississippi, Bragg sent Smith a summary of the crises at Petersburg and Atlanta. He implored Smith to execute the movement of troops across the Mississippi at once. In response, Smith acknowledged the grave conditions in Virginia and Georgia but restated his argument that the planned troop withdrawal rendered the Trans-Mississippi defenseless: "I regret the necessity which compels the removal of the infantry under General Taylor to the east bank of the Mississippi. It leaves me powerless to resist any movement of the enemy made in force." On this contingency, Smith worried needlessly. The mission to transfer Trans-Mississippi infantry did not spark a renewed offensive by the Federals west of the river, but it did reignite the smoldering antagonism between him and Taylor.[25]

Trouble between the generals began almost immediately. Taylor used the proposed crossing to revive his plans for a drive toward New Orleans. On July 29 he informed Smith, "If troops can be crossed at all it can only be effected by a diversion in the direction of New Orleans." All Taylor needed was Smith's cooperation. Taylor also provided a list of staff officers he wished to retain and added that secrecy at department headquarters concerning the mission was crucial to its success. Stealth was one of the few areas of agreement between the generals. One day earlier, Smith had warned Walker that the "success of the movement [to Mississippi] will depend upon its secrecy and dispatch." Taylor pushed the idea one step further by asserting that he should not take control of the operations personally until all preparations were completed and the troops ready to move. Eager to get out from under Smith's authority, Taylor also proposed to cross the Mississippi immediately so as to expedite cooperation east of the river.[26]

Taylor's recommendation was a legitimate one, particularly in light of the security issue. His conspicuous presence in Alexandria after having been removed from command would certainly arouse suspicion among the soldiers. Many troops, the Texans in particular, were reluctant to serve in a theater far from their home state. As early as June 14, word of Taylor's transfer east of the Mississippi had begun to circulate throughout Confederate campsites in Louisiana, and desertion rates rose amid reports of a mass crossing. Smith shared Taylor's concerns but on July 31 declared that secrecy was impossible. As a solution, he suggested "an appeal to the patriotism of the men" and urged Taylor to deal "openly and frankly with the troops." Enclosing a copy of a special order sent to Walker, which explained the necessity of sending reinforcements to the East, Smith recommended its publication for the troops. On August 1 Taylor met with Walker, and both generals decided against publication. Its distribution, Walker insisted, would only confirm the suspicions of the men and be "fatal to the success of the contemplated movement."[27]

In the July 31 correspondence, Smith also patently rejected Taylor's other suggestions. He overruled his request to operate near New Orleans and characterized the region as a "distant and sickly country." Despite his letters to Davis and Bragg announcing a suspension of the planned campaign through Arkansas, Smith explained to Taylor that a move toward New Orleans would waste troops that were "needed for operations in Arkansas and Missouri." More important, Smith demanded that Taylor remain in Alexandria to supervise preparations for the crossing. While refusing to grant Taylor permission to cross the river in advance, Smith agreed to allow the Louisianan's staff to cross and to establish lines of communication.[28]

Taylor did not want to serve as Smith's lieutenant during the crossing operation. Walker was the district commander and as such should oversee the arrangements and manage the preparations. On the night of July 30 Taylor met with Walker to review the situation. The following day Taylor reported that he and Walker were in agreement on how best to handle the assignment. "General Walker coincides with me in opinion that the command of the troops should remain with him until everything is in readiness to attempt the passage," he announced to Smith. Taylor also requested that an additional brigade, under Allen Thomas, join the exodus into Mississippi. In the three days since his reinstatement, Taylor had pressured Smith to endorse a variety of schemes ranging from a campaign in the Lafourche to the assignment of troops. To Smith, these requests signaled another challenge to his supremacy in the Trans-Mississippi.[29]

Taylor's sudden return to active duty, his promotion to lieutenant general, and his orders from Richmond to cross the Mississippi created confusion and insta-bility within the department command structure. Smith responded accordingly, with an autocratic assertion of his authority. Although he insisted that Taylor direct operations, Smith issued instructions for the logistics directly to Walker. In addition, he gave Walker permission to hold any member of Taylor's staff. These instructions came four days after Smith had directed Taylor to reassemble his staff to help facilitate the crossing. Yet when Walker requested the services of A. H. Mason, the chief commissary officer, Smith refused. Several days later he reversed himself and this time refused Taylor's request to assign Mason and ord-nance chief Joseph Brent to his staff. Ignoring the importance of Taylor's mission to the Confederate hopes of victory in the East, Smith claimed that Mason and Brent were "essentially necessary" to the war effort in the Trans-Mississippi.[30]

To add to the turmoil, Smith pressured Walker to join the march to Missis-sippi. In a patriarchal tone he told the general, "Your influence with your old command is deservedly great, and can be made a powerful auxiliary in securing its cheerful acquiescence in the movement." Implying that the decision was Walker's alone, Smith urged him to assume command of the division temporarily to assist Taylor.[31]

Smith's proposal to Walker was less than forthright. It was a ploy to convince him that as district commander he had far greater control over the situation than he really did. Smith also notified Taylor that he would order Walker to accompany the Texas division across the river if Taylor so desired. This directive too was a ma-nipulative ploy, an attempt on Smith's part to exercise his prerogative as the senior officer and ensure that Taylor played a subordinate role. One way or the other, Walker would cross the river. Either he would go on his own initiative, or Taylor would issue orders through Smith for him to cross. Thus, Smith played the innocent. He absolved himself of the responsibility for Walker and retained control over Taylor. Richmond may have instructed Taylor to march the troops across the river, but Smith still held sway in the Trans-Mississippi. While Walker believed that the decision to cross was his to make, Taylor presumed the opposite.[32]

On August 1 Walker rejected Smith's proposition, insinuating that a district commander did not have the authority to make such decisions. Rather, Walker considered himself the "channel through which General Taylor would communicate his orders." Walker could have chosen to leave the decision up to Smith but instead advised the commanding general that he would be "guided entirely by [Taylor's] suggestions." The rebuff stung Smith, but he acceded promptly to Walker's argument and stated that the War Department had in fact ordered Taylor to direct the crossing. Thus, Smith implied the decision was Taylor's and not his. On this point, Smith misrepresented the messages from Bragg, Lee, and Davis. While they affirmed that Taylor was to cross the river with infantry, their letters did not dictate that he select the troops or coordinate the movement. In fact, the instructions indicated that Smith should direct the operations. Smith was acting in a duplicitous manner. In his dealings with Taylor he claimed authority over the operation. Yet he sought to convince Walker that Taylor was responsible for all aspects of the crossing.[33]

Smith had hoped that Walker would volunteer for the mission. His reluctance to do so put the commanding general in a bind. If he insisted that Walker accompany the Texans, Taylor could exercise his authority to countermand the order, but if he let Taylor make the decision, he was yielding power to his adversary. In an attempt to maintain some degree of influence, Smith prodded Walker to offer Taylor "every facility and assistance, and if necessary bring the strength of your whole district to bear upon the undertaking." Two days later Smith decided that Thomas's brigade would indeed join the forces moving into Mississippi. That brought the total number to nearly ten thousand and reduced the department's strength to twenty-eight hundred troops in Texas and fifty-four hundred in Arkansas.[34]

Despite Smith's attempt to manipulate Walker and control Taylor, the problem of how to cross the troops remained paramount to all concerned. Less than one week after receiving orders to devise a means of crossing, H. T. Douglas completed his proposal. Instead of presenting the plans to Walker as Smith had ordered, Douglas submitted his ideas directly to Taylor. The engineer intended to span the river with an immense pontoon bridge that would enable the infantry to cross en masse rather than in successive waves. The ambitious design seemed feasible to Taylor, who had witnessed firsthand the accomplishments of Federal engineers working to free the fleet at Alexandria. Declaring, "I heartily approve of colonel Douglas' plan," he forwarded the information to Smith on August 4.[35]

Three days later Smith asked why Taylor had not yet begun to cross. He dismissed the plan to bridge the Mississippi and contended that Douglas already had enough boats to carry nearly a thousand men at a single crossing. Douglas's job, according to Smith, was merely to assist Taylor in selecting the point of crossing, not to concoct an ostentatious engineering scheme. He also announced that Thomas's brigade was no longer a part of the mission, but that the Crescent Regiment would move from Shreveport and rejoin Polignac to cross the river. "You will conduct the operation of crossing in person," Smith reminded Taylor sternly. Since Taylor's return to duty, the correspondence between him and Smith had remained relatively cordial. Smith's August 7 letter, however, was antagonistic. Despite his demand that Taylor control operations, Smith insisted on his own plan for moving the troops in boats. He also began to shuffle regiments in and out of Taylor's jurisdiction without consultation. His renewed hostility toward Taylor is evident in his condescending tone: "The importance of the expedition in crossing the infantry . . . must have impressed itself upon you."[36]

By this time Walker had informed Smith of his decision to remain in Louisiana rather than accompany the Texans to Mississippi. Although Taylor did not object, Smith resented this turn of events and attempted to reassert strict control over the general officers in his department. On the same day that Smith voiced his displeasure with Taylor and Douglas, he sent a curt letter to Walker with instructions to select and position four batteries to protect the crossing points. Smith provided his subordinate with a list of artillery companies from which to choose. Enclosed in the correspondence was a copy of the August 7 letter to Taylor, and Smith addressed Walker in the same condescending tone. "You will perceive from my letter to General Taylor that I have directed the immediate crossing of the troops," he announced. Smith also derided Douglas's bridge and Taylor's endorsement of the design as folly. "The collection of material and the preparations necessary for throwing a bridge across the Mississippi River necessitate a delay of at least thirty days, and I believe is of doubtful success," he scoffed. The objection was not without merit. The logistics involved in such a project were formidable indeed, and the critical situation east of the river demanded that the troops cross as soon as possible. Yet a piecemeal crossing of one or two thousand troops, landing in Mississippi at different times, as Smith proposed, would hardly make a difference to the struggle in the East. Taylor sought to cross ten thousand soldiers in one large-scale operation and deliver immediate aid to the cause.[37]

Taylor responded angrily to Smith's August 7 letter. "The importance of the expedition in crossing the infantry has fully impressed itself on me," he retorted. His misgivings concerned only the means of effecting the crossing and the lack of cooperation from headquarters. As he had done in his letters to Smith at the close of the Red River campaign, Taylor related the chain of events that had brought the planned operation to a standstill. He stressed that nearly eight weeks had elapsed between his relief from command and his return to active duty. The forced seclusion at Natchitoches had left him out of touch with developments in the district and unprepared to supervise the complex task that Smith had assigned. Taylor affirmed that without a staff he had no means of ascertaining the strength of enemy positions, the locations of enemy gunboats, and "such other necessary facts as would enable . . . [him] to fix upon suitable places for crossing." By assigning him a difficult mission and then undermining his ability to direct the department's resources, Smith had set Taylor up to fail.[38]

Also in dispute was Smith's contention that the War Department had issued specific instructions for Taylor to direct the troop movement personally. Taylor had read the dispatches and challenged Smith's interpretation of the orders: "I can perceive nothing therein which instructs that the troops should 'cross under my orders' and that 'I should conduct the operation of crossing in person.'" Further, Taylor contended that Smith had not permitted him to carry out his assigned responsibilities. "Simply to cross the men is but a portion of the movement," he argued. Once in Mississippi, according to Richmond's plan, the troops were to march eastward and join Confederate forces near Atlanta. Consequently, the network of roads and supply depots in Mississippi and Alabama became exceedingly important to the overall success of the mission. These factors, Taylor insisted, required his immediate presence across the river. By prohibiting him from crossing, Taylor alleged, Smith jeopardized the entire mission and undermined the chances for success in Mississippi. In addition, he insinuated that Smith's reluctance to grant him permission to cross immediately violated orders from the War Department.[39]

More than the transport of ten thousand troops, Taylor's own crossing emerged as a crucial point of contention in the power struggle between the generals. Taylor insisted that his assignment as a departmental commander meant that the War

Department wanted him across the river as soon as possible. To the contrary, Smith reasoned that as long as Taylor remained in the Trans-Mississippi, the Louisianan was subject to his instructions. On August 3, in an attempt to circumvent Smith's authority, Taylor asked Bragg to clarify his orders. Did Bragg want him to cross ahead of the infantry? Should he cross, even if the troops could not? While awaiting a response, there was little Taylor could do beyond renewing his criticism of Smith's imperious control of the Trans-Mississippi Department.[40]

In a flagrant challenge to both Smith's veracity and his judgment, Taylor accused the general of using the mission to undermine his authority on both sides of the river. "So long as the command is within this department it is subject to your orders, and without dispositions made by you as commanding general I am powerless to effect anything," he fumed. Smith's refusal to let him cross, Taylor charged, put essential preparations across the river beyond his control. The letter closed with another defiant outburst. While he vowed to carry out Smith's orders to the best of his ability, Taylor condemned his superior for interfering with the operation and disavowed any accountability for the crossing: "I deem it proper to state to you that . . . I do not deem myself responsible either for the failure or success of the undertaking which you direct."[41]

On August 11 Smith issued an uncompromising reply to Taylor's attacks. He dismissed Douglas's plan for bridging the Mississippi as "impracticable and visionary" and enumerated the various obstacles that would impede construction. Even under the most favorable conditions, Smith scoffed, the construction required setting up a navy yard at Shreveport, requisitioning supplies from Texas, and reassigning laborers and engineers from across the department to construct the bridge. He estimated that completion could take up to two months and would delay the troops' arrival east of the river past the point of usefulness. "You certainly could not have carefully examined the plan proposed," he scolded Taylor.[42]

Smith insisted that he had complied with instructions that required Taylor to organize and supervise the crossing. Even if Richmond had left the choice to him, Smith affirmed, he would have ordered Taylor to direct the operation. "Your experience on the Mississippi, your knowledge of the country, and your personal interest in the success of the movement, make you the proper officer to command, even had the dispatches from the War Department not so directed," he explained impatiently. On the issue of operational control, Smith maintained that Taylor already commanded all aspects of the crossing. He claimed that Taylor could have launched a feint toward New Orleans if he had so desired and that he himself had merely recommended against the plan, not expressly forbidden it. In closing, Smith renewed his demand for an immediate crossing and warned against further procrastination: "If there is any unnecessary delay the authorities in Richmond can judge where the fault lies and upon whom the responsibility rests."[43]

The crossing quagmire had a ripple effect throughout the Trans-Mississippi, and on August 4 Smith ordered a shake-up among his district commanders. In part because of his reluctance to accompany the Texas infantry into Mississippi, Smith transferred Walker to the District of Texas, New Mexico, and Arizona. Veteran Simon B. Buckner, recently arrived from Tennessee, took command in western Louisiana, while Magruder moved from Texas to Arkansas to replace Price. Taylor feared that Smith would send Price across the river to rid himself of the troublesome officer. "Unless ordered to remain, the general will be sent over, as General E. K. Smith is anxious to get rid of him," Taylor insisted to Bragg. Smith, however, had other things in mind for Price.[44]

The intradepartmental shift allowed Smith to launch a campaign into Missouri. Although he no longer controlled the infantry necessary for a large operation, a full-scale invasion was unnecessary, according to fresh intelligence from Price. Immediately following the Red River campaign, Smith had ordered Price to gather information on conditions in Missouri. Several weeks later Price met with Missouri governor Thomas Reynolds to discuss a campaign to liberate the state. Reynolds and Price agreed that a cavalry raid, with Price in command, could accomplish two objectives. The raid would divert Federal troops away from operations east of the river, and Price's celebrity would attract a new wave of volunteers to the colors. Reports from Joseph O. Shelby, whose cavalry patrolled the Arkansas-Missouri border, supported both contentions. In fact, Shelby claimed he could deliver twenty thousand recruits if Smith took immediate action. The horse-soldier believed that Smith should throw the entire force of the Trans-Mississippi into Missouri to "seize St. Louis, hold it, fortify it, and cross over into Illinois." In late July, Price, Reynolds, and Shelby petitioned Smith to approve a Missouri raid. With the infantry in Louisiana preparing to cross the Mississippi, and with the War Department insisting on action to ease the pressure on Confederate armies east of the river, Smith saw Missouri as a solution to his predicament.[45]

Smith assigned Price to field command and ordered him to prepare for a sweeping cavalry raid. He gave the Missourian specific instructions for the operation and emphasized the political and military importance of the mission. "Make

Saint Louis the objective point of your movement," he directed, "which, if rapidly made, will put you in possession of that place, its supplies, and military stores, and which will do more toward rallying Missouri to your standard than the possession of any other point." Price's raid, while not an operation of grand proportions, was part of the campaign that Smith had envisioned since coming to the Trans-Mississippi. Responsibilities as departmental commander, however, would prevent him from personally leading the troops. So while Price remained in Camden awaiting supplies from Shreveport, Smith reluctantly shifted his attention back to Louisiana.[46]

Although Taylor was not involved directly in Smith's realignment, the changes affected him and the Texans under his control. Smith gave permanent command of Walker's old division to John H. Forney, a veteran of Vicksburg who had just arrived in the Trans-Mississippi. On August 12, before Forney took command, reports reached department headquarters of a mutiny within the ranks. According to a message from Walker, "great opposition" to Forney's appointment had surfaced among the officers, and trouble was imminent. Smith warned Taylor to expect "serious difficulty . . . among the troops" once Forney took command. He then abdicated responsibility for the problem and instructed Taylor to assess the situation upon Forney's arrival. Afterward, once the Texans had crossed the Mississippi, Taylor could relieve Forney at his discretion.[47]

Smith then turned to Walker and asked him to reconsider his decision not to accompany the Texans into Mississippi. "The troops of your division might cross the river with you in command," he suggested, but with Forney at the helm, Smith feared, "the greater part would refuse to cross or desert." He appealed to Walker's sense of patriotism and implied that anything less than a return to field command was selfishness: "It is your duty to cross with your troops and you should retain command of your division, though it be a sacrifice of private feelings." Smith then gave Walker the authority to relieve Forney if he so desired. Thus, Smith again sought to sidestep his duty as department commander. Taylor could dismiss Forney east of the river and Walker could remove him west of the Mississippi, but in either case, Smith would not intercede.[48]

Walker did not respond immediately to Smith's request, nor did he relieve Forney. Instead, on August 13 he advised Smith that Taylor's direct involvement in the crossing and his presence among the troops was essential to the success of the movement. However, Walker also disclosed that according to William M. Levy, Taylor's adjutant, the Louisianan intended to leave the next day "to assume command of the Department of Mississippi and await the arrival of the troops on the other side." Walker cited Levy's claim that Taylor had received direct orders from Bragg to cross the river without further delay.[49]

On the same day that Walker sent his message to headquarters, Taylor addressed Smith's assessment of the plan to bridge the Mississippi. He pointed out that Douglas was chief engineer of the department and a member of Smith's staff. Without personal knowledge of the department's resources, Taylor argued, he was forced to rely on Douglas's judgment to devise a plan that best utilized the assets at his immediate disposal. Insisting that he had done nothing to retard the troop movement, Taylor offered a facetious apology for the "unfortunate . . . manner of expression" that had led to the latest misunderstanding.[50]

The following day, August 14, Taylor confronted Smith about the Forney affair. He alleged that Smith had blundered in appointing Forney to lead the reluctant Texans on a hazardous mission hundreds of miles from their home state. While Smith demanded an immediate movement of the troops, Taylor charged that the commander had assigned an unpopular officer whose presence would only inhibit the movement. Taylor thought he knew why Forney had received the assignment and accused Smith of trying to "get rid of an officer" whose services he did not want by sending him across the river. He acknowledged Smith's right to assign officers within the Trans-Mississippi but, asserting that his was an independent command, refused to allow Forney to participate in the operation. "As soon as the troops reach the [west] bank of the Mississippi River I shall order General Forney to report to your headquarters as I do not require him to cross with the division," he assured Smith.[51]

Sending Forney back to Shreveport was only part of Taylor's revolt against Smith's authority. Since his return to active duty, Taylor had argued that Walker, as district commander, had a better grasp of available resources and thus should direct the troop movement. In the August 14 letter he insisted that Smith should have ordered Walker to resume control of his old division with instructions to supervise operations on the west bank. Meanwhile, Taylor contended that he would have crossed the Mississippi, assumed command of his new department, and coordinated the operation from the east bank. Taylor believed that Smith's responsibility as commander of the Trans-Mississippi was to direct troops in the department. His own command obligations lay east of the river. Taylor reasoned that it was Smith's failure to follow this course that had led to the multitude of "embarrassments and difficulties," including the troubles with Forney and Walker.[52]

Convinced that Smith had botched the crossing effort, Taylor resolved to escape the Trans-Mississippi at once. His August 14 letter to Smith contained a copy of a dispatch from Bragg that authorized him to cross the river as soon as practicable. Taylor vowed to leave Alexandria immediately to inspect the troops and complete arrangements for their crossing. Following this discharge of duty, he would cross the Mississippi without delay.[53]

Prior to receiving Taylor's letter and the dispatch from Bragg, Smith wrote Taylor to address Levy's claim that Taylor planned to cross ahead of the army. "I learn that you contemplate leaving the troops here under your command and crossing the Mississippi," he declared accusingly. "This I positively forbid." Smith demanded to see any recent correspondence Taylor might have received from Bragg but even so insisted that Taylor stay in Louisiana. Smith planned to file a protest with the War Department and challenge Bragg's authority in the Trans-Mississippi. "You will still remain in command of the troops until further orders," he directed Taylor, "as I shall object to a compliance of those instructions until the crossing of the troops shall have been effected." Smith gave the letter to Buckner with instructions to deliver it to Taylor only if the rumors of his crossing proved to be true.[54]

Taylor left Alexandria just ahead of Buckner and began his inspection of the troops scheduled to make the crossing. On the evening of April 16 he arrived at the Texas campsite above Harrisonburg, less than twenty-five miles west of the Mississippi. Confederate pickets along the river reported the presence of enemy ironclads stationed at twelve-mile intervals and determined that gunboats on patrol between Vicksburg and the Red River passed by the crossing site every four hours. After conferring with several officers, Taylor decided to remain with the army and cross the river with the troops. He cited an "unwillingness to cast unpleasant responsibilities upon other officers" as justification for his change of heart. Taylor promptly sent word to Walker and requested that he apprise Smith of the situation.[55]

Two days later Taylor informed Smith that conditions along the river posed a serious threat to the operation. The presence of the Federal navy and the enemy's apparent knowledge of the crossing sites made the transfer impossible. Taylor also disclosed that he had advised Richmond that moving troops across the river was no longer feasible. "I hope the receipt of my dispatch will induce the War Department to countermand the order [to cross]," he stated. The attempted crossing would, according to Taylor, almost certainly result in calamitous failure. He cautioned Smith to guard against desertions and lamented the waste of man-power. These soldiers "might be of some service elsewhere in this department," Taylor suggested, and he reported that he had already sent William H. Parsons's brigade of Texas cavalry to Arkansas. In doing so, Taylor acknowledged the vi-ability of Smith's proposed Missouri campaign relative to the fruitless operation along the Mississippi. Whether as a conciliatory gesture or a strategic imperative, he implored Smith to consider shifting the disposable infantry to Arkansas: "I beg leave respectfully to submit my opinion that if any movement of troops in this department is in contemplation it should not be delayed on account of the proposed crossing of the infantry from this district, which I believe to be at pres-ent impossible."[56]

Late on the night of August 18 a member of Buckner's staff delivered Smith's August 15 letter to Taylor at Harrisonburg. Evidently the officer had misunder-stood his orders to suspend delivery if Taylor had decided to remain with the troops. Once Taylor read the letter, the amicable disposition toward Smith that he had exhibited earlier in the day vanished instantly. "I cannot recognize the propriety of expression used in your letter in which you state that you 'positively forbid' my crossing the river," he shot back. Taylor detailed the recent chaos that had beset the crossing attempt and tied the crisis to the stormy conclusion of the Red River campaign. In doing so, he positioned Bragg, Davis, and the power of the presidency directly between himself and Smith.[57]

Taylor refused to concede Smith's authority to prevent compliance with orders "emanating directly from the President of the Confederate States." To Taylor, a di-rective from Bragg, Davis's director of military operations, carried the same weight as an order from the president himself. Accordingly, to ignore Bragg's August 9 dispatch and forbid Taylor to cross violated the wishes of the president. If the way in which Davis conveyed his wishes was objectionable to Smith, Taylor suggested that he complain to "the higher authority." Brazenly, he pointed to the dispute over the Red River campaign as a reminder of Davis's favorable disposition toward him: "I was relieved by you from the command of the district to which I had been assigned by the President and ordered to 'await his pleasure.' That pleasure has been indicated by assignment of me to another command and department." Once orders from the president reached him, Taylor vowed, he would either obey them and cross the river at once or, at his discretion, cancel the operation entirely. It is evident that Taylor's personal animosity toward Smith and his recent restoration to command had colored his judgment. While he may have had the authority to defy orders from Smith that ran contrary to Bragg's instructions, Taylor certainly had no legal justification for disobeying orders from the president. Regardless of their personal relationship, Davis could not allow a subordinate to disobey a direct order. In threatening to defy instructions from the War Department, Taylor drew dangerously close to sedition.[58]

Whether Taylor would have disobeyed orders from Davis soon became a moot point. After sending the scurrilous letter to Smith, Taylor requested permission from Bragg to halt the crossing. Meanwhile, Smith had no time to draft a response to Taylor's threats. On August 21, the day Smith read Taylor's letter, a dispatch from the president arrived at headquarters. Davis had composed the response one week after Smith's July 30 inquiry regarding troop withdrawals from the department. The president informed Smith, "[I could] find no record of a telegram ordering you to send General Taylor and infantry from the Trans-Mississippi across the Mississippi River." Davis emphasized positively, "No such order was ever given by me." He disclosed that instructions to send troops across the Mississippi had been discretionary. Since Smith and Taylor agreed that the crossing was unwise, they should have simply declined the request rather than use the proposed movement as an excuse to resume their personal war.[59]

The president also questioned Smith's concern that the transfer of infantry from Louisiana would prevent a campaign into Arkansas and Missouri. Davis declared that Smith had not presented Richmond with plans for an offensive into either state. Even if he had, Davis wondered how the success of the campaign, the arrangements for which Smith said had been perfected, "could depend on infantry which was below the Lower Red River." He scolded Smith for his failure to initiate a campaign west of the river as a means to ease the pressure on Confederate armies in Virginia and Georgia. Davis emphasized that if Smith's forces threatened enemy positions in the Trans-Mississippi, the Federals could not send troops across the river to reinforce armies in the East. "This was so obvious that I expected you to act without waiting for orders," Davis admonished him.[60]

The rebuke from the president, arriving on the heels of Taylor's vitriolic letter, delivered a staggering blow to Smith. He took immediate action and ordered Taylor to suspend all plans to move troops across the Mississippi. A prompt redeployment was in order, Smith announced, and he instructed Taylor to send the infantry north to Monroe. Enclosed with the orders was a telegram addressed to Smith from Samuel Cooper, the Confederacy's adjutant and inspector general. Written on July 18, Cooper's message had arrived at Shreveport along with the letter from Davis. The dispatch directed Smith to send Taylor across the river if his services were not essential to operations within the department. Smith's refusal to recognize Bragg's authority in the Trans-Mississippi had prevented Taylor from crossing the river for nearly one month. Cooper's message, however, provided a codicil that left the decision up to Smith. Taylor was clearly no longer indispensable to the department. To the contrary, he had become a threat to Smith's authority. Smith cited Cooper's dispatch as his authorization to transfer Taylor, and so on August 22 he ordered the disgruntled general across the Mississippi.[61]

Considering the date of Cooper's message, it is apparent that neither he nor Davis realized that Smith had relieved Taylor from command on June 10. When the War Department issued orders for Taylor to assume control of the Department of Mississippi, Alabama, and Eastern Louisiana, the general was essentially under arrest for insubordination. The dates of early dispatches to Smith from Bragg and Stephen D. Lee concerning Taylor's reassignment also indicate that the news had not yet reached the Confederate commanders. Taylor admitted as much on August 8 when he disclosed to Smith that the War Department had issued orders for his transfer, "evidently under the belief" that he commanded the District of Western Louisiana or a corps. Similarly, one week later he indicated that Bragg had based his orders "on the supposition" that he still commanded the troops. This information throws an entirely different light on Taylor's August 19 boast to Smith that the president had indicated his "pleasure" by assigning him to another command. Taylor suspected that word of his dismissal had not yet reached Richmond and sought to use the circumstances to his advantage. Taylor's boast was no mere display of bravado but a calculated bluff designed to secure his immediate passage across the river.[62]

On August 26 Taylor visited the camp of the Louisiana brigade, where he dined with a few of the officers. Several hours later, accompanied only by his servant Tom Strother, Taylor slipped quietly across the Mississippi in a leaky old pirogue. In Shreveport, Smith tried to busy himself with last-minute arrangements for the Missouri raid, but he was in ill health. Dr. Sol Smith examined the general and returned a diagnosis of acute dysentery. Apparently exhausted by the Red River campaign and by his battles with Taylor, Smith went into seclusion for several days to rest and recover.[63]

The crossing fiasco reflected poorly on both Smith and Taylor. Neither general devoted sufficient time or effort to advance the project beyond the preliminary stages. Taylor acknowledged that he had been out of touch with developments in the district since June 10. Accordingly, he turned over most of the logistics for the crossing to chief engineer Douglas. This decision was out of character for Taylor, who throughout the previous campaign had seen to many of the details personally. In his memoirs Taylor asserted that while "a knowledge of details will not make a great general . . . there can be no greatness in war without such knowledge." By his own definition, the crossing was not one of Taylor's shining moments. Had he taken a more active role in the project, he might have recognized the futility of large-scale pontoon construction across a wide river teeming with enemy warships.[64]

Smith's plan to ferry the men across in a fleet of rowboats was just as impractical as the Douglas bridge. The task would have required dozens of trips across the river, and the forces would still have had to contend with numerous enemy river patrols. Further, the incremental crossing of mutinous Trans-Mississippi troops would have made discipline on the west bank difficult and reorganization along the east bank a haphazard endeavor at best. Yet Smith saw no other solution and would consider no plan besides his own.[65]

Taylor claimed that if he crossed in advance of the infantry he could secure arrangements east of the river. While this was undoubtedly true, his primary concern was to escape Smith's influence. To this end, he was willing to forgo the prospect of taking ten thousand troops into his new department. Smith, for his part, was angry at the developments beyond his control that restored Taylor to active duty. Refusing to recognize Bragg's authority, he held Taylor until he received direct orders from the War Department to send the general across the river. Had Smith allowed Taylor to cross before the troops, the Louisianan would have established immediate communications with Bragg and the War Department. By relaying intelligence of the problems involved with the crossing, Taylor would have secured permission to call off the maneuver. This would have freed Smith to take the infantry to Arkansas and join Price. Ironically, Smith's preoccupation with Taylor undermined his own cherished goal of leading a campaign into Missouri.[66]

12

A Commander without an Army

After the end of the Red River campaign, Smith's private correspondence took on an increasing tone of pessimism and distrust of those around him. The stress of command and his battle with Taylor had taken a toll on his outlook. Letters written to his family during the dispute over Walker's division contained far more complaints about Smith's personal well-being than those written earlier in the campaign. "I was sad and out of spirits yesterday," he confided to his wife on May 25, after receipt of a venomous letter from Taylor. In a letter to his mother written during the failed attempt to cross troops into Mississippi, Smith admitted to a "great anxiety" for the future of the Confederacy. He also complained of a physical and emotional decline. "I feel lonely and miserable," he wrote to his wife on August 4, adding that the constant exposure to sickness in Shreveport caused him much dread. "I am positively suffering from martyrdom," he wrote the following day, claiming that he was "persecuted" by a rheumatic attack. This was the same affliction that plagued Taylor. Curiously, although Smith complained of pains in his shoulders, arms, legs, and back, symptoms that are consistent with rheumatoid arthritis, his surgeon diagnosed the affliction as dysentery.[1]

Ordered to rest, Smith retired to his quarters and took the opportunity to sift through the "gossip and scandal" that surrounded his quarrel with Taylor. On August 20, in an exasperated letter to his wife, Smith disclosed that censure of his strategy in the Red River campaign was the topic of intense discussions within the Confederate government. "Taylor's friends have made a violent and bitter attack upon me in Congress," he complained. Yet upon learning that Florida congressman Robert B. Hilton had spoken out in his defense, Smith criticized him for having acted "without knowing the circumstances or having data." Smith's illness left him weakened, confused, and suspicious of friends and family. "I fear you don't know what a good husband you have," he whined to his wife. "You don't appreciate and confide in me as I do in you. I have been sick."[2]

The following day, under peculiar circumstances, Smith dictated a lengthy account of his strategy during the Red River campaign for a report to Jefferson

Davis. Fear among Smith's inner circle that pro-Taylor operatives had infiltrated department headquarters led the general to take precautions to ensure against a leak to the Louisianan's political allies. Rather than assign the duty of writing the report to his chief of staff, an aide, or an adjutant, Smith had his surgeon and confidant Sol Smith transcribe the letter. This effectively removed William Boggs from any involvement with the correspondence. Boggs's previous support for many of Taylor's positions had provoked an unsuccessful attempt by Smith to remove him and appoint Sol Smith as chief of staff. Davis had personally denied the request. By having his confidant write the report, Smith both protected its contents from Taylor's spies and demonstrated to Davis his steadfast dependence on Sol Smith.[3]

Smith began the letter by referring to the president's August 8 dispatch. He expressed shock that Davis had not directly ordered Trans-Mississippi troops to cross the river. In addition, Smith disputed the president's implication that he had not properly utilized departmental resources to prevent the Federals from shifting troops to eastern theaters. He explained that military circumstances had prevented the Confederates from holding the enemy west of the river. Smith traced strategic movements in the Trans-Mississippi from the fall of 1863 up to the recent attempt to cross the troops. While he did not criticize Taylor directly, Smith portrayed himself as an accomplished strategist and tactician whose plans had fallen victim to events beyond his immediate control.[4]

When the narrative reached the April 9 battle of Pleasant Hill, a turning point in the campaign, Smith paused and posed a rhetorical question to Davis concerning his strategic options. "The question may be asked why the enemy was not pursued at once," he offered in reference to the decision against implementing Taylor's strategy of continued concentration. "I answer, because our troops were completely paralyzed by the repulse at Pleasant Hill." Smith's portrayal of Pleasant Hill as a defeat contradicted his earlier assessments of the battle. In his April 12 letter to Samuel Cooper in Richmond and in an April 14 letter to Missouri governor Thomas Reynolds, each written just days after the fighting, Smith had characterized Pleasant Hill as a Confederate victory. Smith's revisionist interpretation of the battle as a defeat was designed to defend his decision to move against Steele rather than to present Davis with an accurate account of the operations.[5]

The letter's question-and-answer format gave Smith an opportunity to present his strategy in a favorable light. Eager to dispel criticism of his decision to send troops from Louisiana to Arkansas, he presented Davis with another leading question: "Should I with the bulk of my forces pursue Banks until he left the Red River Valley, or should I march against Steele, who threatened my depots and workshops, the loss of which would well-nigh have closed operations in this department?" The detailed response delivered an elaborate justification of the Arkansas campaign. Smith provided a geographical analysis of the Red River Valley and emphasized that his strategic use of interior lines had played an essential role in the successful effort to thwart the two-pronged Federal invasion.[6]

The assessment was technically accurate but limited in scope. The flaw in Smith's argument lay in his failure to adequately address Taylor's strategic position. According to Taylor, once Steele began to retreat, Walker should have returned immediately to Louisiana to operate against Banks and Porter. Smith continued to insist that only by concentrating his forces in Arkansas could he end the threat from Steele, and that to return Walker to Louisiana would have placed the entire department in grave danger.[7]

Notwithstanding Smith's own faith in his decision, the recent criticism of the Arkansas strategy had undermined his self-assuredness. He closed the letter to Davis by repeating his June 11 offer to resign. "I care not for the censure of those who allege that I have exhibited a want of capacity," Smith stated. "You Mr. President, have honored me with your confidence. . . . I beg if at any time I lose this that you will relieve me of the weighty responsibilities with which I am now intrusted."[8]

Before Davis could respond, another conflict arose within Smith's department. Like the firestorm over the Red River strategy, this too directly involved criticism from Taylor. Upon his arrival in Mississippi, Taylor told Braxton Bragg that he "would have been over [the river] four weeks ago but was positively forbidden by department commander, General E. Kirby Smith." This prompted an angry directive from Bragg to Smith that called for a full report of "any and every action . . . taken in regard to General Taylor's movements" since the Louisianan received orders to cross the river. Bragg soon had copies of the letters exchanged by Smith and Taylor during the operation. Secretary of State Judah Benjamin, at Davis's insistence, also requested that Taylor provide Richmond with information on the undertaking to cross troops into Mississippi. Taylor's adjutant, William Levy, furnished Benjamin with a synopsis of events that focused on Walker, Forney, and the apparent mishandling of the Texas division. Quoting Smith's own words from dispatches sent to Taylor, Levy effectively portrayed the commanding general as indecisive and manipulative. Upon receipt of the letter, Benjamin passed the information on to Davis and added that Smith had "countermanded all he had done."[9]

Even with the Mississippi River as a barrier, Taylor continued to snipe at his former commander. He lodged a protest with Bragg over allegations that Smith had pardoned deserters who fled the army during preparations to cross into Mississippi. The complaint, though, contained just partially accurate information regarding Smith's proposed amnesty plan. Immediately after he had rescinded the orders for the troops to cross, Smith suggested the idea of pardons to Simon Buckner, commander of Taylor's former district. He urged Buckner to intercept deserters and inform them "that if they will return at once to duty no notice will be taken of their absence." Following a conference with his division commanders, however, Buckner nixed the idea. "Such a course at present would destroy the discipline of the command," he cautioned. Buckner agreed that only for the purposes of punishment would he make a distinction between those who had turned themselves in voluntarily and those returned forcibly by patrols. Smith's orders to pardon deserters were discretionary, and Buckner declined to obey them.[10]

Unaware that Buckner had refused to enact the liberal amnesty program, Taylor complained that Smith's directive ended any hope of support from the Trans-Mississippi. Bragg passed Taylor's message to Secretary of War Seddon and attached a note calling the plan "unfortunate." Seddon turned the matter over to the president, who responded sharply. In an October 7 memorandum to Seddon, Davis condemned Smith's actions and accused him of placing a premium on desertion. He also declared that by allowing the troops to evade orders to cross the river, Smith had put the interests of the Trans-Mississippi above those of the Confederacy. "Require General Smith to explain his conduct," Davis instructed Seddon.[11]

His health and vigor restored, Smith responded to the allegations of misconduct with another attack on Taylor. He "respectfully returned" all inquiries regarding the alleged pardons to Richmond and called the charges of impropriety "a misrepresentation." Smith flatly denied issuing amnesty orders and maintained that, to the contrary, "measures were taken to arrest and punish the deserters." The beleaguered general then linked the accusations to Taylor and cautioned Davis against relying on his enemies for intelligence: "In acting on any communication personal to myself from General Taylor I beg the President to remember that General Taylor's systematic misrepresentation of my motives and acts exhibits a violence and prejudice restrained neither by respect for himself nor his superiors."[12]

After studying the information concerning Smith's struggles during the summer, Davis wrote the general a ponderous letter that addressed several points of contention. Dated December 24, the letter offered an explanation of the mix-up in orders to cross troops. The president asserted that the operation fell under Bragg's jurisdiction. He emphasized that Bragg was aware of his views "concerning the importance of re-enforcements from the Trans-Mississippi Department." Accordingly, the president had authorized Bragg to take any steps necessary to provide additional manpower for the armies in the East. However, Smith's telegrams to Richmond regarding the movement had neglected to stipulate that orders for the crossing came directly from Bragg. In fact, Davis claimed that the July 30 message from Smith marked the first time that he had heard of the proposed operations. He blamed Smith's telegrams for creating the confusion and forcing an executive "investigation" into the matter.[13]

Davis's criticism of Smith was unfair. Responsibility for notifying Richmond of the operation ultimately belonged to Bragg, not Smith. Further, Davis's contention that he was unaware of the proposed movement until receiving Smith's correspondences seems suspect. On July 16 Robert Garlick Hill Kean, a senior member of the War Department, recorded in his diary that Bragg had "carried out orders for General E. K. Smith to make a demonstration by crossing over a part of his force" to the east side of the Mississippi. Thus, three weeks before Davis informed Smith that he could find "no record" of orders for the movement, a War Department bureaucrat indicated that instructions to launch the operation had come from Davis and Seddon.[14]

While Kean may have misinterpreted Davis's recommendation to Bragg as a direct order, diaries written by other government officials support the contention that Richmond knew of the proposed crossing. John B. Jones, an assistant to Seddon, wrote on August 14, "General Taylor will cross the Mississippi with 4,000 on the 18th of this month." An entry in Josiah Gorgas's diary dated August 17 corroborated Jones's notation. Gorgas, the Confederacy's chief ordnance officer, asserted that "a division of the Trans-Mississippi Army [is] to cross the River tomorrow." On August 18, the crossing date projected by Jones and Gorgas, Taylor apprised the War Department of the "impracticability of moving troops . . . to the east bank of the Mississippi." Even if Taylor's message had taken several weeks to reach Richmond, Davis had become aware of the problems by August 8 and certainly had time to offer advice long before his Christmas Eve letter condemning Smith's conduct.[15]

Davis continued the correspondence by renewing his objections to Smith's strategy during the latter stages of the Red River campaign. "Vigorous measures did not rapidly follow your victories in April as would have prevented the enemy from sending troops to re-enforce his armies elsewhere," complained the president. In Davis's opinion, Smith had blundered in seeking to drive the Federals out of Arkansas and Louisiana rather than engaging the enemy to prevent him from crossing the Mississippi. A reluctance to engage the Federals west of the river, and the subsequent inability to send infantry east, signaled to Davis that Smith did not understand his role in the Confederacy's grand strategy. "I have not failed to appreciate the tendency of a commander whose mind is properly concentrated upon the necessities of his own position to overlook the wants which may exist elsewhere," he admonished Smith. The Trans-Mississippi's function was twofold: first, to prevent Federal forces west of the river from reinforcing the war effort in the East, and second, to serve as a conduit for troops and supplies for Confederate armies in Georgia and Virginia. Thus far, in Davis's estimation, Smith had failed to carry out either mission. The president urged him, "Spare no effort to afford assistance where it is so much needed for the maintenance of the common defense."[16]

Davis closed by offering encouragement for future operations and expressing great confidence in Smith's "zeal and ability." The president praised Smith for his "earnest desire . . . to sacrifice every personal consideration" to ensure the success of the Confederate cause. One week later, on New Year's Eve, he expanded Smith's authority to include "military operations on both banks of the Mississippi." The Federals had reportedly shifted a large number of troops from Tennessee to Virginia. To counterbalance the threat, Davis advised Smith to cross the river with as large a force as possible. However, Smith questioned the wisdom of this suggestion. Compliance with Davis's request would reduce the Confederate military presence in the Trans-Mississippi to a skeleton force. Despite the waning of Confederate fortunes on both sides of the river, Smith remained reluctant to acknowledge that his department was now a source of strategic supply rather than a true theater of operations. Neither Smith nor any significant number of troops would cross the Mississippi.[17]

Since the Red River campaign, military operations in the department had not gone well for Smith. The campaign into Missouri that he so desperately wanted to succeed failed to reach St. Louis and nearly ended in complete disaster. Led by Sterling Price, the newly christened Army of Missouri left Camden on August 28 and crossed into Missouri on September 19. Of the twelve thousand troops under Price's command, nearly one-third were ill equipped, untrained conscripts. One week later Price suffered a calamitous defeat at Pilot Knob, sixty-five miles south of St. Louis, after which he veered west and skirmished his way across Missouri until the Federals intercepted him south of Kansas City. On October 23, at West-port, Price fought his way out of a Union trap and raced southwest through Indian Territory and into Texas before finally returning to Camden on December 2. By then his army could muster just six thousand troops.[18]

Although Price did succeed in diverting a Union corps from operations east of the river, the raid had little impact on the war, and St. Louis remained fixed under Federal control. Partially because of his problems with Taylor, Smith failed to pro-vide Price with all of the department's available resources, including the infantry necessary to execute a full-scale invasion. Nevertheless, Smith portrayed the raid as a success: "I consider General Price as having effected the objects for which he was ordered into Missouri," he announced to the War Department.[19]

But the raid had not been a success, and Smith knew it. Upon Price's return to Shreveport, Smith refused to receive him. This snub, coupled with criticism from Reynolds, so offended Price that he requested a court of inquiry. Smith agreed and in March began arrangements for a hearing. Although the issue was never resolved, the bitterness between the commanders accentuated the factionalism that undermined efficient management of the department. By this time the Trans-Mississippi Department had come to be known derisively as the Kirby Smithdom. Smith sought to direct every aspect of the department but refused to shoulder blame for any failures. It was his unwillingness to support the raid combined with Price's incompetence that had led to defeat in Missouri.[20]

The most important resource that Smith neglected to provide was personal leadership. His decision to remain in Louisiana while Price led the raid compro-mised the campaign from the outset. Smith was well aware of Price's weaknesses as a field general and thus should have taken command himself. Price should have accompanied the column for recruiting purposes only. By assigning Price to command, Smith undermined the campaign's chances for success and in effect abandoned the Missouri politicians whose support he had enjoyed since assum-ing control of the Trans-Mississippi. Smith may have recognized the futility of the campaign from the outset and decided to divorce himself from field operations entirely. If Price achieved any degree of success, there would still be time for Smith to join the campaign and take his share of the accolades. But such thinking was backwards. Without Smith's direct involvement on the field, the campaign was doomed to failure. "General Smith had no correct idea himself of what was necessary in Missouri," complained a cavalry officer. "He had slept too long in Shreveport among the perfumes of its wonderful flowers and beneath the soft languor of its delicious skies."[21]

While the Federals continued to garrison St. Louis, most Union military efforts in the West turned toward key transportation and supply centers still under
Rebel control. To hold these points, Davis needed daring generalship rather than
the conservative approach demonstrated by Smith in the Trans-Mississippi. By
the time Taylor reached his headquarters in Meridian, Mississippi, the Federals
had secured Mobile Bay, and the Army of Tennessee had evacuated Atlanta. Additional manpower for the defense of these strongholds was the primary reason
Davis and Bragg wanted Taylor to take troops from the Trans-Mississippi across
the river. A tour of his new department only served to convince Taylor that without reinforcements from the Trans-Mississippi, the Confederates had little hope
of victory. He also knew that these prospects were highly unlikely. During a meeting with Davis in Montgomery, Alabama, on September 27, Taylor advised the
president that the Trans-Mississippi could provide no more assistance to armies
east of the river and that, in fact, states west of the Mississippi "clamored for the
return of those [troops] already there." Taylor also pointed out that the citizens
of the Trans-Mississippi felt neglected and abused by Richmond and that several
politicians had proposed secession from the Confederacy.[22]

These claims represented an indirect attack on Smith's ability to run the department. In a letter to Bragg written two days before the meeting with Davis, Taylor
offered an unequivocal challenge to Smith's authority. He unveiled a plan for Bragg
to take command of the Trans-Mississippi and, with his own help, renew operations
west of the river. Although the plan was motivated partially by Taylor's disdain for
Smith, it also had considerable strategic value. The vast territory and resources of the
Trans-Mississippi could afford the Confederacy both the time and the wherewithal
to shift the center of gravity away from the East and turn a war of attrition to their
advantage. The attention of both Bragg and Davis, however, remained fixed on territory east of the river rather than on the strategic alternatives posed by developments to the west. Accordingly, Taylor received instructions to support and supply
John B. Hood's foray into Tennessee. "I did not disguise my conviction that the best
we could hope for was to protract the struggle until spring," Taylor later wrote. "It
was for statesmen, not soldiers, to deal with the future." The autumn of 1864, marred
by Hood's campaign, would prove to be the swan song for the Confederacy.[23]

During the fall, the Louisiana ballot box became a new battleground for the
feud between Taylor and Smith. Across the state, Taylor remained the hero of
the Red River campaign, while Smith emerged increasingly as the villain who
had allowed the marauding Federals to despoil the countryside and escape unpunished. On October 17 Louisiana held a special election to fill a congressional

seat left vacant by the death of Benjamin Hodge. Widely viewed as a referendum on Smith's policies, the contest pitted John Langdon Lewis, portrayed as a pro-Smith candidate, against Taylor's former lieutenant Henry Gray. An experienced politician and friend of Jefferson Davis, Gray had raised a regiment from the state's northwestern parishes early in the war. During the Teche and Red River campaigns, his Twenty-eighth Louisiana Infantry had established itself as one of Taylor's most reliable fighting forces. Moreover, at Mansfield, Gray had conspired with Taylor to violate Smith's orders and confront the Federals at the Moss plantation. With the northwestern portion of the state suffering from the aftermath of Banks's raids and the congressional seat representing these parishes up for grabs, Gray seemed a wise choice to represent the growing number of Louisianans who deplored Smith's authority over their state.[24]

As an officer serving within Smith's jurisdiction, however, Gray could not openly conduct a campaign against the policies of the department commander. Although the public did not receive an official acknowledgment of Gray's candidacy until several weeks before the election, his subordinates and supporters canvassed the parishes on his behalf. The Louisiana media helped define the election as a referendum on Smith's conduct versus Taylor's. As early as September 6, newspapers in Natchitoches and Shreveport had asked their readers to scrutinize the achievements of the Smith administration before casting their vote. "Do you endorse the military administration of General E. Kirby Smith?" asked the *Natchitoches Times*. The *Shreveport News* reminded its readers that the outcome of the election would depend on voters' interpretation of events.[25]

Bitter electioneering between pro-Smith and pro-Taylor factions divided Louisiana during the fall of 1864. A leading citizen indicated to former governor Thomas Moore that contempt for Taylor would prevent at least one man from voting for Gray. Frank Biosset pledged that he had "learned to hate Genl. Taylor so . . . that he would support the devil if he thought it would mortify Taylor." Sol Smith complained openly about Taylor's influence in the election and declared that minds had been "poisoned against Genl. Smith." He urged the electorate to "resist belief in the accusations" against Smith and reminded Moore of the truth of the proverb, "A prophet finds honor save in his own country." On the other side of the debate, E. Warren Moise, a prominent magistrate, announced, "I have no sympathy for those who are willing & knowing victims of [Smith's] immeasurable stupidity." In a fiery letter to Moore, he described an exchange between Lewis and electors in Rapides Parish in which the candidate "was asked directly if he sustained Genl. Smith." Lewis replied that he was "not aware of the charges against Genl. Smith," but that he would study the topic before making up his mind. "And this is the candidate . . . for congress," Moise roared in disgust. "What we want now, of all other things, is to send to congress a bitter opponent of Smith, & this we have in Gray."[26]

Several days later Moore received information that Lewis did not in fact support the Smith administration. In reference to the Red River campaign, a Lewis supporter, I. D. Harper, insisted that his candidate favored Taylor's policies and had been, from the outset of Banks's invasion, "opposed to drawing the enemy into the interior." Further, he claimed that the alleged association with Smith disturbed Lewis. Nevertheless, Lewis could not dispel the perception that he had endorsed Smith's policies. By October 5 Gray had publicly acknowledged his candidacy, and on October 17 he trounced Lewis by a three-to-one margin. The connection to Taylor and Mansfield, combined with widespread support from those who had suffered at the hands of the Federal invasion, gave Gray a decisive victory. Shortly afterward, Gray left Louisiana to take his seat in what would be the last session of the Confederate Congress.[27]

Gray's support for Taylor and his animus toward Smith did not end with his departure for Richmond. Rather, he carried the battle with Smith onto the floor of the Congress. Gray's focus was not military strategy but cotton and trade with the enemy. Accusations surfaced in Richmond that during the Red River campaign Smith had intentionally devised his strategy of retreat into the Louisiana interior so as to allow Banks and Porter to procure twenty-five thousand bales of Confederate cotton. The allegation that Smith had received a share of the profits in exchange for his cooperation severely damaged his reputation. In January 1865 Davis received a letter from a prominent Arkansan that directly implicated Smith as a principal in the illegal cotton trade. Robert W. McHenry advised the president that during the previous spring campaign, Smith had approved the sale of "thousands of bales of cotton to the enemy on the Mississippi."[28]

Although the charges of collusion with the Federals were never proved, repeated complaints of graft in Smith's department compelled Congress to act. In March the legislature passed a joint resolution authorizing the chief executive to investigate the allegations of corruption. Davis appointed a presidential commission to investigate charges against the Cotton Bureau in the Trans-Mississippi. Gray protested that the measure was not strong enough to curb the treasonous practice of selling cotton to the Federals. He spoke to the representatives "at considerable length, giving what he had seen of this traffick with the enemy while he was with the army in Louisiana." Gray's persistence was instrumental in passing a bill aimed directly at Smith's authority over the Cotton Bureau. Signed into law on March 18, the measure ordered that "suit be brought against persons connected with the Cotton Bureau and Cotton Office" by attorneys representing the Trans-Mississippi states. A friend in Richmond, privy to governmental affairs, passed along some timely advice to Smith: "If [you] can find anybody who has been acting the rascal about cotton . . . have him shot."[29]

In the months before the collapse of the Confederacy, Smith did in fact sanction the export of cotton across enemy lines. A Confederate treasury agent serving in the Trans-Mississippi vetoed the writ and forced Smith to halt the practice. Still, the exchange of cotton between the lines became increasingly common during the final days of the Trans-Mississippi. The treasury agent, Judge P. W. Gray (no relation), resigned soon after issuing his directive against the illicit trade. Judge Gray claimed that he could not handle the overwhelming pressure of the job. As newspapers throughout the Confederacy argued about Smith's complicity in the illegal cotton trade, the San Antonio News called upon Davis to remove him from command.[30]

Smith's prestige was beginning to suffer east of the river as well. The Richmond Whig delivered a series of stinging editorials directed at Smith's administration, praising Taylor for engineering the victories at Mansfield and Pleasant Hill and denouncing Smith for the failure to destroy Banks and Porter. The Whig blamed the Confederate misfortunes in the East on the results of the Red River campaign and Smith's inability to send reinforcements across the Mississippi. "The loss of Atlanta [and] General Sherman's march through Georgia . . . are directly traceable to the unaccountable blunder committed by Lieut. Gen. Kirby Smith in Louisiana," the paper trumpeted. Accordingly, as Confederate fortunes waned, Smith's prestige among easterners began to suffer amid his censure over cotton, troops, and strategy.[31]

The escape of Banks and Porter notwithstanding, when the Shreveport News reprinted the Richmond Whig's criticisms of Smith, the articles elicited a dramatically different response from Louisiana's citizenry. For months the War Department, to no avail, had implored Smith to send troops across the Mississippi to replenish the eastern armies. This did not endear him to Confederates in Virginia, but his failure to deliver troops enhanced Smith's status among Louisianans. The security of their own territory was the greatest concern for most Trans-

Mississippians, and Smith's reluctance to send Louisiana boys across the river was for many a matter of protecting the state's right to self-defense. In February, Governor Henry Watkins Allen joined the state legislature in issuing a protest over Richmond's continued attempts to sustain the war effort in the East with soldiers from the Trans-Mississippi. Yet despite the tenuous shift in public opinion in Smith's favor, Arkansas's *Washington Telegraph* indicated that the general's enormous responsibilities were too much for any one person to handle.[32]

Nevertheless, troop movement was but one issue for the citizens of the Trans-Mississippi, and support for Smith remained relatively weak. Louisiana state representatives endorsed Taylor's proposal that Bragg cross the river and take command of the department. Missouri congressman Thomas Snead agreed that Smith must go, but he represented a political faction that was "violently opposed" to Bragg. He therefore suggested that Davis install Joseph E. Johnston as commander. Ultimately, Snead's wing believed that the Trans-Mississippi was too vast for any one general to oversee effectively. Snead argued that Richmond should divide the department's leadership tasks between two generals, one to handle military affairs and another to execute administrative and political duties. But Snead had little hope that Davis would heed his recommendation and believed that, to the detriment of the Confederacy, Smith would retain sole power. "The people of the South have very little administrative ability," he lamented, "and the President has less of it than almost any other man."[33]

The concept of concurrent command in the Trans-Mississippi surfaced in some military circles as well. Bragg's adjutant, George W. Brent, brought up the possibility to P. G. T. Beauregard, commanding the Military Division of the West: "It would be well to recommend . . . that General Bragg be sent at once to relieve Smith, and organize and administer trans-Mississippi, and General R. Taylor to command troops. This would be a strong concentration and secure prompt action." While nothing tangible came of the idea, Richmond continued to grapple with Smith's administrative deficiencies. Seddon warned Beauregard not to count on succor from across the river. He confessed that Smith had "failed heretofore to respond" to such requests and stated plainly, "no plans should be based on his compliance." As the crisis in Virginia worsened, Davis counseled Robert E. Lee to expect nothing from Smith. He held the Trans-Mississippi commander responsible for failing to aid the Army of Northern Virginia and reminded Lee "of the extent to which I have urged General Smith to send troops from the west to the east side of the Mississippi River." The president suggested that the only way to rectify the situation was to replace Smith with Bragg, a commander "whose views were sufficiently comprehensive to embrace the whole question of defense in the Confederate States." [34]

Anti-Smith sentiment seemed to be contagious, and the general felt increasingly persecuted by adversaries and allies alike. In a March 9 letter to Davis, Smith defended himself against the numerous allegations of impropriety. Complaining, "I have been attacked in the columns of the Richmond Whig," he challenged the veracity of the editorials. The derisive articles appearing in newspapers across the South were, he claimed, part of a conspiracy by his enemies to "prejudice the public mind and destroy confidence" in his "motives and . . . ability to command." Assuring the president that he understood the strategic needs of the war effort, Smith insisted that he had "never failed to co-operate with the means at [his] disposal in insuring its success." As he had done earlier when his leadership came under fire, Smith offered to resign his post. "I desire to aid and not embarrass you in your action," he pledged, and he suggested that Davis regard the letter as "an application to be relieved from the command of the department whenever you believe that the public interests will be advanced thereby." [35]

In a subsequent letter written on March 11 Smith offered a response to the criticisms contained in Davis's December 24 letter. On Christmas Eve the president had condemned Smith for his failure to follow up battlefield victories during the spring and for the fruitless effort to send troops across the Mississippi. Smith defended his actions on both fronts and emphasized that Davis did not fully appreciate the degraded conditions in the Trans-Mississippi. The general insisted that when Banks and Porter evacuated Alexandria, in mid-May 1864, he had planned to lead a campaign through Arkansas and into Missouri. This campaign would have met Davis's demand for "vigorous measures" to prevent the Federals from using their Trans-Mississippi units in other theaters. Smith cited "the exhausting effects of [the Red River] campaign on both men and material" to explain his hesitation in launching the proposed operation. To support this argument, he enclosed a letter from Taylor written soon after the close of affairs on the Red River. On May 24 Taylor had expressed his support for a drive into Missouri. However, he had also described his divisions as "utterly worn down" and insisted that the troops were in dire need of rest and resupply before beginning another campaign. Accordingly, Smith postponed the movement into Arkansas and Missouri and busied himself with the "task of preparing for active operations late in August." [36]

Smith reminded Davis that the instructions issued in July to send troops across the Mississippi had disrupted his plans. Smith blamed the failure to launch a summer campaign through Arkansas on the wasted efforts to secure safe passage across the Mississippi for Taylor and his troops. His decision to turn the invasion into a cavalry raid rested on the assumption that the crossing would deprive the Trans-Mississippi of its infantry. Still, Smith considered the raid a success in that Price had forced the Federals to divert troops from the East to meet the threat in Missouri. Moreover, Smith challenged the president's impression that he remained indifferent to the struggles across the river. "The Mississippi was an impassable barrier," Smith reasoned, and he insisted that "by the expedition into Missouri I made the only diversion in my power."[37]

As he had done two days earlier, Smith again offered Davis the opportunity to remove him from command. Unlike the previous letter, in which Smith confessed that he did not wish to "embarrass" Davis, this time he put the onus of replacing him squarely on the president's shoulders. While expressing a desire to "promote the common welfare" and a willingness to "sacrifice every personal consideration," he refused to accept responsibility for the strategic failures in the Trans-Mississippi. Rather than address the president in the sympathetic manner that characterized the March 9 letter, Smith stated plainly that he would "as a soldier strive honestly and faithfully to obey" his orders. He then issued a challenge to the president: "If you doubt my ability or believe that another can better execute [your orders], I request that he may be sent to relieve me of the responsible and onerous duties with which I am charged."[38]

Apart from his misuse of Walker's division during the Red River campaign and his reluctance to lead the Missouri raid, the failures in the Trans-Mississippi were not entirely Smith's fault. From the very beginning of his tenure in the Trans-Mississippi, the weak military infrastructure of the department and the strong Federal presence along the Mississippi had posed an enormous challenge. Disappointment over setbacks on the battlefield and frustration over the running battle with Taylor had further eroded Smith's hopes of success. The barbed criticism of the eastern press and the indirect rebuke at the ballot box in Louisiana had brought his administration to the brink of collapse, and now the commander in chief himself had impugned Smith's honor and ability. The allegations of unprofessional conduct were particularly galling in light of the president's reluctance to reprimand Taylor for his insubordination following the Red River campaign.

As he had demonstrated during the quarrel with Taylor, Smith was slow to anger. Davis's Christmas Eve letter might not have so rankled him had it not come on the heels of the other recent attacks on his character. As it was, the letter provoked a contentious response.[39]

A firm belief that he had done nothing wrong and had carried out orders implicitly emboldened Smith to turn the question of his competency over to the president. By now the rumors of Bragg or Taylor or Johnston coming to take command in the department had reached Smith's ears. The March 9 letter suggests that he was confident Davis would not appoint a new commander for the Trans-Mississippi. Yet by using Taylor's May 24 letter to illustrate the degraded state of his department, Smith risked undermining his own argument. While Taylor's letter affirmed the jaded condition of his troops, it also laid the blame for the declining state of the Trans-Mississippi directly on Smith's headquarters. The Louisianan listed numerous weaknesses in the department and insisted that the problems all stemmed from Shreveport. "No campaign dependent on the present system of [bureaucracy] will succeed," Taylor had emphasized. Upon receiving Taylor's letter, Smith had initially composed an angry challenge to dispute the charges. He never sent the letter to Taylor, but he did forward a copy to Davis along with copies of Taylor's disparaging letters, including the one of May 24. Smith had used that series of communications as evidence to support his decision to relieve Taylor from command in June 1864. Nine months later, with Taylor ensconced across the Mississippi, Smith sent Davis another copy of the May 24 letter, but this time for a far different purpose: to use Taylor as an ally *in absentia*. It was an action that put Smith's credibility at considerable risk.[40]

After sending the dispatches to Davis, Smith turned his attention to the pressing needs of his department. To the west he made defensive arrangements to safeguard Texas from invasion, and to the east he ordered fortifications strengthened at Monroe. To remedy the department's shortage of manpower, he revisited the notion of "training negroes under command by their masters." Smith also began preparations to take the offensive against the Federals at Little Rock, in hopes of paving the way for a Missouri campaign during the summer of 1865. He apprised Davis of the operation and requested a conference with the president in Richmond. Davis's focus, however, was elsewhere. On March 24 Robert E. Lee sent word to Smith imploring him to cross the Mississippi "with as large a force as may be prudently withdrawn" from the Trans-Mississippi. None of these plans had time to develop. Like the struggles between Confederate leaders, campaigns in the Trans-Mississippi became moot with news of Lee's surrender at Appomattox.[41]

Word of Lee's surrender "burst like a thunderbolt on the Trans-Mississippi Department," in the words of one Missourian. Another, upon hearing the news, confided to his diary, "This is a sad and I fear almost fatal blow to the prospects of our cause." Confronting the specter of defeat, many of Smith's detractors began to take a milder stance. "We are just as capable of distrust of Robert E. Lee as of Kirby Smith," editorialized one Texas newspaper, while another acknowledged the "absurdity of supposing that he would do any act to tarnish the brilliant military reputation which secures . . . the confidence and esteem of his countrymen and the gratitude of posterity." On April 21 Smith ordered his army to remain in the field and told his men that Lee and the Army of Northern Virginia were prisoners of war. "The crisis of the revolution is at hand," he announced defiantly. Declaring that the fate of the Confederacy depended upon the Trans-Mississippi, he entreated the soldiers, "Stand by your colors [and] maintain your discipline." Smith's plea did little to motivate the troops. Despondency in the dwindling ranks soon yielded to "apathy and indifference." From Shreveport, a Union scout observed that "the Army of the Trans-Mississippi was in spirit crushed."[42]

At headquarters, Smith met repeatedly with senior officers and politicians in an attempt to consolidate military and civilian control over the department. The efforts failed, and Federal overtures to open surrender negotiations put Smith under increased pressure to act. Some in the Trans-Mississippi hierarchy opposed capitulation entirely, and Smith learned that a handful of disgruntled officers, including Price, had met to discuss a coup d'état. Still others urged Smith to seek the best possible terms of surrender.[43]

Smith declared Houston the new capital of the department and on May 20 abandoned Shreveport for Texas. He believed that Trans-Mississippi troops would follow him across the Sabine and hoped that the weight of their numbers would compel the Federals to offer better terms or risk a resumption of hostilities. The gamble did not pay off. Smith arrived at Houston on May 27 only to find that his soldiers had not followed en masse. To the contrary, a steady flow of reports confirmed the breakup of commands across the department. Three days later Smith addressed his men for the last time and declared, "I am left a commander without an army—a General without troops." Rather than acknowledge the futility of a protracted war that would carry the Confederates into the Southwest, he blamed the common soldier for failing to stand by a cause irrevocably lost. "You have made your choice," he chided them. "It is unwise and unpatriotic, but it is final. I pray you may not live to regret it." Smith urged the men to return to their homes and families and to "resume occupations of peace." On June 2, on board the ship *Fort Jackson* anchored off Galveston, Smith signed the documents of surrender presented by Federal general Edward R. S. Canby. Two months earlier in Alabama, the same Federal officer had accepted the surrender of Taylor's command.[44]

By the time of his surrender, Taylor commanded very few troops. After the destruction of Hood's army at Nashville in December, Davis assigned Taylor command of the Army of Tennessee. The president also issued instructions for the bulk of the forces, numbering only about seventeen thousand, to march east and reinforce efforts to stop Sherman in the Carolinas. Taylor relinquished field command to Beauregard, the ranking officer in the theater, and as the army moved east, Taylor worked to strengthen defenses in southern Alabama. "The duty of a soldier in the field is simple," he recalled, "to fight until stopped by the civil arm of his government or his government has ceased to exist." By the spring of 1865 the Confederate government was teetering on the brink of extinction, and Taylor acknowledged that "the struggle was virtually over."[45]

On April 9, one year after Pleasant Hill, Taylor received word that Richmond had fallen, and he soon learned of Lee's and Johnston's surrender. Admitting that "there was no room for hesitancy," he agreed to an immediate truce with Canby, adding, "Folly and madness combined would not have justified an attempt to prolong a hopeless contest." On April 29 the generals met at Magee's farm near Mobile to discuss terms that would "soothe the pride of the vanquished." Taylor recalled that in the days that surrounded the negotiations many members of the Confederate Congress who had fled Richmond sought refuge at his headquarters. He implored the representatives to return to their homes and, by example, "teach the people to submit to the inevitable, obey the laws, and resume the peaceful occupations on which society depends." On May 6, at Citronelle, Alabama, forty miles northwest of Mobile, Taylor signed the surrender papers. "We could only secure honorable interment for the remains of our cause," he later conceded. Unlike Smith's outburst against his own troops at the end of the war, Taylor praised his men and declared that he would share the fate of his soldiers. "I delivered the epilogue of the great drama in which I had played a humble part," he recalled. "All were weary of strife," he told Canby.[46]

Upon completion of the surrender formalities, Taylor directed Canby to supply depots across the department and helped transfer thousands of bales of Confederate cotton to United States authorities. Afterward, Canby escorted Taylor and Tom Strother, now a free man, to New Orleans, where the former Confederate general and his former slave awaited reunion with their family. Within days, word reached Taylor that several high-ranking officers from the Trans-Mississippi had arrived in New Orleans under a flag of truce and requested a meeting with him. Price, Buckner, and Joseph Brent wanted to discuss their remaining options. Taylor met with the generals and helped arrange an interview with Canby. Both Union and Confederate principals requested Taylor's presence at the meeting. Buckner suggested that he had the authority to negotiate terms for the Trans-Mississippi, and on May 26 he surrendered the department to Canby, contingent upon Smith's approval. One week after the New Orleans meeting, Canby secured Smith's signature on the documents. Smith's was the last Confederate command to surrender.[47]

During the negotiations in New Orleans, Taylor learned that "some generals of the highest rank had found it convenient to fold their tents and quietly leave for the Rio Grande." On June 26, astride an army mule, Smith crossed the river and entered Mexico. "I have left everything behind," he wrote, "except a clear conscience."[48]

13

Denouement

OF MEN AND MEASURES

Edmund Kirby Smith based his decision to flee to Mexico primarily upon reports that Federal authorities had arrested Robert E. Lee. Aware that President Andrew Johnson's amnesty proclamation excluded general officers, Smith decided not to risk the uncertainty that faced many Confederates in the reunited states. He set out on his journey on June 15, stopping briefly at San Antonio. There, several ex-Confederates, including Price, Reynolds, Allen, and Moore, joined him on the trek across the Rio Grande. The group reached Mexico City on July 16. To his disappointment, Smith found Mexican authorities unreceptive to the presence of former Rebel leaders, and in late July he sailed for Cuba.[1]

Smith lived on the island in relative comfort but soon began to make inquiries about the process of repatriation. He wanted to return home "without dishonor or humiliation" and wrote a series of letters to United States government officials offering to take the oath of allegiance if permitted to repatriate without penalty. On July 31 Smith pleaded his case to Ulysses S. Grant: "I wish to return home, will give my parol take the oath of allegiance and quietly and peaceably settle down at some occupation." A letter from Grant arrived in late October informing Smith that once he took the oath, his status would be the same as any other parolee. On November 14 he returned to his wife and family in Lynchburg, Virginia. For Smith, the war was finally over.[2]

Taylor traveled to Washington soon after the war to lobby Grant, Johnson, and others in the government for the release of Jefferson Davis, imprisoned since his capture in Georgia on May 10, 1865. For two years he persisted in pressuring Washington officials in behalf of his brother-in-law. In 1867 the United States freed the former Confederate president, and Davis returned to Mississippi. Throughout Reconstruction, Taylor worked as a lobbyist for the Democratic Party in Louisiana and spoke out against the vigilantism of the Ku Klux Klan, whose members he portrayed as assassins and criminals. During that time, he and his brother-in-law Duncan Kenner launched two business ventures, both of which failed. Upon the death of his wife in March 1875, Taylor left New Orleans and relocated to Winchester, Virginia, near the home of his sister. Two years later he began work on his memoirs. "One who has made history, even in a small way, is rarely happy writing it," Taylor told an associate before he began work on the manuscript. "An intelligent intermediate is more likely to do justice to a campaign than a commander, as he writes from an impersonal standpoint." The task took nearly two years, and his book, *Destruction and Reconstruction*, was published in April 1879. On April 12, several days after the book's release, Taylor died at the home of a friend in New York City. He was fifty-three years old.[3]

Smith learned of Taylor's death while employed as a mathematics professor at the University of the South in Sewanee, Tennessee. He had decided to return to the world of academics in 1875 after several failed attempts at business. Smith never directly answered Taylor's allegations of incompetence. Instead, he wrote a brief synopsis of the Red River campaign as part of the series "Battles and Leaders of the Civil War" published in *Century* magazine. The article, titled "The Defense of the Red River," also gave Smith an opportunity to defend himself against charges of corruption in the cotton trade. The series of articles, including Smith's piece, was later published collectively in book form. The last living full Confederate general, Smith died on March 28, 1893, at his home in Sewanee. Although he never met with Taylor after the war, Smith was aware, at the time of his death, of the impression that *Destruction and Reconstruction* had left on veterans and historians.[4]

The release of *Destruction and Reconstruction* elicited both praise and criticism of Taylor. While the *New York Herald* portrayed the book as "the most credible attempt made by a Southerner" to interpret the war, the *Nation* cautioned its readers that although Taylor's work was "useful," it was also "mischievous." Privately, William T. Sherman admitted that even though Taylor's memoir slandered many good men, *Destruction and Reconstruction* was generally "honest, fair, and just." Louisianan P. G. T. Beauregard, however, denounced the book. In personal correspondence he criticized it as inaccurate and cited Grant's impression of Taylor as a "great talker" who often substituted "imagination for facts."[5]

From Virginia, the Southern Historical Society, an organization of former Confederates dedicated to preserving the history of their short-lived nation, presented a relatively balanced review of Taylor's work. The *Southern Historical Society Papers*, the organization's monthly publication, characterized *Destruction and Reconstruction* as riveting, filled with vivid descriptions of campaigns and personalities. "If the style is sometimes pedantic, flippant, and occasionally even coarse, it is always sprightly, often sparkling, and throughout decidedly entertaining," the *Papers* editorialized. This tacit endorsement of Taylor's book helped to nurture the myth of the Lost Cause. Among other things, *Destruction and Reconstruction* corroborated the image of Robert E. Lee as an American icon, supported the concept of James Longstreet as the villain of Gettysburg, and established the notion that Stonewall Jackson sucked lemons. The *Southern Historical Society Papers* cautioned, however, that some of Taylor's pronouncements were historically imprecise. Citing the account of First Manassas, in which Taylor failed to credit Smith for a timely arrival at the front, the review of *Destruction and Reconstruction* alerted the reader, "[Taylor] has not always verified his facts and is sometimes inaccurate in his statements."[6]

That admonition aside, Taylor's book became a manifesto upon which countless former Confederates relied for their own reminiscences of the war. In the *Southern Historical Society Papers* and in *Confederate Veteran*, a magazine that served as an outlet for the reminiscences of old soldiers, numerous articles cited *Destruction and Reconstruction* to support their assertions and anecdotes. Like many veterans and their families, the periodicals embraced Taylor's book as a source of "valuable material for the future historian."[7]

At meetings of the United Daughters of the Confederacy, women read aloud from Taylor's book and entered passages into the record as a part of the proceedings. In later years the organization sponsored essay contests in Louisiana schools based on Taylor's exploits during the war. In one such essay an eighth-grader explained that Taylor "was opposed to war but when his state seceded he joined the Confederates [and] defeated General Banks at Sabine Cross Roads." Another described the Louisianan as "one of the bravest generals in the army," while a third student postulated, "Taylor's skillful management prevented the federals from spreading all over the state." The students emphasized repeatedly that Taylor had engineered the victories at Mansfield and Pleasant Hill, "thereby making it necessary for the federal General to give up the Red River expedition and retreat." While these pronouncements possessed a degree of historical accuracy, they also mirrored Taylor's point of view as expressed in *Destruction and Reconstruction*.[8]

Despite the assessments of Taylor's memoir as an important reference for students of the war, the *Southern Historical Society Papers* issued a warning to society members: "General Taylor's criticisms of men and measures are trenchant, sharp and decided, and there will be, of course, difference of opinion as to whether they are always just." No man suffered more under the weight of Taylor's acerbic pen than Smith. *Destruction and Reconstruction* offered venomous condemnations of him as an administrator, a strategist, and a leader. Taylor asserted that Smith established a vast departmental bureaucracy in the Trans-Mississippi that functioned primarily to support his administration rather than to serve the needs of the soldiers. Further, he accused his former commanding officer of sacrificing the Confederacy's strengths in Louisiana and Texas to pursue personal glory in Union-occupied Missouri and Arkansas.[9]

Taylor's criticism was harshest in his examination of Smith's strategy during the Red River campaign. Describing Smith's policy as one of "sheer stupidity and pig-headed obstinacy," he claimed that the withdrawal of Walker's division for the Arkansas campaign wasted the advantage that the army had gained with its blood in Louisiana. Smith's strategy had the effect of protecting rather than destroying the Federal army and fleet. According to Taylor's analysis, Smith had based the plan not on sound military strategy but rather on his consuming desire to recover the "lost empire" of the Trans-Mississippi: Arkansas and Missouri. As Taylor put it, in a particularly biting passage, "General Kirby Smith had a wonderful plan for the destruction of the enemy which I had disturbed rashly by beating his army at Mansfield and Pleasant Hill."[10]

The widespread acceptance of Taylor's memoir and its use as a standard resource helped foster a negative perception of Smith among many veterans of the Red River campaign. In *Confederate Veteran,* Texan W. T. Shaw scrutinized the campaign and reached a conclusion consistent with Taylor's view: "Had not Kirby Smith persisted in withdrawing more than two-thirds of Taylor's force to Arkansas, it is practically certain [the Federals] would not have escaped." H. T. Douglas, former chief engineer in the Trans-Mississippi, directly addressed the question of Smith's strategy in his article for the magazine. "I am inclined to think that the move against General Steele was a mistake," Douglas announced. He tempered the criticism, however, by portraying Smith as a brave and honest soldier who put forth an "earnest effort to achieve success for his army and his cause." Douglas concluded that "all generals make mistakes" and that by pursuing Steele instead of allowing Taylor to continue concentration against Banks, Smith "may have made one." Another veteran drew a similar conclusion. John Witherspoon Dubose blamed Smith for failing to allow Taylor "to control the situation and its logic" immediately following Pleasant Hill. "General Taylor, on the very evening of his great victory, in the act of giving orders to drive the enemy out of the Mississippi Valley and New Orleans, was arbitrarily displaced," argued Dubose. From Taylor's home state, Louisianan Frank D. Henderson did not hesitate to cite *Destruction and Reconstruction* to support his interpretation of the campaign:

"Taylor tells in his memoirs that except for Kirby Smith's restraint and lack of support, he could have captured Banks's army. I think so too."[11]

While other veterans analyzed the Red River campaign without casting blame on Smith, most articles heaped praise on Taylor. Several of the general's former troops boasted proudly that Taylor had disobeyed orders at Mansfield and deliberately provoked a fight with Banks. In his exposé on the battle, J. E. Hewitt characterized Taylor as "one of the most successful and resourceful officers in the Confederate service." Others echoed Hewitt's sentiments. In the *Southern Historical Society Papers,* Dabney H. Maury, a friend of Taylor and an influential member of the society, provided readers with a biographical sketch that dripped with sentimentality. Maury reminded his readers that while in command in Louisiana, Taylor's "history was a brilliant record of incessant activity and unfailing success, culminating in the remarkable victories of Mansfield and Pleasant Hill." In a veiled criticism of Smith, Maury contended that unlike most Confederate commanders, Taylor sought to follow up his victories rather than allow the enemy to escape without a fight.[12]

While some society members continued to praise Taylor for his "marvelous energy" and quoted liberally from *Destruction and Reconstruction,* an interview with Benjamin Ewell, brother of Confederate general Richard Ewell, appeared to raise questions about the effect of wartime stress on the Louisianan's mental state. Originally published in 1892 by the *Richmond Times,* the piece was reprinted by the Southern Historical Society later that same year. Although not overtly critical of Taylor, Ewell revealed that during the months his brother served with the Louisianan, General Ewell feared that Taylor was so eccentric that "his mind would lose its balance." David French Boyd, an officer who served under Taylor in Louisiana and during the Shenandoah Valley campaign, supported Ewell's contention. In an article published in 1897 by the *New Orleans Times-Democrat,* Boyd indicated that Taylor rarely permitted himself to go "off duty." He also recalled that because of rheumatoid arthritis, Taylor endured constant pain and partial paralysis. The combination of physical pain and emotional stress contributed to Taylor's quick temper and mordant disposition. "In his moments of intense bodily suffering he was cross and irritable," Boyd confessed, and he admitted that many soldiers tried to stay away from Taylor during his bouts with rheumatoid arthritis. Boyd reminded his readers of "what a treat it was to sit around the campfire at night and listen to Dick Taylor—when he wasn't suffering." However, Boyd emphasized, "Taylor sick was not a pattern of patience and amiability."[13]

Taylor's physical and emotional condition did not improve during his tenure under Smith. The feud with his commanding officer combined with pressure from the Federals to keep Taylor in a constant state of agitation. In a tract published by the Southern Historical Society, Xavier DeBray recalled his first meeting with Taylor six days before the battle of Mansfield. The cavalry officer and his command had arrived at the front after two weeks of hard riding from Houston. Furious at Smith for the delay in sending reinforcements, Taylor directed his anger toward DeBray and threatened to arrest and court-martial the officer for his tardiness. Years later a Louisianan suggested that Taylor behaved like a determined soldier who had suffered a wound during combat, "crippled but full of fight and blasphemy."[14]

During the war Smith acknowledged that illness affected Taylor's judgment. In the spring of 1864 he had defended Taylor against criticism from other officers and repeatedly overlooked instances of insubordination. Only when the violations of military decorum degenerated into vitriolic personal attacks that threatened Smith's authority did he relieve Taylor from command. Smith's tolerant nature was evident to many who served under him during the war. *Confederate Veteran* articles often characterized him as a true "Christian Soldier" and pointed to his forgiving spirit as evidence of a strong religious faith. An obituary published in *Confederate Veteran* reprinted the eulogies delivered at the general's funeral service. Each one emphasized Smith's devotion to the Confederacy and to his church. Another article in the magazine anointed Smith as a "'praying' soldier" and asserted reverently that he was among the "cream of the staff." An essay in the *Southern Historical Society Papers* also surrounded Smith with an aura of holiness. Paul F. Hammond described the general as "an earnest Christian and a gentleman" and contended, "Pleasant manners flow naturally from the goodness of his heart, while an impulsive temper is kept under almost perfect control."[15]

Most articles in the Confederate journals continued to venerate Smith's character rather than discuss his generalship. His attempt to hold out against pressure to surrender in 1865 embodied for many veterans the very spirit of the Confederate Lost Cause. Other contributors cited Federal general Edward R. S. Canby's description of Smith as "the soul of honor" during surrender negotiations. Smith's active participation in the United Confederate Veterans contributed to his growing postwar prestige, as did a sketch written by his cousin and printed in *Confederate Veteran*. Eleanor G. Kirby, a historian with the Tennessee chapter of the United Daughters of the Confederacy, depicted Smith as a "great military genius" whose Christian leadership "left the imprint of a noble life on our Southern manhood." In him she saw the ideal blend of warrior and holy man, someone to be revered by future generations: "He had the nobility of Lee, the intense religious fervor of Jackson, [and] the dash of Stuart."[16]

In 1911 the town of Bossier City, Louisiana, christened Fort Smith Memorial Park to honor the general's contributions to the Trans-Mississippi. In the keynote speech, titled "The Last Confederate Army to Surrender and Its General," the speaker praised Smith's efforts to build a military-industrial complex that kept the Confederacy supplied with food, munitions, and troops. As a result of this success, the orator professed, Smith predicted the Federal movement to reduce Shreveport and devised his Red River strategy accordingly. "Fort Smith is a fitting memorial," he declared, for a general whose "record as a man and as a soldier is one that we do well to honor."[17]

Few articles from Trans-Mississippians, however, mirrored the sentiments expressed by their compatriots who served across the river or by the good people of Bossier City. In fact, immediately following the war one southern historian recalled that during the Red River campaign, "there was no enthusiasm for Smith among the troops," especially those from Louisiana. In other postwar recollections written by Trans-Mississippi veterans, the general's record mustered only mild support. One biographical sketch praised Smith's organizational talents but believed that during the Red River campaign it was the "measures of defense," rather than Smith's initiative, that "resulted in the decisive victory." Another piece, written by Texan P. S. Hagy, insisted that the strategic retreat had been Smith's idea and that the commanding general had wanted to "draw the enemy farther away from their gunboats in the Red River before engaging them." Hagy gave Taylor credit for the tactical victory at Mansfield but asserted, "General Smith (at least it was so reported) had determined to give battle" at the Sabine Crossroads.[18]

In the postwar analyses, Smith's reputation fared worse within the officer corps than among the common soldiers. Missourian Thomas L. Snead, one of Sterling Price's staff officers, echoed the harsh criticism of the Trans-Mississippi bureaucracy found in *Destruction and Reconstruction*. In a *Century* magazine article, Snead alleged that Smith disregarded the military necessities of the Trans-Mississippi and instead "kept very busy at Shreveport organizing bureaus and sub-bureaus; fortifying his capital; issuing orders and countermanding them; and planning campaigns that were never to be fought." Snead argued that Smith's weak leadership allowed the illegal cotton trade to flourish throughout the department. Another Missouri officer, John Newman Edwards, also chronicled the events surrounding Smith's involvement with cotton. In his memoirs, published just two years after the war, Edwards stated clearly that while Smith never profited from the sale of cotton, the illicit trade thrived under his watch and served as "another fruitful source of demoralization and distrust" among Trans-Mississippi soldiers. He insisted that by the latter stages of the war, the army had lost faith in Smith.[19]

Edwards traced this loss of faith back through the Missouri raid, through the failed attempt to send troops across the Mississippi, and finally to Smith's quarrel with Taylor during the Red River campaign. Although he considered Smith patriotic and well versed in military theory, Edwards charged that the commanding general was a poor leader whose failure to grasp the practical realities of war undermined his relationship with his men and led ultimately to his downfall. The Missourian accused Smith of letting his ego dictate policy and declared, "When a vain, weak man hesitates he invariably fails." In a blistering characterization of Smith's strategy and tactics during the Red River campaign, Edwards wrote, "While being pure, and true to the cause as any officer in the army, the unfortunate dispositions and maneuvers of General Smith placed him in a position to be violently criticized, and this criticism not unfrequently took the form of abuse or denunciation." Edwards argued that Smith stubbornly refused to alter his strategy after Taylor drove Banks from Pleasant Hill. Thus, Smith squandered an opportunity to destroy the Federals along the Red River and wasted Trans-Mississippi troop strength in the pointless pursuit of Steele in Arkansas.[20]

Edwards also acknowledged that Taylor had committed an "open violation of orders" by precipitating a fight at Mansfield: "The attack of Taylor involves serious considerations of unfortunate impetuosity and rash and hasty judgment." Edwards concluded that it was up to Smith to determine campaign strategy, even if that strategy was flawed, and that Taylor had no right to disobey orders. Nevertheless, he maintained that Taylor could not be held responsible for Smith's failure to inspire and enforce discipline among his lieutenants.[21]

Particularly among the general officers who served in the Trans-Mississippi, there emerged a view more consistent with the interpretation Taylor expressed in *Destruction and Reconstruction*. Camille J. Polignac, division commander during the latter stages of the Red River campaign, stated that Taylor showed "great judgment and remarkable insight into the enemy's designs." Smith's former chief of staff, William R. Boggs, noted a singular lack of such qualities in the commanding general. Once Steele began his retreat, Boggs maintained, Smith "ought to have

known that his army should have been pushed across country toward Alexandria."
John G. Walker, whose division was at the core of the dispute between Smith
and Taylor, weighed the relative merits of the debate and delivered his analysis
in support of the latter. "If on one hand, Banks was defeated, Steele was not sufficiently strong to advance alone," Walker asserted. "If on the other hand, Banks
should defeat Taylor, Steele's defeat would not retrieve the disaster, or save . . .
Western Louisiana and Eastern Texas from Federal invasion." Indeed, Walker disclosed that he had fully expected Smith to order the pursuit of Banks and that the
general's insistence on withdrawing most of Taylor's infantry and marching after
the Federals in Arkansas had surprised him. He characterized Smith's decision as
a calamitous "blunder" and insisted that "if the whole force of the Confederates
had been thrown upon [Banks's] shattered and demoralized army, its escape as an
organized force would have been almost impossible."[22]

Among the department's general officers, only Thomas J. Churchill expressed
unqualified support for Smith's strategy. During the campaign Churchill's Arkansas and Missouri troops had fought under Taylor at Pleasant Hill and with Smith
at Jenkins' Ferry. The Kentucky general charged that Taylor had done more than
merely commit a breach of protocol in initiating a battle below Shreveport. In disobeying orders, Churchill argued, Taylor wrecked Smith's strategy to lure Banks
deep into the Louisiana interior and strike him at Keachi. Churchill complained
rancorously, "Had Taylor carried out Gen Smiths instructions we would have
captured Banks entire army."[23]

Given Churchill's professional relationship with Smith, his complaints are less
than objective. During the Kentucky campaign Churchill had led a division under
Smith and performed admirably. In his official report on the battle of Richmond
Smith cited Churchill for his "bold" actions and commended him for displaying
"promptness and intelligence" in executing orders. In the opening stages of the
Red River campaign, Smith gave him command over the department's Arkansas
and Missouri infantry, and following the campaign he asked the War Department
to promote him to major general. Churchill identified Smith as an ally and remained devoted to his commander even after the war. Moreover, Churchill resented Taylor and held him responsible for the calamity on the Confederate right
at Pleasant Hill. The combination of loyalty to Smith and antipathy toward Taylor
colored the Kentuckian's analysis of events on the Red River.[24]

In contrast, St. John R. Liddell, who detested Taylor, did not hesitate to assign
Smith a large share of the blame: "General Smith, it is clear, should have kept

his forces together and pushed these successes [at Mansfield and Pleasant Hill], and will always be censured for this neglect." Liddell saved his harshest criticism, however, for Taylor. In many instances his memoirs surpassed *Destruction and Reconstruction* for sarcasm and vitriol directed toward a superior officer. He asserted that Taylor was unfit to lead troops and, attributing the general's rank to nepotism, charged that Taylor had "pocketed all sense of honor in taking the command." Liddell also contended that despite Smith's blunder, Taylor had a "splendid opportunity" to destroy Banks and Porter. He insisted that while the cavalry drove Banks toward Alexandria, Taylor's infantry should have occupied the town ahead of the retreat, seized Federal supplies, and cut the enemy lines of communication. Taylor's failure to adopt this strategy, Liddell believed, was at least in part to blame for the escape of Banks and Porter. He claimed that Smith had supported this plan but that Taylor, "carried away by childish elation and vain glory," resolved to chase Banks into Alexandria. According to Liddell, once Taylor recognized his mistake, he "had to exercise all his cunning to find some one to bear the blame." Taylor therefore "bitterly complained to the world that General Smith had taken away his troops."[25]

Liddell's continued insistence on his own strategy indicates that he was unaware of the arrangement between Smith and Taylor. On April 13, twelve days before the Federals occupied Alexandria, Smith agreed to return Walker's division to Louisiana once the Federal column in Arkansas began to retreat. He reiterated the agreement during a meeting with Taylor days later. His April 25 letter to Smith established that Taylor had based his plan to drive Banks into Alexandria on assurances that Walker's division would be at his disposal.[26]

Liddell's proposal to occupy Alexandria ahead of the Federals was not worth the strategic risks. With only three thousand Texas cavalry troopers guarding the road to Shreveport, Banks could have simply turned and, using his superior numbers, overwhelmed the cavalry and resumed the campaign. Further, the operation would have exposed the infantry at Alexandria to fire from Porter's fleet. Given the experiences with gunboats at Blair's Landing on April 12 and at Milliken's Bend during the summer of 1863, there is no indication that the infantry could have held Alexandria against Porter's ships. In addition, Steele would have received intelligence of Banks's advance, halted his retreat, and engaged Smith near Camden. Even if Smith had prevailed in Arkansas, Banks would still have taken Shreveport, cut Confederate lines of communication, and seized the vital Trans-Mississippi supply depots. With the Trans-Mississippi forces divided, it is unlikely that Smith could have prevented the Federals from marching into Texas and achieving their objective in the Red River campaign. Moreover, the Confederate strategy of concentration and the use of interior lines throughout the campaign belies Liddell's contention that Smith endorsed the plan to occupy Alexandria. As a strategist, Liddell was simply not on a par with either Smith or Taylor. Like Taylor, Liddell carried a personal grudge. He used his memoir as an opportunity to attack Taylor in much the same way Taylor used *Destruction and Reconstruction* as an opportunity to attack Smith. Unlike Taylor's criticism of Smith, however, Liddell's criticism of Taylor was militarily unjustified.[27]

Liddell's condemnation of Taylor stretched beyond disagreement over strategy at Alexandria. Liddell implied that he was privy to information from the Trans-Mississippi medical staff and maintained that illness made Taylor's "conduct and arrogance . . . intolerable." Liddell also alleged that Dr. David W. Yandell, the department's medical director, had little sympathy for Taylor and considered him selfish and egotistical—unlike Smith, whom Yandell called the most modest and devoted man he had ever met.[28]

Liddell also recalled a discussion with Dr. Sol Smith, the commanding general's surgeon and confidant. Sol Smith had insisted that Taylor did not become enraged over the Arkansas campaign until Smith refused to give him field command. A letter written by Lieutenant Edward Cunningham, also a member of Smith's staff, made the same claim. "Certainly, I never heard a word of [Taylor's] disapproval of the movement [to Arkansas] until . . . it was determined that he would remain in Louisiana," Cunningham asserted at the close of the campaign. That two members of Smith's staff gave the same account of events suggests that both were echoing the opinion of the commanding general. Taylor's recollections and his correspondence with Smith, however, indicate that he had voiced disapproval of the plan as early as April 10, five days before Smith ordered him to remain in Louisiana.[29]

Liddell also claimed to have met with Louisiana governor Henry Watkins Allen, who indicated that he did not get along with Taylor, either. Allen allegedly confided that he had urged Smith to remove Taylor from command in western Louisiana because, as Liddell put it, "Taylor's senselessness kept the whole department in an uproar. His insults had no other effect than to gain the ill will of everyone and to injure greatly the public service."[30]

Sarah Anne Dorsey, who compiled Allen's memoirs immediately following the war, disputed the notion that the governor disliked Taylor. To the contrary, she insisted, Allen maintained that Taylor was among the best military leaders in the Trans-Mississippi and called his transfer a "misfortune." Dorsey acknowledged that the dispute between Smith and Taylor divided the department, and she sought to clarify Allen's understanding of their differences in campaign strategy. "Taylor did not like giving up the men" for operations in Arkansas while he still had a chance to destroy the Federals in Louisiana, she recalled. Smith, however, maintained that the threat to Shreveport from Arkansas outweighed the advantages of continued concentration against Banks and Porter. "At last they compromised," Dorsey wrote, confirming that Smith promised to return Walker's division if Steele retreated. Once the Federals in Arkansas began their movement away from Shreveport, "Taylor expected his men to be restored" at once. His festering anger over the removal of his infantry turned to outrage when Smith suspended Walker's return and waged a meaningless and costly battle along the Saline River. Allen lamented the heavy losses among Walker's officer corps at Jenkins' Ferry and confessed that "Smith fought gallantly, if not discreetly."[31]

The governor believed that Taylor had taken Smith's offer of promotion to lieutenant general as an insult, and that he had misconstrued the offer of temporary department command as mere appeasement for the loss of Walker. "Taylor had no fancy for administrative duties," Dorsey reflected. "He wanted to get back to Banks." Once Banks and Porter escaped the Red River, Taylor "had time . . . to give expression to the wrath he had been nursing against Smith." According to Dorsey, Allen believed that while "Smith [had] behaved with more amiability than Taylor," Taylor's strategy would have aided the Confederate war effort east of the Mississippi.[32]

Dorsey disclosed that Allen understood Smith's rationale for the Arkansas campaign. The security of Shreveport was the most important task for the department commander. The governor acknowledged Smith's vast responsibilities in the Trans-Mississippi and insisted that no other department commander, east or west of the river, had more "varied and onerous" duties. Allen conceded, however, that Smith's military insight did not measure up to Taylor's. Whereas Taylor's "skill and gallantry" made him a successful field commander, Smith was unable "in some respects . . . to fill his most difficult position."[33]

Although Smith was not Taylor's equal in military skill, Allen recognized that he had the personal qualities it took to run the Trans-Mississippi Department. As Dorsey put it, "History must acknowledge that *no other Confederate officer* in the Trans-Mississippi Department was Smith's superior in general administrative qualities or *personal* purity and courage." Allen also believed that Taylor's "impatience" and "audacity" at Mansfield had put Shreveport in danger and jeopardized the security of the entire department. Although the Arkansas campaign allowed Banks and Porter to escape, Smith's strategy did ensure the protection of Shreveport. "Whether Steele's retreat was materially hastened by Smith's following him, and fighting him [at Jenkins' Ferry], is a question for military critics," Dorsey concluded.[34]

Allen's recollections defined the three main areas of conflict between Smith and Taylor: first, the removal of Walker's division for operations in Arkansas; second, Smith's proposal that Taylor join the expeditionary force, followed by his withdrawal of the offer; and third, Smith's failure to return the infantry to Taylor in time for operations against Banks and Porter. With Confederate forces concentrated in Louisiana after victories at Mansfield and Pleasant Hill, pursuit of Banks's routed columns seemed strategically sound. Taylor was confident that when word of Banks's defeat reached the Federals in Arkansas, Steele would abandon the campaign. Smith's obligation as department commander, however, demanded that he shift the primary theater of operations to Arkansas in order to guarantee that Steele would not continue his advance on Shreveport. With Banks crippled and the southern flank relatively secure, Smith insisted that Steele's presence north of Shreveport presented the only remaining threat in the Trans-Mississippi. Accordingly, he planned to continue the strategic use of interior lines to concentrate against the more immediate danger to the department.[35]

Despite Taylor's protests, Smith faced the formidable task of a war on two fronts. Taylor was responsible solely for the defense of Louisiana, but Smith was accountable for the security of the entire department. While the pursuit of Banks was Taylor's priority, concentration against Steele was necessary to secure the safety of Shreveport. To rely exclusively on Price for operations in Arkansas was to leave the northern front vulnerable. To engage Banks and suffer defeat was to open the southern front to a renewed Federal invasion. With Banks dug in along the Red River under the shield of Porter's fleet, Taylor's plan of attack presented considerable risk. Although Taylor had gambled and won at Mansfield and Pleasant Hill, Smith would have jeopardized the security of the department had he neglected Steele for the sake of continued concentration in Louisiana.[36]

Although he was under no obligation to consider any suggestions that challenged his plan, Smith indulged Taylor's sharp criticism of the strategy. As Lee had done with Longstreet at Gettysburg, Smith allowed Taylor to articulate his position, out of respect for his subordinate's knowledge, skill, and patriotism. Taylor's reluctant acceptance of the Arkansas campaign was in fact a mere technicality. Smith could have ordered Walker's, Polignac's, or any other Trans-Mississippi command to Arkansas without Taylor's approval. His decision to allow Taylor to select and accompany the troops for the campaign indicated that Smith tried to salve their differences. Yet on the eve of the march his sudden decision to leave Taylor behind only served to worsen the problems between the generals. Smith asserted that Taylor's continued presence in Louisiana, "on the line he knew so well," would strengthen the operation against Banks. However, he did not order Taylor to take command of the forces along the Red River. Instead, Smith gave him the option of either remaining at department headquarters in Shreveport or joining Polignac and John A. Wharton in the field.[37]

His refusal to allow Taylor to go to Arkansas and the discretionary orders for operations in Louisiana undermined Smith's credibility. If Arkansas was the true theater of operations, Smith should have thrown every resource in the department against Steele's army, including the talented but quarrelsome Taylor. Whatever his idiosyncrasies, Taylor possessed far greater skill than either Price or Churchill, the two generals upon whom Smith relied most heavily in Arkansas. Similarly, if Smith wanted Taylor to remain in Louisiana for operations against Banks, he should have ordered him to take command of the troops along the Red River. If Smith believed that Banks would resume the advance, then Taylor's presence in Shreveport was immaterial. If he did not expect a renewed advance from Louisiana, then Taylor should have accompanied the troops to Arkansas.

Although Smith may have feared that Banks would resume his march toward Shreveport, his decision to keep Taylor in Louisiana indicates that he also feared Taylor's presence in Arkansas. Another show of defiance like the one that had led to Mansfield and Pleasant Hill could potentially undermine Smith's leadership in the field. The stakes in the department were too high for Smith to risk an episode of insubordination in Arkansas. Smith simply did not know how to handle Taylor and thus chose to exclude him from the campaign despite the advantage that his intuition and experience would have brought to the battlefield.[38]

Smith had another, more personal reason to fear Taylor's presence in Arkansas. Ever since First Manassas, Smith had been trying to recapture the fame he had won for his role in that victory. The near-miss in Kentucky only intensified his craving for accolades. Prior to the battle at Mansfield, Smith had planned to ride down with reinforcements at a suitable moment during Banks's advance and "carry off the glory," just as he had done at First Manassas, but his hopes were dashed by Taylor's unauthorized action along the Sabine Crossroads. Smith stood a better chance of capturing the limelight in the Arkansas campaign if he led his troops into battle without the aid of his most capable, though impetuous, lieutenant.[39]

The single concession Smith made to Taylor was the agreement that Walker would return to Louisiana if the Federal columns in Arkansas began to retreat. Taylor had assured the commanding general that Steele would turn away from Shreveport as soon as he learned of Banks's fate. It would be pointless to follow Steele, he insisted, as long as Banks and Porter remained targets on the Red River. The agreement placated Taylor to some degree without compromising Smith's overall strategy. Throughout the campaign Smith made adroit use of the department's disposable force along interior lines. Given the logistical difficulties and contingencies of fighting a two-front campaign, the decision to return Walker was strategically sound.[40]

On April 12 Steele turned away from Shreveport and began to march his army toward Camden, still unaware of Banks's retreat. Two days later Smith learned of the movement but refused to send Walker back to Taylor. Although Taylor complained that Smith had violated their agreement, Smith maintained that the Federal flight to Camden did not signal a full-fledged withdrawal to Little Rock. Taylor continued to argue that without support from Banks in Louisiana, Steele would not resume the advance on Shreveport. Yet when Steele did order a retreat to Little Rock, it was not solely because of Banks's defeat. On April 16, the day Steele's army took possession of Camden, Banks's defeat was just a camp rumor. The following day, as Smith's infantry moved to join Price, the Federals suffered a devastating loss at Poison Spring. On April 18 Steele received confirmation of the Confederate triumphs at Mansfield and Pleasant Hill, and four days later he learned that Smith's infantry was closing in on his position. "Although I believe we can beat Price," he reported on April 22, "I do not expect to meet successfully the whole force which Kirby Smith could send against me, if Banks should let him go." Although Steele did not initiate the retreat to Little Rock until after the April 25 defeat at Marks' Mills, it was the combination of Smith's pursuit and Banks's defeat that persuaded the Federals to abandon the campaign.[41]

With the Arkansas Federals in full retreat and Shreveport secure, the destruction of Banks and Porter became the priority for the department and for the Confederacy. According to his own plans, Smith was obligated to return Walker to Louisiana for operations along the Red River. He had argued this strategy in a meeting with Taylor hours before leaving for Arkansas and reaffirmed his intentions in a private correspondence sent from the field. On April 16 Smith had assured Taylor that if Steele retreated across the Ouachita River, northwest of Camden, the infantry would march to Louisiana in time to operate against Banks and Porter. Two days later Smith confided to his wife that, should Steele withdraw from Camden before the Confederates arrived, he would return to Shreveport. His failure to honor the terms of his agreement did more than deprive Taylor of an opportunity to secure the fruits of Mansfield by striking Banks and Porter. Smith's stubborn insistence on chasing Steele past Camden supports Taylor's contention that the general was more concerned with enhancing his reputation as a battle-field hero than with maintaining the security of the department.[42]

Steele's late-night decision on April 25 to abandon Camden ended the Federal threat in Arkansas. Despite Steele's retreat, Smith could still have pursued the Federals with some impunity if he had divided his force. By sending Walker back to Louisiana and retaining the rest of the infantry, along with Price's cavalry, Smith could have seized the initiative along both fronts. Continued concentration against Steele was no longer necessary for the security of Confederate workshops and warehouses in Shreveport. The threat from Arkansas no longer existed, and the strategic complexion of Confederate operations on both fronts thus shifted from defensive to offensive. This is precisely what Davis's August 8 letter to Smith had characterized as "obvious." Smith, however, failed to grasp this transition. While Steele hastened his army toward Little Rock, Banks and Porter lay trapped at Alexandria, and despite their firepower, they presented a far more vulnerable target for attack. Smith's inability to adapt to the changing situation in Arkansas and his reluctance to part with Walker prevented Taylor from exploiting the advantage in Louisiana.[43]

By dividing his force in Arkansas and sending Walker back to Taylor, Smith would have refined his use of interior lines and established control of an extended front running from Camden to Alexandria. The participation of the Texas division at Jenkins' Ferry merely helped close the door on the Federal retreat at the Saline River. Walker's presence with Taylor at Alexandria could have wrecked Banks's army and crippled Porter's fleet. Smith would then have received credit for crush-ing the Federals in the Red River Valley rather than blame for allowing Banks and Porter to escape. Moreover, he would have given the Confederacy much-needed help from west of the Mississippi by preventing Banks and Porter from moving to support Union operations in the East.[44]

Smith opposed hazarding an attack against an entrenched enemy under the protection of gunboats. Despite the tactical risks involved in striking the Federals along the Red River, the Confederate war effort was in desperate need of more than frontal attacks and battlefield glory. Destruction of the joint Federal forces at Alexandria would have provided a crucial strategic and psychological victory for the Confederates. Waiting for Walker outside Alexandria, Taylor stressed this in a letter to Smith written the day after Steele evacuated Camden: "The moral effect on the North [of Banks's and Porter's defeat] and the shock to public credit would have seriously affected the war." In his memoirs Taylor charged that Smith had wasted a rare opportunity to strike a decisive blow for the Confederacy from the Trans-Mississippi. He asserted that the Federal Nineteenth Corps would not have reached Washington in time to help defend the city against Jubal Early's raid. Likewise, three other Union corps would not have joined William T. Sherman in Georgia. Instead, Taylor declared, "Johnston would have been reenforced from west of the Mississippi, and thousands of absent men, with fresh hope, would have rejoined Lee." Taylor also argued that had he captured even a portion of Porter's fleet, the Confederates "would have at once recovered possession of the Mississippi, from the Ohio to the sea."[45]

A few years before beginning work on his memoirs, Taylor admitted that "the military operations in the Trans-Miss. . . . were credible to the troops engaged, though, like all events, outside the two armies of Lee and Johnston, without influence on the issue of the War." However, once he began to scrutinize the emerging literature on the war and to analyze his own role in the conflict, he apparently altered his perspective. In claiming that the outcome of the war had been influenced by Smith's failure to sustain his action against Banks and Porter, Taylor in effect gave the Lost Cause a Trans-Mississippi component. His plans were much more in keeping with the "political and military points of view" held by Davis in 1864 than was Smith's cautious and conservative approach.[46]

Indeed, Taylor had a valid point, in that his operations against Banks and Porter could have influenced the course of the war, if not the outcome. On April 28, the day Taylor berated Smith for failing to support his efforts against the Federals in Alexandria, Porter sent a letter to United States Secretary of the Navy Gideon Welles that in many ways confirmed Taylor's view of the situation. Porter described the Red River campaign as the worst Union defeat of the war, and he confirmed that if he was forced to scuttle his fleet, the Confederates would have "material enough to build a half-dozen iron-clads." Ten thousand troops detached from Sherman languished in Alexandria, unable to join the proposed campaign through Mississippi, and unless they could be freed, Porter feared, the Union's "prestige" would receive a shock from which it would "be long in recovering."[47]

Many leaders on both sides of the conflict understood that events in the field would influence the upcoming elections in the United States. Had Taylor destroyed the joint Federal force at Alexandria, and had the Confederates gone on to threaten New Orleans and St. Louis, the Union's "prestige" might have suffered irreparable damage. Without the timely capitulation of Atlanta, Abraham Lincoln would certainly have been more vulnerable to defeat in 1864. While such considerations did not necessarily fuel Taylor's determination to crush Banks and Porter, the campaign labored under the weight of Smith's refusal to implement a strategy that could have achieved these ends.[48]

Months after the campaign had ended, Smith reflected, "I have honestly done what appeared to me to be right and proper . . . and beg to doubt whether more could have been accomplished." The Confederates could certainly have accomplished more if Smith had not been so preoccupied with victory in Arkansas and Missouri as a means of restoring his faded reputation. After the war Taylor charged that Smith's strategy seemed designed "to throw a protecting shield around the Federal army and fleet" at Alexandria. He blamed Smith for allowing personal ambition to dictate strategy and scoffed that the Confederate victories at Mansfield and Pleasant Hill had upset the commander's "wonderful plan" to recapture glory in the Red River campaign. Smith's pride, poor judgment, and lack of military skill prevented Taylor from turning those victories into a campaign that would aid the Confederate war effort east of the river. Although Smith's failings do not excuse Taylor's insubordinate behavior, they explain his bitterness.[49]

Smith's decision to lead the infantry into Arkansas while Banks and Porter remained along the Red River may not have been insightful, but it was strategically justifiable. The same cannot be said, however, of his refusal to return Walker's division to Louisiana after Steele had begun his retreat to Little Rock. Smith could not see beyond his myopic focus on Arkansas and Missouri as his personal road to glory. A weary veteran of the war between Smith and Taylor, Walker concluded, "Unfortunately for the Confederates, Gen. E. K. Smith was not the leader to comprehend the true line of action."[50]

NOTES

Abbreviations

B&L	Battles and Leaders of the Civil War
CGEN	The Confederate General, ed. William C. Davis
CVET	Confederate Veteran
DUKE	Duke University, Perkins Library Special Collections
ENCC	Encyclopedia of the Confederacy, ed. Richard N. Current
HEH	Henry E. Huntington Library
LAGO	Louisiana Adjutant General's Office at Jackson Barracks
LOC	Library of Congress Manuscript Division
LSA	Louisiana State Archives and Records
LSMHC	Louisiana State Museum and Historical Center
LSU	Louisiana State University, Hill Memorial Library Louisiana and Lower Mississippi Valley Collection
MHS	Missouri Historical Society
MSHS	Mansfield State Historic Site Archives and Records
OR	Official Records of the Union and Confederate Armies
ORN	Official Records of the Union and Confederate Navies
PHS	Pennsylvania Historical Society
RJC	Report of the Joint Committee on the Conduct of the War
SBIV	Southern Bivouac
SHSP	Southern Historical Society Papers
TUL	Tulane University, Howard Tilton Memorial Library Special Collections
UARK	University of Arkansas, David W. Mullins Library Special Collections
UMO	University of Missouri, Ellis Library Western Historical Manuscript Collection
UNC	University of North Carolina, Wilson Library Southern Historical Collection
USMA	United States Military Academy Archives
USAMHI	United States Army Military History Institute, Carlisle Barracks
USNA	United States National Archives
UTEX	University of Texas, Center for American History
WRC	Williams Research Center, Historic New Orleans Collection

Introduction

1. Joseph T. Glatthaar, *Partners in Command: The Relationship between Leaders in the Civil War* (New York: Free Press, 1994).

2. Douglas Southall Freeman, *Lee's Lieutenants: A Study in Command,* 3 vols. (New York: Charles Scribner's Sons, 1944); Kenneth P. Williams, *Lincoln Finds a General: A Military Study of the Civil War,* 5 vols. (New York: Macmillan, 1949–1959); Richard M. McMurry, *Two Great Rebel Armies: An Essay in Confederate Military History* (Chapel Hill: University of North Carolina Press, 1989); James M. McPherson, *Battle Cry of Freedom: The Civil War Era* (New York: Oxford University Press, 1988).

3. Terry L. Jones, "The Twenty-eighth Louisiana Volunteers in the Civil War," *North Louisiana Historical Association Journal* 9 (1978): 85.

4. Archer Jones, *Civil War Command and Strategy: The Process of Victory and Defeat* (New York: Free Press, 1992), 220; Emory M. Thomas, *The Confederate Nation, 1861–1865* (New York: Harper and Row, 1979), 256, 285; Gary W. Gallagher, *The Confederate War* (Cambridge: Harvard University Press, 1997), 36–39.

5. M. Jane Johansson, *Peculiar Honor: A History of the Twenty-eighth Texas Cavalry, 1862–1865* (Fayetteville: University of Arkansas Press, 1998); Stanley S. McGowen, *Horse Sweat and Powder Smoke: The First Texas Cavalry and the Civil War* (College Station: Texas A&M University Press, 1999); Richard Lowe, *Walker's Texas Division C.S.A.: Greyhounds of the Trans-Mississippi* (Baton Rouge: Louisiana State University Press, 2004); Anne J. Bailey, *Between the Enemy and Texas: Parsons's Texas Cavalry in the Civil War* (Fort Worth: Texas Christian University Press, 1989); Jeff Kinard, *Lafayette of the South: Prince Camille de Polignac and the American Civil War* (College Station: Texas A&M University Press, 2001); Arthur W. Bergeron Jr., ed., *The Civil War Reminiscences of Major Silas T. Grisamore C.S.A.* (Baton Rouge: Louisiana State University Press, 1993).

6. Robert L. Kerby, *Kirby Smith's Confederacy: The Trans-Mississippi South, 1863–1865* (New York: Columbia University Press, 1972); John D. Winters, *The Civil War in Louisiana* (Baton Rouge: Louisiana State University Press, 1963).

7. Ludwell Johnson, *Red River Campaign: Politics and Cotton in the Civil War* (Baltimore: Johns Hopkins Press, 1958; reprint, Kent, OH: Kent State University Press, 1993), 283; William Riley Brooksher, *War along the Bayous: The 1864 Red River Campaign in Louisiana* (Washington, DC: Brassey's, 1998), 233–234; Gary Dillard Joiner, *One Damn Blunder from Beginning to End: The Red River Campaign of 1864* (Wilmington, DE: Scholarly Resources, 2003), 156, 173–174.

8. T. Michael Parrish, *Richard Taylor: Soldier Prince of Dixie* (Chapel Hill: University of North Carolina Press, 1992), 403, 501; Joseph H. Parks, *General Edmund Kirby Smith C.S.A.* (Baton Rouge: Louisiana State University Press, 1954), 413.

9. Arthur W. Hyatt Diaries, pt. 2, 58–59, LSU.

1. Prologue: The Gentleman and the Officer

1. *OR,* vol. 15, 789, 802; Richard Taylor, *Destruction and Reconstruction: Personal Experiences of the Civil War* (New York: Appleton, 1879; reprint, New York: Da Capo, 1995), 62–63, 81, 102; Parrish, *Richard Taylor,* 240. Tom Strother was Taylor's servant and remained with him for the duration of the war.

2. Parrish, *Richard Taylor,* 16–21, 33, 64–67; Jackson Beauregard Davis, "The Life of Richard Taylor," *Louisiana Historical Quarterly* 24 (January 1941): 54–55; Moses Greenwood Papers, 44–52, WRC. Taylor called his plantation Fashion.

3. Taylor, *Destruction and Reconstruction,* 11–13; Parrish, *Richard Taylor,* 68–76.

4. Taylor, *Destruction and Reconstruction*, 12–14; Parrish, *Richard Taylor*, 104–106, 124–125; Bragg to Wife, March 11, April 11, April 19, May 25, 1861, Braxton Bragg Papers, MHS; Grady McWhiney, *Braxton Bragg and Confederate Defeat* (New York: Columbia University Press, 1969), 145–146, 182.

5. Taylor, *Destruction and Reconstruction*, 15–16; Parrish, *Richard Taylor*, 12–13, 127–135; McWhiney, *Braxton Bragg*, 182; Terry L. Jones, *Lee's Tigers: The Louisiana Infantry in the Army of Northern Virginia* (Baton Rouge: Louisiana State University Press, 1987), 10–11; Clyde L. Cummer, ed., *Yankee in Gray: The Civil War Memoirs of Henry E. Handerson, with a Selection of His Wartime Letters* (Cleveland: Press of Western Reserve University, 1962), 91.

6. Taylor, *Destruction and Reconstruction*, 23; Jack D. Welsh, *Medical Histories of Confederate Generals* (Kent, OH: Kent State University Press, 1995), 210–211; Harris D. Riley Jr., "General Richard Taylor, C.S.A.: Louisianan, Distinguished Military Commander, and Author, with Speculations on His Health," *Southern Studies: An Interdisciplinary Journal of the South* 1 (spring 1990): 67–86.

7. Taylor, *Destruction and Reconstruction*, 23–25; *New Orleans Daily Delta,* November 6, 1861; unidentified newspaper clipping, Confederate States of America Archives, DUKE; Cummer, *Yankee in Gray,* 33; C. Vann Woodward, ed., *Mary Chesnut's Civil War: A Diary from Dixie as Written by Mary Boykin Chesnut* (New Haven: Yale University Press, 1981), 235; Parrish, *Richard Taylor*, 135–142; Jones, *Lee's Tigers,* 40–44. On November 6 the War Department assigned Taylor's brigade to the Fourth Division under Edmund Kirby Smith. Ten days later the Louisiana troops were reassigned to the First Division and then in January were sent back to Smith. Richard Ewell assumed command of Smith's division in February. See Charles L. Dufour, *Nine Men in Gray* (New York: Doubleday, 1963; reprint, Lincoln: University of Nebraska Press, 1993), 15–22.

8. David French Boyd, *Reminiscences of the War in Virginia* (Baton Rouge: Louisiana State University Press, 1994), 13; Taylor, *Destruction and Reconstruction*, 58, 107–108; Parrish, *Richard Taylor*, 151; Jones, *Lee's Tigers,* 64.

9. Taylor, *Destruction and Reconstruction*, 36–40; Benjamin Ewell, "Jackson and Ewell," *SHSP* 20 (1892): 33; Donald C. Pfanz, *Richard S. Ewell: A Soldier's Life* (Chapel Hill: University of North Carolina Press, 1998), 153, 156–157.

10. Taylor, *Destruction and Reconstruction*, 40–41; Arthur W. Bergeron Jr., "General Richard Taylor: A Study in Command" (master's thesis, Louisiana State University, 1972), 20.

11. Boyd, *War in Virginia*, 7–10; Parrish, *Richard Taylor*, 152–154; James I. Robertson Jr., *Stonewall Jackson: The Man, the Soldier, the Legend* (New York: Macmillan, 1997), 367, 447.

12. Taylor, *Destruction and Reconstruction*, 49–51, 54, 80; Parrish, *Richard Taylor*, 156–161; Freeman, *Lee's Lieutenants,* 1:483–484. Jackson's recent biographer challenges Taylor's version of the relationship with the general. See Robertson, *Stonewall Jackson,* 389.

13. Taylor, *Destruction and Reconstruction*, 20; Freeman, *Lee's Lieutenants,* 1:481–485.

14. *OR,* vol. 12, pt. 1, 715, 786, 802–803; Taylor, *Destruction and Reconstruction*, 75–76; Parrish, *Richard Taylor*, 212–214; Jones, *Lee's Tigers,* 91; Pfanz, *Richard S. Ewell,* 217–218; Dufour, *Nine Men in Gray,* 15–22.

15. Parrish, *Richard Taylor*, 240; Jones, *Lee's Tigers,* 92; Dufour, *Nine Men in Gray,* 22.

16. Taylor, *Destruction and Reconstruction*, 64, 79–85; *OR,* vol. 11, pt. 2, 605; Welsh, *Medical Histories of Confederate Generals,* 210–211; Jones, *Lee's Tigers,* 101–111; Parrish, *Richard Taylor*, 231–237.

17. Moore to Davis, October 9, 1862, Jefferson Davis Papers, DUKE; Judah P. Benjamin Papers, WRC; J. T. Batchelor, August 10, 1862, J. T. Batchelor Letters, WRC; *OR,* vol. 15, 748–749, 754, vol. 51, pt. 2, 597; Parrish, *Richard Taylor*, 241.

18. Taylor, *Destruction and Reconstruction*, 99–101; *OR,* vol. 17, pt. 2, 656.

19. Anne J. Bailey, "Edmund Kirby Smith," *CGEN*, 5 : 163.

20. Parks, *Edmund Kirby Smith*, 1–19. Ephraim graduated from West Point in 1826. See ibid., 9.

21. Ibid., 20–38; Official Register of the Officers and Cadets of the United States Military Academy, vol. 3, USMA.

22. Smith to Mother, March 6, 1846, Edmund Kirby Smith Papers, UNC; Emma Jerome Blackwood, ed., *To Mexico with Scott: Letters of Captain E. Kirby Smith to His Wife* (Cambridge: Harvard University Press, 1917), 45–53; Parks, *Edmund Kirby Smith*, 42–51, 69; K. Jack Bauer, *Zachary Taylor: Soldier, Planter, Statesman of the Old Southwest* (Baton Rouge: Louisiana State University Press, 1985), 120–129; K. Jack Bauer, *The Mexican War, 1846–1848* (New York: Macmillan, 1974), 40, 52–62; U. S. Grant, *Personal Memoirs of U. S. Grant* (Cleveland: World, 1952; reprint, New York: Da Capo, 1982), 43–47. It was after these battles that Taylor visited his father's camp. See Parrish, *Richard Taylor*, 19–21.

23. Smith to Mother, September 24, 1846, Kirby Smith Papers, UNC; Parks, *Edmund Kirby Smith*, 53–54; Bauer, *Zachary Taylor*, 177–185, 192–193; John S. D. Eisenhower, *Agent of Destiny: The Life and Times of General Winfield Scott* (New York: Free Press, 1977), 227–234.

24. Blackwood, *To Mexico with Scott*, 197–204, 216–217; Parks, *Edmund Kirby Smith*, 54–64; Timothy D. Johnson, *Winfield Scott: The Quest for Military Glory* (Lawrence: University Press of Kansas, 1998), 181–186, 202–207; Eisenhower, *Agent of Destiny*, 233–244, 251–257; Bauer, *Mexican War*, 263–268.

25. Smith to Mother, April 3, 1847, Kirby Smith Papers, UNC; Parks, *Edmund Kirby Smith*, 63–65; Allan R. Millett and Peter Maslowski, *For the Common Defense: A Military History of the United States of America* (New York: Free Press, 1984), 156–157. For an analysis of the impact of the Mexican War on Civil War strategy and tactics, consult Grady McWhiney and Perry D. Jamieson, *Attack and Die: Civil War Military Tactics and the Southern Heritage* (Tuscaloosa: University of Alabama Press, 1982), 153–169.

26. Grant, *Personal Memoirs*, 75, 83–84; McWhiney, *Braxton Bragg*, 65.

27. Parks, *Edmund Kirby Smith*, 61–63.

28. Ibid., 50.

29. Smith to Mother, September 28, 1852, July 6, 8, 1858, Kirby Smith Papers, UNC; Parks, *Edmund Kirby Smith*, 64–87, 92–98; William C. Davis, *Jefferson Davis: The Man and His Hour* (New York: HarperCollins, 1991), 231.

30. Smith to Mother, November 10, 23, 1859, March, December 24, 1860, May 21, June 2, 1861, Kirby Smith Papers, UNC; Parks, *Edmund Kirby Smith*, 102–111; J. J. Bowden, *The Exodus of Federal Forces from Texas* (Austin: Eakin, 1986), 26.

31. *OR*, vol. 1, 559–560; Smith to Thomas, April 26, 1860, Civil War Collection, HEH; Smith to Mother, February 3, March 3, 1861, Kirby Smith Papers, UNC; Parks, *Edmund Kirby Smith*, 114–119; Bowden, *Exodus of Federal Forces*, 73–76; Davis, *Jefferson Davis*, 314. At this point in his career Smith began to add the name Kirby to his signature, evidently to distinguish himself from others in the military with the same surname. In the interest of continuity, the name Smith is used throughout this work.

32. *OR*, vol. 1, 614–615, ser. 4, vol. 1, 218; Smith to Cooper, April 16, 1861, Gratz Collection, PHS; Parks, *Edmund Kirby Smith*, 119–121; Cyril M. Lagvanec, "Chevalier Bayard of the Confederacy: The Life and Career of Edmund Kirby Smith" (Ph.D. diss., Texas A&M University, 1999), 133–135.

33. Smith to Mother, May 16, 21, June 2, 1861, Kirby Smith Papers, UNC; Parks, *Edmund Kirby Smith*, 122–127.

34. Smith to Mother, June 2, 1861, Kirby Smith Papers, UNC; Parks, *Edmund Kirby Smith*, 126–128; Craig L. Symonds, *Joseph E. Johnston: A Civil War Biography* (New York: W. W. Norton, 1992), 102–104.

35. *OR*, vol. 2, 880–881; Smith to Mother, May 29, June 2, 9, 1861, Kirby Smith Papers, UNC; Joseph E. Johnston, *Narrative of Military Operations during the Civil War* (New York: Appleton, 1874; reprint, New York: Da Capo, 1959), 16, 318.

36. *OR*, vol. 2, 472–473; Johnston, *Military Operations*, 18–19, 33, 38; Bradley T. Johnson, "Memoirs of 1st Md. Regiment: First Manassas and Subsequent Movements," *SHSP* 9 (1881): 481–482; Freeman, *Lee's Lieutenants*, 1:40–41; Parks, *Edmund Kirby Smith*, 130–133; William C. Davis, *Battle at Bull Run* (Mechanicsburg, PA: Stackpole Books, 1977), 132–140. Elzey was humiliated by the loss of his command and pledged that he would earn promotion at Manassas or die trying. See William C. Davis, "Arnold Elzey," *CGEN*, 2:98.

37. Johnson, "1st Md.," 482; *OR*, vol. 2, 476; J. W. Lillard, "Events of 1861–1865 Recalled," *CVET* 21 (1913): 18; Davis, *Bull Run*, 225–226, 248; Parks, *Edmund Kirby Smith*, 135; Johnston, *Military Operations*, 51; Symonds, *Joseph E. Johnston*, 121.

38. *OR*, vol. 2, 476, 522–523; Joseph E. Johnston, "Responsibilities of the First Bull Run," *B&L*, 1:249; D. Augustus Dickert, *History of Kershaw's Brigade* (Newberry: Elbert H. Aull, 1899; reprint, Dayton, OH: Morningside, 1988), 63; T. B. Warder and Jas. M. Catlett, *Battle of Young's Branch or Manassas Plain Fought July 21, 1862* (Richmond: Enquirer Book and Job Press, 1862; reprint, Prince William County Historical Commission, n.d.), 127; Davis, *Bull Run*, 224–226.

39. Smith to Mother, August 16, 1861, Kirby Smith Papers, UNC; Delancey to Bache, July 30, 1861, Rhees Collection, HEH; Nina Kirby-Smith Buck, "Blucher of the Day at Manassas," *CVET* 7 (1889): 108; Parks, *Edmund Kirby Smith*, 136–138.

40. Dunbar Rowland, ed., *Jefferson Davis, Constitutionalist: His Letters, Papers, and Speeches*, 10 vols. (Jackson: Mississippi Department of Archives and History, 1923), 6:493; Johnston, *Military Operations*, 51; "An 'Unseen Message' of President Davis," *CVET* 14 (1906): 365.

41. Smith to Wife, November 27, December 1, 1861, Kirby Smith Papers, UNC; newspaper clipping, Confederate States of America Archives, DUKE; Jones, *Lee's Tigers*, 40–41; James P. Gannon, *Irish Rebels, Confederate Tigers: A History of the Sixth Louisiana Volunteers* (Mason City, IA: Savas, 1998), 14–15, 41–42.

42. *OR*, vol. 53, 182, vol. 5, 914, 1073, vol. 6, 288, 295, vol. 7, 908, vol. 10, pt. 2, 308, 320–21; Smith to Wife, March 1862, March 13, 1862, Kirby Smith Papers, UNC; Parks, *Edmund Kirby Smith*, 138–158; Thomas L. Connelly, *Army of the Heartland: The Army of Tennessee, 1861–1862* (Baton Rouge: Louisiana State University Press, 1967), 187.

43. *OR*, vol. 16, pt. 2, 683–685, 696–697, 701–702, 706–710, 714, 718, 721, 723, 725–727, vol. 17, pt. 2, 651; Smith to Cooper, June 15, 1862, Edmund Kirby Smith Papers, DUKE; Smith to Wife, July 19, 1862, Kirby Smith Papers, UNC; George W. Morgan, "Cumberland Gap," *B&L*, 3:62–64; Connelly, *Army of the Heartland*, 188–194; Parks, *Edmund Kirby Smith*, 159–187, 196.

44. *OR*, vol. 16, pt. 2, 727, 730–731, 734, 739; Connelly, *Army of the Heartland*, 193–194.

45. *OR*, vol. 16, pt. 2, 730–735, 738–739, 745–746, vol. 17, pt. 2, 619, 627, 652, vol. 52, pt. 2, 335; Bragg to Wife, July 22, 1862, Bragg Papers, MHS; Parks, *Edmund Kirby Smith*, 201; Connelly, *Army of the Heartland*, 193–201; McWhiney, *Braxton Bragg*, 266–268, 272–273; James Lee McDonough, *War in Kentucky: From Shiloh to Perryville* (Knoxville: University of Tennessee Press, 1994), 70–72, 79; Kenneth W. Noe, *Perryville: The Grand Havoc of Battle* (Lexington: University Press of Kentucky, 2001), 29–31.

46. *OR*, vol. 16, pt. 2, 741, 748–749; Smith to Wife, August 1, 24, 25, 1862, Kirby Smith Papers, UNC; Parks, *Edmund Kirby Smith*, 201–202; McWhiney, *Braxton Bragg*, 272–278; Connelly, *Army of the Heartland*, 193–194, 205–210; Noe, *Perryville*, 34; Steven E. Woodworth, *Jefferson Davis and His Generals: The Failure of Confederate Command in the West* (Lawrence: University Press of Kansas, 1990), 137–138.

47. *OR*, vol. 16, pt. 1, 918–919, pt. 2, 744–745, 748–749, 752–753, 755–756, 759, 766–769, 775–778; Smith to Davis, August 1862, Kirby Smith Papers, DUKE; Smith to Wife, August 19, 25, September 4, 1862, Kirby Smith Papers, UNC; Edmund Kirby Smith, *Speech to Kentuckians*, n.d., Kirby Smith Papers, UNC; Paul F. Hammond, "Campaign of General E. Kirby Smith in Kentucky," *SHSP* 9 (1881): 230; Paul F. Hammond, "General Edmund Kirby Smith's Campaign in Kentucky," *SHSP* 9 (1881): 247–248; Frank T. Ryan, "The Kentucky Campaign and the Battle of Richmond," *CVET* 26 (1918): 160; William R. Boggs, *Military Reminiscences of General Wm. R. Boggs, C.S.A.* (Durham, NC: Seeman Printery, 1913), 37–41; Noe, *Perryville*, 33–39; Connelly, *Army of the Heartland*, 209–217; Parks, *Edmund Kirby Smith*, 202–208, 211–220; McDonough, *War in Kentucky*, 80–82.

48. *OR*, vol. 16, pt. 1, 932–933, pt. 2, 797, 830, 861; Smith to Bragg, September 15, 1862, Eldridge Collection, HEH; Boggs, *Military Reminiscences*, 35, 41; Parks, *Edmund Kirby Smith*, 202–203, 230; Connelly, *Army of the Heartland*, 218–220; Noe, *Perryville*, 40–41. Paul F. Hammond, one of Smith's aides, noted that the general "placed the greatest trust" in Dr. Smith's "sagacity and judgement." See Hammond, "Campaign of General E. Kirby Smith," 226.

49. *OR*, vol. 16, pt. 1, 968, 1088, 1091, pt. 2, 830, 849, 861, 870–871, 876; Smith to Wife, September 27, 1862, Kirby Smith Papers, UNC; Parks, *Edmund Kirby Smith*, 231; Connelly, *Army of the Heartland*, 220–228, 231–235; McWhiney, *Braxton Bragg*, 283–286, 293–294, 297.

50. *OR*, vol. 16, pt. 1, 1094–1095, pt. 2, 891, 896–898, 901–903; Don Carlos Buell, "East Tennessee and the Campaign of Perryville," *B&L*, 3 : 47; McWhiney, *Braxton Bragg*, 297–300; Parks, *Edmund Kirby Smith*, 232–233; Connelly, *Army of the Heartland*, 241, 247, 251–252; McDonough, *War in Kentucky*, 189, 199–200; Noe, *Perryville*, 125.

51. *OR*, vol. 16, pt. 1, 1092–1093, 1095–1096, 1110, 1120, pt. 2, 912, 915, 918, 920, 925; Paul F. Hammond, "General Kirby Smith's Campaign in Kentucky," *SHSP* 10 (1882): 71, 73; McWhiney, *Braxton Bragg*, 308–316; Connelly, *Army of the Heartland*, 254–263; Noe, *Perryville*, 132–133, 215–305.

52. *OR*, vol. 16, pt. 1, 1135–1136, pt. 2, 925, 927–928; Connelly, *Army of the Heartland*, 270; Noe, *Perryville*, 329; McWhiney, *Braxton Bragg*, 319–320.

53. *OR*, vol. 16, pt. 2, 943, 949, 959, 975; Hammond, "Kirby Smith's Campaign," 73, 75; Parks, *Edmund Kirby Smith*, 237–243; Noe, *Perryville*, 330; McWhiney, *Braxton Bragg*, 320–321.

54. *OR*, vol. 16, pt. 2, 979; Parks, *Edmund Kirby Smith*, 242–243; Davis, *Jefferson Davis*, 473.

55. *OR*, vol. 15, 948; 18 : 856; Boggs, *Military Reminiscences*, 51; Lagvanec, "Chevalier Bayard," 354–356.

56. *OR*, vol. 19, pt. 2, 643, vol. 22, pt. 2, 787; Boggs, *Military Reminiscences*, 51; Parks, *Edmund Kirby Smith*, 251–252; Kerby, *Kirby Smith's Confederacy*, 1. Smith's servant Aleck accompanied him throughout the war.

2. To Baffle the Enemy in His Designs

1. *OR*, vol. 15, 838; Moore to Davis, October 9, 1862, Davis Papers, DUKE; Taylor, *Destruction and Reconstruction*, 102; Jefferson Davis Bragg, *Louisiana in the Confederacy* (Baton Rouge: Louisiana State University Press, 1941), 107–138; Winters, *Civil War in Louisiana*, 125–148.

2. *OR*, vol. 15, 16–17, 777–778, 786, 794–795, vol. 52, pt. 2, 334; Taylor, *Destruction and Reconstruction*, 103; Ezra J. Warner, *Generals in Gray: Lives of the Confederate Commanders* (Baton Rouge: Louisiana State University Press, 1959), 141; Welsh, *Medical Histories of Confederate Generals*, 104; Herman Hattaway and Archer Jones, *How the North Won: A Military History of the Civil War* (Urbana: University of Illinois Press, 1983), 429.

3. *OR*, vol. 15, 791, 779; Winters, *Civil War in Louisiana*, 152.

4. *OR*, vol. 15, 754, 786, 795, 802, 804, 810; George Green Shackelford, *George Wythe Randolph and the Confederate Elite* (Athens: University of Georgia Press, 1988), 129, 141; Jones, *Confederate Strategy from Shiloh to Vicksburg* (Baton Rouge: Louisiana State University Press, 1961), 72–74; Frank E. Vandiver, *Rebel Brass: The Confederate Command System* (Baton Rouge: Louisiana State University Press, 1956; reprint, 1984), 51–53; Parrish, *Richard Taylor*, 249–250; William Royston Geise, "The Confederate Military Forces in the Trans-Mississippi West" (Ph.D. diss., University of Texas, 1974), 109–110.

5. *OR*, vol. 15, 777, 791, 802, 806–807, 810, 817, 839–840; Daniel Ruggles Papers, DUKE; Parrish, *Richard Taylor*, 250; Dufour, *Nine Men in Gray*, 25; Shackelford, *George Wythe Randolph*, 129; Jones, *Confederate Strategy*, 73. For an analysis of the Randolph-Davis Plan, see Shackelford, *George Wythe Randolph*, 123–141. On September 1 Randolph instructed Henry H. Sibley in Marshall, Texas, and John H. Forney in Mobile, Alabama, to prepare their brigades for a march to Louisiana to support Taylor. See *OR*, vol. 15, 804, 819.

6. Taylor, *Destruction and Reconstruction*, 108. Vermilionville has been renamed Lafayette, and Brashear City is now called Morgan City.

7. Taylor, *Destruction and Reconstruction*, 111–113; *OR*, vol. 15, 133–137; George R. Morris, "The Battle of Bayou Des Allemands," *CVET* 34 (1926): 14–16; Parrish, *Richard Taylor*, 254; Winters, *Civil War in Louisiana*, 155–156; William Arceneaux, *Acadian General Alfred Mouton and the Civil War* (Lafayette: University of Southwestern Louisiana, 1981), 54–56; Morris Raphael, *The Battle in Bayou Country* (Detroit: Harlo, 1975), 33–36.

8. *OR*, vol. 15, 133; Taylor, *Destruction and Reconstruction*, 111–112; Morris, "Bayou Des Allemands," 15; Parrish, *Richard Taylor*, 255–259.

9. *OR*, vol. 15, 820; Joseph L. Brent, Ordnance Rules and Regulations, November 1862, and P. B. Leeds to J. L. Brent, March 14, 21, 1863, Joseph L. Brent Papers, LAGO; "Career of Gen. Joseph Lancaster Brent," *CVET* 17 (1909): 345; Taylor, *Destruction and Reconstruction*, 117–118; Geise, "Confederate Military Forces," 110–111.

10. *OR*, vol. 15, 855, 868, vol. 23, pt. 2, 641; Taylor, *Destruction and Reconstruction*, 115; Rowland, *Jefferson Davis, Constitutionalist*, 5 : 381; Parrish, *Richard Taylor*, 251–252; Jones, *Confederate Strategy*, 73. As late as February 1863, Davis expressed his disappointment that "nothing has been heard of the plan proposed [for the recapture of New Orleans] . . . which should have been executed before this date." See *OR*, vol. 23, pt. 2, 641.

11. Edmund T. King Memoir, 1–2, Civil War Manuscript Series, TUL; Taylor, *Destruction and Reconstruction*, 113; Arceneaux, *Acadian General*, 53–57; Parrish, *Richard Taylor*, 260.

12. *OR*, vol. 15, 174–175, 868, 873, vol. 17, pt. 2, 717; Taylor, *Destruction and Reconstruction*, 115; Parrish, *Richard Taylor*, 251, 261–262.

13. *OR*, vol. 15, 176–180, 860; John William DeForest, *A Volunteer's Adventures: A Union Captain's Record of the Civil War*, ed. James H. Croushore (New Haven: Yale University Press, 1946), 86; F. S. Twitchell Letter, December 12, 1863, Miscellaneous Manuscript Collection, WRC; Taylor, *Destruction and Reconstruction*, 113–114, 118; Arceneaux, *Acadian General*, 62.

14. *OR*, vol. 15, 855, 859–861, 868; Taylor, *Destruction and Reconstruction*, 116–117, 119; Parrish, *Richard Taylor*, 263–264.

15. *OR*, vol. 15, 590–591; Parrish, *Richard Taylor*, 264; James G. Hollandsworth, *Pretense of Glory: The Life of General Nathaniel P. Banks* (Baton Rouge: Louisiana State University Press, 1998), 62–69, 84–85.

16. *OR*, vol. 15, 948, 972, 1005, vol. 17, pt. 2, 767; Taylor, *Destruction and Reconstruction*, 120, 127, 164; Raphael, *Bayou Country*, 89; Jerry Thompson, *Henry Hopkins Sibley: Confederate General of the West*

(Natchitoches, LA: Northwestern State University Press, 1987), 320; Edwin C. Bearss, *The Campaign for Vicksburg*, 3 vols. (Dayton, OH: Morningside, 1985), 3 : 57; Kerby, *Kirby Smith's Confederacy*, 53, 98.

17. *OR*, vol. 22, pt. 2, 802–803; Smith to Wife, March 19, 1863, Kirby Smith Papers, UNC; "The Last Confederate Army to Surrender and Its General," J. Fair Hardin Collection, LSU; William A. Freret Letter, Robert A. Brock Collection, HEH; Boggs, *Military Reminiscences*, 54; Parks, *Edmund Kirby Smith*, 252–257; Kerby, *Kirby Smith's Confederacy*, 53.

18. *OR*, vol. 22, pt. 2, 802–803; Boggs, *Military Reminiscences*, 54–56; Parks, *Edmund Kirby Smith*, 257.

19. *OR*, vol. 22, pt. 2, 802–803; R. W. Johnson, Charles B. Mitchel, et al. to Jefferson Davis, February 2, 1863, Davis Papers, DUKE; Edward Younger, ed., *Inside the Confederate Government: The Diary of Robert Garlick Hill Kean, Head of the Bureau of War* (New York: Oxford University Press, 1957; reprint, Baton Rouge: Louisiana State University Press, 1993), 38, 45; Frank Vandiver, ed., *The Civil War Diary of Josiah Gorgas* (Tuscaloosa: University of Alabama Press, 1947), 28; Boggs, *Military Reminiscences*, 56. Kerby, *Kirby Smith's Confederacy*, 53; Michael B. Dougan, *Confederate Arkansas* (Tuscaloosa: University of Alabama Press, 1976), 102.

20. *OR*, vol. 22, pt. 2, 802–803.

21. Ibid., 781–782, 791; Reynolds to Price, January 30, 1862, Reynolds to J. D. B. DeBow, February 4, 1862, Eldridge Collection, HEH; Reynolds to Davis, January 30, 1862, Davis Papers, DUKE; Reynolds to Seddon, January 31, 1863, Reynolds to Thornton, February 17, 1863, Thomas C. Reynolds Papers, LOC; Thomas C. Reynolds, "General Sterling Price and the Confederacy," typescript, 42–71, MHS; Albert Castel, *General Sterling Price and the Civil War in the West* (Baton Rouge: Louisiana State University Press, 1968), 134–138. The department covered over one million square miles yet had only 50,000 Confederate soldiers, including 25,300 in Arkansas, 11,600 in Texas, and just 9,000 in Louisiana. See Kerby, *Kirby Smith's Confederacy*, 53.

22. Boggs, *Military Reminiscences*, 54–56; Reynolds to Smith, May 13, 1863, Reynolds Papers, LOC; Castel, *Sterling Price*, 142; Parks, *Edmund Kirby Smith*, 258.

23. Smith acknowledged that "each district was acting independently." See *OR*, vol. 22, pt. 2, 872.

24. *OR*, vol. 15, 388.

25. Ibid., 388–389; Bergeron, *Silas T. Grisamore*, 111; Parrish, *Richard Taylor*, 270; Raphael, *Bayou Country*, 94; Kerby, *Kirby Smith's Confederacy*, 53.

26. *OR*, vol. 15, 389; Taylor, *Destruction and Reconstruction*, 129–130.

27. Taylor, *Destruction and Reconstruction*, 129–130; *OR*, vol. 15, 388–389; Sibley to Brent, February 21, 1863, Davis Papers, DUKE; Parrish, *Richard Taylor*, 271–272; Thompson, *Henry Hopkins Sibley*, 322, 325.

28. *OR*, vol. 15, 389–391; Taylor, *Destruction and Reconstruction*, 130–131; Thompson, *Henry Hopkins Sibley*, 325; Parrish, *Richard Taylor*, 272–273.

29. *OR*, vol. 15, 358–359, 391–392, 398–399, vol. 53, 466–468; Taylor, *Destruction and Reconstruction*, 133–134; Winters, *Civil War in Louisiana*, 227–229; Morris Raphael, *A Gunboat Named Diana* (Detroit: Harlo, 1993), 146–156; Dana Mangham, *Oh for the Touch of the Vanished Hand: Discovering a Southern Family and the Civil War* (Murfreesboro: Southern Heritage, 2000), 589–590; Arthur W. Bergeron Jr., "Yellow Jacket Battalion," in *Louisianans in the Civil War*, edited by Lawrence Lee Hewitt and Arthur W. Bergeron Jr. (Columbia: University of Missouri Press, 2002), 63–64.

30. *OR*, vol. 15, 392–393, 399, 1092–1096; Richard B. Irwin, *History of the Nineteenth Army Corps* (Baton Rouge: Louisiana State University Press, 1985), 115; A. S. Gates, "A Lost Flag," *SBIV* 3 (1884): 367; Raphael, *Battle in the Bayou Country*, 101–120; Arceneaux, *Acadian General*, 84; Parrish, *Richard*

Taylor, 277–278; Thompson, *Henry Hopkins Sibley,* 326–331. Sibley was acquitted in court-martial proceedings. See ibid., 330–331.

31. *OR,* vol. 15, 1041–1043, vol. 22, pt. 2, 828; Kerby, *Kirby Smith's Confederacy,* 105–106; Parks, *Edmund Kirby Smith,* 257, 260–261. The Federal movements were designed to pass through northeastern Louisiana and cross the Mississippi below Vicksburg. See *OR,* vol. 24, pt. 1, 46–48.

32. *OR,* vol. 15, 1044–1050; Taylor, *Destruction and Reconstruction,* 135; Parks, *Edmund Kirby Smith,* 261–263; Parrish, *Richard Taylor,* 279.

33. *OR,* vol. 15, 1044–1059; Taylor, *Destruction and Reconstruction,* 125–126; Woodworth, *Davis and His Generals,* 204; Bearss, *Campaign for Vicksburg,* 3 : 1153–1157; Michael B. Ballard, *Pemberton: A Biography* (Jackson: University Press of Mississippi, 1991), 137, 144.

34. *OR,* vol. 15, 1054, vol. 22, pt. 2, 871; Boggs, *Military Reminiscences,* 57, 60; Parks, *Edmund Kirby Smith,* 259, 416; Waldo M. Moore, "The Defense of Shreveport: The Confederacy's Last Redoubt," in *Military Analysis of the Civil War: An Anthology* (Millwood, NY: KTO, 1977), 396.

35. Taylor, *Destruction and Reconstruction,* 136.

36. *OR,* vol. 15, 386–387; Hyatt Diaries, 2 : 6, LSU; Kerby, *Kirby Smith's Confederacy,* 106–107.

37. *OR,* vol. 26, pt. 2, 30; Taylor, *Destruction and Reconstruction,* 136–137; Parrish, *Richard Taylor,* 281–284.

38. Hyatt Diaries, 2 : 4–5, LSU; *OR,* vol. 15, 311, 701; David C. Edmunds, ed., *The Conduct of Federal Troops in Louisiana during the Invasions of 1863 and 1864* (Lafayette, LA: Acadiana, 1988), 145; Winters, *Civil War in Louisiana,* 235–238; Hollandsworth, *Pretense of Glory,* 115–116.

39. *OR,* vol. 15, 1054, 1084; Taylor, *Destruction and Reconstruction,* 134; *RJC,* 2 : 311; Hollandsworth, *Pretense of Glory,* 119.

40. *OR,* vol. 15, 791; Taylor, *Destruction and Reconstruction,* 138; Kerby, *Kirby Smith's Confederacy,* 109–110.

41. *OR,* vol. 22, pt. 2, 802–803, vol. 26, pt. 2, 12–13.

42. Ibid., vol. 26, pt. 2, 12–13.

3. The Golden Opportunity Has Passed

1. *OR,* vol. 24, pt. 3, 846, vol. 26, pt. 2, 13, 15; Taylor, *Destruction and Reconstruction,* 137–138; Winters, *Civil War in Louisiana,* 198.

2. *OR,* vol. 22, pt. 2, 855–856, 872–873, 948, vol. 26, pt. 2, 41; Taylor, *Destruction and Reconstruction,* 139; Johansson, *Peculiar Honor,* 53; Kerby, *Kirby Smith's Confederacy,* 114. Young's Point remained a link in Grant's supply system. See Bearss, *Campaign for Vicksburg,* 3 : 1174.

3. *OR,* vol. 26, pt. 2, 15, 41; Taylor, *Destruction and Reconstruction,* 138. Tappan arrived on June 17 and did not participate in the operation. See *OR,* vol. 24, pt. 2, 460, and Bearss, *Campaign for Vicksburg,* 3 : 1195.

4. *OR,* vol. 24, pt. 2, 449, 458–460; Taylor, *Destruction and Reconstruction,* 139; Joseph P. Blessington, *Campaigns of Walker's Texas Division* (New York: Lange, Little, 1875; reprint, Austin: State House Press, 1994), ix–xi, 93–94; Arthur W. Bergeron Jr., *Guide to Louisiana Confederate Military Units, 1861–1865* (Baton Rouge: Louisiana State University Press, 1989), 60–61. Before his assignment to the Trans-Mississippi, Walker had served with distinction in the Army of Northern Virginia. Among his brigadiers, only Hawes, a West Point graduate, had seen action during the Civil War. Along with McCulloch and Randal, also a West Pointer, all had seen combat during the Mexican War. How-

ever, except for Walker, none had commanded significant numbers of troops on the battlefield. See Norman D. Brown, "John George Walker," *CGEN*, 6:88–89; William C. Davis, "James Morrison Hawes," ibid., 3:74–75; Anne J. Bailey, "Henry Eustace McCulloch," ibid., 4:120–121; and Bruce S. Allardice, *More Generals in Gray* (Baton Rouge: Louisiana State University Press, 1995), 192–193.

5. *OR*, vol. 24, pt. 2, 447, 458–459, 469; *ORN*, ser. 1, vol. 25, 163; Blessington, *Walker's Texas Division*, 101; Winters, *Civil War in Louisiana*, 199.

6. *OR*, vol. 24, pt. 2, 459–470; Blessington, *Walker's Texas Division*, 95–109; Mamie Yeary, ed., *Reminiscences of the Boys in Gray* (McGregor, TX, 1912; reprint, Dayton, OH: Morningside, 1986), 610; Taylor, *Destruction and Reconstruction*, 139; Bearss, *Campaign for Vicksburg*, 3:1179–1182; Johansson, *Peculiar Honor*, 54; Winters, *Civil War in Louisiana*, 199–201. For more on the battle at Milliken's Bend, see Richard Lowe, "Battle on the Levee: The Fight at Milliken's Bend," in *Black Soldiers in Blue: African American Troops in the Civil War Era*, ed. John David Smith (Chapel Hill: University of North Carolina Press, 2002), 107–135.

7. *OR*, vol. 24, pt. 2, 448–449, 458–460, 471–472; Taylor, *Destruction and Reconstruction*, 139; Bearss, *Campaign for Vicksburg*, 3:1183–1187; Winters, *Civil War in Louisiana*, 201–202.

8. *OR*, vol. 24, pt. 3, 827, 845, 948; Reynolds to Smith, May 13, 1863, Reynolds to R. W. Johnson, February 22, 1864, Reynolds Papers, LOC; Symonds, *Joseph E. Johnston*, 199–201, 210, 214; Parks, *Edmund Kirby Smith*, 258.

9. *OR*, vol. 26, pt. 2, 41–42; Taylor, *Destruction and Reconstruction*, 126; Parrish, *Richard Taylor*, 287.

10. *OR*, vol. 26, pt. 2, 13; Taylor, *Destruction and Reconstruction*, 138.

11. Taylor, *Destruction and Reconstruction*, 139.

12. Ibid.; *OR*, vol. 15, 392, vol. 24, pt. 2, 460, 464, 469, 471.

13. *OR*, vol. 24, pt. 2, 460–462, 465.

14. Ibid., 457–462, 465.

15. *OR*, vol. 26, pt. 2, 29–30; Parrish, *Richard Taylor*, 288; Parks, *Edmund Kirby Smith*, 272.

16. *OR*, vol. 22, pt. 2, 990, ser. 2, vol. 6, 21–22; Joseph T. Glatthaar, *Forged in Battle: The Civil War Alliance of Black Soldiers and White Officers* (New York: Free Press, 1990), 155. Grant received a report that some Confederate units at Milliken's Bend carried a black flag with a skull and crossed bones as a sign of no quarter toward black Federal troops. However, Smith's reaction to Taylor's failure to issue such a call undermines these Federal claims. A more likely explanation for the high Union casualties at Milliken's Bend is Confederate obedience to Taylor's instructions to carry the works at the point of the bayonet, as well as the inexperienced and ill-equipped black Federal recruits' motivation to fight. See *OR*, vol. 24, pt. 1, 102, pt. 2, 459, pt. 3, 425.

17. *OR*, vol. 24, pt. 2, 459, 468–469, ser. 2, vol. 5, 797, vol. 6, 21–22.

18. *OR*, vol. 22, pt. 2, 965, ser. 2, vol. 5, 797, vol. 6, 21–22, 115; Parks, *Edmund Kirby Smith*, 267–268; Kerby, *Kirby Smith's Confederacy*, 111–112. For more on the evolution of the Confederate government's position regarding black Union soldiers, see Herman Hattaway and Richard E. Beringer, *Jefferson Davis, Confederate President* (Lawrence: University Press of Kansas, 2002), 191–192.

19. *OR*, vol. 24, pt. 3, 425–426; Parrish, *Richard Taylor*, 293. For the Federal policy toward prisoners of war, see *OR*, ser. 3, vol. 3, 153–155. Grant sent colonels Kilby Smith and John Riggin.

20. *OR*, vol. 24, pt. 3, 425–426, 443–444. Grant allegedly sentenced at least one Confederate prisoner to death as retribution for the purported incidents surrounding the battle of Milliken's Bend. See M. W. Sims, "Reminiscence of Johnson's Island Prison," *CVET* 13 (1905): 253, and Sims, "Interesting Story of Prison Experience," *CVET* 14 (1906): 502.

21. *OR*, vol. 26, pt. 2, 26, 43, vol. 22, pt. 2, 868; Surget to Brent, June 5, 1863, Brent Papers, LAGO; Parks, *Edmund Kirby Smith*, 274.

22. *OR*, vol. 22, pt. 2, 868, vol. 24, pt. 2, 460–461; Taylor, *Destruction and Reconstruction*, 139. Contrary to Taylor's reminiscences, it was he rather than Smith who first ordered Walker back to northeast Louisiana. On June 5 Smith assured Holmes that he had no intention of incorporating Tappan's brigade into Taylor's army. However, he notified Richmond of Walker's transfer to the District of Western Louisiana on June 16, after Taylor had ordered the division to remain in northern Louisiana. See *OR*, vol. 22, pt. 2, 857, 873.

23. *OR*, vol. 22, pt. 2, 885–886, 914, vol. 24, pt. 3, 979, vol. 26, pt. 1, 211, pt. 2, 71.

24. Ibid., vol. 22, pt. 2, 868, 871–872, 904, 915–916; Walker to Smith, July 3, 1864, Eldridge Collection, HEH; Symonds, *Joseph E. Johnston*, 200; Parks, *Edmund Kirby Smith*, 276; Kerby, *Kirby Smith's Confederacy*, 115. For more on Smith's concerns over the situation in Missouri and Arkansas, see *OR*, vol. 22, pt. 2, 855–857, 859–860, 864–865, 889–890.

25. *OR*, vol. 26, pt. 1, 209–210; Taylor, *Destruction and Reconstruction*, 139–140; Irwin, *Nineteenth Army Corps*, 236–237; Kerby, *Kirby Smith's Confederacy*, 115–116.

26. *OR*, vol. 26, pt. 1, 217–218; Taylor, *Destruction and Reconstruction*, 140–141; Anne J. Bailey, "James Patrick Major," *CGEN*, 4:148–149. Major was Green's brother-in-law.

27. *OR*, vol. 26, pt. 1, 215, 223–226; Joseph A. Breaux, "Reminiscences," Louisiana Historical Association Collection, TUL; Taylor, *Destruction and Reconstruction*, 140–141; Raphael, *Bayou Country*, 167; Winters, *Civil War in Louisiana*, 287.

28. *OR*, vol. 26, pt. 1, 215, 217–220, 223–224; Irwin, *Nineteenth Army Corps*, 240–241; "Capture of Brashear City: A Rebel Account," in *The Rebellion Record: A Diary of American Events, with Documents, Narratives, Illustrative Incidents, Poetry, etc.*, 12 vols., ed. Frank Moore (G. P. Putnam's Sons: New York, 1861–1864), 8:78; Taylor, *Destruction and Reconstruction*, 140–142; Raphael, *Bayou Country*, 168–171; Parrish, *Richard Taylor*, 297–299.

29. *OR*, vol. 26, pt. 1, 210–211, pt. 2, 106–107; Taylor, *Destruction and Reconstruction*, 142–143; Frank M. Flinn, *Campaiging with Banks in Louisiana in '63 and '64, and with Sheridan in the Shenandoah Valley in '64 and '65* (Lynn, MA: Thomas P. Nichols, 1887), 89; Parrish, *Richard Taylor*, 298–299.

30. *OR*, vol. 26, pt. 1, 217, 220.

31. Taylor, *Destruction and Reconstruction*, 143.

32. Ibid.; *OR*, vol. 26, pt. 1, 211; John Q. Anderson, *A Texas Surgeon in the C.S.A.* (Tuscaloosa: Confederate Publishing Co., 1957), 61–66; Kerby, *Kirby Smith's Confederacy*, 118; Parrish, *Richard Taylor*, 299–300.

33. *OR*, vol. 26, pt. 2, 26, 107, vol. 24, pt. 3, 979, vol. 22, pt. 2, 916; Walker to Smith, July 3, 1863, Eldridge Collection, HEH.

34. Blessington, *Walker's Texas Division*, 112–115; John G. Walker, "The War of Secession West of the Mississippi River during the Years 1863–4 & 5," typescript, 31–33, Myron Gwinner Collection, USAMHI; Bailey, *Between the Enemy and Texas*, 134, 138–147. For more on these operations, see *OR*, vol. 22, pt. 2, 856–857, 990, vol. 24, pt. 2, 158, 450–451, 457, 466, vol. 26, pt. 2, 107; *ORN*, 25:215–216; John Q. Anderson, ed., *Campaigning with Parsons' Texas Cavalry Brigade, CSA: The War Journals and Letters of the Four Orr Brothers, Twelfth Texas Cavalry Regiment* (Hillsboro, TX: Hill Junior College Press, 1976), 111–112; and Bearss, *Campaign for Vicksburg*, 3:1199–1202.

35. *OR*, vol. 26, pt. 1, 213; Parrish, *Richard Taylor*, 302–303.

36. *OR*, vol. 26, pt. 1, 213, 226–229; Joseph Lancaster Brent, *Memoirs of the War between the States* (New Orleans: Fontana, 1940), 55–56; Irwin, *Nineteenth Army Corps*, 242–246; Odie B. Faulk, *General Tom Green: A Fightin' Texan* (Waco, TX: Texian, 1963), 56–57; Parrish, *Richard Taylor*, 301; Winters, *Civil War in Louisiana*, 290–291.

37. *OR*, vol. 26, pt. 1, 220–222, 230; Irwin, *Nineteenth Army Corps*, 247–249; Parrish, *Richard Taylor*, 301–302; Winters, *Civil War in Louisiana*, 291.

38. *OR*, vol. 26, pt. 1, 535–536; Irwin, *Nineteenth Army Corps*, 249; Richard B. Irwin, "The Capture of Port Hudson," *B&L*, 3:596–597; *RJC*, 2:313; Alvin M. Josephy Jr., *The Civil War in the American West* (New York: Vintage Books, 1991), 176; Parrish, *Richard Taylor*, 302.

39. *OR*, vol. 24, pt. 2, 466, vol. 26, pt. 1, 211–214, pt. 2, 108–109.

40. *OR*, vol. 26, pt. 1, 204–208, 222–223, 230–232, pt. 2, 110–111; Taylor, *Destruction and Reconstruction*, 139, 145; Walker, "War of Secession," 28, Gwinner Collection, USAMHI; Winters, *Civil War in Louisiana*, 292–293; Curtis W. Milbourn, "The Lafourche Offensive," *North and South* 7, no. 5 (2004): 80–81.

41. *OR*, vol. 22, pt. 1, 407–412; Thomas L. Snead, "The Conquest of Arkansas," *B&L*, 3:456; Thomas A. DeBlack, "1863: We Must Stand or Fall Alone," *Rugged and Sublime: The Civil War in Arkansas*, ed. Mark K. Christ (Fayetteville: University of Arkansas Press, 1994), 74–89; Castel, *Sterling Price*, 140–152; Parks, *Edmund Kirby Smith*, 278–280; Gregory J. W. Urwin, "A Very Disastrous Defeat: The Battle of Helena," *North and South* 6, no. 1 (2002): 26–39.

42. *OR*, vol. 26, pt. 1, 214, pt. 2, 109. The letters are in ibid., vol. 22, pt. 2, 885–886, 914.

4. The Devil's Own Time

1. *OR*, vol. 22, pt. 2, 948–950; Parks, *Edmund Kirby Smith*, 280–282.

2. Freret Letter, Brock Collection, HEH; Lawson H. Deck to Sister, June 24, 1863, Confederate States of America Archives, DUKE; "The Last Confederate Army to Surrender."

3. "Last Confederate Army to Surrender"; *OR*, vol. 22, pt. 2, 948–950, 992–994; vol. 53, 885; Parks, *Edmund Kirby Smith*, 280–305.

4. *OR*, vol. 22, pt. 2, 952–953. For a partial list of state concerns, see ibid., 945–947, and Parks, *Edmund Kirby Smith*, 311–317.

5. *OR*, vol. 26, pt. 2, 194, 232, 241; Hyatt Diaries, 2:59, LSU.

6. *OR*, vol. 22, pt. 2, 994–995, 1035–1036, vol. 26, pt. 2, 258; Kerby, *Kirby Smith's Confederacy*, 254–255. Also see D. Walker to "Dear David," August 2, 1864, Walker Family Letters, Gwinner Collection, USAMHI, and Edward Spencer, "Confederate Negro Enlistments," in *The Annals of the Civil War* (Philadelphia: Times, 1878; reprint, New York: Da Capo, 1994), 537–553. For insight into Smith's appointment, see Johnson, Mitchel, et al. to Davis, February 2, 1863, Davis Papers, DUKE.

7. Smith to Cushing, September 21, 1863, Kirby Smith Papers, UNC; *OR*, vol. 22, pt. 2, 990; Walker, "War of Secession," 29; Kerby, *Kirby Smith's Confederacy*, 239; Parks, *Edmund Kirby Smith*, 321.

8. *OR*, vol. 22, pt. 1, 520, pt. 2, 916, 942, 955, 990, 997, 1026, vol. 53, 884; Parks, *Edmund Kirby Smith*, 310. Smith sent Smith P. Bankhead's brigade from Texas. *OR*, vol. 22, pt. 2, 955, 997.

9. *OR*, vol. 22, pt. 1, 520–522, pt. 2, 920, 942, 945, 1014, vol. 53, 884, 897–898; Walker, "War of Secession," 34–35, Gwinner Collection, USAMHI; Reynolds, "Sterling Price," 88–89, MHS; Kerby, *Kirby Smith's Confederacy*, 226–233; Castel, *Sterling Price*, 153–170.

10. *OR*, vol. 22, pt. 2, 982, vol. 26, pt. 1, 294–299, 302–303, pt. 2, 203–204; Washington J. Smith, "Battle of Sabine Pass," *CVET* 27 (1919): 461; Parks, *Edmund Kirby Smith*, 326; Josephy, *American West*, 180–184.

11. *OR*, vol. 26, pt. 2, 218–221, 224, 231, 233, 245; Kerby, *Kirby Smith's Confederacy*, 189–190; Parks, *Edmund Kirby Smith*, 329–330.

12. *OR*, vol. 26, pt. 2, 221–222.

13. Ibid.; Parks, *Edmund Kirby Smith*, 327–328. Several weeks earlier Smith told Magruder, "Should Vicksburg fall, I regard an attempt to occupy Louisiana by the enemy as certain." See Smith to Magruder, June 27, 1863, Eldridge Collection, HEH.

14. *OR*, vol. 22, pt. 2, 1023, 1027, vol. 26, pt. 2, 242, 256.

15. *OR*, vol. 26, pt. 2, 241–242, 244, 256; Parks, *Edmund Kirby Smith*, 330–331.

16. *OR*, vol. 22, pt. 2, 1034–1036; Parks, *Edmund Kirby Smith*, 332–333.

17. *OR*, vol. 22, pt. 2, 1035–1036; Parks, *Edmund Kirby Smith*, 333.

18. *OR*, vol. 22, pt. 2, 1036, vol. 26, pt. 1, 328–330, 386–387, pt. 2, 255, 293; Taylor, *Destruction and Reconstruction*, 150; Norman D. Brown, *Journey to Pleasant Hill: Civil War Letters of Captain Elijah P. Petty, Walker's Texas Division, C.S.A.*, 2 vols. (San Antonio: Institute of Texan Cultures, 1982), 2:261; David C. Edmonds, *Yankee Autumn in Acadiana* (Lafayette: Acadiana, 1979), 153; Parrish, *Richard Taylor*, 308–309; Kerby, *Kirby Smith's Confederacy*, 242–234.

19. *OR*, vol. 26, pt. 1, 292, 732–738, 783; Ezra J. Warner, *Generals in Blue: Lives of the Union Commanders* (Baton Rouge: Louisiana State University Press, 1964; reprint, 1992), 159; Hollandsworth, *Pretense of Glory*, 138–140; Richard Lowe, *The Texas Overland Expedition of 1863* (Fort Worth: Ryan Place, 1996), 44–48.

20. *OR*, vol. 26, pt. 1, 386–387, pt. 2, 294–295. Father Raymond of St. Landry's Catholic Church in Opelousas had spent several weeks in New Orleans and returned to his parish by way of the Lafourche, Berwick Bay, and Plaquemine. Raymond's contact in Opelousas was Judge E. C. Dupre, who in turn reported directly to Taylor's adjutant, William Levy. See ibid., 294–295, and Edmonds, *Yankee Autumn*, 211, 255–256, 276.

21. *OR*, vol. 26, pt. 2, 323–324.

22. Ibid., pt. 1, 393, pt. 2, 291, 327; Lowe, *Texas Overland Expedition*, 49; Mark A. Snell, *From First to Last: The Life of Major General William B. Franklin* (New York: Fordham University Press, 2002), 288.

23. *OR*, vol. 26, pt. 1, 386–388, pt. 2, 294–295; Brown, *Journey to Pleasant Hill*, 2:265; Edmonds, *Yankee Autumn*, 163–172; Lowe, *Texas Overland Expedition*, 53–58.

24. *OR*, vol. 26, pt. 1, 386–390; Taylor to Moore, October 23, 1863, Thomas O. Moore Papers, LSU; Walker, "War of Secession," 38, Gwinner Collection, USAMHI.

25. *OR*, vol. 26, pt. 2, 341, 364.

26. Ibid., 294, 364.

27. Ibid., vol. 22, pt. 2, 1034–1036.

28. Ibid., vol. 26, pt. 2, 293, 341–342.

29. Ibid., pt. 1, 390–391, 393–394; Hyatt Diaries, 2:47, LSU.

30. Blessington, *Walker's Texas Division*, 135–136; Brown, *Journey to Pleasant Hill*, 2:271; Edmonds, *Yankee Autumn*, 239–241.

31. *OR*, vol. 26, pt. 1, 19–21, 292, 340–342; Lowe, *Texas Overland Expedition*, 60–62; Josephy, *American West*, 186–187; Snell, *First to Last*, 288–289.

32. *OR*, vol. 26, pt. 1, 359, 393–395, pt. 2, 341; Taylor, *Destruction and Reconstruction*, 150; Brown, *Journey to Pleasant Hill*, 2:279; Lowe, *Texas Overland Expedition*, 39–41, 56–57, 80–100; Snell, *First to Last*, 289–291; Lowe, *Walker's Texas Division*, 135–145.

33. *OR*, vol. 26, pt. 1, 384–385.

34. Ibid., pt. 2, 394–395, 468; Taylor, *Destruction and Reconstruction*, 152; Parrish, *Richard Taylor*, 314–315; Kerby, *Kirby Smith's Confederacy*, 247–248. The first editorial criticism occurred on June 3. See *OR*, vol. 26, pt. 2, 29–30. For Smith's response to Moore's concerns, see ibid., 221–222.

35. *OR*, vol. 22, pt. 2, 1110–1111, vol. 26, pt. 2, 439, 508; Parks, *Edmund Kirby Smith*, 339, 342.

36. *OR*, vol. 26, pt. 2, 439.

37. Freret Letter, Brock Collection, HEH.

38. *OR*, vol. 22, pt. 2, 988–990.

39. Ibid.

40. Ibid., 952, 989.

41. Ibid., vol. 26, pt. 2, 111; Freret Letter, Brock Collection, HEH; Smith to Wife, September 10, 1863, Kirby Smith Papers, UNC.

5. A Battle for Louisiana

1. *OR*, vol. 34, pt. 1, 573, pt. 2, 879, 1024; Taylor, *Destruction and Reconstruction*, 154. For specifics on the Union plans, see *RJC*, 2:5–6, 270, and *OR*, vol. 34, pt. 2, 15–16, 41–42, 267, 351, 494, 514–515.

2. Allen to Taylor, January 26, 1864, Brent Papers, LAGO; Sarah A. Dorsey, *Recollections of Henry Watkins Allen* (New York: M. Doolady, 1866), 234–235, 260.

3. *OR*, vol. 34, pt. 2, 991–992, 999–1000, 1027; Taylor, *Destruction and Reconstruction*, 154; Kerby, *Kirby Smith's Confederacy*, 287–288. Through fits and starts, the Red River campaign got under way on March 7 as Albert Lee's Union cavalry rode north from Baton Rouge. Andrew Jackson Smith, with elements from Sherman's Sixteenth and Seventeenth corps, left Vicksburg three days later for a rendezvous with Porter's fleet at the confluence of the Red and Mississippi. The command spread into Louisiana on March 12. William B. Franklin brought up the infantry on March 15 with his Nineteenth Corps and a detachment from the Thirteenth Corps. All three Federal columns converged slowly on Alexandria, the first target of the campaign. For Federal itineraries, see *OR*, vol. 34, pt. 1, 162, 170, 177, 444, pt. 2, 545, and Johnson, *Red River Campaign*, 89–91, 98–99. The Arkansas arm of the movement did not get under way until March 21. See ibid., 171.

4. *OR*, vol. 34, pt. 2, 895, 1028–1029; Taylor, *Destruction and Reconstruction*, 153; Parrish, *Richard Taylor*, 320. For more on Smith's fortifications, see Boggs, *Military Reminiscences*, 71, 74, and Joiner, *One Damn Blunder*, 19–29.

5. *OR*, vol. 34, pt. 1, 489, pt. 2, 1024, 1027; Surget to Brent, January 21, 24, 1864, Walker to Brent, February 8, 1864, Brent Papers, LAGO; Taylor, *Destruction and Reconstruction*, 153. Porter agreed with Taylor's assessment of Confederate fortifications along the river. See James K. Ewer, *The Third Massachusetts Cavalry in the War for the Union* (Maplewood, MA: Perry, 1903), 139–140.

6. *OR*, vol. 34, pt. 1, 573–574.

7. Taylor to Smith, February 28, 1864, Smith to Taylor, March 4, 1864, Richard Taylor Papers, LAGO; Parrish, *Richard Taylor*, 319.

8. *OR*, vol. 34, pt. 1, 489, 491–493, 573–575, 597–598, pt. 2, 1024; William H. Stewart Diary, March 20, 1864, UNC; Henry C. Fike Diary, UMO; Taylor, *Destruction and Reconstruction*, 154–155; Blessington, *Walker's Texas Division*, 166–167.

9. *OR*, vol. 34, pt. 1, 491–493, 561, 597–599; Blessington, *Walker's Texas Division*, 169.

10. *OR*, vol. 34, pt. 1, 561, 597–600; King Memoir, 8–11, Civil War Manuscript Series, TUL; William S. Burns, "The Red River Expedition," in *B&L*, 5:576–578; Johnson, *Red River Campaign*, 89–94; Shelby Foote, *The Civil War: A Narrative*, 3 vols. (New York: Random House, 1958–1974), 3:30; Lowe, *Walker's Texas Division*, 173–177.

11. *OR*, vol. 34, pt. 1, 492, 575–578, 599; King Memoir, 8–11, Civil War Manuscript Series, TUL; Camille Armand Jules Marie de Polignac Diary, April 7, 1864, Civil War Times Illustrated Collection,

USAMHI; Walker, "War of Secession," 42, Gwinner Collection, USAMHI; Taylor, *Destruction and Reconstruction*, 154–155; Kinard, *Lafayette of the South*, 131.

12. *OR*, vol. 34, pt. 1, 478, 484, 561; Blessington, *Walker's Texas Division*, 175; Taylor, *Destruction and Reconstruction*, 156; Boggs, *Military Reminiscences*, 74; Joiner, *One Damn Blunder*, 53; Johnson, *Red River Campaign*, 96.

13. *OR*, vol. 34, pt. 1, 501; Charles F. Sherman to Father, April 26, 1864, Charles F. Sherman Letters, WRC; Benjamin F. McDaniel Memoir, 64–65, Money Collection, UTEX; Polignac Diary, April 7, 1864, Civil War Times Illustrated Collection, USAMHI; Stewart Diary, March 22, 1864, UNC; Ewer, *Third Massachusetts Cavalry*, 137–139; Burns, "Red River Expedition," *B&L*, 5:579; Taylor, *Destruction and Reconstruction*, 156–157; Joiner, *One Damn Blunder*, 54.

14. *OR*, vol. 34, pt. 1, 491, 501, pt. 2, 1027, pt. 4, 654; Taylor, *Destruction and Reconstruction*, 157. Additional cavalry units moved from Texas to Louisiana on March 16. See *OR*, vol. 34, pt. 2, 1048.

15. *OR*, vol. 34, pt. 1, 494, 501, pt. 2, 852–853, 871, 971–972, 978, 982; Burrud to Wife, April 1, 1864, John B. Burrud Collection, HEH; Edwin C. Bearss, ed., *A Louisiana Confederate: Diary of Felix Pierre Poche* (Natchitoches, LA: Northwestern State University, 1972), 102–103; Brown, *Journey to Pleasant Hill*, 2:384; Parks, *Edmund Kirby Smith*, 352–356; Susan E. Dollar, "The Red River Campaign: Natchitoches Parish, Louisiana: A Case of Equal Opportunity Destruction," *Louisiana History* (fall 2002): 416–418.

16. *OR*, vol. 34, pt. 1, 488, 514, pt. 2, 977.

17. *OR*, vol. 34, pt. 1, 514, pt. 2, 1009, 1023, 1026–1027, 1055–1056, 1059–1060, 1096. On March 16 Smith told Taylor that Magruder was to blame for the delay in the arrival of reinforcements. See ibid., pt. 1, 496, pt. 2, 1044, 1048.

18. *OR*, vol. 34, pt. 2, 935, 1021–1022, 1035.

19. Ibid., 1021, 1035, vol. 22, pt. 2, 942, vol. 53, 897–898; Brown, *Journey to Pleasant Hill*, 2:151, 153; Parks, *Edmund Kirby Smith*, 368–369; Castel, *Sterling Price*, 152, 162–163.

20. Reynolds to Smith, May 23, 24, 1863, Reynolds to Johnson, December 24, 1863, Reynolds Papers, LOC; *OR*, vol. 22, pt. 2, 802–803; Kerby, *Kirby Smith's Confederacy*, 289; Parks, *Edmund Kirby Smith*, 369; Castel, *Sterling Price*, 163; Dougan, *Confederate Arkansas*, 121.

21. *OR*, vol. 22, pt. 2, 1110–1111, vol. 34, pt. 2, 870, 1028–1029, 1047; Castel, *Sterling Price*, 142, 162–163, 171.

22. *OR*, vol. 34, pt. 2, 1028–1029, 1043–1044, 1095, 1102; Castel, *Sterling Price*, 172–173; Parks, *Edmund Kirby Smith*, 373. For reports on the Federal movements, see *OR*, vol. 34, pt. 2, 638, 657, 692, 704, 707, and Johnson, *Red River Campaign*, 170–171.

23. *OR*, vol. 34, pt. 2, 1056, 1059–1060, 1062–1063, 1102, pt. 1, 484, 516; Castel, *Sterling Price*, 173; Johnson, *Red River Campaign*, 119; Kerby, *Kirby Smith's Confederacy*, 300.

24. *OR*, vol. 34, pt. 1, 514–515, 516.

25. Ibid., 490, 494, 515.

26. Brown, *Journey to Pleasant Hill*, 2:2, 386; Blessington, *Walker's Texas Division*, 179; Frank L. Richardson, "Mansfield Campaign," 3, Louisiana Historical Association Collection, TUL.

27. *OR*, vol. 34, pt. 1, 511; Richardson, "Mansfield Campaign," 3, Louisiana Historical Association Collection, TUL; Ewer, *Third Massachusetts Cavalry*, 142.

28. *OR*, vol. 34, pt. 1, 511–513; Parrish, *Richard Taylor*, 42. Kenner's assertion that the troops had been in Shreveport for a week is unsupported. The infantry left Arkansas on March 20 and arrived at Shreveport on March 24 and 25. See *OR*, vol. 34, pt. 1, 563; William N. Hoskin Diary, typescript, 52, UMO; and William McPheeters Diary, March 20–March 25, 1864, William McPheeters Collection, MHS. The McPheeters diary has recently been published by the University of Arkansas

Press: Cynthia DeHaven Pitcock and Bill J. Gurley, eds., *I Acted from Principle: The Civil War Diary of William McPheeters, Confederate Surgeon in the Trans-Mississippi* (Fayetteville: University of Arkansas Press, 2002).

29. *OR*, vol. 34, pt. 1, 513–515, pt. 2, 1078; Hoskin Diary, 52–53, UMO; McPheeters Diary, March 28, 1864, McPheeters Collection, MHS; John P. Quesenberry Diary, March 28, 1864, UMO; Parrish, *Richard Taylor*, 333; Parks, *Edmund Kirby Smith*, 380–381. After the war Smith admitted that he had held the troops at Shreveport because "it seemed probable at this time that Steele would advance first." See Edmund Kirby Smith, "The Defense of the Red River," *B&L*, 4 : 370–371.

30. Boggs, *Military Reminiscences*, 75–76.

31. *OR*, vol. 34, pt. 1, 494, 513, 516; Boggs, *Military Reminiscences*, 76.

32. Smith to Johnston, December 26, 1862, Joseph E. Johnston Papers, HEH; Boggs, *Military Reminiscences*, 41; Parks, *Edmund Kirby Smith*, 203, 242–243, 346; Archie McDonald, "William Robertson Boggs," *CGEN*, 1 : 107.

33. *OR*, vol. 34, pt. 2, 870, 897; Boggs, *Military Reminiscences*, 76, 82; Freret Letter, Brock Collection, HEH; Parks, *Edmund Kirby Smith*, 346–347; Brooksher, *War along the Bayous*, 28–29.

34. *OR*, vol. 34, pt. 1, 513, 519; Johnson, *Red River Campaign*, 121.

35. Boggs, *Military Reminiscences*, 76; *OR*, vol. 34, pt. 1, 505, 513; Parrish, *Richard Taylor*, 333–334.

36. *OR*, vol. 34, pt. 1, 517.

37. Ibid., 519.

38. Ibid., 514–515; Thomas L. Connelly and Archer Jones, *The Politics of Command: Factions and Ideas in Confederate Strategy* (Baton Rouge: Louisiana State University Press, 1973), 10.

39. *OR*, vol. 34, pt. 1, 516.

40. Ibid., 515.

6. To Whip the Scoundrels Here

1. *OR*, vol. 34, pt. 1, 518–521; Joiner, *One Damn Blunder*, 52.

2. *OR*, vol. 34, pt. 1, 517–518, 520–521; Norman C. Delaney, ed., "The Diary and Memoirs of Marshall Samuel Pierson Company C, 17th Reg., Texas Cavalry, 1862–1865," *Military History of Texas and the Southwest* 13, no. 3 (1976): 33. Taylor's anger over the delay in receiving reinforcements led him to threaten the colonel of a tardy Texas regiment with arrest. See Xavier DeBray, *A Sketch of the History of DeBray's Twenty-sixth Regiment of Texas Cavalry* (Austin: Eugene Von Boeckmann Book and Job Printer, 1884; reprint, Waco: Waco Village, 1961), 15–16, and Parrish, *Richard Taylor*, 337.

3. *OR*, vol. 34, pt. 2, 869.

4. Ibid., pt. 1, 521–522.

5. Ibid., 522–523.

6. Ibid., 521–524; Parks, *Edmund Kirby Smith*, 384–385; Johnson, *Red River Campaign*, 121–122. The idea for sinking the ship *New Falls City* originated with Smith. See *OR*, vol. 34, pt. 2, 1056–1057, 1068, and Joiner, *One Damn Blunder*, 66–67.

7. *OR*, vol. 34, pt. 1, 519–520, 563; McPheeters Diary, April 3, April 5, 1864, McPheeters Collection, MHS. The April 3 date attributed to Taylor's correspondence to Smith (Boggs) in *OR*, vol. 34, pt. 1, 519, is incorrect. Diaries written by members of Churchill's command reveal that the men arrived in Keachi on April 5. See Hoskin Diary, 53–53, UMO; McPheeters Diary, April 3, April 5, 1864, McPheeters Collection, MHS.

8. *OR*, vol. 34, pt. 1, 480, 484–485, 525–526, pt. 3, 733; Hoskin Diary, 54, UMO.

9. *OR*, vol. 34, pt. 1, 480, 484–485, 525–526; Taylor, *Destruction and Reconstruction*, 159–160; Johnson, *Red River Campaign*, 122–123. Although Smith later reported that the meeting took place on April 5, dispatches from his headquarters in Shreveport dated April 5 instruct Taylor to prepare for a conference "to-morrow morning at your headquarters near Mansfield," making the date of the meeting April 6. See *OR*, vol. 34, pt. 1, 480, 526.

10. Taylor, *Destruction and Reconstruction*, 159; J. E. Hewitt, "The Battle of Mansfield, LA," *CVET* 33 (1925): 172.

11. *OR*, vol. 34, pt. 1, 480, 485, pt. 3, 733; Churchill to My Dear Colonel, September 6, 1885, Eldridge Collection, HEH; McPheeters Diary, April 6, 1864, McPheeters Collection, MHS; Hoskin Diary, 54, UMO; Smith, "Defense of the Red River," *B&L*, 4:371; Taylor, *Destruction and Reconstruction*, 159.

12. *OR*, vol. 34, pt. 1, 485; Churchill to Colonel, September 6, 1885, Eldridge Collection, HEH; Xavier DeBray, "A Sketch of DeBray's Twenty-sixth Texas Cavalry," *SHSP* 13 (1885): 157; Taylor, *Destruction and Reconstruction*, 159–160; Smith, "Defense of the Red River," *B&L*, 4:371; Curtis Milbourn, "Fighting for Time," *North and South* 5, no. 4 (2002): 69–70.

13. *OR*, vol. 34, pt. 1, 480; Taylor, *Destruction and Reconstruction*, 159; Smith, "Defense of the Red River," *B&L*, 4:370–371.

14. For an examination of Banks's decision, see Johnson, *Red River Campaign*, 113–116, and Joiner, *One Damn Blunder*, 75–80.

15. *OR*, vol. 34, pt. 1, 179, 485; *RJC*, 2:35, 286–287; *ORN*, 26:60; Snell, *From First to Last*, 302.

16. *OR*, vol. 34, pt. 1, 450, 454, 563, 616–617; *RJC*, 2:58; Taylor, *Destruction and Reconstruction*, 160; Bearss, *Louisiana Confederate*, 105; DeBray, "DeBray's Twenty-sixth," 157; Milbourn, "Fighting for Time," 70–76.

17. *OR*, vol. 34, pt. 1, 450, 455, 617; *RJC*, 2:58–59; Taylor, *Destruction and Reconstruction*, 160; Milbourn, "Fighting for Time," 73–75.

18. *RJC*, 2:58–60; Stewart Diary, March 25, 1864, UNC; Patten to Mother, March 15, 1864, Patten to Family, April 12, 1864, George D. Patten Papers, HEH; Tibbetts to Family, April 4, 1864, Melvan Tibbetts Letters, WRC; Irwin, *Nineteenth Army Corps*, 298; Taylor, *Destruction and Reconstruction*, 160; Bearss, *Louisiana Confederate*, 105; Johnson, *Red River Campaign*, 124–126.

19. *OR*, vol. 34, pt. 1, 518–521; Walker, "War of Secession," 49; Taylor, *Destruction and Reconstruction*, 159–161; *RJC*, 2:201. Taylor later scoffed that the strategic significance of Mansfield "was pointed out to the 'Aulic Council' at Shreveport, but failed to elicit any definite response." See Taylor, *Destruction and Reconstruction*, 159. Many Federal sources place the Sabine Crossroads either in Mansfield itself or directly along the northern edge of the Moss plantation. One Federal map, however, shows the road nearly three miles south of the Fincher farm at Pleasant Grove, where the third stage of the battle took place. While it is doubtful that Federal cartographers would have had sufficient time to acquire detailed information on the area between Mansfield and Pleasant Hill, several Confederate sources locate the crossroads below Mansfield and south of Fincher's farm. A Confederate engineer's map drawn by Major Richard M. Venable, a member of the Crescent Regiment, put the road near present-day Louisiana state route 522, a location that marks the second phase of the fighting. A map drawn in 1914 under the auspices of the United Confederate Veterans Camp Mouton and the United Daughters of the Confederacy Kate Beard Chapter also pinpoints the road just south of the site of the second phase. However, seven years earlier J. A. Jarratt, another veteran from the Crescent regiment who was from De Soto Parish, claimed that "the Sabine Cross Roads was over six miles from Mansfield." The secondary literature on the battle reflects these disagreements between the veterans, and the road network has become a subject of controversy among scholars and buffs of the campaign.

The consensus is that current-day highway 522 marks the site of the crossroads. These interpretations were garnered by the author from the files of the Mansfield State Historical Area and discussions with historians Arthur Bergeron, Steve Bounds, Scott Dearman, and Gary Joiner.

20. OR, vol. 34, pt. 1, 563; Taylor, *Destruction and Reconstruction*, 40, 160–161; Blessington, *Walker's Texas Division*, 181; J. A. Jarratt, *Reminiscences of a Great Struggle by the Heroes of the Confederacy* (privately published, 1907), 11–13; Alonzo Plummer, *Confederate Victory at Mansfield* (Mansfield, LA: United Daughters of the Confederacy, 1969), 19; Joiner, *One Damn Blunder*, 94–95.

21. Taylor, *Destruction and Reconstruction*, 161; Delaney, "Marshall Samuel Pierson," 33–34; Blessington, *Walker's Texas Division*, 181; Bearss, *Louisiana Confederate*, 105; Bergeron, *Silas T. Grisamore*, 145; P. H. Goodloe, "Service in the Trans-Mississippi," *CVET* 23 (1915): 31; Dorsey, *Henry Watkins Allen*, 260; Beard to Wife, April 2, 1864, Consolidated Crescent File, MSHS. Beard was killed in the battle of Mansfield. See Carl Moneyhon and Bobby Roberts, *Portraits of Conflict: A Photographic History of Louisiana in the Civil War* (Fayetteville: University of Arkansas Press, 1990), 281.

22. OR, vol. 34, pt. 1, 521; Walker, "War of Secession," 49–50, Gwinner Collection, USAMHI; Taylor, *Destruction and Reconstruction*, 160–161; J. E. Sliger, "How General Taylor Fought the Battle of Mansfield," *CVET* 31 (1923): 457; Joiner, *One Damn Blunder*, 94–95.

23. OR, vol. 34, pt. 1 290; *RJC*, 2:58; Walker, "War of Secession," 49–50, Gwinner Collection, Sliger, "How General Taylor Fought," 457; DeBray, "DeBray's Twenty-sixth," 557–558; M. Jane Johansson, ed., *Widows by the Thousands: The Civil War Letters of Theophilus and Harriet Perry, 1862–1864* (Fayetteville: University of Arkansas Press, 2000), 232; Johnson, *Red River Campaign*, 118; Joiner, *One Damn Blunder*, 82; Snell, *From First to Last*, 305–306.

24. Sliger, "How General Taylor Fought," 457; Hewitt, "Battle of Mansfield," 172; Blessington, *Campaigns of Walker's Texas Division*, 182–183.

25. OR, vol. 34, pt. 1, 526; Taylor, *Destruction and Reconstruction*, 161; Sliger, "How General Taylor Fought," 457; Parrish, *Richard Taylor*, 339–340; Johnson, *Red River Campaign*, 131–132.

26. OR, vol. 34, pt. 1, 519–520, 526; Taylor, *Destruction and Reconstruction*, 161.

27. Sliger, "How General Taylor Fought," 457; Moise to Moore, September 24, 1864, Moore Papers, LSU; Taylor, *Destruction and Reconstruction*, 115; Brooksher, *War along the Bayous*, 88. A typographical error in *Confederate Veteran* changed Sligh's name to Sliger. The name Sligh is used throughout this work in the text, but the author is cited as Sliger in the notes. See "A Correction," *CVET* 32 (1924): 46.

28. Sliger, "How General Taylor Fought," 457; Bergeron, *Louisiana Confederate Military Units*, 138–139; Thesta Kennedy Scogland, *The Garlington Family* (Baltimore: Gateway, 1976), 367–369. William R. Kennedy "served as a courier for the Confederates in Louisiana" and enjoyed a reputation as a person of daring exploits. Reportedly, he arrived in Mansfield on April 8 just after the battle had started. Despite the designation "Co. D, Col Gray's 28th Regt" in family records, Kennedy did not appear on the official regimental roles. See ibid. and Office of Board of Pension Commissioners, State of Louisiana, "William R. Kennedy, Claibourne Parish," document numbers 15363, 15073, LSA. For other examples of Taylor's unconventional courier system, see "The Nankeen Shirt," *CVET* 33 (1925): 183, 198. Also see Boggs, *Military Reminiscences*, 69.

29. Equestrian distance rider Mike Marino contributed to this assessment.

30. OR, vol. 34, pt. 2, 1057; Dorsey, *Henry Watkins Allen*, 263. On the night of April 7 one of Taylor's men commented on the peculiar situation: "We have orders to suspend all military duties tomorrow, it being fast day, and have orders to load up and be ready to march at a moment's notice. Which don't respond with fasting." See Delaney, "Marshall Samuel Pierson," 33–34.

31. OR, vol. 34, pt. 1, 528; Johnson, *Red River Campaign*, 123–124; Parrish, *Richard Taylor*, 339–340.

32. *OR*, vol. 34, pt. 1, 528; Boggs, *Military Reminiscences,* 76.

33. In his letter of April 8 Smith wrote that he would reinforce Taylor with all the armed cavalry from Marshall, Texas, and forward Pratt's battery from Shreveport. *OR*, vol. 34, pt. 1, 485, 528; Smith, "Defense of the Red River," *B&L*, 4:371; Boggs, *Military Reminiscences,* 76.

7. Too Late, Sir, the Battle Is Won

1. Louis Hall, "The Battle of Mansfield: Experience of a Veteran," *Shreveport Enterpriser,* March 4, 1910, Consolidated Crescent File, MSHS; James Crayton Carroll Memoir, 12, Fourteenth Texas File, MSHS; Blessington, *Walker's Texas Division,* 181–183; Bearss, *Louisiana Confederate,* 105–106.

2. *OR*, vol. 34, pt. 1, 563; Taylor, *Destruction and Reconstruction,* 161; Dorsey, *Henry Watkins Allen,* 261; "Map of the Mansfield Battlefield," Fiftieth Anniversary Association, April 8, 1914, MSHS; Johnson, *Red River Campaign,* 132–133; Brooksher, *War along the Bayous,* 91–92. There are indications that numerous Louisiana partisans, irregulars, and parolees joined Taylor's ranks at Mansfield. See Joiner, *One Damn Blunder,* 96.

3. *OR*, vol. 34, pt. 1, 526; Taylor, *Destruction and Reconstruction,* 162, 132; Dorsey, *Henry Watkins Allen,* 260.

4. *OR*, vol. 34, pt. 1, 602, 604; McPheeters Diary, April 8, 1864, McPheeters Collection, MHS; Taylor to Walker, April 9, 1864, John G. Walker Papers, UNC; Walker, "War of Secession," 49–50, Gwinner Collection, USAMHI; John R. House III, "Battle of Mansfield Numbers Were Off," *Civil War News,* December 1996, 8; interview with Gary Joiner and Scott Dearman, spring 2004.

5. Taylor, *Destruction and Reconstruction,* 162; Hyatt Diaries, 2:71, LSU; S. A. Poche, Letter to *Picayune Times-Democrat,* July 4, 1864, Eighteenth Louisiana Crescent File, MSHS; Sliger, "How General Taylor Fought," 457; Arthur W. Bergeron Jr., "A Colonel Gains His Wreath: Henry Gray's Louisiana Brigade at Mansfield, April 8, 1864," *Civil War Regiments* 4, no. 2 (1994): 11.

6. John M. Stanyan, *A History of the Eighth Regiment of New Hampshire Volunteers, Including Its Service as Infantry, Second N.H. Cavalry, and Veterans Battalion in the Civil War of 1861–1865* (Concord, NH: Ira C. Evans, 1892), 412.

7. *RJC*, 2:60; Blessington, *Walker's Texas Division,* 182; Patten to Family, April 12, 1864, Patten Papers, HEH; Taylor, *Destruction and Reconstruction,* 20, 162–163; Parrish, *Richard Taylor,* 343. Some Confederates also expected Price. See Beard to Wife, April 2, 1864, Consolidated Crescent File, MSHS.

8. Taylor, *Destruction and Reconstruction,* 20. The Federals had massed forty-eight hundred troops at the front. See Johnson, *Red River Campaign,* 133.

9. *OR*, vol. 34, pt. 1, 564; Taylor, *Destruction and Reconstruction,* 163; Hall, "Battle of Mansfield," Consolidated Crescent File, MSHS; Bergeron, *Silas T. Grisamore,* 145; Jones, "Twenty-eighth Louisiana," 91; Parrish, *Richard Taylor,* 344–346.

10. Dorsey, *Henry Watkins Allen,* 260; DeBray, *DeBray's Twenty-sixth,* 17; Jarratt, *Reminiscences,* 11; John Dimitry, *Confederate Military History: Louisiana,* Clement A. Evans, series ed. (Atlanta: Confederate Publishing Co., 1899; reprint, Wilmington, NC: Broadfoot, 1988), 138–139; "Map of the Mansfield Battlefield," MSHS; Napier Bartlett, "The Trans-Mississippi," in *Military Record of Louisiana* (Baton Rouge: Louisiana State University Press, 1964; reprint, 1992), 13; Johnson, *Red River Campaign,* 135.

11. *OR*, vol. 34, pt. 1, 564; J. T. Woods, *Service of the Ninety-sixth Ohio Volunteers* (Toledo: Blade Printing, 1874), 59; Taylor, *Destruction and Reconstruction,* 163; Charles F. Sherman to Father, April 26,

1864, Sherman Letters, WRC; Bearss, *Louisiana Confederate*, 107; Bergeron, *Silas T. Grisamore*, 146; Bartlett, *Military Record*, 42, 62; Jones, "Twenty-eighth Louisiana," 91–92; Bergeron, "Colonel Gains His Wreath," 12–17.

12. *OR*, vol. 34, pt. 1, 528; Dimitry, *Louisiana*, 138; Dorsey, *Henry Watkins Allen*, 263.

13. Blessington, *Walker's Texas Division*, 186–188; John Thomas Stark Diary, 5–6, Thirteenth Texas Dismounted File, MSHS; *OR*, vol. 34, pt. 1, 564; Parrish, *Richard Taylor*, 347.

14. Walker, "War of Secession," 50, Gwinner Collection, USAMHI; Carroll Memoir, 13, Fourteenth Texas File, MSHS; Blessington, *Walker's Texas Division*, 188–189. The Federal guns captured by Walker's men were from the Second Massachusetts Battery commanded by Ormand F. Nims. See *OR*, vol. 34, pt. 1, 462.

15. *OR*, vol. 34, pt. 1, 564; Dimitry, *Louisiana*, 140–141; Bartlett, *Military Record*, 42; Bergeron, *Silas T. Grisamore*, 146; Jones, "Twenty-eighth Louisiana," 92; Bergeron, "Colonel Gains His Wreath," 13, 21–22. For other estimates of Confederate casualties, see ibid., 21–22, and Steve Bounds and Curtis Milbourn, "The Battle of Mansfield," *North and South* 5, no. 6 (2002): 28. According to Mansfield historian Steve Bounds, the casualty estimate of the veterans for this phase of the battle is high. Interview with Steve Bounds, spring 2004.

16. *OR*, vol. 34, pt. 1, 266, 301, 564; Blessington, *Walker's Texas Division*, 187; Johnson, *Red River Campaign*, 135–136. Although not a West Pointer, Taylor was well versed in military history, and his plan resembled the approach used by Marlborough, the British commander at the battle of Blenheim, in 1704.

17. *OR*, vol. 34, pt. 1, 292, 301, 564; Taylor, *Destruction and Reconstruction*, 163; Delaney "Marshall Samuel Pierson," 34–35; Plummer, *Confederate Victory at Mansfield*, 23; Johnson, *Red River Campaign*, 142; Joiner, *One Damn Blunder*, 99; Bounds and Milbourn, "Battle of Mansfield," 34.

18. *OR*, vol. 34, pt. 1, 521, 564.

19. Blessington, *Walker's Texas Division*, 187; Sliger, "How General Taylor Fought," 458; O. W. Wells to Sister, April 12, 1864, Henry Gray File, MSHS; Walker, "War of Secession," 52, Gwinner Collection, USAMHI.

20. Dorsey, *Henry Watkins Allen*, 262; Sliger, "How General Taylor Fought," 458; B. G. Goodrich, "Battle of Mansfield, LA," *CVET* 8 (1900): 103; "The Battle of Mansfield," *SBIV* 3 (1885): 413; Bergeron, *Silas T. Grisamore*, 190; Dimitry, *Louisiana*, 139–142; Edward A. Pollard, *The Lost Cause* (New York: E. B. Treat, 1866), 495; Blessington, *Walker's Texas Division*, 187; Bearss, *Louisiana Confederate*, 107; Richardson, "Mansfield Campaign," 5, Louisiana Historical Association Collection, TUL; Carroll Memoir, 13, Fourteenth Texas File, MSHS; Bartlett, *Military Record*, 41; Taylor, *Destruction and Reconstruction*, 165. Smith also bemoaned the loss of Mouton and urged his soldiers to emulate the Louisianan's "virtues and valor." See Trans-Mississippi Department Papers, 55B, TUL, and *OR*, vol. 34, pt. 1, 549.

21. Sliger, "How General Taylor Fought," 457–458; Taylor, *Destruction and Reconstruction*, 108, 165, 178.

22. Walker, "War of Secession," 49–51, Gwinner Collection, USAMHI.

23. Ibid.; Sliger, "How General Taylor Fought," 457; Blessington, *Walker's Texas Division*, 183, 186.

24. J. H. Beck, "Special to Houston Daily Telegraph," April 15, published April 22, 1864, First Infantry Division, C.S.A. File, MSHS; John Alexander Green, "General Thomas Green," *Biographical Encyclopedia of Texas* (New York, 1880), 131–132; Bounds and Milbourn, "Battle of Mansfield," 32, 38, 40.

25. *OR*, vol. 34, pt. 1, 480, 485, 564, 553; Polignac Diary, 177, Civil War Times Illustrated Collection, USAMHI; Nathaniel C. Hughes, ed., *Liddell's Record* (Dayton, OH: Morningside, 1985), 181; Smith, "Defense of the Red River," *B&L*, 4:371.

26. *OR*, vol. 34, pt. 1, 200–201, 553, 565, 607; Stark Diary, 6–8, Thirteenth Texas Dismounted File, MSHS; Tibbetts to Family, April 12, 1864, Tibbetts Letters, WRC; Patten to Family, April 12, 1864, Patten Papers, HEH; Taylor, *Destruction and Reconstruction*, 164; Parrish, *Richard Taylor*, 349–352; Johnson, *Red River Campaign*, 136–141; Bounds and Milbourn, "Battle of Mansfield," 26–40. The Federals called the fight at Chapman's "Pleasant Grove."

27. John Burrud to Wife, April 12, 1864, Burrud Collection, HEH; Patten to Family, April 12, 1864, Patten Papers, HEH; *Philadelphia Press* article, Shreveport Enterprise File, MSHS; Sherman to Father, April 26, 1864, Sherman Letters, WRC; Harris H. Beecher, *Record of the 114th Regiment, N.Y.S.V.: Where It Went, What It Saw, and What It Did* (Norwich, NY: J. F. Hubbard Jr., 1866), 311–312; Flinn, *Campaigning with Banks*, 108–109; Johnson, *Red River Campaign*, 140; Hollandsworth, *Pretense of Glory*, 187–189; Fred H. Harrington, *Fighting Politician: Major General Nathaniel P. Banks* (Philadelphia: University of Pennsylvania Press, 1948; reprint, Westport: Greenwood, 1970), 156–157.

28. James T. Wallace Diary, April 8, 1864, UNC; Stanyan, *New Hampshire Volunteers*, 404; Yeary, *Boys in Gray*, 627; Blessington, *Walker's Texas Division*, 193–194; Kinard, *Lafayette of the South*, 148–149; Lowe, *Walker's Texas Division*, 199–200.

29. Orton S. Clark, *The One Hundred and Sixteenth Regiment of New York State Volunteers* (Buffalo: Printing House of Mathews and Warren, 1868), 166; Blessington, *Walker's Texas Division*, 189, 193–194; Beck, "Houston Daily Telegraph," First Infantry Division, C.S.A. File, MSHS; *OR*, vol. 34, pt. 1, 201; Parrish, *Richard Taylor*, 349; Harrington, *Fighting Politician*, 156.

30. *OR*, vol. 34, pt. 1, 480, 527.

31. Ibid., 527; Boggs, *Military Reminiscences*, 77; Parks, *Edmund Kirby Smith*, 391.

32. *OR*, vol. 34, pt. 1, 528; Boggs, *Military Reminiscences*, 77; Bearss, *Louisiana Confederate*, 110.

33. Tibbetts to Family, April 12, 1864, Tibbetts Letters, WRC; Sherman to Father, April 26, 1864, Sherman Letters, WRC; Blessington, "Walker's Texas Division," 201.

34. Sliger, "How General Taylor Fought," 458; Hamilton P. Bee, "Battle of Pleasant Hill—An Error Corrected," *SHSP* 8 (1880): 185; *RJC*, 2:13; *OR*, vol. 34, pt. 1, 201.

35. Boggs, *Military Reminiscences*, 77; DeBray, "DeBray's Twenty-sixth," 157; Churchill to Colonel, September 6, 1885, Eldridge Collection, HEH.

36. *OR*, vol. 34, pt. 1, 476, 559; Smith, "Defense of the Red River," *B&L*, 4:372.

37. *OR*, vol. 34, pt. 1, 559; Smith, "Defense of the Red River," *B&L*, 4:372. Taylor noted in his memoirs that his familiarity with Banks's character and his previous experience with the Federal commander during earlier campaigns bolstered his confidence on the eve of the battle. Taylor, *Destruction and Reconstruction*, 161.

38. *OR*, vol. 34, pt. 1, 565–567; Taylor, *Destruction and Reconstruction*, 171.

39. *OR*, vol. 34, pt. 1, 480, 527; Taylor to Walker, April 9, 1864, Walker Papers, UNC.

40. *OR*, vol. 34, pt. 1, 567, 605; Taylor to Walker, April 9, 1864, Walker Papers, UNC; McPheeters Diary, April 9, 1864, McPheeters Collection, MHS; Joiner, *One Damn Blunder*, 104. Walker states in his memoir that Taylor knew the Federals were in retreat at 11:00 P.M. Given the substance of Taylor's 1:30 A.M. letter, Walker's postwar claim seems erroneous. See Walker, "War of Secession," 51.

41. Taylor to Walker, April 9, 1864, Walker Papers, UNC; McPheeters Diary, April 9, 1864, McPheeters Collection, MHS; Bee, "Battle of Pleasant Hill," 18; *OR*, vol. 34, pt. 1, 528, 565, 605, 607; Taylor, *Destruction and Reconstruction*, 165.

42. *OR*, vol. 34, pt. 1, 528–29, 566–567; Taylor, *Destruction and Reconstruction*, 165–167; Joiner, *One Damn Blunder*, 109. Taylor assigned command of Mouton's division to Polignac and held the troops in reserve. Kinard, *Lafayette of the South*, 146–150.

43. *OR*, vol. 34, pt. 1, 201, 566, 607–608; Bee, "Battle of Pleasant Hill," 184; Walker, "War of Secession," 54, Gwinner Collection, USAMHI; Taylor, *Destruction and Reconstruction*, 166; interview with LTC Dana M. Mangham, United States Military Academy, spring 2004.

44. *OR*, vol. 34, pt. 1, 566–568, 602, 605; McPheeters Diary, April 9, 1864, McPheeters Collection, MHS; Joiner, *One Damn Blunder*, 109–110.

45. *OR*, vol. 34, pt. 1, 566–568; Churchill to Colonel. September 6, 1885, Eldridge Collection, HEH; McPheeters Diary, April 9, 1864, McPheeters Collection, MHS; Taylor, *Destruction and Reconstruction*, 166–167; Brooksher, *War along the Bayous*, 113; Johnson, *Red River Campaign*, 155.

46. *OR*, vol. 34, pt. 1, 566–568, 602–605; Tibbetts to Family, April 12, 1864, Tibbetts Letters, WRC; Joiner, *One Damn Blunder*, 114–115.

47. *OR*, vol. 34, pt. 1, 566–568; "Galveston Tri-Weekly News," May 8, 1864, Twelfth Texas File, MSHS; Taylor, *Destruction and Reconstruction*, 168–169; Blessington, *Walker's Texas Division*, 198–199; Brooksher, *War along the Bayous*, 125–138. Walker suffered a painful wound during the battle and retired from the field. Taylor reported that without Walker, the Texans lost their "continuity." See *OR*, vol. 34, pt. 1, 568, and Blessington, *Walker's Texas Division*, 197.

48. *OR*, vol. 34, pt. 1, 566–568, 608, 618; Polignac Diary, 178, Civil War Times Illustrated Collection, USAMHI; Debray, *DeBray's Twenty-sixth*, 18; Patten to Family, April 12, 1864, Patten Papers, HEH; Stark Diary, 6–8, Thirteenth Texas Dismounted File, MSHS; Walker, "War of Secession," 54, Gwinner Collection, USAMHI; Burns, "Red River Expedition," *B&L*, 5:582; Taylor, *Destruction and Reconstruction*, 168–170; Blessington, *Walker's Texas Division*, 200; "Unpublished After-Action Reports," *Civil War Regiments*, 4, no. 2 (1994): 133–134; McGowen, *Horse Sweat and Powder Smoke*, 139–144; Johnson, *Red River Campaign*, 155–169.

49. *OR*, vol. 34, pt. 1, 184–185, 309; Burrud to Wife, April 12, 1864, Burrud Collection, HEH; Patten to Family, April 12, 1864, Patten Papers, HEH; William H. Whitney to Brother, May 23, 1864, Miscellaneous Manuscript Collection, LSU; *RJC*, 2:35, 221–222; Irwin, *Nineteenth Army Corps*, 323; Brooksher, *War along the Bayous*, 141–144. After the battle Banks planned to resume the advance until dissuaded at a council of war. See Banks's testimony in *RJC*, 2:13. Also see Joiner, *One Damn Blunder*, 115–116.

50. Blessington, *Walker's Texas Division*, 200; W. F. Mills to Parents, April 12, 1864, Twenty-eighth Texas Cavalry Division File, MSHS; McPheeters Diary, April 11, 1864, McPheeters Collection, MHS; "Galveston Tri-Weekly News," May 8, 1864, Twelfth Texas File, MSHS; Bearss, *Louisiana Confederate*, 111.

51. Quesenberry Diary, April 8, 1864, UMO; McPheeters Diary, April 10, 1864, McPheeters Collection, MHS. For an analysis of casualty statistics, see Johnson, *Red River Campaign*, 169, and Brooksher, *War along the Bayous*, 135.

52. Taylor, *Destruction and Reconstruction*, 170–171; *OR*, vol. 34, pt. 1, 568.

53. Churchill to Colonel, September 6, 1885, Eldridge Collection, HEH.

54. *OR*, vol. 34, pt. 1,568, 601–606; W. Davidson article, September 13, 1888, "The Overton Sharp-Shooter," MSHS; W. T. Shaw, "The Red River Campaign," *CVET* 25 (1917): 117; Bergeron, "General Richard Taylor," 110–111; Johnson, *Red River Campaign*, 167–169.

55. *OR*, vol. 34, pt. 1, 563, 566; Taylor, *Destruction and Reconstruction*, 40, 171.

56. Taylor, *Destruction and Reconstruction*, 171.

57. Walker, "War of Secession," 52–54, Gwinner Collection, USAMHI; Bee, "Battle of Pleasant Hill," 184.

58. *OR*, vol. 34, pt. 3, 99; *RJC*, 2:176; John D. Imboden, "Stonewall Jackson in the Shenandoah," *B&L*, 2:297; Hollandsworth, *Pretense of Glory*, 182.

59. *OR*, vol. 34, pt. 1, 567; Polignac Diary, 178, Civil War Times Illustrated Collection, USAMHI; Taylor, *Destruction and Reconstruction*, 169; Parrish, *Richard Taylor*, 359–361. Taylor's official report made no mention of Green's condition.

60. Walker, "War of Secession," 54, USAMHI. Walker insisted that Green's repulse "should have convinced Taylor of his error, or, at least, have demonstrated the necessity of ascertaining the enemy's position and strength before attempting a further advance." Ibid.

61. *OR*, vol. 34, pt. 1, 543, 545, 584; Taylor to Walker, April 9, 1864, Walker Papers, UNC.

62. Taylor to Walker, April 9, 1864, Walker Papers, UNC.

63. Ibid.; DeBray, *DeBray's Twenty-sixth*, 19; Taylor, *Destruction and Reconstruction*, 176.

8. The Fruit of Your Victory

1. *OR*, vol. 34, pt. 1, 516, 532–533, 554, pt. 3, 759; Smith, "Defense of the Red River," *B&L*, 4:372.

2. *OR*, vol. 34, pt. 1, 571–572; Walker, "War of Secession," 56–57, Gwinner Collection, USAMHI; Taylor, *Destruction and Reconstruction*, 176.

3. *OR*, vol. 34, pt. 1, 480; Boggs, *Military Reminiscences*, 77; Taylor, *Destruction and Reconstruction*, 176; Parrish, *Richard Taylor*, 370–371; Johnson, *Red River Campaign*, 181–182.

4. *OR*, vol. 34, pt. 1, 530.

5. Ibid.; Parrish, *Richard Taylor*, 371.

6. *OR*, vol. 34, pt. 1, 476, 478, 531–532; Parrish, *Richard Taylor*, 370–371.

7. *OR*, vol. 34, pt. 1, 531; Parks, *Edmund Kirby Smith*, 395–396; Parrish, *Richard Taylor*, 371.

8. *OR*, vol. 34, pt. 1, 530–532; Parrish, *Richard Taylor*, 370–371; Brooksher, *War along the Bayous*, 146–147. Price sent his infantry to Taylor under orders from Smith and would have preferred to keep the force for his own use against Steele. Thus, Smith's characterization of Price's behavior as "unselfish" is at best a stretch. See *OR*, vol. 34, pt. 2, 1043–1044, 1056, 1059–1060.

9. *OR*, vol. 34, pt. 1, 546, 571–572; Smith to Wife, April 12, 1864, Kirby Smith Papers, UNC.

10. *OR*, vol. 34, pt. 1, 480, 546, 572; Taylor, *Destruction and Reconstruction*, 180; Johnson, *Red River Campaign*, 182.

11. *OR*, vol. 34, pt. 1, 530–531, 545–546, 571–572; Taylor, *Destruction and Reconstruction*, 176.

12. *OR*, vol. 34, pt. 1, 572; J. N. Bragg to Wife, April 12, 1864, Thirty-third Arkansas File, MSHS; Johnson, *Red River Campaign*, 182. Churchill and Parsons took the road to Kingston while Walker marched through Keachi. See McPheeters Diary, April 14, 1864, McPheeters Collection, MHS.

13. Hoskin Diary, April 14, 1864, UMO; William Bull, "Reminiscences of the War between the States 1861–1865," 130, UMO; McPheeters Diary, April 13, 1864, McPheeters Collection, MHS; Quesenberry Diary, April 14, 1864, UMO.

14. *OR*, vol. 34, pt. 1, 572; Taylor, *Destruction and Reconstruction*, 180.

15. *OR*, vol. 34, pt. 1, 480–481, 572, 780, 824–825; Taylor, *Destruction and Reconstruction*, 180; Parrish, *Richard Taylor*, 372; Johnson, *Red River Campaign*, 182–183.

16. *OR*, vol. 34, pt. 1, 661, pt. 3, 766, 780–781; Castel, *Sterling Price*, 176; Johnson, *Red River Campaign*, 183.

17. *OR*, vol. 34, pt. 1, 480, pt. 3, 766; Johnson, *Red River Campaign*, 183.

18. *OR*, vol. 34, pt. 3, 766.

19. Ibid., 767.

20. Ibid., pt. 1, 572; Taylor, *Destruction and Reconstruction*, 180.

21. *OR*, vol. 34, pt. 1, 476, pt. 3, 770–771; Taylor, *Destruction and Reconstruction*, 180. Smith ordered Churchill to move into Arkansas along the Red River and then turn east to Magnolia. Parsons marched north through Benton and Walker northeast through Minden. See *OR*, vol. 34, pt. 1, 555.

22. Smith to Wife, April 18, 1864, Kirby Smith Papers, UNC; Hoskin Diary, April 16, 1864, UMO; Quesenberry Diary, April 16, 1864, UMO; Johnson, *Red River Campaign*, 183. Steele's planned junction with John Thayer was over a week late, and the columns did not effect a rendezvous until April 9, twenty miles west of Arkadelphia on the Little Missouri River. The following day Confederate cavalry engaged the Federals in a sharp skirmish at Prairie D'Ane. By that point Steele's main concern was supplies, and he insisted on a train from Little Rock before continuing the campaign. Steele hoped to secure a base at Camden until resupplied. Thus, while the movement by the Federals toward Camden had the outward appearance of a retreat, Steele did not initially intend to abandon the campaign. See ibid., 170–180, and *OR*, vol. 34, pt. 1, 661–662, pt. 3, 77–79.

23. *OR*, vol. 34, pt. 1, 661, pt. 3, 728; Smith to Wife, April 18, April 20, Kirby Smith Papers, UNC; Castel, *Sterling Price*, 185.

24. *OR*, vol. 34, pt. 1, 481, 534, 555, pt. 3, 782; Edwin C. Bearss, *Steele's Retreat from Camden* (Little Rock: Pioneer, 1967), 47–49, 80; Parks, *Edmund Kirby Smith*, 397.

25. *OR*, vol. 34, pt. 1, 534; Parrish, *Richard Taylor*, 380–381.

26. *OR*, vol. 34, pt. 1, 481, 781, 787–788, pt. 3, 766; Boggs, *Military Reminiscences*, 78; Bearss, *Steele's Retreat*, 49–51; Parks, *Edmund Kirby Smith*, 398; Castel, *Sterling Price*, 177–178, 185–186.

27. *OR*, vol. 34, pt. 1, 781, 826, 842. For more on Poison Spring, see Bearss, *Steele's Retreat*, 15–41. For an examination of alleged brutality by the Confederates against the First Kansas Colored Volunteers, see Anne J. Bailey, "Was There a Massacre at Poison Spring?" *Military History of the Southwest* 20 (fall 1990): 1–12, and Gregory J. W. Urwin, "Cut to Pieces and Gone to Hell: The Poison Spring Massacre," *North and South* 3, no. 6 (2000): 45–57.

28. *OR*, vol. 34, pt. 1, 661–663, pt. 3, 267–268; Bearss, *Steele's Retreat*, 42; Johnson, *Red River Campaign*, 188–189.

29. *OR*, vol. 34, pt. 1, 481–482, 665, 712–715, 781, 787–790; Parks, *Edmund Kirby Smith*, 399–400. Steele's loss of material at Poison Springs and Marks' Mill totaled 440 wagons and prompted an Iowa Federal to compare him to "Commissary Banks." See Ira D. Richards, "The Camden Expedition, March 23–May 3, 1864" (master's thesis, University of Arkansas, 1957), 112. For more on the fighting at Marks' Mill, see Bearss, *Steele's Retreat*, 42–86.

30. *OR*, vol. 34, pt. 1, 668, 671; Bearss, *Steele's Retreat*, 87–91; Johnson, *Red River Campaign*, 193–194.

31. *OR*, vol. 34, pt. 1, 481; Boggs, *Military Reminiscences*, 78; Blessington, *Walker's Texas Division*, 247.

32. *OR*, vol. 34, pt. 1, 480–481, 555, 781–782, 788, pt. 3, 766; Boggs, *Military Reminiscences*, 78; John Newman Edwards, *Shelby and His Men, or The War in the West* (Cincinnati: Miami Printing and Publishing Co., 1867; reprint, Waverly, MO: General Joseph Shelby Memorial Fund, 1993), 290; Castel, *Sterling Price*, 177–178, n. 28.

33. *OR*, vol. 34, pt. 1, 481, 555, 764, 790, 840; Walker, "War of Secession," 62, Gwinner Collection, USAMHI; *Washington (Arkansas) Telegraph*, March 22, 1865; Boggs, *Military Reminiscences*, 78; Edwards, *Shelby and His Men*, 290–291; Bearss, *Steele's Retreat*, 95–96, 98–100; Castel, *Sterling Price*, 180–181, n 35.

34. *OR*, vol. 34, pt. 1, 826–827, 829, 834; Edwards, *Shelby and His Men*, 291–293; Castel, *Sterling Price*, 179–180.

35. *OR*, vol. 34, pt. 1, 530, 534, 556; Taylor, *Destruction and Reconstruction,* 180; Smith to J. L. S. Kirby, April 18, 1864, Record Group 109, E-106, Box 52, Department of the Trans-Mississippi, vol. 73 1/2, USNA. For more on the confusion over the pontoon, see correspondences dated April 20 and 21, 1864, found in ibid., 195–197, no. 2722, 2724, 2725, 2728, 2729.

36. *OR*, vol. 34, pt. 1, 780, 845–846; Johnson, *Red River Campaign,* 195; Bearss, *Steele's Retreat,* 100. A rumor that the Federals planned to invade Texas through Indian Territory may have reached Smith's camp in Arkansas and influenced his decision. See *OR*, vol. 34, pt. 3, 773, 794–795, 796–798.

37. *OR*, vol. 34, pt. 1, 668–669, 790, 834, 840; Bearss, *Steele's Retreat,* 96, 99–100.

38. *OR*, vol. 34, pt. 1, 669, 764, 790; Quesenberry Diary, May 3, 1864; Johnson, *Red River Campaign,* 196; Bearss, *Steele's Retreat,* 96, 103.

39. Hoskin Diary, April 27, 28, 1864, UMO; Bull, "Reminiscences," 131, UMO; A. F. Sperry, *History of the Thirty-third Iowa Infantry Volunteer Regiment, 1863–6,* ed. Gregory J. W. Urwin and Cathy Kunzinger Urwin (Fayetteville: University of Arkansas Press, 1999), 95–96; Carl H. Moneyhon, ed., "Life in Confederate Arkansas: The Diary of Virginia Davis Gray, 1863–1865, Part I," *Arkansas Historical Quarterly* 42 (spring 1983): 82–83; *OR*, vol. 34, pt. 1, 782. Steele worried that Fagan had moved to attack Little Rock. See ibid., 669.

40. *OR*, vol. 34, pt. 1, 556, 782; Blessington, *Walker's Texas Division,* 247–248; Bearss, *Steele's Retreat,* 110–111.

41. *OR*, vol. 34, pt. 1, 556, 689, 726, 782, 809; Bearss, *Steele's Retreat,* 106, 116. Walker noted that the land was for cultivation of cotton. See Walker, "War of Secession," 64, Gwinner Collection, USAMHI.

42. *OR*, vol. 34, pt. 1, 556, 689.

43. Ibid., 782, 799–800, 829–830; Wallace Diary, April 30, 1864, UNC; Blessington, *Walker's Texas Division,* 248; Josephy, *American West,* 213–214; Johnson, *Red River Campaign,* 197–198.

44. *OR*, vol. 34, pt. 1, 782, 799–801, 809, 816; Blessington, *Walker's Texas Division,* 248; Bearss, *Steele's Retreat,* 119–120.

45. *OR*, vol. 34, pt. 1, 481, 782, 799, 809; Blessington, *Walker's Texas Division,* 248; Walker, "War of Secession," 63, Gwinner Collection, USAMHI.

46. *OR*, vol. 34, pt. 1, 669, 811, 817; Blessington, *Walker's Texas Division,* 249; Yeary, *Boys in Gray,* 31–32; R. S. Wilson, "The Battle of Jenkins's Ferry," *CVET* 18 (1910): 468.

47. *OR*, vol. 34, pt. 1, 556, 782, 799–808, 829–830; Wiley Britton, *The Civil War on the Border,* 2 vols. (New York: G. P. Putnam's Sons, 1899; reprint, Ottawa: Kansas Heritage, 1994), 2:301–303; Castel, *Sterling Price,* 181–183; Johnson, *Red River Campaign,* 198–199. For a detailed description covering each phase of the battle at Jenkins' Ferry, see Bearss, *Steele's Retreat,* 114–169.

48. *OR*, vol. 34, pt. 1, 556–557, 782, 799–801, 806, 809–816; Britton, *Civil War on the Border,* 2:303–305; Castel, *Sterling Price,* 181–183; Johnson, *Red River Campaign,* 198–199.

49. *OR*, vol. 34, pt. 1, 556–557, 810, 812; Bearss, *Steele's Retreat,* 148–150.

50. *OR*, vol. 34, pt. 1, 556–557, 782, 816–817; Blessington, *Walker's Texas Division,* 249–251; Johnson, *Red River Campaign,* 200.

51. *OR*, vol. 34, pt. 1, 557, 782–783, 817; Johnson, *Red River Campaign,* 200; Norman D. Brown, "Walker's Texas Division," *Confederate History Symposium: Proceedings 1992* (Hillsboro, TX: Hill College, 1992), 45.

52. *OR*, vol. 34, pt. 1, 557, 690, 790, 800, 817–818; Blessington, *Walker's Texas Division,* 253; Richards, "Camden Expedition," 140. There is evidence that black Federal soldiers executed Confederate prisoners and wounded. See *OR*, vol. 34, pt. 1, 813; Hoskin Diary, April 30, 1864, UMO; Milton

P. Chambers to Brother, May 7, 1864, Milton P. Chambers Papers, UARK; Yeary, *Boys in Gray*, 390, 437, 799; and Sperry, *Thirty-third Iowa*, 291–292, nn. 12, 14.

53. Quesenberry Diary, May 1, 3, 1864, UMO; Blessington, *Walker's Texas Division*, 253–255; Wilson, "Battle of Jenkins's Ferry," 468.

54. Walker, "War of Secession," 64, Gwinner Collection, USAMHI. The marshlike condition of the battlefield precluded Smith's effective use of artillery. See *OR*, vol. 34, pt. 1, 812, 816.

55. *OR*, vol. 34, pt. 1, 557, 691, 787–788; Taylor, *Destruction and Reconstruction*, 176; Johnson, *Red River Campaign*, 202–203. During the campaign the Federals lost approximately 2,750 men and the Confederates 2,300. See ibid. The number of Confederates engaged may have been as high as 8,000. See Michael J. Forsyth, *The Camden Expedition of 1864* (Jefferson, NC: McFarland, 2003), 170.

56. *OR*, vol. 34, pt. 1, 531, 550; Geise, "Confederate Military Forces," 241–242.

57. Walker, "War of Secession," 56–57, Gwinner Collection, USAMHI; Taylor, *Destruction and Reconstruction*, 190; Boggs, *Military Reminiscences*, 78–79. For an examination of Taylor's line of reasoning, see Michael J. Forsyth, *The Red River Campaign and the Loss by the Confederacy of the Civil War* (Jefferson, NC: McFarland, 2002).

9. The Path of Glory

1. Smith to Mother, May 5, 1864, Kirby Smith Papers, UNC; *OR*, vol. 34, pt. 1, 477–478. Smith's letter to his mother contained much of the same information as a preliminary report to Jefferson Davis dated May 4. See ibid., 476–477.

2. *OR*, vol. 34, pt. 1, 478. Missouri governor Thomas Reynolds recalled a meeting with Smith in which the general was highly critical of Price's performance during the campaign. See Reynolds, "Sterling Price," 120–122, MHS.

3. *OR*, vol. 34, pt. 1, 481–482; Castel, *Sterling Price*, 185–186.

4. *OR*, vol. 41, pt. 2, 1017; Blessington, *Walker's Texas Division*, 259; Castel, *Sterling Price*, 185–186. Snead was elected to the Confederate Congress in May 1864. See Steven E. Woodworth, "Thomas L. Snead," *ENCC*, 4:1483.

5. *OR*, vol. 34, pt. 1, 482, 537; Trans-Mississippi Department Papers, 55B, TUL; Blessington, *Walker's Texas Division*, 255, 257, 259.

6. *OR*, vol. 34, pt. 1, 537.

7. Ibid., 538. Smith made the decision to countermarch Churchill and Parsons on May 15, two days before he notified Taylor. See Blessington, *Walker's Texas Division*, 262.

8. *OR*, vol. 34, pt. 1, 486, 572; Smith, "Defense of the Red River," *B&L*, 4:372.

9. *OR*, vol. 34, pt. 1, 530, 538, 594–595; Parrish, *Richard Taylor*, 394; Castel, *Sterling Price*, 196–196.

10. Blessington, *Walker's Texas Division*, 262–263; *OR*, vol. 34, pt. 1, 486.

11. *ORN*, 26:60; *OR*, vol. 34, pt. 2, 1056–1057, 1068, pt. 3, 99; Johnson, *Red River Campaign*, 208–209; Chester G. Hearn, *Admiral David Dixon Porter: The Civil War Years* (Annapolis: Naval Institute Press, 1996), 250–251; Joiner, *One Damn Blunder*, 137–144.

12. Taylor to Walker, April 9, 1864, Walker Papers, UNC; *OR*, vol. 34, pt. 1, 530, 570–572; Taylor, *Destruction and Reconstruction*, 177; Johnson, *Red River Campaign*, 211–212.

13. *ORN*, 26:49, 54–55, 60–63; *OR*, vol. 34, pt. 1, 571; Henry C. Sampson Diaries, April 14, 15, 1864, WRC; Taylor, *Destruction and Reconstruction*, 177–178; Bailey, *Between the Enemy and Texas*, 170–179; B. P. Gallaway, *The Ragged Rebel: A Common Soldier in W. H. Parsons' Texas Cavalry* (Austin: University

of Texas Press, 1988), 90–101. The Federal ships involved in the battle with Green were the monitor *Osage*, the tinclad *Lexington*, and the transport *Black Hawk*. See Joiner, *One Damn Blunder*, 144–146. At Grand Ecore a rumor circulated among Federals that Green lay mortally wounded aboard the *Blackhawk*. See Sampson Diaries, April 15, 1864, WRC.

14. Rebecca W. Smith and Marion Mullins, eds. "The Diary of H. C. Medford, Confederate Soldier, 1864," *Southwestern Historical Quarterly* 34 (January 1931): 226; Taylor, *Destruction and Reconstruction*, 178; Hyatt Diaries, 2:74, LSU; Parrish, *Richard Taylor*, 375. On May 3 Smith publicly mourned the loss of Mouton and Green as well as generals Horace Randal and William Scurry, who fell at Jenkins' Ferry. See *OR*, vol. 34, pt. 1, 549.

15. Taylor, *Destruction and Reconstruction*, 179, 190; General Orders 33, April 13, 1864, Confederate District of West Louisiana Record Book, TUL; *OR*, vol. 34, pt. 1, 546, 571–572.

16. *OR*, vol. 34, pt. 1, 476, 481, 572; Taylor, *Destruction and Reconstruction*, 180; Parrish, *Richard Taylor*, 370–372.

17. Taylor to Boggs, June 1, 1864, Joseph L. Brent Collection, TUL; *OR*, vol. 34, pt. 1, 186, 572; Taylor, *Destruction and Reconstruction*, 180; Polignac Diary, April 18, 20, 1864, Civil War Times Illustrated Collection, USAMHI; John C. Murray Diary, April 13, 1864, Civil War Manuscript Series, TUL; Bailey, *Between the Enemy and Texas*, 178–179. Wharton had served previously under Joseph Wheeler and Nathan Bedford Forrest. See Anne J. Bailey, "John Austin Wharton," *CGEN*, 6:122–123.

18. Boyd to Taylor, April 14, 1864, Brent Papers, LAGO. Boyd's letter has recently been printed in Joiner, *One Damn Blunder*, 117–119.

19. Taylor to Boggs, June 1, 1864, Brent Collection, TUL; Taylor, *Destruction and Reconstruction*, 180; *OR*, vol. 34, pt. 1, 190; Johnson, *Red River Campaign*, 214–221; Joiner, *One Damn Blunder*, 146–148.

20. Taylor, *Destruction and Reconstruction*, 181; Johnson, *Red River Campaign*, 220–222. Calhoun's Landing is present-day Colfax.

21. Taylor, *Destruction and Reconstruction*, 181–182; *OR*, vol. 34, pt. 1, 580, 610, 612; Johnson, *Red River Campaign*, 226; Fredericka Meiners, "Hamilton P. Bee in the Red River Campaign," *Lone Star Blue and Gray: Essays on Texas in the Civil War*, ed. Ralph A. Wooster (Austin: Texas State Historical Association, 1995), 301–303; Bergeron, "General Richard Taylor," 117–118. A Federal soldier remarked, "They had a beautiful trap to lead us in. Their fortifications were so arranged as to rake us from all directions, in case we tried to cross." See Dianne E. Green, ed., *The Civil War Diary of Lieutenant Robert Molford Addison Co. E, Twenty-third Wisconsin Infantry* (Westminster, MD: Willow Bend Books, 2001), 49.

22. *OR*, vol. 34, pt. 1, 541–542, 581; Taylor, *Destruction and Reconstruction*, 182, 188–189. Bee insisted that the Union army was not demoralized. See *OR*, vol. 34, pt. 1, 613. The April 23 diary entry of a Federal soldier supports Bee's contention: "The rebels were under the impression that we would surrender on finding a rebel force in our front again, and a large force in our rear. The mistake cost them dear." He testified to the fierce fighting at Monett's Ferry: "I saw more killed and wounded in the space of a few yards than I ever saw before." See Sampson Diaries, April 23, 1864, WRC.

23. Hughes, *Liddell's Record*, 179–180; *OR*, vol. 34, pt. 1, 580, 633; Taylor to Boggs, June 1, 1864, Brent Collection, TUL; Brooksher, *War along the Bayous*, 170.

24. *OR*, vol. 34, pt. 1, 396, 610–614; Woods, *Ninety-sixth Ohio*, 74; Alwyn Barr, ed., "William T. Mechling's Journal of the Red River Campaign," *Texana* 1 (1963): 363–379; Meiners, "Hamilton P. Bee," 303–305; Johnson, *Red River Campaign*, 226–233; Brooksher, *War along the Bayous*, 172–181.

25. Taylor, *Destruction and Reconstruction*, 182; *OR*, vol. 34, pt. 1, 580–581; Taylor to Boggs, June 1, 1864, Brent Collection, TUL; Parrish, *Richard Taylor*, 378. One of Banks's staff officers, captured days

later near Alexandria, confessed that if the Confederates had held out at Monett's Ferry "a few hours longer" the Federals might have been compelled to surrender. See *OR*, vol. 34, pt. 1, 586.

26. *OR*, vol. 34, pt. 1, 613–614; Confederate District of West Louisiana Record Book, April 29, 1864, TUL; Taylor to Brent, June 1, 1864, Brent Collection, TUL; Parrish, *Richard Taylor*, 378–379; Meiners, "Hamilton P. Bee," 306–308.

27. Brent to Surget, May 20, 1864, Brent Collection, TUL; *OR*, vol. 34, pt. 1, 615; Meiners, "Hamilton P. Bee," 308–309.

28. Walker, "War of Secession," 69, Gwinner Collection, USAMHI; *OR*, vol. 41, pt. 2, 1066–1067; Parrish, *Richard Taylor*, 379.

29. Bee to Smith, May 18, 1879, Kirby Smith Papers, UNC; *OR*, vol. 34, pt. 1, 614–615, vol. 53, 1029; Meiners, "Hamilton P. Bee," 309–310; Parrish, *Richard Taylor*, 379. Bee's brother Barnard had been Smith's close friend in the West Point class of 1845. See Lagvanec, *Chevalier Bayard*, 179 n. 107.

30. Taylor, *Deconstruction and Reconstruction*, 182; Jarratt, *Reminiscences*, 24; Taylor to Anderson, April 21, 1864, Trans-Mississippi Department Papers, TUL; *OR*, vol. 34, pt. 1, 534–535.

31. Hughes, *Liddell's Record*, 179–181; *OR*, vol. 34, pt. 1, 634–635; Brooksher, *War along the Bayous*, 170.

32. Burrud to Wife, April 28, 1864, Burrud Collection, HEH; Ewer, *Third Massachusetts Cavalry*, 166; Dorsey, *Henry Watkins Allen*, 279; Taylor, *Destruction and Reconstruction*, 193; *OR*, vol. 34, pt. 1, 419, 581, pt. 3, 307; Walker, "War of Secession," 57, Gwinner Collection, USAMHI; Winters, *Civil War in Louisiana*, 365–366. For testimony on the actions of Banks's soldiers during the retreat, see Edmonds, *Conduct of Federal Troops*.

33. *OR*, vol. 34, pt. 1, 191, 581, 583–585; Fike Diary, April 14, 1864, UMO; McDaniel Memoir, 92, UTEX; Kerby, *Kirby Smith's Confederacy*, 315–316. A rumor spread among Confederates that Porter threatened to fire on Banks if the Union infantry tried to leave Alexandria ahead of the fleet. See Walker, "War of Secession," 71, Gwinner Collection, USAMHI.

34. *OR*, vol. 34, pt. 1, 481, 534, 535, 582.

35. Ibid., 582–583; Confederate District of West Louisiana Record Book, April 26, 1864, TUL; Taylor, *Destruction and Reconstruction*, 182; Parrish, *Richard Taylor*, 38.

36. *OR*, vol. 34, pt. 1, 582–583, 634; Taylor, *Destruction and Reconstruction*, 189; Hughes, *Liddell's Record*, 179–180. Smith detached one section of Archibald Cameron's Louisiana battery and Battery H of Conner's First Mississippi Light Artillery from Liddell's command.

37. *ORN*, 26:74, 79; *OR*, vol. 34, pt. 1, 585; Confederate District of West Louisiana Record Book, April 26, 1864, TUL; Johnson, *Red River Campaign*, 237–238. For a narrative of the Union naval operations between Grand Ecore and Alexandria, see Brooksher, *War along the Bayous*, 186–194.

38. Dorsey, *Henry Watkins Allen*, 265; Henry Rust Diary, April 25, 1864, WRC; Ed Steers, ed., "The Red River Campaign Letters of Lt. Charles Washington Kennedy, 156th New York Volunteer Infantry," *Civil War Regiments* 4, no. 2 (1994): 116; *OR*, vol. 34, pt. 1, 590, pt. 3, 791; Parrish, *Richard Taylor*, 383–384.

39. Taylor, *Destruction and Reconstruction*, 190; Surget to Walker, April 26, 1864, Walker Papers, UNC; Johnson, *Red River Campaign*, 254–255.

40. *OR*, vol. 34, pt. 1, 549, 583–584; Trans-Mississippi Department Papers, TUL; Parrish, *Richard Taylor*, 380–381.

41. *OR*, vol. 34, pt. 1, 534, 535, pt. 3, 782; "Unpublished After–Action Reports," 119–120; Johnson, *Red River Campaign*, 221. After the war Taylor wrote that Banks withdrew hastily from Grand Ecore. See Taylor, *Destruction and Reconstruction*, 183.

42. *OR*, vol. 34, pt. 1, 534.

43. Ibid., 534–535.

44. Ibid., 534–535, 541; Parrish, *Richard Taylor,* 381. Smith's and Taylor's interpretations of the Shreveport Agreement appear in *OR,* vol. 34, pt. 1, 480–481, 584.

45. *OR,* vol. 34, pt. 1, 541, 584; Taylor, *Destruction and Reconstruction,* 188–189.

46. *OR,* vol. 34, pt. 1, 541.

47. Ibid., 541–542.

48. Ibid., 541–542, 634; Taylor, *Destruction and Reconstruction,* 153, 189.

49. *OR,* vol. 34, pt. 1, 534–535, 541–542; Taylor, *Destruction and Reconstruction,* 126.

50. *OR,* vol. 34, pt. 1, 542. Taylor was aware that in the weeks before Mansfield, members of Smith's staff had dismissed his plea for reinforcements and questioned the sincerity of his efforts to stop Banks. See *OR,* vol. 34, pt. 1, 519. Considering his April 27 reaction to General Order 18, Taylor's April 28 assertion that he was not interested in accolades for his achievements seems disingenuous. See ibid., 549, 584.

51. *OR,* vol. 34, pt. 1, 542–543, 584.

52. Ibid., 542–543; Taylor to Smith, April 28, 1864, Joseph L. Brent Collection, HEH; Blessington, *Walker's Texas Division,* 260.

10. This Fatal Blunder

1. *OR,* vol. 34, pt. 1, 402–404, 587, 635–636; Hughes, *Liddell's Record,* 183; "Unpublished After-Action Reports," 122–124; *RJC,* 2:8; Brooksher, *War along the Bayous,* 209–211; Bergeron, "Richard Taylor," 126. For more on Bailey's Dam, see Joiner, *One Damn Blunder,* 159–168.

2. Burrud to Wife, May 20, 1864, Burrud Collection, HEH; H. T. Douglas, "The Trans-Mississippi Department," *CVET* 25 (1917): 153; Taylor, *Destruction and Reconstruction,* 186–189; Johnson, *Red River Campaign,* 258–259.

3. Taylor to Boggs, June 1, 1864, Brent Collection, TUL; *OR,* vol. 34, pt. 1, 584–591; Taylor, *Destruction and Reconstruction,* 189.

4. *OR,* vol. 34, pt. 1, 636; Hughes, *Liddell's Record,* 179–184; Taylor, *Destruction and Reconstruction* 189.

5. Hughes, *Liddell's Record,* 173–174, 181, 183; *OR,* vol. 34, pt. 3, 829–830. Taylor's instructions for control of the district that Liddell found objectionable are in ibid., 953–956.

6. *OR,* vol. 34, pt. 1, 582, 634, 636; Hughes, *Liddell's Record,* 183; Taylor, *Destruction and Reconstruction,* 189. The dates and locations on various correspondences indicate that Smith arrived in Shreveport on May 11.

7. DeBray, *DeBray's Twenty-sixth,* 22; Sampson Diaries, May 2, May 3, 1864, WRC; *OR,* vol. 34, pt. 1, 584, 587, 589.

8. Taylor to Boggs, June 1, 1864, Brent Collection, TUL; *OR,* vol. 34, pt. 1, 584–591; Hughes, *Liddell's Record,* 173; Taylor, *Destruction and Reconstruction,* 189.

9. Hughes, *Liddell's Record,* 184; *OR,* vol. 34, pt. 1, 537; Parrish, *Richard Taylor,* 388–389. Taylor pointed to the shortage of artillery as a factor in the Federal success and criticized Smith's decision to withdraw the guns to Arkansas. See Taylor to Boggs, June 1, 1864, Brent Collection, TUL.

10. Edmonds, *Conduct of Federal Troops,* 151–152, 179–180; *OR,* vol. 34, pt. 1, 591; Taylor, *Destruction and Reconstruction,* 193–194; Dorsey, *Henry Watkins Allen,* 279; Johnson, *Red River Campaign,* 268–272.

11. Polignac Diary, 181, Civil War Times Illustrated Collection, USAMHI; *OR,* vol. 34, pt. 1, 542; Taylor, *Destruction and Reconstruction,* 188–193. A Union soldier who approved of the pillaging

insisted, "Gen. Banks don all he could to prevent it but could not do it." See Burrud to Wife, May 20, 1864, Burrud Collection, HEH. Banks testified that he did not order the burning of Alexandria. See *RJC*, 2 : 23. Walker predicted, "The conduct of the federal army on this retreat will be a standing disgrace to the federal arms for all times, as many generations must pass away before the devastation and wanten destruction of towns, villages, and farm houses will be forgotten and forgiven. The perpetrators of these acts . . . were worse enemies of the cause of Union than the so called 'rebels' in arms." See Walker, "War of Secession," 71, Gwinner Collection, USAMHI.

12. *OR*, vol. 34, pt. 1, 591–592.

13. Ibid., 592; Confederate District of West Louisiana Record Book, May 14, 1864, TUL.

14. Confederate District of West Louisiana Record Book, May 14, 1864, TUL; *OR*, vol. 34, pt. 1, 592, pt. 3, 823.

15. Taylor to Boggs, June 1, 1864, Brent Collection, TUL; *OR*, vol. 34, pt. 1, 325, 593; Bearss, *Louisiana Confederate*, 121; Brooksher, *War along the Bayous*, 218–219.

16. Fike Diary, May 16, 1864, UMO; Tibbetts to Family, May 26, 1864, Tibbetts Letters, WRC; *OR*, vol. 34, pt. 1, 593.

17. Taylor to Boggs, June 1, 1864, Brent Collection, TUL; Burrud to Wife, May 20, 1864, Burrud Collection, HEH; *OR*, vol. 34, pt. 1, 325, 593; Johnson, *Red River Campaign*, 273–274. According to Joseph Brent, Taylor's artillery chief, John Wharton, the ranking cavalry commander, directed him to reconnoiter the ground near Mansura and select a position "suitable for the employment of artillery." See Brent to Surget, June 20, 1864, Brent Collection, TUL.

18. *OR*, vol. 34, pt. 1, 325, 593, pt. 3, 616–617; Burrud to Wife, May 20, 1864, Burrud Collection, HEH; Brooksher, *War along the Bayous*, 218–219. Brent maintained that Wharton ordered the withdrawal. See Brent to Surget, June 20, 1864, Brent Collection, TUL.

19. *OR*, vol. 34, pt. 1, 593.

20. Ibid., 538, 592, pt. 3, 828–829; Boggs to Price, May 19, 1864, Record Group 109, E-106, Box 52, Department of the Trans-Mississippi, vol. 73 1/2, USNA.

21. *OR*, vol. 34, pt. 1, 538, 592, pt. 3, 828–829; Castel, *Sterling Price*, 196–197.

22. *OR*, vol. 34, pt. 1, 487, 538, 593–594.

23. Ibid., 593–594; Irwin, *Nineteenth Army Corps*, 345–347; Brooksher, *War along the Bayous*, 219–220, 223–224.

24. Irwin, *Nineteenth Army Corps*, 346–347; *OR*, vol. 34, pt. 1, 320, 329, 367–368; Winters, *Civil War in Louisiana*, 336–337.

25. *OR*, vol. 34, pt. 1, 594–595, 624, 631; Tibbetts to Family, May 26, 1864, Tibbetts Letters, WRC; "The Battle of Yellow Bayou," *CVET* 25 (1917): 94–95; John Calvin Williams, "The Fire of Hatred," *Civil War Times Illustrated* 17 (1979): 29; Bearss, *Louisiana Confederate*, 122–124; Bailey, *Between the Enemy and Texas*, 186–188; Johnson, *Red River Campaign*, 274–275.

26. *OR*, vol. 34, pt. 1, 594; "Battle of Yellow Bayou," 95; Bergeron, *Silas T. Grisamore*, 159; Goodloe, "Service in the Trans-Mississippi," 32; DeBray, "DeBray's Twenty-sixth," 163; Bailey, *Between the Enemy and Texas*, 188–189; Alwyn Barr, *Polignac's Texas Brigade* (Houston: Texas Gulf Coast Historical Association, 1964), 46–47; Brooksher, *War along the Bayous*, 223; Johnson, *Red River Campaign*, 275. For criticism of Wharton, see Anderson, *Campaigning with Parsons*, 139–140.

27. *OR*, vol. 34, pt. 1, 592; Johnson, *Red River Campaign*, 275–276.

28. *OR*, vol. 34, pt. 1, 538, 542, 547; Taylor, *Destruction and Reconstruction*, 189–190; Imboden, "Jackson in the Shenandoah," 297; Robertson, *Stonewall Jackson*, xiii, 446–450.

29. *OR*, vol. 34, pt. 1, 594–595; Walker, "War of Secession," 57, Gwinner Collection, USAMHI; Johnson, *Red River Campaign*, 278.

30. *OR*, vol. 34, pt. 1, 543, 595. Taylor also notified Smith that Union general Edward R. S. Canby had replaced Banks as commander of the Federal Department of the Gulf. See ibid.

31. Ibid., 538, 543, 592.

32. Ibid., 538, 543–544.

33. Ibid., 543–544, 592. Smith's desire to reclaim Arkansas and Missouri for the Confederacy and Taylor's resistance to the strategy are documented in the following: *OR*, vol. 26, pt. 2, 42; Smith, "Defense of the Red River," *B&L*, 4 : 372; Taylor, *Destruction and Reconstruction*, 126.

34. *OR*, vol. 34, pt. 1, 543, 545.

35. Boggs, *Military Reminiscences*, 60–61, 65–68, 76. Major Ezell was the quartermaster, Colonel Clemsen was the head of the Nitre and Mining Bureau, the commissary officer was Major Thomas, and the three aides were captains Cunningham, Walworth, and Meem. The surgeons were doctors Yandell and Sol Smith. See ibid.

36. Taylor, *Destruction and Reconstruction*, 153.

37. *OR*, vol. 34, pt. 1, 545.

38. Ibid., 540–543, 545–546. Both during and after the war Taylor acknowledged his conditional support for the Arkansas campaign. See ibid., 571–572, and Taylor, *Destruction and Reconstruction*, 179–180. Smith maintained in his official report on the campaign, written on June 11, that Taylor chose Walker for the march to Arkansas. See *OR*, vol. 34, pt. 1, 480.

39. *OR*, vol. 34, pt. 1, 538–540. Taylor's May 24 letter is found in ibid., 543–545.

40. Ibid., 538–540. The *Official Records* show that Smith issued two replies to Taylor's May 24 letter. These replies are designated as inclosures H and K. The *Official Records* indicate that Smith sent H on May 26 and contend that K was not found. It is apparent, however, that Smith's letter of June 5 is inclosure K. Thus, Smith never sent the June 5 letter to Taylor. Instead, upon receipt of Taylor's letter also dated June 5, Smith relieved him of command. These correspondences are found in ibid., 538–546.

41. Ibid., 546.

42. Ibid., 546–547.

43. Ibid.; Taylor, *Destruction and Reconstruction*, 180.

44. Taylor, *Destruction and Reconstruction*, 182, 190.

45. *OR*, vol. 34, pt. 1, 546, 547. Smith halted Walker briefly at Minden, Louisiana, on April 20. See ibid., 534.

46. Ibid., 547.

47. Ibid., 542, 547; Taylor to Boggs, June 1, 1864, Brent Collection, TUL.

48. *OR*, vol. 34, pt. 1, 548.

49. Ibid.; Parrish, *Richard Taylor*, 395–396; Johnson, *Red River Campaign*, 281–282.

50. *OR*, vol. 34, pt. 1, 540–541, 597, pt. 4, 664; Parks, *Edmund Kirby Smith*, 409.

51. *OR*, vol. 34, pt. 4, 653–655. On June 21 Walker notified Smith that the Federals had fortified Morganza "for the purpose of preventing any invasion of the La Fourche country, such as took place last June under General Taylor." Thus, Taylor's willingness to forgo campaigning in the Lafourche was a necessity as well as a concession to Smith. See ibid., 688.

52. Taylor, *Destruction and Reconstruction*, 196.

53. *OR*, vol. 34, pt. 1, 540–548; Trans-Mississippi Department Papers, TUL; Jefferson Davis Papers, TUL.

54. *OR*, vol. 34, pt. 1, 540–541. An annotation on the envelope containing Taylor's April 28 letter reads, "Not to be published until after the death of gnl. S." This was undoubtedly written after the war, perhaps by Joseph L. Brent, in an effort to spare Smith or Taylor from embarrassment.

The envelope also has Smith's personal notation, "Report returned to Gnl. Taylor. This communication is not only improper but unjust." See Taylor to Smith, April 28, 1864, Brent Collection, HEH.

55. *OR*, vol. 34, pt. 1, 540–541.

56. Ibid.

57. Ibid., 480, 482, 545–546.

11. An Unfortunate Manner of Expression

1. *OR*, vol. 34, pt. 1, 540, pt. 4, 664, 681; Taylor, *Destruction and Reconstruction*, 196; Johnson, *Red River Campaign*, 282.

2. *OR*, vol. 34, pt. 1, 548.

3. Ibid., vol. 41, pt. 2, 990–991.

4. Taylor to Brent, July 5, 1864, Brent Collection, HEH. Taylor's argument to Smith on this point appears in *OR*, vol. 34, pt. 1, 542, 547.

5. Kenner to Benjamin, July 31, 1864, MSS 276, WRC. Annotation on the document indicates that Benjamin presented the matter to Davis on October 7, 1864. See ibid. Kenner was Taylor's brother-in-law and later became Brent's father-in-law. See Craig A. Bauer, *A Leader among Peers: The Life and Times of Duncan Farrar Kenner* (Lafayette: University of Southwest Louisiana, 1993), 76, 80, 181, 209, and "Career of Gen. Joseph Lancaster Brent," 346.

6. Egan to Moore, July 9, 1864, Moore Papers, LSU; *OR*, vol. 41, pt. 2, 993; Bragg, *Louisiana in the Confederacy*, 269; Dufour, *Nine Men in Gray*, 34.

7. *OR*, vol. 41, pt. 2, 992–993.

8. Moise to Conrad, July 22, 1864, Davis Papers, DUKE.

9. Woodward, *Mary Chesnut's Civil War*, 627, 639. Also see *OR*, vol. 34, pt. 1, 540–541, 558, and Dufour, *Nine Men in Gray*, 34.

10. Reynolds to Johnson, April 13, July 14, 1864, Reynolds to Charles B. Mitchel, May 21, 1864, Reynolds Papers, LOC; Reynolds Letter, August 22, 1864, Eldridge Collection, HEH; Stewart Sifakis, *Who Was Who in the Confederacy* (New York: Facts on File, 1988), 150, 201.

11. Mrs. E. Kirby Smith to Frances K. Smith, May 1864, Kirby Smith Papers, UNC; Hughes, *Liddell's Record*, 185; Boggs, *Military Reminiscences*, 60–61; Parks, *Edmund Kirby Smith*, 410–411, 416–419; Sifakis, *Who Was Who in the Confederacy*, 313.

12. *OR*, vol. 34, pt. 1, 550–551. Cunningham had served under Smith since early in the war. When Smith was wounded at Manassas in July 1861, his staff took the general to the estate of Cunningham's uncle, thirty miles from the battlefield. See Parks, *Edmund Kirby Smith*, 137–138.

13. *OR*, vol. 34, pt. 1, 551–554, 559–560. One of Taylor's men responsible for coordinating the supply lines indicated that forage below Pleasant Hill was scarce and that the Confederates appropriated supplies as a "tax-in-kind." See J. W. Sims Letterbook, Hardin Collection, LSU.

14. Taylor, *Destruction and Reconstruction*, 176–177.

15. *OR*, vol. 34, pt. 1, 554.

16. Ibid., 555–557. According to Missouri governor Reynolds, Smith was satisfied with the performance of the infantry. See Reynolds to Parsons, August 27, 1864, Eldridge Collection, HEH.

17. *OR*, vol. 34, pt. 1, 481, 482, 554, 557, pt. 3, 802; Smith, "Defense of the Red River," *B&L*, 4:372–373; Parks, *Edmund Kirby Smith*, 400.

18. *OR*, vol. 34, pt. 1, 558.

19. Taylor, *Destruction and Reconstruction*, 179–180; *OR*, vol. 34, pt. 1, 559–560.

20. *OR*, vol. 34, pt. 1, 559–560.

21. U.S. War Department, *Journal of the Congress of the Confederate States of America,* 7 vols. (Washington, DC: U.S. Government Printing Office, 1904–1905), 4:49; Bragg to Davis, July 21, 1864, Davis Papers, TUL; Taylor, *Destruction and Reconstruction,* 196; *OR*, vol. 34, pt. 1, 476, vol. 41, pt. 1, 90; Dufour, *Nine Men in Gray,* 34–35; Parks, *Edmund Kirby Smith,* 420–421. Smith received official notification of Taylor's reassignment on July 22. The decision to promote Taylor did not create as much controversy as did the question of where to send him. Secretary of War Seddon advised Davis that Taylor should command either a corps or a department. When Steven D. Lee, commander of the Department of Alabama, Mississippi, and East Louisiana, received an assignment to corps command in the Army of Tennessee, Taylor became the leading candidate to replace him as department commander. However, Bragg recommended that Taylor join the Army of Tennessee and assume command of William J. Hardee's corps. In Bragg's opinion, the addition of Taylor would make John Bell Hood's army "invincible," and Hood concurred. Hardee agreed to turn his corps over to Taylor and go to the Trans-Mississippi. Davis rejected the plans and sent Taylor to command the Department of Alabama, Mississippi, and East Louisiana. See *OR*, vol. 38, pt. 5, 1030, vol. 39, pt. 2, 760, 832, vol. 52, pt. 2, 713; Richard M. McMurry, *John Bell Hood and the War for Southern Independence* (Lexington: University Press of Kentucky, 1982; reprint, Lincoln: University of Nebraska Press, 1992), 136–137, 152–153.

22. *OR*, vol. 34, pt. 2, 970, pt. 3, 764–765, 41, pt. 1, 90, 92; Parks, *Edmund Kirby Smith,* 420; Kerby, *Kirby Smith's Confederacy,* 324.

23. *OR*, vol. 41, pt. 1, 90–92; Blessington, *Walker's Texas Division,* 271; Johansson, *Peculiar Honor,* 127; Parks, *Edmund Kirby Smith,* 421; Kerby, *Kirby Smith's Confederacy,* 325–327; Lowe, *Walker's Texas Division,* 235.

24. *OR*, vol. 41, pt. 1, 92–93.

25. Ibid., 95–96, pt. 2, 1029–1030; Parks, *Edmund Kirby Smith,* 423.

26. *OR*, vol. 41, pt. 1, 91–92; Taylor to Boggs, July 29, 1864, Davis Papers, TUL.

27. *OR*, vol. 41, pt. 1, 93–94, pt. 2, 1036, 1038; Bearss, *Louisiana Confederate,* 152, 155–156; Blessington, *Walker's Texas Division,* 270, 273; Bergeron, *Silas T. Grisamore,* 164–165.

28. *OR*, vol. 41, pt. 1, 93–94; Parks, *Edmund Kirby Smith,* 423–424.

29. *OR*, vol. 41, pt. 1, 94. Thomas was Taylor's brother-in-law. See Arthur W. Bergeron Jr., "Allen Thomas," *CGEN,* 6:40–41.

30. *OR*, vol. 41, pt. 1, 90–91, 95–96, 100–101, pt. 2, 1036, 1038.

31. Ibid., pt. 1, 91, 94–95.

32. Ibid.

33. Ibid., 90–91, 94–96, pt. 2, 1036.

34. Ibid., pt. 1, 94–97.

35. Ibid., 96–98.

36. Ibid., 99–100. Although Smith specified the Crescent Regiment, these troops had been designated the Consolidated Crescent Regiment since November 1863. The Consolidated Crescent consisted of the old Crescent Regiment (Twenty-fourth Louisiana Infantry) and the Eleventh and Twelfth Louisiana battalions. See Bergeron, *Louisiana Confederate Military Units,* 130–132, 146–147.

37. *OR*, vol. 41, pt. 1, 100; Kerby, *Kirby Smith's Confederacy,* 327.

38. *OR*, vol. 41, pt. 1, 100–101.

39. Ibid., 101–102.

40. Ibid., 103.

41. Ibid., 101–102.

42. Ibid., 103.

43. Ibid., 94, 103–104.

44. Ibid., 105, pt. 2, 1039.

45. Reynolds to Price, July 18, 1864, Reynolds to Smith, July 25, 1864, Reynolds Papers, LOC; Reynolds, "Sterling Price," MHS, 119–120; OR, vol. 34, pt. 4, 642, vol. 41, pt. 2, 1020–1024, 1027–1028; John Newman Edwards, Shelby's Expedition to Mexico: An Unwritten Leaf of the War, ed. Conger Beasley Jr. (Fayetteville: University of Arkansas Press, 2002), 4; Robert E. Shalhope, Sterling Price: Portrait of a Southerner (Columbia: University of Missouri Press, 1971), 256–262.

46. OR, vol. 41, pt. 2, 1039–1041; Castel, Sterling Price, 201–202.

47. OR, vol. 41, pt. 1, 105, pt. 2, 1062–1063; Kerby, Kirby Smith's Confederacy, 327. Forney had a reputation as a strict disciplinarian. See W. W. Draper, "How Forney Saved the Day at Manassas," CVET 15 (1907): 487; Arthur W. Bergeron Jr., "John Horace Forney," CGEN, 2:134–135.

48. OR, vol. 41, pt. 2, 1063; Lowe, Walker's Texas Division, 241–242.

49. OR, vol. 41, pt. 1, 106; Parks, Edmund Kirby Smith, 425–426.

50. OR, vol. 41, pt. 1, 107–108.

51. Ibid., 108–109.

52. Ibid., 109.

53. Ibid.

54. Ibid., 106, 109–110.

55. Ibid., 110, 112; Lowe, Walker's Texas Division, 236–240. For accounts of Confederate camps along the river, see "A Revival in Waterhouse's Brigade, Walker's Division," Louisiana Baptist, August 3, 1864, LSU; Bearss, Louisiana Confederate, 155–156; Bergeron, Silas T. Grisamore, 164–165.

56. OR, vol. 41, pt. 1, 110–111; Bailey, Between the Enemy and Texas, 194. In a letter home a Texan confided that "a great many men pretend to be bitterly opposed to crossing the Miss. River" and that most of them "only wanted an excuse to leave." See Thomas W. Cutrer, ed., "Bully for Flournoy's Regiment, We Are Some Punkins, You'll Bet: The Civil War Letters of Virgil Sullivan Rabb Captain, Company 'I' Sixteenth Texas Infantry, C.S.A.," Military History of the Southwest 20 (1990): 74.

57. OR, vol. 41, pt. 1, 111–112. The officer who gave Taylor the message was Captain Foote.

58. Ibid., 109, 111–112; Kerby, Kirby Smith's Confederacy, 329; For Bragg's relationship with Davis as military adviser, see Judith Lee Hallock, Braxton Bragg and Confederate Defeat: Volume 2 (Tuscaloosa: University of Alabama, 1991), 163–187.

59. OR, vol. 41, pt. 1, 92–93, 102, 117; Kerby, Kirby Smith's Confederacy, 329; Parks, Edmund Kirby Smith, 427. At this point the futility of the mission was the only thing upon which Smith and Taylor agreed. See OR, vol. 41, pt. 1, 100, 112.

60. OR, vol. 41, pt. 1, 92–93, 102.

61. Ibid., 117; Parks, Edmund Kirby Smith, 427.

62. OR, vol. 41, pt. 1, 90, 101, 107, 117. Given Smith's June 11 letter to Davis and the July 4 and 6 letters to Bragg from Taylor and Manning respectively, it is possible that the Confederate brass knew of the situation in the Trans-Mississippi Department. Considering the time it took for a letter to travel from Louisiana to the districts across the Mississippi, however, it is unlikely that Davis and Bragg knew the extent of Smith and Taylor's feud. These letters are in OR, vol. 34, pt. 1, 540–541, vol. 41, pt. 2, 990–991, 992–993. Also see Parks, Edmund Kirby Smith, 421, and Kerby, Kirby Smith's Confederacy, 325.

63. OR, vol. 41, pt. 1, 113, pt. 4, 1068–1069; Taylor, Destruction and Reconstruction, 196–197; Bearss, Louisiana Confederate, 159; Kerby, Kirby Smith's Confederacy, 330; Welsh, Medical Histories of Confederate Generals, 199; Parrish, Richard Taylor, 406–407.

64. *OR,* vol. 41, pt. 1, 96–98, 101; Taylor, *Destruction and Reconstruction,* 40–41.

65. *OR,* vol. 41, pt. 1, 99. Several other Confederates submitted alternative designs for a crossing. All were subsequently rejected by Smith or Taylor. See "Career of General Joseph Lancaster Brent," 346.

66. *OR,* vol. 41, pt. 1, 109.

12. A Commander without an Army

1. Smith to Wife, May 25, August 4–5, 1864, Smith to Mother, August 17, 1864, Kirby Smith Papers, UNC; *OR,* vol. 34, pt. 1, 482, vol. 41, pt. 1, 113; Parks, *Edmund Kirby Smith,* 428; Welsh, *Medical Histories of Confederate Generals,* 198–199.

2. *OR,* vol. 34, pt. 1, 482, vol. 41, pt. 1, 113; Smith to Wife, August 9, 20, 1864, Kirby Smith Papers, UNC; Arch Fredric Blakey, "Robert B. Hilton," *ENCC,* 2:776.

3. *OR,* vol. 34, pt. 2, 870, 897; Boggs, *Military Reminiscences,* 60, 76, 81–84; Parks, *Edmund Kirby Smith,* 346–347, 457. For suspicions of departmental leaks, see *OR,* vol. 34, pt. 1, 550–551.

4. *OR,* vol. 34, pt. 1, 482, vol. 41, pt. 1, 102. The same letter to Davis, dated one week later, also appears in *OR,* vol. 41, pt. 1, 113–117.

5. *OR,* vol. 34, pt. 1, 476, 482–485; Parrish, *Richard Taylor,* 370.

6. *OR,* vol. 34, pt. 1, 485–487.

7. Taylor, *Destruction and Reconstruction,* 179–180; *OR,* vol. 34, pt. 1, 541–542, 584–587, 668–669.

8. *OR,* vol. 34, pt. 1, 487–488.

9. Ibid., vol. 41, pt. 1, 119–121. The date and heading on Levy's letter indicate that he was in Richmond at the time of the correspondence.

10. Ibid., 113, 118, 120; Parks, *Edmund Kirby Smith,* 429–430; Kerby, *Kirby Smith's Confederacy,* 331.

11. *OR,* vol. 41, pt. 1, 121–122; John B. Jones, *A Rebel War Clerk's Diary,* 2 vols. (Philadelphia: J. B. Lippincott, 1866; reprint, Time-Life Books, 1982), 2:302. October 7 was the same day that Benjamin presented Davis with a list of complaints against Smith lodged by Louisiana congressman Duncan Kenner. See Kenner to Benjamin, July 31, 1864, with October 7, 1864, annotation, MSS 276, WRC.

12. *OR,* vol. 41, pt. 1, 122; Smith to Davis, October 10, 1864, Davis Papers, DUKE; Kerby, *Kirby Smith's Confederacy,* 331.

13. *OR,* vol. 41, pt. 1, 92–93, 102, 117, 123–124; Kerby, *Kirby Smith's Confederacy,* 330–331; Parks, *Edmund Kirby Smith,* 431.

14. *OR,* vol. 41, pt. 1, 102, 123–124; Younger, *Inside the Confederate Government,* 166–167.

15. Jones, *Rebel War Clerk,* 2:265; Vandiver, *Josiah Gorgas,* 135; *OR,* vol. 41, pt. 1, 102, 110–111.

16. *OR,* vol. 41, pt. 1, 123–124.

17. Ibid., 124.

18. Ibid., 625–640, 653, 679–680, 707–714, pt. 2, 1041; Edwards to O. M. Watkins, January 3, 1866, Eldridge Collection, HEH; "Battle of Pilot Knob by One Who Was There," UMO; John C. Darr, "Price's Raid into Missouri" *CVET* 11 (1903): 360–362; Edwards, *Shelby and His Men,* 389, 480; Britton, "Operations in Missouri and Arkansas," *B&L,* 4:374–377; Daniel E. Sutherland, "1864: A Strange Wild Time," in *Rugged and Sublime,* ed. Mark K. Christ (Fayetteville: University of Arkansas Press, 1994), 136–142; Daniel O'Flaherty, *General Jo Shelby: Undefeated Rebel* (Chapel Hill: University of North Carolina Press, 1954; reprint, 2000), 216–217; Shalhope, *Sterling Price,* 266–267; Kerby, *Kirby Smith's Confederacy,* 333–352; Castel, *Sterling Price,* 203–245.

19. *OR*, vol. 41, pt. 2, 1023–1024, pt. 4, 1069; Kerby, *Kirby Smith's Confederacy*, 336–337, 342; Hattaway and Jones, *How the North Won*, 637–638.

20. Edwards, *Shelby and His Men*, 517–519; *OR*, vol. 48, pt. 1, 1416, 1442.

21. *OR*, vol. 48, pt. 1, 482; Reynolds, "Sterling Price," 116–120, MHS; Edwards, *Shelby and His Men*, 482; Castel, *Sterling Price*, 201–202. Reynolds nominated Price to lead the raid. See *OR*, vol. 41, pt. 2, 1011–1012, 1020.

22. Davis to Hardee, September 5, 1864, Davis to Hood, September 5, 1864, Davis Papers, TUL; *OR*, vol. 39, pt. 1, 542–549, pt. 2, 816, 818–819, pt. 3, 860–863; Taylor, *Destruction and Reconstruction*, 197–201, 205; Thomas D. Osborne, "Kentucky's Gifts to the Confederacy," *CVET* 13 (1905): 200; Parrish, *Richard Taylor*, 406–408, 413–414.

23. Taylor to Bragg, September 25, 1864, Richard Taylor Letterbook, TUL; Taylor, *Destruction and Reconstruction*, 206; Parrish, *Richard Taylor*, 412; Dufour, *Nine Men in Gray*, 36.

24. Trans-Mississippi Department Papers, 55B, TUL; Moise to Moore, September 24, 1864, Moore Papers, LSU; Ezra J. Warner and W. Buck Yearns, *Biographical Register of the Confederate Congress* (Baton Rouge: Louisiana State University Press, 1975), 105; Kerby, *Kirby Smith's Confederacy*, 407–408; Bragg, *Louisiana in the Confederacy*, 268–270; Parrish, *Richard Taylor*, 397. Lewis served briefly as a captain in the Eighth Louisiana, a part of Taylor's brigade in Virginia. See Bergeron, *Louisiana Confederate Military Units*, 90, 120. Immediately following the victories at Mansfield and Pleasant Hill, Taylor recommended Gray for promotion, only to have Smith decline, blaming Gray's "habits." Although Smith may have suspected Gray's role in bringing on a fight at Mansfield, he later approved the promotion. See *OR*, vol. 34, pt. 1, 531, pt. 3, 764, 768. For more on Gray, see Bergeron, "Henry Gray," *CGEN*, 3:26–27, and Thomas J. Legg, "Henry Gray," *ENCC*, 2:709–710.

25. Warner and Yearns, *Biographical Register*, 105–106; *Shreveport News*, September 6, 1864; *Louisiana Democrat*, October 5, 1864, Moore Papers, LSU; Bragg, *Louisiana in the Confederacy*, 269–270. In a letter to former governor Moore, E. Warren Moise warned that Gray risked court martial if he came out against Smith. See Moise to Moore, September 24, 1864, Moore Papers, LSU. Historians Ezra J. Warner and W. Buck Yearns assert that Gray did not know that he was on the ballot for the congressional seat until after he had won the election. However, an entry in the diary of Captain Felix Pierre Poche, a member of Gray's staff, refutes that contention. Writing three weeks before the election, Poche disclosed that Gray planned to send him to the northwestern parishes with instructions to "busy myself with his candidacy." See Warner and Yearns, *Biographical Register*, 105–106, and Bearss, *Louisiana Confederate*, 167.

26. Moise to Moore, September 24, 1864, S. A. Smith to Moore, October 5, 1864, Moore Papers, LSU.

27. I. D. Harper to Moore, September 30, 1864, *Louisiana Democrat*, October 5, 1864, Moore Papers, LSU; *Shreveport News*, November 1, 1864; *Houston Daily Telegraph*, October 19, 1864; Bragg, *Louisiana in the Confederacy*, 270. The final session of Congress convened on November 9, and Gray was sworn in on December 28. See Warner and Yearns, *Biographical Register*, 106.

28. Smith, "Defense of the Red River," *B&L*, 4:373–374; Arthur Howard Noll, *General Edmund Kirby-Smith* (Sewanee, TN: University of the South, 1907), 242–243; *OR*, vol. 48, pt. 1, 1316; Boggs, *Military Reminiscences*, 109–111.

29. Frank E. Vandiver, ed., "Proceedings of the Second Confederate Congress Second Session in Part December 15, 1864–March 18, 1865," *SHSP* 52 (1959): 214, 476; Kerby, *Kirby Smith's Confederacy*, 409–410; Geise, "Confederate Military Forces," 262.

30. *OR*, vol. 48, pt. 1, 1364–1365, 1389, 1414–1415, 1417, 1428–1429, pt. 2, 239; Arndt M. Stickles, *Simon Bolivar Buckner: Borderland Knight* (Chapel Hill: University of North Carolina Press,

1940), 262–263; Kerby, *Kirby Smith's Confederacy,* 407–409; Geise, "Confederate Military Forces," 262–266.

31. Articles in the *Richmond Whig* contained erroneous reports of Smith's conduct. *Richmond Whig,* December 14, 1864, January 18, 1865; Dorsey, *Henry Watkins Allen,* 268–277; Michael Bedout Chesson and Leslie Jean Roberts, eds., *Exile in Richmond: The Confederate Journal of Henri Garidel* (Charlottesville: University Press of Virginia, 2001), 280; Kerby, *Kirby Smith's Confederacy,* 408; Parks, *Edmund Kirby Smith,* 445–446.

32. *OR,* vol. 41, pt. 1, 123–124, vol. 45, pt. 2, 639–640, 764–767, vol. 48, pt. 1, 1406; *Washington Telegraph,* March 8, 1865; Parks, *Edmund Kirby Smith,* 444–445.

33. *OR,* vol. 48, pt. 1, 1321; Hallock, *Braxton Bragg,* 250.

34. *OR,* vol. 45, pt. 2, 647, 665, vol. 49, pt. 2, 1140–1141; Hallock, *Braxton Bragg,* 228, 250. Also see Walker, "War of Secession," 22, Gwinner Collection, USAMHI.

35. *OR,* vol. 48, pt. 1, 1417. Smith's previous offers to resign are in ibid., vol. 34, pt. 1, 487–488, 541.

36. Ibid., vol. 34, pt. 1, 543–545, vol. 41, pt. 1, 123–124, vol. 48, pt. 1, 1418–1419. Although Davis sent the letter to Smith in December, the correspondence took three months to reach the Trans-Mississippi.

37. Ibid., vol. 48, pt. 1, 1418–1419.

38. Ibid., 1417–1419.

39. Ibid., vol. 41, pt. 1, 123–124, vol. 48, pt. 1, 1417–1419; Parks, *Edmund Kirby Smith,* 328, 446–448.

40. *OR,* vol. 34, pt. 1, 538–540, 543–545, vol. 48, pt. 1, 1417.

41. Ibid., vol. 48, pt. 1, 1336–1340, 1351–1353, 1362–1363, 1411–1412, pt. 2, 1262–1263, 1276–1277, 1281; Maury to Granger, March 6, 1865, Joseph L. Brent Papers, LSMHC; Lee to Smith, March 24, 1865, Brent Papers, LAGO; Kerby, *Kirby Smith's Confederacy,* 397, 406–407; Parks, *Edmund Kirby Smith,* 452–455; Geise, "Confederate Military Forces," 267.

42. McPheeters Diary, April 20, 1865, McPheeters Collection, MHS; Edwards, *Shelby and His Men,* 516; Edwards, *Shelby's Expedition,* 4–5; Noll, *Edmund Kirby-Smith,* 247–248; Winchester Hall, *The Story of the Twenty-sixth Louisiana Infantry* (1890; reprint, Gaithersburg, MD: Butternut, 1984), 128, 132–137; Smith to Soldiers of the Trans-Mississippi Army, April 21, 1865, Simon B. Buckner Papers, HEH; *OR,* vol. 48, pt. 2, 400, 1284; Kerby, *Kirby Smith's Confederacy,* 412–418; Parks, *Edmund Kirby Smith,* 455–472; Geise, "Confederate Military Forces," 268–275.

43. *OR,* vol. 48, pt. 1, 183–193; Allen to Reynolds, May 13, 1865, Eldridge Collection, HEH; Edwards, *Shelby and His Men,* 519–523; Dorsey, *Henry Watkins Allen,* 288–289; Parks, *Edmund Kirby Smith,* 458–472; Robert A. Hasskarl and Lief R. Hasskarl, *Waul's Texas Legion, 1862–1865* (Ada, OK: privately published, 1985), 95; Wallace Putnam Reed, "Last Forlorn Hope of the Confederacy," *SHSP* 30 (1902): 117–120.

44. Smith to Governor, May 1865, Smith [to Soldiers], May 30, 1865, Kirby Smith Papers, UNC; Smith to Sprague, May 30, 1865, Gratz Collection, PHS; Simon B. Buckner Letter, May 19, 1865, Buckner Papers, HEH; *OR,* vol. 48, pt. 1, 189–194, pt. 2, 600–602; John C. Walker, "Reconstruction in Texas," *SHSP* 24 (1896): 41–52; Parks, *Edmund Kirby Smith,* 472–478; Parrish, *Richard Taylor,* 441. For the surrender of Trans-Mississippi districts, see Kerby, *Kirby Smith's Confederacy,* 422–431.

45. *OR,* vol. 45, pt. 2, 778–779, 784–785, 789, 805; Taylor, *Destruction and Reconstruction,* 216–218, 223; Bergeron, "General Richard Taylor," 144–147; Parrish, *Richard Taylor,* 427–437; Wiley Sword, *Embrace an Angry Wind: The Confederacy's Last Hurrah: Spring Hill, Franklin, and Nashville*

(New York: HarperCollins, 1992), 427–429; Thomas L. Connelly, *Autumn of Glory: The Army of Tennessee, 1862–1865* (Baton Rouge: Louisiana State University Press, 1985), 513–518.

46. Surget to Taylor, April 9, 1865, Brent Papers, LSMHC; *OR*, vol. 49, pt. 2, 1283–1284; Richard Taylor, "The Last Confederate Surrender," in *The Annals of the Civil War* (Philadelphia: Times, 1878; reprint, New York: Da Capo, 1994), 69–70; Taylor, *Destruction and Reconstruction*, 223–227; Parrish, *Richard Taylor*, 437–441.

47. *OR*, vol. 48, pt. 1, 191–194, pt. 2, 600–602, 673–675; Taylor, *Destruction and Reconstruction*, 63, 227–229; Parks, *Edmund Kirby Smith*, 477; Kerby, *Kirby Smith's Confederacy*, 424–426; Geise, "Confederate Military Forces," 278.

48. *OR*, vol. 48, pt. 2, 600–602; Taylor, *Destruction and Reconstruction*, 229; Parks, *Edmund Kirby Smith*, 476–479, 482.

13. Denouement: Of Men and Measures

1. Smith to Robert Rose, February 1, 1865, Kirby Smith Papers, UNC; Edwards, *Shelby's Expedition*, 22, 24; O'Flaherty, *Jo Shelby*, 242–243; Parks, *Edmund Kirby Smith*, 481–482; Kerby, *Kirby Smith's Confederacy*, 374–375.

2. Smith to Grant, July 31, 1865, Eldridge Collection, HEH; Parks, *Edmund Kirby Smith*, 483–492.

3. Taylor to Maury, May 8, 1876, Brock Collection, HEH; Dabney H. Maury, *Recollections of a Virginian* (New York: Charles Scribner's Sons, 1894), 224–230; Taylor, *Destruction and Reconstruction*, 239–250; Parrish, *Richard Taylor*, 447–496.

4. Parks, *Edmund Kirby Smith*, 496–509. Hamilton Bee and Dabney Maury were among those who urged Smith to challenge Taylor's interpretation of events.

5. Cited in Parrish, *Richard Taylor*, 492–493.

6. "Editorial Paragraphs," *SHSP* 7 (1879): 256; Taylor, *Destruction and Reconstruction*, 19, 50, 96, 230–231; Parrish, *Richard Taylor*, 493–494. Taylor was a founding member of the Southern Historical Society and provided the *Papers* with excerpts from *Destruction and Reconstruction* in advance of the book's publication. See Taylor to Maury, May 8, 1876, Brock Collection, HEH; "Advance Sheets of 'Reminiscences of Secession, War, and Reconstruction,'" *SHSP* 5 (1877): 136–140; "The Southern Historical Society: Its Origin and History," *SHSP* 18 (1880): 350–351.

7. "Editorial Paragraphs," 256, 343–345; W. L. Ritter, "Sketch of the Third Battery of Maryland Artillery," *SHSP* 10 (1882): 467; Ewell, "Jackson and Ewell," 33; John C. Stiles, "Longstreet at Gettysburg," *CVET* 23 (1915): 508; Y. R. LeMonnier, "Gen. Leonidas Polk at Chickamagua," *CVET* 24 (1916): 19; S. A. Ashe, "How President Davis Became Free," *CVET* 36 (1928): 412–413.

8. United Daughters of the Confederacy Collection, TUL; "U. D. C. Notes," *CVET* 36 (1928): 152.

9. "Editorial Paragraphs," 256; Taylor, *Destruction and Reconstruction*, 126, 153.

10. Taylor, *Destruction and Reconstruction*, 126, 158–159, 176, 179, 180, 182, 188–190. Although Taylor also criticized Smith for the failed attempt to relieve Vicksburg in the summer of 1863, he did not mention the attempt to cross the Mississippi during the summer of 1864. Similarly, Taylor did not detail his quarrel with Smith. Instead, he maintained that he "applied for relief from duty." See ibid., 137–138, 196.

11. Shaw, "Red River Campaign," 117; Douglas, "Trans-Mississippi Department," 153–154; John Witherspoon DuBose, "Maj. Gen. Joseph Wheeler," *CVET* 25 (1917): 460; Frank D. Henderson, "Boys of '63," *CVET* 32 (1924): 86. When weighing the influence of Taylor's memoir on veterans, it is significant to note that on the eve of the war the literacy rate of the free population in the South

was 83 percent. See James M. McPherson, *Ordeal by Fire: The Civil War and Reconstruction,* 3rd ed. (New York: McGraw-Hill, 1982), 28.

12. L. T. Wheeler, "General Wilbur Hill King," *CVET* 19 (1911): 172; Sliger, "How General Taylor Fought," 456–458; Hewitt, "Battle of Mansfield," 172; Dabney H. Maury, "Sketch of General Richard Taylor," *SHSP* 7 (1879): 343–345. For examples of nonpartisan accounts by veterans of the campaign, see S. T. Rufner, "Sketch of First Missouri Battery, C.S.A.," *CVET* 20 (1912): 417–420, and Goodloe, "Service in the Trans-Mississippi," 31–32.

13. John William Jones, "Capture of the Indianola," *SHSP* 1 (1876): 93; Ritter, "Maryland Artillery," 466; Ewell, "Jackson and Ewell," 33; Boyd, *War in Virginia,* 13, 32. Taylor's health is examined in Riley, "General Richard Taylor," 67–86.

14. Henderson, "Boys of '63," 86; DeBray, "DeBray's Twenty-sixth," 157, DeBray, *DeBray's Twenty-sixth,* 15–16.

15. *OR,* vol. 34, pt. 1, 540, 543; Hughes, *Liddell's Record,* 184; S. A. Cunningham, "Funeral of Gen. E. Kirby-Smith," *CVET* 1 (1893): 100–101; "Hemming Monument for Florida," *CVET* 7 (1899): 110; C. R. Spenser Jr., "The Morale of the Confederate Soldier," *CVET* 27 (1919): 52; Hammond, "General Edmund Kirby Smith's Campaign," 246.

16. "Ninety-third Anniversary of the Birth of Pres. Jefferson Davis," *SHSP* 29 (1901): 5; Anne Bachman Hyde, "U.D.C. Program for May, 1918," *CVET* 26 (1918): 179; "United Confederate Veterans," *SHSP* 18 (1890): 290–292; Eleanor G. Kirby, "Edmund Kirby Smith," *CVET* 32 (1924): 340; Cunningham, "Funeral of Gen. E. K. Smith," 99; "Honor to Memory of a Prison Officer," *CVET* 19 (1911): 150; "Gen. Edmund Kirby Smith," *CVET* 22 (1914): 178; Parks, *Edmund Kirby Smith,* 478–479. There are numerous examples of attempts by soldiers to reach Smith. See Sam Box, "End of the War—Exiles in Mexico," *CVET* 11 (1903): 121–123; "Scouts Who Tried to Go to Gen. Kirby-Smith," *CVET* 21 (1913): 19, 121; James H. M'Neilly, "Surrender and Homeward Bound," *CVET* 26 (1918): 514; Joseph Pollock, "Shelby's Old Iron Brigade," *CVET* 32 (1924): 50; Inslee Deaderick, "A Long Way to the Trans-Mississippi," *CVET* 34 (1926): 179–180.

17. "The Last Confederate Army to Surrender."

18. "Gen. Edmund Kirby Smith," *CVET* 22 (1914): 178; P. S. Hagy, "Military Operations of the Lower Trans-Mississippi Department, 1863–1864," *CVET* 24 (1916): 546; Dorsey, *Henry Watkins Allen,* 278. For favorable views on Smith's generalship in Virginia, see Washington Hands, "From Baltimore to First Bull Run," *CVET* 7 (1899): 62–63; J. William Jones, "Reminiscences of the Army of Northern Virginia," *SHSP* 9 (1881): 130; and Winfield Peters, "First Battle of Manassas," *SHSP* 34 (1906): 175. For accounts that did not criticize Smith's Tennessee and Kentucky campaigns, see Luke W. Finley, "The Battle of Perryville," *SHSP* 30 (1902): 241–242, and Hammond, "Campaign of Gen. Edmund Kirby Smith," 225–233, 246–254.

19. Snead, "Conquest of Arkansas," *B&L,* 3 : 454, 458–459; Edwards, *Shelby and His Men,* 511, 521. Smith answered charges of corruption six years before his death in the article published by *Century* magazine. See Smith, "Defense of the Red River," *B&L,* 4 : 374.

20. Edwards, *Shelby and His Men,* 285–286, 288, 296, 380, 482–483, 515. Edwards's account of the Red River campaign is in ibid., 250–298.

21. Ibid., 285, 296.

22. Polignac Diary, 181, Civil War Times Illustrated Collection, USAMHI; Boggs, *Military Reminiscences,* 78–79; Walker, "War of Secession," 47, 57, Gwinner Collection, USAMHI. In 1880 General Hamilton Bee wrote a piece for the *Southern Historical Society Papers* on the battle of Pleasant Hill, but despite his contempt for Taylor, and his admiration of Smith, he did not comment on the leadership of either officer during the campaign. See Bee, "Battle of Pleasant Hill," 184–186.

23. Churchill to Colonel, September 6, 1885, Eldridge Collection, HEH.

24. Ibid.; *OR*, vol. 16, 934–935; Parks, *Edmund Kirby Smith*, 204–206, 213–215, 417.

25. Hughes, *Liddell's Record*, 179–181, 184. Taylor refrained from criticizing Liddell in his memoir. See Taylor, *Destruction and Reconstruction*, 183, 185–186, 191.

26. *OR*, vol. 34, pt. 1, 571–572, 582–583.

27. Ibid., 572; Johnson, *Red River Campaign*, 214–221.

28. Hughes, *Liddell's Record*, 184–185. For a contemporary view of Yandell, see "Surgeons of the Confederacy," *CVET* 34 (1926): 254–256.

29. Hughes, *Liddell's Record*, 185; *OR*, vol. 34, pt. 1, 558, 570–572, 582–583 ; Taylor, *Destruction and Reconstruction*, 176, 179–180.

30. Hughes, *Liddell's Record*, 186. In July 1864 Liddell received a transfer to the Department of Alabama, Mississippi, and East Louisiana. Several weeks later, to Liddell's dismay, Taylor crossed the Mississippi and assumed command of the department. See ibid., 187–190.

31. Dorsey, *Henry Watkins Allen*, 263, 266; Bertram Wyatt-Brown, "Sarah Anne Dorsey," *ENCC*, 2:492. Dorsey mistakenly labeled the climactic battle of the Arkansas campaign Marks' Mills rather than Jenkins' Ferry.

32. Dorsey, *Henry Watkins Allen*, 263–266. Taylor's reply to Smith's offer of promotion and command is found in *OR*, vol. 34, pt. 1, 542.

33. Dorsey, *Henry Watkins Allen*, 266–267.

34. Ibid.

35. Ibid., 266–268; Taylor, *Destruction and Reconstruction*, 176; Smith, "Defense of the Red River," *B&L*, 4:372.

36. For an explanation of Smith's strategy by a member of the general's staff, see *OR*, vol. 34, pt. 1, 559–560.

37. Ibid., 545–546; Taylor, *Destruction and Reconstruction*, 180. For information on the disagreement between Lee and Longstreet at Gettysburg, see Freeman, *Lee's Lieutenants*, 2:106–111.

38. Dorsey, *Henry Watkins Allen*, 267.

39. Ibid.; Smith, "Defense of the Red River," *B&L*, 4:371; Boggs, *Military Reminiscences*, 76. For insight into Smith's ego, see Smith to Wife, August 24, 25, 1862, April 22, 1864, Kirby Smith Papers, UNC.

40. *OR*, vol. 34, pt. 1, 480–481; Taylor, *Destruction and Reconstruction*, 179.

41. *OR*, vol. 34, pt. 1, 480–481, 663; Taylor, *Destruction and Reconstruction*, 179–180.

42. *OR*, vol. 34, pt. 1, 480–481; Smith to Wife, April 18, 1864, Kirby Smith Papers, UNC; Taylor, *Destruction and Reconstruction*, 190.

43. Taylor, *Destruction and Reconstruction*, 179–180; *OR*, vol. 34, pt. 1, 541–542, 584–587, 668–669, vol. 41, pt. 1, 102.

44. *OR*, vol. 34, pt. 1, 542; Taylor, *Destruction and Reconstruction*, 188–189.

45. *OR*, vol. 34, pt. 1, 483–484, 541–542; Taylor, *Destruction and Reconstruction*, 189. For an account of the Nineteenth Corps in Washington, see Irwin, *Nineteenth Corps*, 355–367.

46. Taylor to Maury, May 8, 1876, Brock Collection, HEH; *OR*, vol. 34, pt. 1, 541; Taylor, *Destruction and Reconstruction*, 189. Also see Davis's letter of August 8, 1864, in *OR*, vol. 41, pt. 1, 102.

47. *RJC*, 2:250–253; *OR*, vol. 34, pt. 1, 541–542.

48. *RJC*, 2:252; *OR*, vol. 34, pt. 1, 542. For an overview of the northern political situation, see McPherson, *Battle Cry of Freedom*, 721, 771–776.

49. *OR*, vol. 34, pt. 1, 487; Taylor, *Destruction and Reconstruction*, 189–190.

50. Walker, "War of Secession," 56–57, Gwinner Collection, USAMHI.

BIBLIOGRAPHY

PRIMARY SOURCES

MANUSCRIPTS AND DOCUMENTS

Duke University, Perkins Library Special Collections (Durham, North Carolina)
Confederate States of America Archives
Jefferson Davis Papers
Edmund Kirby Smith Papers
Daniel Ruggles Papers

Henry E. Huntington Library (San Marino, California)
Joseph L. Brent Collection
Robert A. Brock Collection
Simon B. Buckner Papers
John B. Burrud Collection
Civil War Collection
Eldridge Collection
Joseph E. Johnston Papers
George D. Patten Papers
Rhees Collection

Library of Congress Manuscript Division (Washington, DC)
Thomas C. Reynolds Papers

Louisiana Adjutant General's Office at Jackson Barracks (New Orleans)
Joseph L. Brent Papers
Richard Taylor Papers

Louisiana State Archives and Records (Baton Rouge)
Office of Board of Pension Commissioners, "William R. Kennedy, Claibourne Parish," document nos. 15073 and 15363

Louisiana State Museum and Historical Center (New Orleans)
Joseph L. Brent Papers

Louisiana State University, Hill Memorial Library Louisiana and
Lower Mississippi Valley Collection (Baton Rouge)
J. Fair Hardin Collection
"The Last Confederate Army to Surrender and Its General"
J. W. Sims Letterbook
Arthur W. Hyatt Diaries
Miscellaneous Manuscript Collection
William H. Whitney Letters
Thomas O. Moore Papers
"A Revival in Waterhouse's Brigade, Walker's Division," *Louisiana Baptist*, August 3, 1864

Mansfield State Historical Site Archives and Records (Mansfield, Louisiana)
Consolidated Crescent File
James H. Beard Letter
Lewis Hall, "The Battle of Mansfield: Experience of a Veteran," *Shreveport Enterpriser*,
    March 4, 1910
W. Davidson, "The Overton Sharp-Shooter"
Eighteenth Louisiana Crescent File
S. A. Poche Letter to *Picayune Times-Democrat*, July 4, 1864
First Infantry Division, C.S.A. File
J. H. Beck, "Special to Houston Daily Telegraph," April 15, 1864
Fourteenth Texas File
James Crayton Carroll Memoir
Henry Gray File
O. W. Wells Letter
"Map of the Mansfield Battlefield," Fiftieth Anniversary Association, April 8, 1914
Shreveport Enterprise File
Philadelphia Press article
Thirteenth Texas Dismounted File
John Thomas Stark Diary
Thirty-third Arkansas File
J. N. Bragg Letter
Twelfth Texas File
"Galveston Tri-Weekly News," May 8, 1864
Twenty-eighth Texas Cavalry Division File
W. F. Mills Letter

Missouri Historical Society (St. Louis)

Braxton Bragg Papers
William McPheeters Collection
William McPheeters Diary
Thomas C. Reynolds, "General Sterling Price and the Confederacy"

Pennsylvania Historical Society (Philadelphia)

Gratz Collection

Tulane University, Howard Tilton Memorial Library Special Collections
(New Orleans, Louisiana)

Joseph L. Brent Collection
Civil War Manuscript Series
Edmund T. King Memoir
John C. Murray Diary
Confederate District of West Louisiana Record Book
Jefferson Davis Papers
Louisiana Historical Association Collection
Joseph A. Breaux, "Reminiscences"
Frank L. Richardson, "Mansfield Campaign"
Richard Taylor Letterbook
Trans-Mississippi Department Papers
United Daughters of the Confederacy Collection

United States Army Military History Institute, Carlisle Barracks (Carlisle, Pennsylvania)
Civil War Times Illustrated Collection
Camille Armand Jules Marie de Polignac Diary
Myron Gwinner Collection
Walker Family Letters
John G. Walker, "The War of Secession West of the Mississippi River during the Years 1863–4 & 5"

United States Military Academy Archives (West Point, New York)
Official Register of the Officers and Cadets of the United States Military Academy, 1838–1847

United States National Archives (Washington, DC)
Record Group 109, E-106, Box 52, Trans-Mississippi Department, vol. 73 1/2

University of Arkansas, David W. Mullins Library
Special Collections (Fayetteville)

Milton P. Chambers Papers

University of Missouri, Ellis Library Western Historical
Manuscript Collection (Columbia)

"Battle of Pilot Knob by One Who Was There"
William Bull, "Reminiscences of the War between the States 1861–1865"
Henry C. Fike Diary
William N. Hoskin Diary
John P. Quesenberry Diary

University of North Carolina, Wilson Library Southern
Historical Collection (Chapel Hill)

Edmund Kirby Smith Papers
William H. Stewart Diary
John G. Walker Papers
James T. Wallace Diary

University of Texas, Center for American History (Austin)

Money Collection
Benjamin F. McDaniel Memoir

Williams Research Center, Historic New Orleans Collection
(New Orleans, Louisiana)

J. T. Batchelor Letters
Judah P. Benjamin Papers
Moses Greenwood Papers
Duncan Kenner Letter to Judah Benjamin
Miscellaneous Manuscript Collection
Henry Rust Diary and Related Papers
Henry C. Sampson Diaries and Related Papers
Charles F. Sherman Letters
Melvan Tibbetts Letters

BOOKS

Anderson, John Q., ed. *Brokenburn: The Journal of Kate Stone, 1861–1868*. Baton Rouge: Louisiana State University Press, 1972.

————, ed. *Campaigning with Parsons' Texas Cavalry Brigade, CSA: War Journals and Letters of* the Four Orr Brothers, Twelfth Texas Cavalry Regiment. Hillsboro, TX: Hill Junior College Press, 1967.

——, ed. A Texas Surgeon in the C.S.A. Tuscaloosa: Confederate Publishing Co., 1957.

Bartlett, Napier. Military Record of Louisiana. New Orleans: L. Graham, 1874; reprint, Baton Rouge: Louisiana State University Press, 1992.

Battles and Leaders of the Civil War. Edited by Robert U. Johnson and Clarence C. Buell. 4 vols. New York: Century, 1887; reprint, New York: Yoseloff, 1956.

Battles and Leaders of the Civil War. Vol. 5. Edited by Peter Cozzens. Chicago: University of Illinois Press, 2002.

Bearss, Edwin C., ed. A Louisiana Confederate: Diary of Felix Pierre Poche. Natchitoches: Northwestern State University, Louisiana Studies Institute, 1972.

Beecher, Harris H. Record of the 114th Regiment, N.Y.S.V.: Where It Went, What It Saw, and What It Did. Norwich, NY: J. F. Hubbard Jr., 1866.

Benson, Solon F. Civil War Battle of Pleasant Hill. Des Moines: Historical Department of Iowa, 1906; reprint, Shreveport: Briner Printing, 1972.

Bergeron, Arthur W., Jr., ed. The Civil War Reminiscences of Major Silas T. Grisamore C.S.A. Baton Rouge: Louisiana State University Press, 1993.

Biographical Encyclopedia of Texas. New York: Southern Publishing Co., 1880.

Blackwood, Emma Jerome. To Mexico with Scott: The Letters of Captain E. Kirby Smith to His Wife. Cambridge: Harvard University Press, 1917.

Blessington, Joseph P. The Campaigns of Walker's Texas Division. New York: Lange, Little and Co., 1875; reprint, with introductory essays by Norman D. Brown and T. Michael Parrish, Austin: State House Press, 1994.

Boggs, William R. Military Reminiscences of General Wm. R. Boggs, C.S.A. Edited by William K. Boyd. Durham: Seeman Printery, 1913.

Boyd, David French. Reminiscences of the War in Virginia. Edited by T. Michael Parrish. Austin: Jenkins, 1989.

Brent, Joseph Lancaster. Capture of the Ironclad Indianola. New Orleans: Seares and Pfaff, 1926.

——. Memoirs of the War between the States. New Orleans: Fontana Printing Co., 1940.

Britton, Wiley. The Civil War on the Border. 2 vols. New York: G. P. Putnam's Sons, 1899; reprint, Ottawa: Kansas Heritage, 1994.

Brown, Norman D., ed. Journey to Pleasant Hill: Civil War Letters of Captain Elijah P. Petty, Walker's Texas Division, C.S.A. 2 vols. San Antonio: University of Texas Institute of Texan Cultures, 1982.

Chesson, Michael Bedout, and Leslie Jean Roberts, eds. Exile in Richmond: The Confederate Journal of Henri Garidel. Charlottesville, University Press of Virginia, 2001.

Clark, Orton S. The One Hundred and Sixteenth Regiment of New York State Volunteers. Buffalo: Printing House of Mathews and Warren, 1868.

Condensed History of Parsons' Texas Cavalry Brigade, 1861–1865. Corsicana, TX, 1903.

Cummer, Clyde L., ed. *Yankee in Gray: The Civil War Memoirs of Henry E. Handerson, with a Selection of His Wartime Letters.* Cleveland: Press of Western Reserve University, 1962.

Cutrer, Thomas W., and T. Michael Parrish, eds. *Brothers in Gray: The Civil War Letters of the Pierson Family.* Baton Rouge: Louisiana State University Press, 1997.

Davis, Jefferson. *The Rise and Fall of the Confederate Government.* 2 vols. New York: D. Appleton, 1881; reprint, New York: Da Capo, 1990.

DeBray, Xavier B. *A Sketch of the History of DeBray's Twenty-sixth Regiment of Texas Cavalry.* Austin: Eugene Von Boeckman Book and Job Printer, 1884; reprint, Waco: Waco Village, 1961.

DeForest, John William. *A Volunteer's Adventures: A Union Captain's Record of the Civil War.* Edited by James H. Croushore. New Haven: Yale University Press, 1946.

Dickert, D. Augustus. *History of Kershaw's Brigade.* Newberry: Elbert H. Aull, 1899; reprint, Dayton, OH: Morningside, 1988.

Dimitry, John. *Confederate Military History: Louisiana.* Edited by Clement A. Evans. Atlanta: Confederate Publishing Co., 1899; reprint, Wilmington, NC: Broadfoot, 1988.

Dorsey, Sarah A. *Recollections of Henry Watkins Allen.* New York: M. Doolady, 1866.

Edmonds, David C., ed. *The Conduct of Federal Troops in Louisiana during the Invasion of 1863 and 1864.* Lafayette, LA: Acadiana, 1988.

Edwards, John Newman. *Shelby and His Men, or The War in the West.* Cincinnati: Miami Printing and Publishing Co., 1867; reprint, Waverly, MO: General Joseph Shelby Memorial Fund, 1993.

——. *Shelby's Expedition to Mexico: An Unwritten Leaf of the War.* Edited by Conger Beasley Jr. Fayetteville: University of Arkansas, 2002.

Ewer, James K. *Third Massachusetts Cavalry in the War for Union.* Maplewood, MA: Perry, 1903.

Fay, Edwin Hedge. *This Infernal War: The Confederate Letters of Edwin H. Fay.* Edited by Bell Irvin Wiley with the assistance of Lucy E. Fay. Austin: University of Texas Press, 1958.

Flinn, Frank M. *Campaigning with Banks in Louisiana in '63 and '64, and with Sheridan in the Shenandoah Valley in '64 and '65.* Lynn, MA: Thomas P. Nichols, 1887.

Freeman, Douglas Southall, ed. *Lee's Dispatches: Unpublished Letters of General Robert E. Lee.* New York: Putnam, 1957.

Frey, Jerry, ed. *In the Woods before Dawn: The Samuel Richey Collection of the Southern Confederacy.* Gettysburg: Thomas Publications, 1994.

Grant, U. S. *Personal Memoirs of U. S. Grant.* Edited by E. B. Long. Cleveland: World, 1952; reprint, with an introduction by William S. McFeely, New York: Da Capo, 1982.

Greene, Dianne E., ed. *The Civil War Diary of Lieutenant Robert Molford Addison Co. E, Twenty-third Wisconsin Infantry.* Westminster, MD: Willow Bend Books, 2001.

Hall, Winchester. *The Story of the Twenty-sixth Louisiana Infantry.* With an introduction by Edwin C. Bearss. Gaithersburg, MD: Butternut, 1984.

Haskell, John Cheves. *The Haskell Memoirs.* Edited by Gilbert E. Govan and James W. Livingood. New York: G. P. Putnam and Sons, 1960.

Heartsill, W. W. *Fourteen Hundred and Ninety-one Days in the Confederate Army.* Marshall, TX: 1867; reprint, edited by Bell Irvin Wiley, Jackson, TN: McCowat Mercer, 1953; second reprint, Wilmington, NC: Broadfoot, 1992.

Howard, McHenry. *Recollections of a Confederate Soldier and Staff Officer under Johnston, Jackson, and Lee.* Baltimore: Williams and Wilkins, 1941.

Hughes, Nathaniel C., ed. *Liddell's Record.* Dayton, OH: Morningside, 1985.

Irwin, Richard B. *History of the Nineteenth Army Corps.* New York: 1892; reprint, with an introduction by Lawrence L. Hewitt, Baton Rouge: Elliot's Book Shop, 1985.

Jarratt, J. A. *Reminiscences of a Great Struggle by the Heroes of the Confederacy.* Privately published, 1907.

Johansson, M. Jane. *Widows by the Thousands: The Civil War Letters of Theophilus and Harriet Perry, 1862–1864.* Fayetteville: University of Arkansas Press, 2000.

Johnston, Joseph E. *Narrative of Military Operations during the Civil War.* 1874; reprint, with an introduction by Frank E. Vandiver, New York: Da Capo, 1959.

Jones, John B. *A Rebel War Clerk's Diary.* 2 vols. Philadelphia: J. B. Lippincott, 1866; reprint, Alexandria: Time-Life Books, 1982.

Jones, Terry L., ed. *Campbell Brown's Civil War: With Ewell and the Army of Northern Virginia.* Baton Rouge: Louisiana State University Press, 2002.

Keefe, James F., and Lynn Morrow. *A Connecticut Yankee in the Frontier Ozarks: The Writings of Theodore Pease Russell.* Columbia: University of Missouri Press, 1988.

Lowe, Richard, ed. *A Texas Cavalry Officer's Civil War: The Diary and Letters of James C. Bates.* Baton Rouge: Louisiana State University Press, 1999.

MacLean, David G., ed. *Prisoner of the Rebels in Texas: The Civil War Narrative of Aaron T. Sutton, Corporal, Eighty-third Ohio Volunteer Infantry.* Decatur, IN: Americana Books, 1978.

Maury, Dabney H. *Recollections of a Virginian.* New York: Charles Scribner's Sons, 1894.

Moore, Frank, ed. *The Rebellion Record: A Diary of American Events, with Documents, Narratives, Illustrative Incidents, Poetry, etc.* 11 vols. New York: G. P. Putnam's Sons, 1861–1863, and D. Van Nostrand, 1864–1868; supplemental volume published New York: G. P. Putnam's Sons and Henry Holt, 1864.

Nisbet, James Cooper. *Four Years on the Firing Line.* Chattanooga: Imperial, 1914; reprint, edited by Bell I. Wiley, Jackson, TN: McCowat Mercer; second reprint, Wilmington, NC: Broadfoot, 1991.

Noel, Theo. *A Campaign from Santa Fe to the Mississippi, Being a History of the Old Sibley*

Brigade. Edited and with an introduction by Martin Hardwick Hall and Edwin Adams Davis. Houston: Stagecoach, 1961.

Parker, William Harwar. *Recollections of a Naval Officer, 1841–1865*. New York: Charles Scribner's Sons, 1883.

Pitcock, Cynthia DeHaven, and Bill J. Gurley, eds. *I Acted from Principle: The Civil War Diary of William McPheeters, Confederate Surgeon in the Trans-Mississippi*. Fayetteville: University of Arkansas Press, 2002.

Polignac, Camille Armand Jules Marie. *L'Union américaine*. Paris, 1866.

Pollard, Edward A. *The Lost Cause*. New York: E. B. Treat, 1866.

Porter, David Dixon. *Incidents and Anecdotes of the Civil War*. New York: Appleton, 1885.

————. *The Naval History of the Civil War*. New York: Sherman, 1887.

Rowland, Dunbar, ed. *Jefferson Davis, Constitutionalist: His Letters, Papers, and Speeches*. 10 vols. New York: J. J. Little and Ives, 1923.

Simon, John Y. *The Papers of Ulysses S. Grant*. Carbondale: University of Illinois Press, 1990.

Sperry, A. F. *History of the Thirty-third Iowa Infantry Volunteer Regiment, 1863–6*. Edited by Gregory J. W. Urwin and Cathy Kunzinger Urwin. Fayetteville: University of Arkansas Press, 1999.

Stanyan, John M. *A History of the Eighth Regiment of New Hampshire Volunteers, Including Its Service as Infantry, Second N.H. Cavalry, and Veterans Battalion in the Civil War of 1861–1865*. Concord: Ira C. Evans, 1892.

Taylor, Richard. *Destruction and Reconstruction: Personal Experiences of the Civil War*. New York: Appleton, 1879; reprint, with an introduction by T. Michael Parrish, New York: Da Capo, 1995.

Tunnard, Willie H. *A Southern Record: The Story of the Third Louisiana Infantry, C.S.A.* Baton Rouge: 1866; reprint, edited by Edwin C. Bearss, Dayton, OH: Morningside, 1988.

United States Congress. *Report of the Joint Committee on the Conduct of the War at the Second Session Thirty-eighth Congress: Red River Expedition, Fort Fisher Expedition, Heavy Ordnance*. Washington, DC: U.S. Government Printing Office, 1865.

United States War Department. *Journal of the Congress of the Confederate States of America*. 7 vols. Washington, DC: U.S. Government Printing Office, 1904–1905.

————. *Official Records of the Union and Confederate Navies in the War of the Rebellion*. 31 vols. Washington, DC: U.S. Government Printing Office, 1894–1927.

————. *The War of the Rebellion: A Compilation of the Official Records of the Union and Confederate Armies*. 128 vols. Washington, DC: U.S. Government Printing Office, 1880–1901.

————. *Supplement to the Official Records of the Union and Confederate Armies*. Part 1, Reports. Vol. 6, *Addendum Series I vols. 31–37* (series nos. 54–55, 57, 60–61, 65, 67–68, 70). Wilmington, NC: Broadfoot, 1996.

Vandiver, Frank, ed. *The Civil War Diary of General Josiah Gorgas*. Tuscaloosa: University of Alabama Press, 1947.

Warder, T. B., and Jas. M. Catlett. *Battle of Young's Branch or Manassas Plain, Fought July 21, 1861*. Richmond: Enquirer Book and Job Press, 1862; reprint, Prince William County Historical Commission, n.d.

Wells, Carol, ed. *War, Reconstruction, and Redemption on the Red River: The Memoirs of Dosia Williams Moore*. Ruston: Louisiana Tech University, 1990.

Woods, J. T. *Service of the Ninety-sixth Ohio Volunteers*. Toledo: Blade Printing, 1874.

Woodward, C. Vann. *Mary Chesnut's Civil War: A Diary from Dixie as Written by Mary Boykin Chesnut*. New Haven: Yale University Press, 1981.

Worsham, John H. *One of Jackson's Foot Cavalry*. New York: Neale, 1912; reprint, Alexandria, VA: Time-Life Books, 1982.

Yeary, Mamie, ed. *Reminiscences of the Boys in Gray*. McGregor, TX: 1912; reprint, Dayton, OH: Morningside, 1986.

Younger, Edward, ed. *Inside the Confederate Government; The Diary of Robert Garlick Hill Kean, the Head of the Bureau of War*. New York: Oxford University Press, 1957.

ARTICLES

"Advance Sheets of 'Reminiscences of Secession, War, and Reconstruction.'" *Southern Historical Society Papers* 5 (1877): 136–140.

Asbury, Ai Edgar. "My Experiences in the War of 1861–1865." *Confederate Veteran* 20 (1912): 242–243.

Ashe, S. A. "How President Davis Became Free." *Confederate Veteran* 36 (1928): 411–413.

Barr, Alwyn, ed. "The Civil War Diary of James Allen Hamilton." *Texana*, summer 1964, 132–145.

———, ed. "William T. Mechling's Journal of the Red River Campaign." *Texana* 1 (1963): 363–379.

"The Battle of Mansfield." *Southern Bivouac* 3 (1884–1885): 412–414.

"The Battle of Yellow Bayou." *Confederate Veteran* 25 (1917): 94–95.

Beauregard, G. T. "The First Battle of Bull Run." In *Battles and Leaders of the Civil War*, 1:196–227.

Bee, Hamilton P. "Battle of Pleasant Hill—An Error Corrected." *Southern Historical Society Papers* 8 (February 1880): 184–186.

Box, Sam. "End of the War—Exiles in Mexico." *Confederate Veteran* 11 (1903): 121–123.

Boyd, D. F. "Gen. Richard Taylor, C.S.A." *Confederate Veteran* 36 (1928): 412–413.

Brent, Joseph L. "Operations of the Artillery of the Army of Western Louisiana, after the Battle of Pleasant Hill." *Southern Historical Society Papers* 9 (1881): 257–264.

Britton, Wiley. "Resume of Military Operations in Missouri and Arkansas." In *Battles and Leaders of the Civil War*, 4:374–377.

Buck, Nina Smith. "Blucher of the Day at Manassas." *Confederate Veteran* 7 (March 1889): 108–109.

Buell, Don Carlos. "East Tennessee and the Campaign of Perryville." In *Battles and Leaders of the Civil War*, 3 : 31–51.

Burns, William S. "The Red River Expedition." In *Battles and Leaders of the Civil War*, 5 : 574–601.

"Capture of Brashear City: A Rebel Account." In *The Rebellion Record: A Diary of American Events, with Documents, Narratives, Illustrative Incidents, Poetry, etc.*, edited by Frank Moore, 7 : 75–84, 173–175. 12 vols. New York: G. P. Putnam's Sons, 1861–1864.

"Career of Gen. Joseph Lancaster Brent." *Confederate Veteran* 17 (1909): 345–347.

"Col. Fred L. Robertson." *Confederate Veteran* 7 (1899): 161.

Combs, D. S. "Texas Boys in the War." *Confederate Veteran* 35 (1927): 265.

Cunningham, S. A. "Funeral of Gen. E. Kirby-Smith." *Confederate Veteran* 1 (1893): 99–101.

Cutrer, Thomas W., ed. "Bully for Flournoy's Regiment, We Are Some Punkins, You'll Bet: The Civil War Letters of Virgil Sullivan Rabb Captain, Company 'I' Sixteenth Texas Infantry, C.S.A." *Military History of the Southwest* 20 (1990): 60–96.

Darr, John C. "Price's Raid into Missouri." *Confederate Veteran* 11 (1903): 359–362.

Deaderick, Inslee. "A Long Way to the Trans-Mississippi." *Confederate Veteran* 34 (1926): 179–180.

DeBray, Xavier B. "A Sketch of the History of DeBray's Twenty-sixth Regiment of Texas Cavalry." *Southern Historical Society Papers* 13 (1885): 153–165.

Delaney, Norman C., ed. "The Diary and Memoirs of Marshall Samuel Pierson, Company C, 17th Reg., Texas Cavalry, 1862–1865." *Military History of Texas and the Southwest* 13, no. 3 (1976): 23–38.

Douglas, H. T. "The Trans-Mississippi Department." *Confederate Veteran* 25 (1917): 153–154.

Draper, W. W. "How Forney Saved the Day at Manassas." *Confederate Veteran* 15 (1907): 487.

DuBose, John Witherspoon. "Maj. Gen. Joseph Wheeler." *Confederate Veteran* 25 (1917): 460–463.

Duke, Basil W. "After the Fall of Richmond." *Southern Bivouac* 5 (1886–1887): 156–166.

———. "Bragg's Campaign in Kentucky." *Southern Bivouac* 4 (1885–1886): 161–167, 217–222, 232–240.

Eaton, T. T. "An Incident." *Southern Bivouac* 2 (1883–1884): 310–311.

"Editorial Paragraphs." *Southern Historical Society Papers* 7 (1879): 253–256.

Evans, J. W. "With Hampton's Scouts." *Confederate Veteran* 32 (1924): 470.

Ewell, Benjamin. "Jackson and Ewell." *Southern Historical Society Papers* 20 (1903): 26–33.

"Federal Occupation of Camden as Set Forth in the Diary of a Union Officer." *Arkansas Historical Quarterly* 9 (1950): 214–219.

Fenner, Charles E. "Richard Taylor." In *The Library of Southern Literature*, edited by Edwin A. Alderman and Joel Chandler Harris, 12 : 5199–5203. 17 vols. Atlanta, 1908–1913.

Finley, Luke W. "The Battle of Perryville." *Southern Historical Society Papers* 30 (1902): 238–250.

Gates, A. S. "A Lost Flag." *Southern Bivouac* 3 (1884–1885): 367.

"Gen. Edmund Kirby Smith." *Confederate Veteran* 22 (1914): 178.

Gilbert, C. C. "Bragg's Invasion of Kentucky." *Southern Bivouac* 6 (1887–1888): 296–301, 336–342, 550–556.

Goffe, Charles H. "The Old South in Peace and War: Confiscation of Plantations." *Confederate Veteran* 29 (1921): 16–18.

Goodloe, P. H. "Service in the Trans-Mississippi." *Confederate Veteran* 23 (1915): 31–32.

Goodrich, B. G. "Battle of Mansfield, LA." *Confederate Veteran* 8 (1900): 103.

Green, John Alexander. "General Thomas Green." In *Biographical Encyclopedia of Texas*, 131. New York: Southern Publishing Co., 1880.

Green, Thomas. "Battle of Atchafalaya River—Letter from General Thomas Green." *Southern Historical Society Papers* 3 (1877): 62–63.

Hagy, P. S. "Military Operations in the Lower Trans-Mississippi Department, 1863–1864." *Confederate Veteran* 24 (1916): 545–549.

Hammond, Paul F. "Campaign of Gen. E. K. Smith in Kentucky in 1862." *Southern Historical Society Papers* 9 (1881): 225–233.

———. "General Edmund Kirby Smith's Campaign in Kentucky in 1862: Paper No. 2." *Southern Historical Society Papers* 9 (1881): 246–254.

———. "General Kirby Smith's Campaign in Kentucky: Paper No. 5." *Southern Historical Society Papers* 10 (1882): 70–76.

———. "General Kirby Smith's Kentucky Campaign: No. 4." *Southern Historical Society Papers* 9 (1881): 455–462.

———. "The Kentucky Campaign: No. 6, Conclusion." *Southern Historical Society Papers* 10 (1882): 158–161.

———. "Kirby Smith's Kentucky Campaign: Paper No. 3." *Southern Historical Society Papers* 9 (1881): 289–297.

Hands, Washington. "From Baltimore to Bull Run." *Confederate Veteran* 7 (1899): 62–63.

Harcourt, A. P. "Terry's Texas Rangers." *Southern Bivouac* 1 (1882–1883): 89–97.

"Hemming Monument for Florida." *Confederate Veteran* 7 (1899): 110.

Henderson, Frank D. "Boys of '63." *Confederate Veteran* 32 (1924): 86.

Hewitt, J. E. "The Battle of Mansfield, LA." *Confederate Veteran* 33 (1925): 172–173, 198.

Hogan, George M. "Parsons's Brigade of Texas Cavalry." *Confederate Veteran* 33 (1925): 17–20.

"Honor to Memory of a Prison Officer." *Confederate Veteran* 19 (1911): 150–151.

Hyde, Anne Bachman. "U.D.C. Program for May, 1918." *Confederate Veteran* 16 (1918): 179.

Imboden, John D. "Stonewall Jackson in the Shenandoah." In *Battles and Leaders of the Civil War*, 2:282–298.

Irwin, Richard B. "The Capture of Port Hudson." In *Battles and Leaders of the Civil War*, 3:586–598.

Johansson, Jane Harris, and David H. Johansson, eds. "Two Lost Battle Reports: Horace Randal's and Joseph L. Brent's Reports of the Battles of Mansfield and Pleasant Hill 8 and 9 April 1864." *Military History of the West* 23 (1993): 169–180.

Johnson, Bradley T. "Memoirs of the First Md. Regiment: First Manassas and Subsequent Movements." *Southern Historical Society Papers* 9 (1881): 481–488.

Johnston, Joseph E. "Responsibilities of the First Bull Run." In *Battles and Leaders of the Civil War*, 1:240–259.

Jones, J. William. "Reminiscences of the Army of Northern Virginia." *Southern Historical Society Papers* 9 (1881): 129–134.

Jones, John William. "Capture of the Indianola." *Southern Historical Society Papers* 1 (1876): 91–99.

Kennedy, Edward. "Last Work of Wheeler's Special Confederate Scouts." *Confederate Veteran* 32 (1924): 60–61.

Kirby, Eleanor G. "Edmund Kirby Smith." *Confederate Veteran* 32 (1924): 340–341.

Kolman, F. C. "Confederate Monuments at Mansfield." *Confederate Veteran* 33 (1925): 170–172.

LeMonnier, Y. R. "General Leonidas Polk at Chickamauga." *Confederate Veteran* 24 (1916): 17–19.

Lillard, J. W. "Events of 1861–1865 Recalled." *Confederate Veteran* 21 (1913): 18.

"Lost Chapter in History." *Southern Historical Society Papers* 38 (1910): 241–242.

McCready, William. "Louisville during the War." *Southern Bivouac* 1 (1882–1883): 157–160.

Martin, Charles L. "The Red River Campaign." *Confederate Veteran* 33 (1925): 169–170.

Maury, Dabney H. "Sketch of General Richard Taylor." *Southern Historical Society Papers* 7 (1879): 343–345.

M'Neily, James H. "Surrender and Homeward Bound." *Confederate Veteran* 26 (1918): 514–515.

Moneyhon, Carl H., ed. "Life in Confederate Arkansas: The Diary of Virginia Davis Gray, 1863–1865, Part I." *Arkansas Historical Quarterly* 42 (spring 1983): 47–85.

———. "Life in Confederate Arkansas: The Diary of Virginia Davis Gray, 1863–1865, Part II." *Arkansas Historical Quarterly* 42 (summer 1983): 134–169.

Morgan, George W. "Cumberland Gap." In *Battles and Leaders of the Civil War*, 3:62–69.

Morris, George R. "The Battle of Bayou Des Allemands." *Confederate Veteran* 34 (1926): 14–16.

"The Nankeen Shirt." *Confederate Veteran* 33 (1925): 183, 198.

"Ninety-third Anniversary of the Birth of Pres. Jefferson Davis." *Southern Historical Society Papers* 29 (1901): 1–33.

"Operations of the Artillery of the Army of Western Louisiana, after the Battle of Pleasant Hill." *Southern Historical Society Papers* 9 (1881): 257–264.

Osborne, Thomas D. "Kentucky's Gifts to the Confederacy." *Confederate Veteran* 13 (1905): 200–204.

Parsons, W. H. "Inside History and Heretofore Unwritten Chapters on the Red River Campaign of 1864 and the Participation Therein of Parsons Texas Cavalry Brigade." In *Condensed History of Parsons' Texas Cavalry Brigade, 1861–1865*, 65–106. Corsicana, TX, 1903.

Peake, John W. "Recollections of a Boy Cavalryman." *Confederate Veteran* 34 (1926): 260–262.

Peters, Winfield. "First Battle of Manassas." *Southern Historical Society Papers* 34 (1906): 170–178.

Polignac, Camille J. "Polignac's Mission." *Southern Historical Society Papers* 32 (1904): 364–371.

——. "Polignac's Mission." *Southern Historical Society Papers* 35 (1907): 326–334.

Pollock, Joseph. "Shelby's Old Iron Brigade." *Confederate Veteran* 32 (1924): 50–51.

Reed, Wallace Putnam. "Last Forlorn Hope of the Confederacy." *Southern Historical Society Papers* 30 (1902): 117–121.

Ritter, W. L. "Sketch of the Third Battery of Maryland Artillery." *Southern Historical Society Papers* 10 (1882): 328–332.

Rufner, S. T. "Sketch of First Missouri Battery, C.S.A." *Confederate Veteran* 20 (1912): 417–420.

Ryan, Frank T. "The Kentucky Campaign and Battle of Richmond." *Confederate Veteran* 26 (1918): 158–160.

Sanders, D. W. "Hood's Tennessee Campaign." *Southern Bivouac* 3 (1884–1885): 97–104.

——. "Hood's Tennessee Campaign." *Southern Bivouac* 4 (1885-1886): 242–252.

"Scouts Who Tried to Go to Gen. Kirby Smith." *Confederate Veteran* 21 (1913): 19, 121.

Selvage, Edwin. "A Reunion at the Reunion." *Confederate Veteran* 37 (1929): 326–327.

Shaw, William T. "The Red River Campaign." *Confederate Veteran* 25 (1917): 116–118.

Sims, M. W. "Interesting Story of Prison Experience." *Confederate Veteran* 14 (1906): 502.

——. "Reminiscence of Johnson's Island Prison." *Confederate Veteran* 13 (1905): 253.

"A Sketch of the Life of General Josiah Gorgas, Chief of Ordnance of the Confederate States." *Southern Historical Society Papers* 13 (1885): 216–228.

Sliger, J. E. "How General Taylor Fought the Battle of Mansfield, La." *Confederate Veteran* 31 (1923): 456–458.

Smith, Edmund Kirby. "The Defense of the Red River." In *Battles and Leaders of the Civil War,* 4:369–374.

Smith, Rebecca W., and Marion Mullins, eds. "The Diary of H. C. Medford, Confederate Soldier, 1864." *Southwestern Historical Quarterly* 34 (January, 1931): 203–230.

Smith, Washington J. "Battle of Sabine Pass." *Confederate Veteran* 27 (1919): 461–462.

Snead, Thomas L. "The Conquest of Arkansas." In *Battles and Leaders of the Civil War,* 3:441–461.

"The Southern Historical Society: Its Origin and History." *Southern Historical Society Papers* 18 (1890): 349–365.

Spencer, Edward. "Confederate Negro Enlistments." In *The Annals of the Civil War,* 536–553. Philadelphia: Times, 1878; reprint, New York: Da Capo, 1994.

Spenser, C. R., Jr. "The Morale of the Confederate Soldier." *Confederate Veteran* 27 (1919): 49–52.

Steers, Edward, ed. "The Red River Campaign Letters of Lt. Charles Washington Kennedy, 156th New York Volunteer Infantry." *Civil War Regiments: A Journal of the American Civil War* 4, no. 2 (1994): 104–117.

Stiles, John C. "In the Years of War." *Confederate Veteran* 26 (1918): 402–403.

———. "Longstreet at Gettysburg." *Confederate Veteran* 23 (1915): 507–508.

"Surgeons of the Confederacy." *Confederate Veteran* 34 (1926): 254–256.

Sykes, E. T. "A Correction Explained—Gov. I. G. Harris." *Confederate Veteran* 6 (1898): 525.

Taylor, Richard. "The Last Confederate Surrender." In *The Annals of the Civil War,* 67–71. Philadelphia: Times, 1878; reprint, New York: Da Capo, 1994.

"United Confederate Veterans." *Southern Historical Society Papers* 18 (1890): 289–293.

"United Daughters of the Confederacy: Notes." *Confederate Veteran* 36 (1928): 152–154.

"Unpublished After–Action Reports from the Red River Campaign." *Civil War Regiments: A Journal of the American Civil War* 4, no. 2 (1994): 118–135.

"An 'Unseen Message' of President Davis." *Confederate Veteran* 14 (1906): 364–371.

Vandiver, Frank E., ed. "The Proceedings of the Second Confederate Congress Second Session in Part December 15, 1864–March 18, 1865." *Southern Historical Society Papers* 52 (1959).

Walker, John C. "Reconstruction in Texas." *Southern Historical Society Papers* 24 (1896): 41–72.

Wheeler, L. T. "General Wilbur Hill King." *Confederate Veteran* 19 (1911): 172–173.

White, Lonnie J., ed. "A Bluecoat's Account of the Camden Expedition." *Arkansas Historical Quarterly* 24 (1965): 82–89.

Williams, John Calvin. "The Fire of Hatred." *Civil War Times Illustrated* 17 (January 1979): 20–31.

Wilson, R. S. "The Battle of Jenkins's Ferry." *Confederate Veteran* 18 (1910): 468.

Wright, J. M. "A Glimpse of Perryville." *Southern Bivouac* 6 (1887–1888): 129–134.

Zorn, Roman J., ed. "Campaigning in Southern Arkansas: A Memoir by C. T. Anderson." *Arkansas Historical Quarterly* 8 (1949): 240–244.

NEWSPAPERS

Houston Daily Telegraph
Louisiana Baptist
Louisiana Democrat
New Orleans Daily Delta
Richmond Whig
Shreveport News
Washington (Arkansas) Telegraph

SECONDARY SOURCES

BOOKS

Allardice, Bruce S. *More Generals in Gray.* Baton Rouge: Louisiana State University Press, 1995.

Anders, Curt. *Disaster in Damp Sand: The Red River Expedition.* Indianapolis: Guild Press of Indiana, 1997.

Arceneaux, William. *Acadian General: Alfred Mouton and the Civil War.* Lafayette: University of Southwestern Louisiana, 1981.

Bailey, Anne J. *Between the Enemy and Texas: Parsons's Cavalry in the Civil War.* Fort Worth: Texas Christian University Press, 1989.

———. *Texans in the Confederate Cavalry.* Civil War Campaigns and Commanders Series, ed. Grady McWhiney. Fort Worth: Ryan Place, 1995.

Bailey, Anne J., and Daniel E. Sutherland, eds. *Civil War Arkansas: Beyond Battles and Leaders.* Fayetteville: University of Arkansas Press, 2000.

Ballard, Michael B. *Pemberton: A Biography.* Jackson: University Press of Mississippi, 1991.

Barr, Alwyn. *Polignac's Texas Brigade.* Houston: Texas Gulf Coast Historical Association, 1964.

Bauer, Craig A. *A Leader among Peers: The Life and Times of Duncan Farrar Kenner.* Lafayette: University of Southwestern Louisiana, 1993.

Bauer, K. Jack. *The Mexican War, 1846–1848.* New York: Macmillan, 1974.

———. *Zachary Taylor: Soldier, Planter, Statesman of the Old Southwest.* Baton Rouge: Louisiana State University Press, 1985.

Bearss, Edwin C. *The Campaign for Vicksburg.* 3 vols. Dayton, OH: Morningside, 1985–1986; reprint, 1991.

———. *Steele's Retreat from Camden and the Battle of Jenkins Ferry.* Little Rock: Pioneer, 1961.

Bergeron, Arthur W., Jr. *Guide to Louisiana Confederate Military Units*. Baton Rouge: Louisiana State University Press, 1989.

Bowden, J. J. *The Exodus of Federal Forces from Texas*. Austin: Eakin, 1986.

Bragg, Jefferson Davis. *Louisiana in the Confederacy*. Baton Rouge: Louisiana State University Press, 1941.

Brooksher, William Riley. *War along the Bayous: The 1864 Red River Campaign in Louisiana*. Washington, DC: Brassey's, 1998.

Cassidy, Vincent H., and Amos E. Simpson. *Henry Watkins Allen of Louisiana*. Baton Rouge: Louisiana State University Press, 1964.

Castel, Albert. *Decision in the West: The Atlanta Campaign of 1864*. Lawrence: University Press of Kansas, 1992.

———. *General Sterling Price and the Civil War in the West*. Baton Rouge: Louisiana State University Press, 1968; reprint, 1993.

Christ, Mark K., ed. *Rugged and Sublime: The Civil War in Arkansas*. Fayetteville: University of Arkansas Press, 1994.

Connelly, Thomas L. *Army of the Heartland: The Army of Tennessee, 1861–1862*. Baton Rouge: Louisiana State University Press, 1967; reprint, 1993.

———. *Autumn of Glory: The Army of Tennessee, 1862–1865*. Baton Rouge: Louisiana State University Press, 1971; reprint, 1995.

Connelly, Thomas L., and Archer Jones. *The Politics of Command: Factions and Ideas in Confederate Strategy*. Baton Rouge: Louisiana State University Press, 1972.

Crute, Joseph H., Jr. *Confederate Staff Officers*. Powhatan, VA: Derwent Books, 1982.

Current, Richard N., ed. *Encyclopedia of the Confederacy*. 4 vols. New York: Simon and Schuster, 1993.

Cutrer, Thomas W. *Ben McCulloch and the Frontier Military Tradition*. Chapel Hill: University of North Carolina Press, 1993.

Davis, William C. *Battle at Bull Run*. Mechanicsburg: Stackpole Books, 1977; reprint, 1995.

———. *Jefferson Davis: The Man and His Hour*. New York: HarperCollins, 1991.

———, ed. *The Confederate General*. 6 vols. Harrisburg: National Historical Society, 1991.

DeBlack, Thomas A. *With Fire and Sword: Arkansas, 1861–1874*. Fayetteville: University of Arkansas Press, 2003.

Dougan, Michael B. *Confederate Arkansas*. Tuscaloosa: University of Alabama Press, 1976; reprint, 1991.

Dufour, Charles L. *Nine Men in Gray*. Garden City, NY: Doubleday, 1963; reprint, with an introduction by Gary W. Gallagher, Lincoln: University of Nebraska Press, 1993.

Edmonds, David C. *Yankee Autumn in Acadiana*. Lafayette, LA: Acadiana, 1979.

Eisenhower, John S. D. *Agent of Destiny: The Life and Times of General Winfield Scott*. New York: Free Press, 1977.

Faulk, Odie. *General Tom Green: A Fightin' Texan.* Waco: Texian, 1963.

Foote, Shelby. *The Civil War: A Narrative.* 3 vols. New York: Random House, 1958; reprint, 1986.

Forsyth, Michael J. *The Camden Expedition of 1864 and the Opportunity Lost by the Confederacy to Change the Civil War.* Jefferson, NC: McFarland, 2003.

———. *The Red River Campaign of 1864 and the Loss by the Confederacy of the Civil War.* Jefferson, NC: McFarland, 2002.

Freeman, Douglas Southall. *Lee's Lieutenants: A Study in Command.* 3 vols. New York: Charles Scribner's Sons, 1942–1944.

Gallagher, Gary W. *The Confederate War.* Cambridge: Harvard University Press, 1997.

Gallaway, B. P. *The Ragged Rebel: A Common Soldier in W. H. Parsons' Texas Cavalry, 1861–1865.* Austin: University of Texas Press, 1988; reprint, 1991.

Gannon, James P. *Irish Rebels, Confederate Tigers: A History of the Sixth Louisiana Volunteers.* Mason City, IA: Savas, 1998.

Glatthaar, Joseph T. *Forged in Battle: The Civil War Alliance of Black Soldiers and White Officers.* New York: Free Press, 1990.

———. *Partners in Command: The Relationships between Leaders in the Civil War.* New York: Free Press, 1994.

Gosnell, H. Allen. *Guns on the Western Waters.* Baton Rouge: Louisiana State University Press, 1949; reprint, 1993.

Groce, W. Todd. *Mountain Rebels: East Tennessee Confederates and the Civil War, 1860–1870.* Knoxville: University of Tennessee Press, 1999.

Hallock, Judith Lee. *Braxton Bragg and Confederate Defeat: Volume 2.* Tuscaloosa: University of Alabama Press, 1991.

Harrington, Fred Harvey. *Fighting Politician: Major General N. P. Banks.* Philadelphia: University of Pennsylvania Press, 1948; reprint, Westport: Greenwood, 1970.

Hasskarl, Robert A., and Lief R. Hasskarl. *Waul's Texas Legion, 1862–1865.* Ada, OK: privately published, 1985.

Hattaway, Herman, and Richard Beringer. *Jefferson Davis, Confederate President.* Lawrence: University Press of Kansas, 2002.

Hattaway, Herman, and Archer Jones. *How the North Won: A Military History of the Civil War.* Urbana: University of Illinois Press, 1983; reprint, 1991.

Hearn, Chester G. *Admiral David Dixon Porter: The Civil War Years.* Annapolis: Naval Institute Press, 1966.

———. *The Capture of New Orleans, 1862.* Baton Rouge: Louisiana State University Press, 1995.

Heidler, David S., and Jeanne T. Heidler, eds. *Encyclopedia of the American Civil War: A Political, Social, and Military History.* 5 vols. Santa Barbara: ABC-CLIO, 2000.

Heleniak, Roman J., and Lawrence L. Hewitt. *Leadership during the Civil War: The 1989 Deep Delta Civil War Symposium: Themes in Honor of T. Harry Williams.* Shippensburg, PA: White Mane, 1992.

Hess, Earl J. *Banners to the Breeze: The Kentucky Campaign, Corinth, and Stones River.* Lincoln: University of Nebraska Press, 2000.

Hewitt, Lawrence Lee. *Port Hudson: Confederate Bastion on the Mississippi.* Baton Rouge: Louisiana State University Press, 1987.

Hewitt, Lawrence Lee, and Arthur W. Bergeron, eds. *Louisianans in the Civil War.* Columbia: University of Missouri Press, 2002.

Hollandsworth, James G., Jr. *Pretense of Glory: The Life of General Nathaniel P. Banks.* Baton Rouge: Louisiana State University Press, 1998.

Johansson, M. Jane. *Peculiar Honor: A History of the Twenty-eighth Texas Cavalry, 1862–1865.* Fayetteville: University of Arkansas Press, 1998.

Johnson, Ludwell. *Red River Campaign: Politics and Cotton in the Civil War.* Baltimore: Johns Hopkins Press, 1958; reprint, Kent, OH: Kent State University Press, 1993.

Johnson, Timothy D. *Winfield Scott: The Quest for Military Glory.* Lawrence: University Press of Kansas, 1998.

Joiner, Gary Dillard. *One Damn Blunder from Beginning to End: The Red River Campaign of 1864.* Wilmington, DE: Scholarly Resources, 2003.

Jones, Archer. *Civil War Command and Strategy: The Process of Victory and Defeat.* New York: Free Press, 1992.

———. *Confederate Strategy from Shiloh to Vicksburg.* Baton Rouge: Louisiana State University Press, 1961; reprint, 1991.

Jones, Terry L. *Lee's Tigers: The Louisiana Infantry in the Army of Northern Virginia.* Baton Rouge: Louisiana State University Press, 1987.

Josephy, Alvin M., Jr. *The Civil War in the American West.* New York: Alfred A. Knopf, 1991.

———. *War on the Frontier: The Trans-Mississippi West.* The Civil War Series. Alexandria: Time-Life Books, 1986.

Kerby, Robert Lee. *Kirby Smith's Confederacy: The Trans-Mississippi South, 1863–1865.* New York: Columbia University Press, 1972.

Kinard, Jeff. *Lafayette of the South: Prince Camille de Polignac and the American Civil War.* College Station: Texas A&M University Press, 2001.

Korn, Jerry. *War on the Mississippi.* The Civil War Series. Alexandria: Time-Life Books, 1985.

Long, E. B., and Barbara Long. *The Civil War Day by Day: An Almanac, 1861–1865.* Foreword by Bruce Catton. New York: Doubleday, 1971; reprint, New York: Da Capo, n.d.

Lonn, Ella. *Foreigners in the Confederacy.* Chapel Hill: University of North Carolina Press, 1940.

———. *Salt As a Factor in the Confederacy.* New York: Neale, 1933; reprint, Tuscaloosa: University of Alabama Press, 1965.

Lowe, Richard. *The Texas Overland Expedition of 1863.* Civil War Campaigns and Commanders Series. Edited by Grady McWhiney. Fort Worth: Ryan Place, 1996.

———. *Walker's Texas Division C.S A.: Greyhounds of the Trans-Mississippi.* Baton Rouge: Louisiana State University Press, 2004.

McDonough, James Lee. *War in Kentucky: From Shiloh to Perryville.* Knoxville: University of Tennessee Press, 1994.

McGowen, Stanley S. *Horse Sweat and Powder Smoke: The First Texas Cavalry in the Civil War.* College Station: Texas A&M University Press, 1999.

McMurry, Richard M. *John Bell Hood and the War for Southern Independence.* Lexington: University Press of Kentucky, 1982; reprint, Lincoln: University of Nebraska Press, 1992.

———. *Two Great Rebel Armies: An Essay in Confederate Military History.* Chapel Hill: University of North Carolina Press, 1989.

McPherson, James M. *Battle Cry of Freedom: The Civil War Era.* New York: Oxford University Press, 1988.

———. *Ordeal by Fire: The Civil War and Reconstruction.* 3rd ed. New York: McGraw-Hill, 1992.

McWhiney, Grady. *Braxton Bragg and Confederate Defeat.* Vol. 1, *Field Command.* New York: Columbia University Press, 1969.

McWhiney, Grady, and Perry D. Jamieson. *Attack and Die: Civil War Military Tactics and the Southern Heritage.* Tuscaloosa: University of Alabama Press, 1982.

Mangham, Dana M. *Oh, for a Touch of the Vanished Hand: Discovering a Southern Family and the Civil War.* Murfreesboro: Southern Heritage, 2000.

Martin, Samuel J. *The Road to Glory: Confederate General Richard S. Ewell.* Indianapolis: Guild, 1991.

Military Affairs. *Military Analysis of the Civil War: An Anthology.* Introduction by T. Harry Williams. Millwood, NY: KTO, 1977.

Millett, Allan R., and Peter Maslowski. *For the Common Defense: A Military History of the United States of America.* New York: Free Press, 1984.

Monaghan, Jay. *Civil War on the Western Border, 1854–1865.* Boston: Little, Brown, 1955; reprint, Lincoln: University of Nebraska Press, 1984.

Moneyhon, Carl H., and Bobby Roberts. *Portraits of Conflict: A Photographic History of Louisiana in the Civil War.* Fayetteville: University of Arkansas Press, 1990.

Noe, Kenneth W. *Perryville: This Grand Havoc of Battle.* Lexington: University Press of Kentucky, 2001.

Noll, Arthur H. *General Kirby-Smith.* Sewanee, TN, 1907.

Oates, Stephen B. *Confederate Cavalry West of the River*. Austin: University of Texas Press, 1961; reprint, 1992.

O'Flaherty, Daniel. *General Jo Shelby: Undefeated Rebel*. Chapel Hill: University of North Carolina Press, 1954; reprint, with a foreword by Daniel E. Sutherland, 2000.

Parks, Joseph H. *General Edmund Kirby Smith C.S.A.* Baton Rouge: Louisiana State University Press, 1954; reprint, 1982.

Parrish, Michael T. *Richard Taylor: Soldier Prince of Dixie*. Chapel Hill: University of North Carolina Press, 1992.

Pfanz, Donald C. *Richard S. Ewell: A Soldier's Life*. Chapel Hill: University of North Carolina Press, 1998.

Plummer, Alonzo H. *Confederate Victory at Mansfield*. Mansfield: Kate Beard Chapter of the United Daughters of the Confederacy, 1969.

Raphael, Morris. *The Battle in the Bayou Country*. Detroit: Harlo, 1975; reprint, 1990.

———. *A Gunboat Named Diana*. Detroit: Harlo, 1993.

Roberts, Bobby, and Carl Moneyhon. *Portraits of Conflict: A Photographic History of Arkansas in the Civil War*. Fayetteville: University of Arkansas Press, 1987.

Robertson, James I., Jr. *Stonewall Jackson: The Man, the Soldier, the Legend*. New York: Macmillan, 1997.

Scogland, Thesta Kennedy. *The Garlington Family*. Baltimore: Gateway, 1976.

Shackelford, George Green. *George Wythe Randolph and the Confederate Elite*. Athens: University of Georgia Press, 1988.

Shalhope, Robert E. *Sterling Price: Portrait of a Southerner*. Columbia: University of Missouri Press, 1971.

Sifakis, Stewart. *Who Was Who in the Confederacy*. New York: Facts on File, 1988.

Smith, John David, ed. *African American Troops in the Civil War Era*. Chapel Hill: University of North Carolina Press, 2002.

Snell, Mark A. *From First to Last: The Life of Major General William B. Franklin*. New York: Fordham University Press, 2002.

Spencer, John W. *Terrell's Texas Cavalry*. Austin: Eakin, 1982.

Starr, Stephen Z. *The Union Cavalry in the Civil War*. 3 vols. Baton Rouge: Louisiana State University Press, 1985.

Stephens, Robert W. *August Buchel: Texas Soldier of Fortune*. Dallas: privately published, 1970.

Stickles, Arndt M. *Simon Bolivar Buckner: Borderland Knight*. Chapel Hill: University of North Carolina Press, 1940.

Stokes, Anson Phelps. *Memorials of Eminent Yale Men*. 2 vols. New Haven: Yale University Press, 1914.

Sutherland, Daniel E., ed. *Guerrillas, Unionists, and Violence on the Confederate Home Front*. Fayetteville: University of Arkansas Press, 1999.

Sword, Wiley. *Embrace an Angry Wind: The Confederacy's Last Hurrah: Spring Hill, Franklin, and Nashville.* New York: HarperCollins, 1992.

Symonds, Craig L. *Joseph E. Johnston: A Civil War Biography.* New York: W. W. Norton, 1992.

Tanner, Robert G. *Stonewall in the Valley: Thomas J. "Stonewall" Jackson's Shenandoah Valley Campaign, Spring 1862.* New York: Doubleday, 1976.

Thomas, Emory M. *The Confederate Nation, 1861–1865.* New York: Harper and Row, 1979.

Thompson, Jerry. *Henry Hopkins Sibley: Confederate General of the West.* Natchitoches, LA: Northwestern State University Press, 1987.

Vandiver, Frank E. *Rebel Brass: The Confederate Command System.* Baton Rouge: Louisiana State University Press, 1956; reprint, 1984.

Warner, Ezra J. *Generals in Blue: Lives of the Union Commanders.* Baton Rouge: Louisiana State University Press, 1964; reprint, 1992.

———. *Generals in Gray: Lives of the Confederate Commanders.* Baton Rouge: Louisiana State University Press, 1959; reprint, 1992.

Warner, Ezra J., and W. Buck Yearns. *Biographical Register of the Confederate Congress.* Baton Rouge: Louisiana State University Press, 1975.

Welsh, Jack D. *Medical Histories of Confederate Generals.* Kent, OH: Kent State University Press, 1995.

———. *Medical Histories of Union Generals.* Kent, OH: Kent State University Press, 1996.

Williams, Kenneth P. *Lincoln Finds a General: A Military Study of the Civil War.* 5 vols. New York: Macmillan, 1949–1959.

Williams, T. Harry. *P. G. T. Beauregard: Napoleon in Gray.* Baton Rouge: Louisiana State University Press, 1955; reprint, 1995.

Winters, John D. *The Civil War in Louisiana.* Baton Rouge: Louisiana State University Press, 1963.

Woodworth, Steven E. *Jefferson Davis and His Generals: The Failure of Confederate Command in the West.* Lawrence: University of Kansas Press, 1990.

———, ed. *Leadership and Command in the American Civil War.* Campbell, CA: Savas Woodbury, 1995.

Wooster, Ralph A., ed. *Lone Star Blue and Gray: Essays on Texas in the Civil War.* Austin: Texas State Historical Association, 1995.

Yearns, W. Buck, ed. *The Confederate Governors.* Athens: University of Georgia Press, 1995.

ARTICLES

Atkinson, James Harris. "The Action at Prairie de Ann." *Arkansas Historical Quarterly* 19 (1960): 40–50.

Bailey, Anne J. "The Abandoned Western Theater: Confederate Policy toward the Trans-Mississippi Region." *Journal of Confederate History* 5 (1990): 35–54.

———. "Chasing Banks out of Louisiana: Parsons's Texas Cavalry in the Red River Campaign." *Civil War Regiments: A Journal of the American Civil War* 2 (1992): 212–233.

———. "A Texas Cavalry Raid: Reaction to Black Soldiers and Contraband." In *Lone Star Blue and Gray: Essays on Texas in the Civil War,* edited by Ralph Wooster, 257–272. Austin: Texas State Historical Association, 1995.

———. "Was There a Massacre at Poison Spring?" *Military History of the Southwest* 20 (fall 1990): 1–12.

Barr, Alwyn. "Confederate Artillery in Western Louisiana, 1862–1863." *Civil War History* 5 (1963): 74–85.

———. "Texan Losses in the Red River Campaign, 1864." *Texas Military History* 3 (1963): 103–113.

Bearss, Edwin C. "Marmaduke Attacks Pine Bluff." *Arkansas Historical Quarterly* 23 (1964): 291–313.

Bergeron, Arthur W., Jr. "A Colonel Gains His Wreath: Henry Gray's Louisiana Brigade at the Battle of Mansfield, April 8, 1864." *Civil War Regiments: A Journal of the American Civil War* 4, no. 2 (1994): 1–25.

———. "General Richard Taylor as a Military Commander." *Louisiana History* 23, no. 1 (1982): 35–47.

Berwanger, Eugene H. "Union and Confederate Reactions to French Threats against Texas." *Journal of Confederate History* 7 (1991): 97–112.

Bounds, Steve, and Curtis Milbourn. "The Battle of Mansfield." *North and South: The Official Magazine of the Civil War Society* 5, no. 6 (2002): 26–40.

Brown, Norman D. "Walker's Texas Division." In *Confederate History Symposium: Proceedings 1992,* B. D. Patterson, dir., 29–50. Hillsboro, TX: Harold B. Simpson Confederate Research Center, 1992.

Burgess, Stephen. "Campfires, Canteen, and Southern Wit: A Selection of Southern Soldiers' Jokes from the Trans-Mississippi Department of the Confederacy." *Confederate Veteran,* July–August 1992, 14–19.

Coulter, E. Merton. "Commercial Intercourse with the Confederacy in the Mississippi Valley." *Mississippi Valley Historical Review* 5 (1919): 377–395.

Davis, Jackson Beauregard. "The Life of Richard Taylor." *Louisiana Historical Quarterly* 24 (January 1941): 49–126.

Dollar, Susan E. "The Red River Campaign, Natchitoches, Louisiana: A Case of Equal Opportunity Destruction." *Louisiana History,* fall 2002, 411–432.

Frazier, Donald S. "Texans on the Teche: The Texas Brigade at the Battle of Bisland and Irish Bend, April 12–14 1863." *Louisiana History,* fall 1991, 417–435.

Hatton, Roy O. "Prince Camille de Polignac and the American Civil War, 1863–1865." *Louisiana Studies* 3 (summer 1964): 163–195.

Holladay, Florence Elizabeth. "The Powers of the Commander of the Confederate Trans-Mississippi Department, 1863–1865." *Southwestern Historical Quarterly* 21 (January 1918): 279–359.

House, John R., III. "Battle of Mansfield Numbers Were Off." *Civil War News*, December 1996, 8.

Huffstodt, James T. "Ransom at the Crossroads: One Man's Ruin on the Red River." *Civil War Times Illustrated* 19 (1980): 9–17.

Johnson, Ludwell. "A Campaign That Failed." In *The Image of War, 1861–1865: The South Besieged*, edited by William C. Davis, 346–377. New York: Doubleday, 1983.

Joiner, Gary D., and Charles E. Vetter. "The Union Naval Expedition on the Red River, March 12–May 22, 1864." *Civil War Regiments: A Journal of the American Civil War* 4, no. 2 (1994): 26–67.

Jones, Terry L. "The Twenty-eighth Louisiana Volunteers in the Civil War." *North Louisiana Historical Association Journal* 9 (1978): 85–95.

Lale, Max S. "For Lack of a Nail." *East Texas Historical Journal* 30 (1992): 34–43.

————. "New Light on the Battle of Mansfield." *East Texas Historical Journal* 25 (1987): 43–41.

Landers, Col. H. L. "Wet Sand and Cotton: Banks' Red River Campaign." *Louisiana Historical Quarterly* 19 (1936): 150–195.

McWhiney, Grady. "Controversy in Kentucky: Braxton Bragg's Campaign of 1862." *Civil War History* 6 (1960): 5–42.

Martin, David. "The Red River Campaign." *Strategy and Tactics* 106 (March–April 1986): 11–20.

Milbourn, Curtis W. "Fighting for Time." *North and South: The Official Magazine of the Civil War Society* 5, no. 4 (2002): 68–76.

————. "The Lafourche Campaign." *North and South: The Official Magazine of the Civil War Society* 7, no. 5 (2004): 70–83.

Moore, Waldo M. "The Defense of Shreveport: The Confederacy's Last Redoubt." In *Military Analysis of the Civil War: An Anthology*, 394–404. Millwood, NY: KTO, 1977.

Pittman, Walter E. "Trading with the Devil: The Cotton Trade in Civil War Mississippi." *Journal of Confederate History* 2, no. 1 (1989): 133–142.

Richards, Ira Don. "The Battle of Jenkins Ferry." *Arkansas Historical Quarterly* 20 (1961): 3–16.

————. "The Battle of Poison Spring." *Arkansas Historical Quarterly* 18 (1959): 336–349.

————. "The Engagement at Marks' Mill." *Arkansas Historical Quarterly* 19 (1960): 51–60.

Riley, Harris D., Jr. "General Richard Taylor, C.S.A.: Louisianan, Distinguished Military Commander, and Author, with Speculations on His Health." *Southern Studies: An Interdisciplinary Journal of the South* 1 (spring 1990): 67–86.

Savas, Theodore P. "A Death at Mansfield: Col. James Hamilton Beard and the Consolidated Crescent Regiment." *Civil War Regiments: A Journal of the American Civil War* 4, no. 2 (1994): 68–103.

Shea, William L. "The Camden Fortifications." *Arkansas Historical Quarterly* 51 (1959): 318–345.

Urwin, Gregory J. W. "Cut to Pieces and Gone to Hell: The Poison Spring Massacre." *North and South: The Official Magazine of the Civil War Society* 3, no. 6 (2000): 45–57.

———. "A Very Disastrous Defeat: The Battle of Helena." *North and South: The Official Magazine of the Civil War Society* 6, no. 1 (2002): 26–39.

Woodworth, Steven E. "Dismembering the Confederacy: Jefferson Davis and the Trans-Mississippi West." *Military History of the Southwest* 20 (spring 1990): 1–22.

UNPUBLISHED MATERIALS

Bergeron, Arthur W., Jr. "General Richard Taylor: A Study in Command." Master's thesis, Louisiana State University, 1972.

Geise, William Royston. "The Confederate Military Forces in the Trans- Mississippi West, 1861–1865: A Study in Command." Ph.D. diss., University of Texas at Austin, 1974.

Lagvanec, Cyril M. "Chevalier Bayard of the Confederacy: The Life and Career of Edmund Kirby Smith." Ph.D. diss., Texas A&M University, 1999.

Richards, Ira D. "The Camden Expedition, March 23–May 3, 1864." Master's thesis, University of Arkansas, 1958.

United States Military Academy. Red River Campaign IPB Briefing. Spring 2004.

INTERVIEWS WITH AUTHOR

Arthur W. Bergeron Jr. Louisiana State Parks. Fall 1994 and spring 2003.

Steven Bounds. Mansfield State Historic Site. Spring 2004.

Scott Dearman. Mansfield State Historic Site. Spring 2004.

Gary D. Joiner. Louisiana State University, Shreveport. Spring 2004.

Dana M. Mangham. United States Military Academy, West Point. Spring 2003 and spring 2004.

Mike Marino. Red Buffalo Ranch, Skippack, Pennsylvania. Spring 2004.

Barron T. Smith. Sons of Confederate Veterans, Los Angeles. Summer 1993.

INDEX